LANGUAGE COMPREHENSION AND THE ACQUISITION OF KNOWLEDGE

LANGUAGE COMPREHENSION AND THE ACQUISITION OF KNOWLEDGE

EDITED BY JOHN B. CARROLL and ROY O. FREEDLE

EDUCATIONAL TESTING SERVICE, PRINCETON, NEW JERSEY

V. H. WINSTON & SONS

1972   Washington, D.C.

DISTRIBUTED BY THE HALSTED PRESS DIVISION OF

JOHN WILEY & SONS

New York   Toronto   London   Sydney

V. H. Winston & Sons, Inc., Publishers
1511 K St. N.W., Washington, D.C. 20005

Distributed solely by Halsted Press Division, John Wiley & Sons, Inc.,
New York.

ISBN 0-470-13585-9

Library of Congress Catalog Card Number: 72-6708

Printed in the United States of America

CONTENTS

Preface   ix

1   DEFINING LANGUAGE COMPREHENSION: SOME
    SPECULATIONS, *John B. Carroll*   1
    The Problem of Defining Language Comprehension   5
    The Testing of Comprehension   14
    Summary   24
    Conference Discussion   24
    References   26

2   THE CONCEPT OF COMPREHENSION: FROM SEMANTICS
    TO SOFTWARE, *Michael Scriven*   31
    Introduction   31
    Conference Discussion   37
    References   39

3   DISCOURSE STRUCTURE AND HUMAN KNOWLEDGE,
    Wallace L. Chafe   41
    Semantic Resources   42
    Variability   46
    Tense   48
    Foregrounding   50
    Definiteness   56
    Conference Discussion   68
    References   69

4   SOME SEMANTIC STRUCTURES FOR REPRESENTING ENGLISH MEANINGS, *Robert F. Simmons*   71

Introduction   71
A Semantic Structure for Discourse   73
Lexical Structure   83
Discussion and Conclusions   94
Conference Discussion   95
References   96

5   PERCEPTIONS, THOUGHT, AND LANGUAGE, *Thomas G. Bever*   99

Introduction and Summary   99
The Structure of Speech Perception   104
Codability and Thought   110
References   111

6   MENTAL OPERATIONS IN LANGUAGE COMPREHENSION, *Tom Trabasso*   113

Encoding Stage   115
Response Change Model   116
An Optional Recoding Model   121
To What Extent does the Encoding Affect Processing?   131
Conference Discussion   135
References   136

7   LANGUAGE USE FOR COMMUNICATING, INSTRUCTING, AND THINKING, *David R. Olson*   139

Sentences as Descriptions: Mapping Sentences onto
      Perception   139
Sentences as Propositions: Mapping Sentences onto
      Sentences   156
Conference Discussion   164
References   165

8   LANGUAGE USERS AS FALLIBLE INFORMATION-PROCESSORS: IMPLICATIONS FOR MEASURING AND MODELING COMPREHENSION, *Roy O. Freedle*   169

Introduction   169
Olson's Cognitive Theory of Reference   170
Experimental Studies   174
Factors in Comprehension   182
The Anthropologist's Contribution to Comprehension   203
Appendix A   205
Conference Discussion   207
References   209

9   EFFECTS OF TASK-INDUCED COGNITIVE OPERATIONS
     ON COMPREHENSION AND MEMORY PROCESSES,
     Carl H. Frederiksen.   211
        An Outline of a Model for Comprehension and
            Memory Processes   213
        The Measurement of Comprehension and Memory
            Processes   218
        Effects of Task Induced Cognitive Operations on Processes
            in Comprehension and Memory   224
        Some Selected Results   228
        Concluding Remarks   232
        Conference Discussion   243
        References   244

10   MEMORY STRUCTURE AND THE RECALL OF DISCOURSE,
     Edward J. Crothers   247
        Introduction   247
        Method   248
        Linguistic Analysis of Nebulae Paragraph   249
        Results and Discussion   260
        Structure and Recall: Empirical Correlation   273
        Implications and Conclusions   276
        Conference Discussion   277
        References   278
        Appendix I   279
        Appendix II   280

11   LEARNING BY LISTENING, *Thomas G. Sticht*.   285
        Introduction   285
        Some Relationships of Reading and Listening   286
        Experimental Studies of Learning by Listening to Rate
            Controlled Recordings   299
        Conference Discussion   311
        References   312

12   STRUCTURAL TEXT FEATURES AND THE CONTROL OF
     PROCESSES IN LEARNING FROM WRITTEN MATERIALS,
     Ernst Z. Rothkopf   315
        Introduction   315
        The Concept of Mathemagenic Activities   322
        Experimental Evidence for the Mathemagenic Concept   324
        Conclusion   330
        Conference Discussion   322
        References   334

13   MAINTENANCE AND CONTROL IN THE ACQUISITION
     OF KNOWLEDGE FROM WRITTEN MATERIALS,
     Lawrence T. Frase   337
         Some Preliminary Studies   335
         Going Beyond the Information in Text   340
         Studies with Adults   242
         Studies with Children   348
         Summary   354
         Conference Discussion   355
         References   356

14   LANGUAGE COMPREHENSION AND THE ACQUISITION
     OF KNOWLEDGE: REFLECTIONS, *Roy O. Freedle and*
     John B. Carroll   361
         Language Competence and Language Understanding   361
         Some Covert Semantic Assumptions and Presuppositions in
             Language Discourse   362
         Information-Processing Approaches to Discourse   365
         The Maintenance of Comprehension Behavior   368
         Conclusion   369
         References   369

Author Index   369
Subject Index   375

PREFACE

Since the revolution in psycholinguistics that was initiated primarily by George Miller in 1962, psychologists have witnessed an intense growth of interest in problems of language production and comprehension. Much of the research on these problems understandably began with the study of the production and comprehension (particularly the latter) of single sentences, and took its inspiration from the theory of transformational grammar as formulated by Noam Chomsky. During this period empirical studies involving multisentence comprehension and production were few and far between because it was taken for granted that problems involving single sentences needed to be well understood first. But it was further assumed that once these problems were understood it would be a simple matter to extend this knowledge base to the problem of discourse comprehension.

In actuality, it has turned out that problems involving just single sentences were more complicated than they were originally thought to be. The initial faith in the close connection between transformational theory and psychological comprehension processes has been badly shaken by difficulties in interpreting experimental findings in this light, but psychologists have managed to salvage some of the empirical regularities that emerged from the work of the last decade by reconceptualizing the processes of language comprehension so as to highlight the possible roles of perceptual and information-processing strategies in comprehension. With this new emphasis, psychological mechanisms are viewed as being of an importance equal to that of linguistic constructs. In the meantime, on the linguistic front, semantic case theories have begun to compete strongly with the classic transformational approach, a fact which many psychologists (among them the editors of this volume) warmly welcome since these formulations appear to reflect more closely our intuitive grasp of what language behavior is all about—the communication of semantic relations concerning various states of the environment. Along with the emphasis on semantics in linguistics there has been an interest in theoretical investigations into the semantic constraints that exist across sentence boundaries. Considering these recent developments both in psychology and in linguistics one has the feeling that language behavior has at last been given back to the psychologists to study. Perhaps that is putting the matter too strongly. At the very least one can say that whereas many psycholinguists were inclined to be uncomfortable about merely borrowing the theoretical paradigms of linguistics in interpreting behavioral language data, they now believe that with the new orientation they have derived from their own discipline, they have as much to offer as linguists do in explaining the regularities in language data.

The time seemed ripe for bringing together a group of language specialists to consider discourse comprehension in order to lay bare both the special linguistic (semantic) problems that occur when interconnected strings of sentences constitute the data base and the special psychological problems (of memory, inference, and motivation) that occur when human subjects are exposed to discourse materials in laboratory or real-life settings. We felt in addition that the resulting analyses would greatly benefit the consideration of complex learning processes in general as well as the psychology of education. It is self-evident that much of the learning that takes place in schools is accomplished by means of exposure to discourse of some kind—whether in classroom lectures and discussions, educational media presentations, or textbooks and other reading material. It was thus our hope that a conference on discourse comprehension would accrue not only to the development of special tools and methods in linguistics and psycholinguistics for the analysis of discourse structure but also to the furtherance of general and educational psychology, particularly the study of how discourse comprehension relates to complex learning.

A wide variety of language experts were encouraged to speculate on these issues, and if possible to report empirical data in support of theoretical positions regarding discourse comprehension. To provide some guidelines to our prospective authors and discussants we submitted to them the following major problem and questions to be explored:

> This workshop is addressed to the general problem of how we gain knowledge through language—how we learn from messages of sentence or of discourse length. We should like the following questions to be considered: (1) Exactly what is "comprehension" of language? (2) Can one identify distinct processes in comprehension? (3) In what senses can there be different degrees, levels, or types of comprehension? (4) How can we measure comprehension in terms of these levels or types? (5) What factors in the language stimulus, the situation, or the receiver influence degree and manner of comprehension? and (6) What is the relation between immediate comprehension and its representation in memory either on a long or a short term basis?

Each author was left free to attempt to answer these questions from whatever points of view he could muster.

The conference itself took the form of a research workshop held at the Quail Roost Conference Center of the University of North Carolina in Rougemont, North Carolina from March 31 through April 3, 1971, under the direction of John B. Carroll. Roy Freedle served as the conference coordinator. In all, sixteen papers, commissioned in advance, were presented at the workshop as draft manuscripts and in oral summaries, leading to lively discussions both in the regular sessions and in informal gatherings.

In editing the present volume we have found it impossible to include all the papers. Of the thirteen papers presented here, twelve have been revised by their authors in the light of the stenographically transcribed discussions and after editorial suggestions that we made. Also we have attempted to summarize after each paper the major points raised in the discussions that took place at the workshop. Dr. Bever's paper as printed here represents a major departure from what he presented at the conference and consequently no discussion summary has been appended to his chapter.

The chapters are presented in the order in which they were given at the workshop. We thought that a review of the literature which summarized results and theory for both single- and multisentence (discourse) experiments should begin the conference (Carroll's chapter). Next, Scriven's chapter was intended to provide some philosophical underpinnings for the concepts of comprehension and knowledge. Following this are two contributions by the linguist Wallace Chafe and a computational linguist Robert Simmons. These two chapters reflect the renewed emphasis on semantic analysis in current linguistic theory.

The remaining chapters report new empirical findings or develop psycholinguistic theories of single- as well as multisentence contexts. Bever's chapter is a theoretical account of some interrelations among thought, perception, and language. Trabasso and Olson each present new data and theory for an information-processing analysis of, for example, the cognitive operations that occur in matching pictorial and sentential content. In addition, Olson contrasts two uses of language—instructional and inferential. Freedle presents new data and theory for message-writing, subject-matter identification, and story comprehension tasks. Frederiksen and Crothers each develop a semantic analysis of discourse passages by which the written recalls of experimental subjects can be evaluated; Crothers' analysis emphasizes hierarchical structure while Frederiksen utilizes a graph-theoretical approach. The chapters by Sticht, Rothkopf, and Frase represent educational applications which offer both data and theory for a variety of studies using discourse. Sticht's chapter investigates, in part, the effect of message and situational factors on learning through listening. Rothkopf and Frase summarize a number of studies which investigate how the structural features of prose and the types of questions asked of subjects influence what they remember. The final chapter by the editors attempts to pull together the major themes of the conference in such a way as to suggest further approaches to the study of discourse.

The workshop held at the Quail Roost Conference Center was one of a series of such conferences, on various topics in the social and biological sciences relating to education, sponsored by the Committee on Basic Research in

Education, which was funded by the United States Office of Education through a grant to the National Academy of Education and the National Academy of Sciences, National Research Council. We are pleased to acknowledge the generous support provided in this way, and also the assistance given by Dr. Sherman Ross, Executive Secretary of the Committee, and Dr. Barbara Meeker, a member of the Committee staff.

Roy Freedle
John B. Carroll

Princeton, July 1972

LIST OF WORKSHOP PARTICIPANTS

Thomas G. Bever, Department of Psychology, Columbia University, New York, New York

John B. Carroll, Division of Psychological Studies, Educational Testing Service, Princeton, New Jersey

Wallace L. Chafe, Department of Linguistics, University of California, Berkeley, California

Edmund B. Coleman, Department of Psychology, University of Texas, El Paso, Texas

Edward J. Crothers, Department of Psychology, University of Colorado, Boulder, Colorado

Lawrence T. Frase, Learning and Instructional Processes Research Group, Bell Laboratories, Murray Hill, New Jersey

Carl Frederiksen, Institute of Human Learning, University of California, Berkeley, California

Roy Freedle, Division of Psychological Studies, Educational Testing Service, Princeton, New Jersey

Kenneth S. Goodman, College of Education, Wayne State University, Detroit, Michigan

Peter Herriot, Hester Adrian Research Centre, University of Manchester, Manchester, England

David R. Olson, Ontario Institute for Studies of Education, Toronto, Canada

William Page, Department of Education, University of Chicago, Chicago, Illinois

Ernst Z. Rothkopf, Learning and Instructional Processes Research Group, Bell Laboratories, Murray Hill, New Jersey

Michael Scriven, Department of Philosophy, University of California, Berkeley, California

Robert Simmons, Department of Computer Science, University of Texas, Austin, Texas

Thomas G. Sticht, Human Resources Research Organization, Presidio of Monterey, California

Thomas Trabasso, Department of Psychology, Princeton University, Princeton, New Jersey

LANGUAGE COMPREHENSION AND THE ACQUISITION OF KNOWLEDGE

1
DEFINING LANGUAGE COMPREHENSION: SOME SPECULATIONS

John B. Carroll
Educational Testing Service

The concept of comprehension is of major relevance to education. In the most general sense of "being educated," an "educated" person possesses a certain body of knowledge, competences, abilities, and skills. On the one hand, this implies some sort of structure that has been laid down in the individual, presumably in his nervous system, or, one might say, in a memory store, as a result of his whole prior development and experience, including educational experiences. Let us assume that this structure includes, among other things, a "cognitive structure" that consists of a large number of "comprehensions" or "understandings" of the almost infinitely diverse phenomena to which the individual has been, or is likely to be exposed. In the study of comprehension processes we must take account of the nature of this structure—noting, however, that it is with the structure of the individual's knowledge that we are concerned, not the "structure of knowledge" in general, for that is an abstraction that may or may not have any isomorphism with the individual's cognitive structure. On the other hand, "being educated" implies a capacity for acquiring new understandings and integrating them in some valid way with the knowledge already acquired. One aspect of this capacity is certainly the ability to understand language (normally, at least the native language, but other languages may be included in the individual's repertoire), and through that ability to acquire new knowledge. It is with this language comprehension process, and the process of acquiring knowledge through language, that this volume is concerned. We recognize, of course, that there are other modes of acquiring knowledge, but we limit ourselves to the consideration of comprehension through language except to the extent that such comprehension is supported, facilitated, or otherwise affected by these other modes of apprehending.

Educators have long wrestled with the problem of language comprehension. They have recognized that the child's competence in his native language, at the time

1

of school entrance, is far from sufficient to permit him to acquire, through language, the range and complexity of knowledge and skills that are contained in the total school program. Consequently, a major concern of the school curriculum is with the promotion of what are essentially language comprehension skills at progressively higher levels of grammatical, lexical, and semantic knowledge. Beyond the process of teaching the child to decode print into some analogue of spoken language, educators find that there still remains the problem of teaching the child to "understand" the language thus decoded. "Listening comprehension" and "reading comprehension" are two phrases that appear very frequently in educational literature, but there is much study and debate as to what those phrases might mean. Their definition becomes particularly problematical when one attempts to develop measures of listening comprehension or of reading comprehension. Davis (1941) was able to assemble a list of several hundred "reading comprehension skills," but since many of these overlapped, he grouped them into nine "testable skills," and in a factor analytic study (Davis, 1944) he felt he had confirmed the independent existence of these nine skills. Using a different factor-analytic approach, Thurstone (1946) claimed that these nine skills represented only one, or at most two independent factors of reading ability. In subsequent work, Davis (1968) reaffirmed the independent existence of eight of these skills, but if one considers the amount of unique variance residing in the tests of these skills one is tempted to conclude that perhaps only four or five of them merit recognition as distinct skills, and even these are rather highly correlated in high-school populations. These "factors" are: "remembering word meanings," "following the structure of a passage," "finding answers to questions answered explicitly or in paraphrase," "recognizing a writer's purpose, attitude, tone and mood," and "drawing inferences from the content."

The story is roughly the same in the field of "listening comprehension" testing. In planning the development of the so-called *STEP Tests of Listening* published by ETS (Educational Testing Service, 1956-59), a committee drew up an impressive list of "listening comprehension skills" that were to be represented in these tests, skills such as "plain-sense comprehension" (identifying main ideas, remembering details and simple sequences of ideas, understanding word meanings); "interpretation" (understanding implications of main ideas and significant details, interrelationships among ideas, and connotative meanings of words); and "evaluation and application" (judging validity of ideas, distinguishing fact from fancy, noting contradictions, judging whether the speaker has created the intended mood or effect, etc.). It can be seen that this is a true hodge-podge, but in view of the fact that the test committee had no real theory of listening comprehension on which to draw, this is pardonable. Other listening comprehension tests have been devised, such as the Brown-Carlsen test (Brown & Carlsen, 1953); what is rather disturbing, however, is that the various tests of "listening ability" tend to show no higher intercorrelations among themselves than they show with reading and intelligence tests (Kelly, 1965). The evidence suggests that listening tests measure a mixed bag of functions (Bateman, Frandsen, & Dedmon, 1964; Freshley & Anderson, 1968), but are mainly measures of "verbal ability."

In this connection it is necessary to point out that tests of listening comprehension and reading comprehension are designed to measure generalized skills of comprehension *ability*. The test maker is not concerned with measuring how well the examinee comprehends a *particular* spoken or written text; rather, he is concerned with the examinee's ability to comprehend a sample of such texts, in order to infer the examinee's ability to understand additional texts. Measuring comprehension *ability* is in some respects a problem quite different from that of measuring the degree of comprehension that a subject has when exposed to a *given* language stimulus. This latter problem will be considered in another section of this paper. But with regard to ability measurements, it should be mentioned that most presently available tests do not permit a satisfactory assessment of the individual's "absolute" level of comprehension ability. Even if it is assumed that comprehension ability is a unitary dimension of individual differences, tests do not permit the placement of an individual on a scale that would indicate in meaningful terms, for example, the difficulty level of textual materials that the individual would be able to comprehend to some desired criterion. The lack of such tests has made it difficult to assess accurately the distribution of levels of "literacy" in the U.S. population at different age levels.

Comprehension ability, however, is more likely a multidimensional affair. Whether one is concerned with spoken or printed language, the evidence suggests that the individual may have different levels of ability with respect to vocabulary, grammatical features, and other characteristics of texts. In listening comprehension, attentional, motivational, auditory, and memory factors may be involved (Spearritt, 1962). In reading comprehension, speed and level of comprehension have long been recognized as conceptually distinct even if they are not statistically independent (Blommers & Lindquist, 1944). Comprehension ability tests tend to be substantially correlated with "intelligence" tests, even those of a nonverbal character, such as a figure analogies test. This is not the place to try to interpret such a finding in depth. However, it is *à propos* to mention that one possible source of this correlation is the fact that reading and listening comprehension tests do not measure *only* what may be called "pure" comprehension of language; because of the way in which they are constructed, and the kind of items they include, they tend also to measure ability to make inferences and deductions from text content. A question that researchers should address is whether it is possible in fact to distinguish "pure" comprehension of language texts from processes of inference, deduction, and problem solving that often accompany the reception of language. An empirical research question would be to see whether it would be possible to decrease the correlation of comprehension ability tests with intelligence tests by eliminating or reducing those elements of comprehension tests that call for inferential processes that go beyond sheer comprehension. This problem has not, to my knowledge, been investigated.

Depending on the method of their administration, comprehension ability tests may also involve memory abilities. Research is needed to see to what extent it is possible to reduce their dependence on memory.

An adequate theory of language comprehension would undoubtedly be of help in the construction of comprehension ability tests. Bormuth (1970) has attempted to develop a systematic theory for this purpose. His approach utilizes the theory of transformational-generative grammar. In essence, he recommends that if one is interested in testing comprehension of a sentence or a longer discourse (or, indeed, a complete course of instruction in a subject-matter), the test questions should be based on transformations of sentences in the text to which the student has been exposed. For example, given the base sentence (1):

(1)   A very old man who lives up the street led his dog up to a store window one day.

one could form, through systematic applications of transformation rules, such questions as (1a − 1c):

(1a) Who led his dog?
(1b) What did the man lead?
(1c) Where does the man live?

Thus far Bormuth has offered only very simple examples of his technique, employing relatively simple grammatical transformations. One might suppose that such simple transformations would be within the reach of almost any native speaker beyond the stage of primary language acquisition. Nevertheless, in a study of fourth-grade children's ability to understand various syntactic structures, using these techniques, Bormuth, Manning, Carr, and Pearson (1970) concluded that "large proportions of the children were unable to demonstrate a comprehension of even these basic structures by which information is signaled . . . ." I suspect, however, that much more elaborate transformations, probably of a "semantic" character, would be required to provide effective comprehension test questions at higher levels of ability. Further development of Bormuth's approach would undoubtedly require a considerable amount of special-purpose linguistic research, as well as research in the psychometric application of the results.

Another important educational problem for which a theory of language comprehension might be able to give solutions is the problem that is referred to by the phrase "mere verbalization." By this is meant a kind of learning that goes only so far as to observe the words, and not the meaningful content, of didactic discourse. It is commonly noted that children can memorize rules and definitions without any evidence of true comprehension of them or of ability to apply them properly. How should we interpret this phenomenon? Is it simply another case of deficient language comprehension competence, is it a function of "set" or motivation, or is it a case of poor performance, i.e., errors in the application of knowledge?

This leads us to the more general problem of how we understand language and what we mean when we say we derive knowledge from language. Obviously this problem pervades education at all levels, because in view of the way in which educational programs are conducted, with lectures, readings, film narrations, and manifold other uses of language, it must be the case that educators have high expectations as to the efficacy of language communications. Yet it is obvious that learning from language does not always occur efficaciously. How shall we analyze these failures? To what extent are they due to deficits in language competence, and to what extent are they due to performance factors, the conditions of instruction, etc.? Questions such as these, it seems to me, are within the purview of this volume.

THE PROBLEM OF DEFINING
LANGUAGE COMPREHENSION

In approaching the definition of language comprehension, we may start with the observation that a mature language user can and often does render a judgment as to whether he does or does not comprehend a particular stretch of discourse. He may render this judgment with respect to a particular word, a phrase, a clause, a whole sentence, or a longer discourse. If a reader fails to understand a particular word, perhaps he will go and look it up in a dictionary or other reference work. Failure to understand a phrase or some longer stretch of discourse may prompt the reader to reinspect the preceding context, exhibiting "regressive" eye movements. In the case of a hearer, failure to understand something may prompt him to request clarification from the speaker (if present and available). Such behaviors are at least evidence for the proposition that an attentive language receiver continually monitors his own comprehension processes and is generally aware of whether he "comprehends" or not. It is also evidence that suggests that comprehension is an internal, subjective process that is in general not open to external observation. Even the detection of subvocal speech movements during silent reading by electromyography (Edfeldt, 1960; McGuigan, Keller, & Stanton, 1964) is only a very indirect and unreliable method of indexing comprehension.

At this stage of the discussion I am not claiming that the language receiver's judgment is veridical. At any point he may be misunderstanding the intent of the discourse even though he believes himself to be comprehending (the false positive case), and it is even possible that he actually understands even though he believes himself not to understand (the false negative case). Nevertheless, let us assume that in most cases the language receiver's judgments are reliable and veridical.

The simplest possible test of comprehension, therefore, is to have the language receiver render his subjective judgments of comprehension in an overt manner. This idea has been applied in certain kinds of experimental settings. For example, in unpublished work on "comprehension tracking" done by Daniel Forsyth and Herbert Rubenstein at the Harvard Center for Cognitive Studies (see the Center's *7th Annual Report*, 1966-67, pp. 26–27) sentences are presented one, two, and four words at a time by means of a computer-controlled CRT display. The subject observes the display and presses a button as soon as he thinks he comprehends it, causing the next segment to appear. The time that each segment is displayed, i.e., the time taken by S to report comprehension, is recorded by the computer and these times can be related to characteristics of the sentence fragments that have been presented—their length, their position in the sentence, their grammatical characteristics, etc. Danks (1969) presented subjects with short printed sentences and measured "comprehension time" by asking them to press a key as soon as they comprehended a given sentence. Some of the sentences were grammatically well-formed, meaningful sentences; others were deviant with respect to either grammar or meaning, or both. Danks found that the latencies for sentence comprehension were primarily a function of their meaningfulness; grammaticalness was only of secondary importance. He insured that the Ss kept "honest" in their reports of comprehension by requiring them to paraphrase the sentences on 40% of the trials. It is interesting, incidentally, that *S*s reported "comprehension" even of presumably meaningless, ungrammatical sentences such as "Guests tall fair sail goats." They did this either by misperceiving words (e.g., mistaking *goats* for *boats*) or by conjuring up highly fanciful interpretations (e.g., "Tall fair guests sail ships in the shape of goats"). This suggests that comprehension contains an element of problem solving.

There are obvious difficulties with subjective reports, even when accompanied by test probes, latency measurements, and the like. It would be inappropriate to use subjective reports in an adversary testing situation: imagine the chaos that would result if ETS asked students taking the SAT simply to report how well they understood reading comprehension paragraphs! Therefore we will want to consider more objective methods of testing comprehension.

Before doing so, perhaps we should make a preliminary characterization of language comprehension so that we may have some idea of what we are after in attempting to select more objective techniques of testing. It is particularly important to identify what accompanying processes we may wish *not* to test or measure. I can think of two candidates for such processes: memory and inference.

Memory. If comprehension is a process that occurs more or less simultaneously with the reception of a message, we would be interested in the occurrence or nonoccurrence of that process only during the reception of the message or at least within a very short time lag. Thus, if memory is to be involved at all, it should be only what has been called *short-term* memory, i.e., memory that can fade within a few seconds. As soon as longer time-intervals are involved in the testing of comprehension, there is the possibility that we are studying memory processes along with, or in place of, comprehension processes. For example, it is conceivable that there could be completely satisfactory comprehension at the time of message reception, but complete or nearly complete loss of that comprehension after the fading of short-term memory.

Some of the methodological problems in the use of memorial techniques to assess the comprehension of syntactic structures have been elucidated by Fillenbaum (1970). He shows, for example, that affirmative and negative yes/no questions are actually understood in different ways even though they appear to be similar in certain studies employing memory techniques. One may also be reminded of Epstein's (1969) experiment that suggested that the Savin and Perchonock (1965) "effect," whereby different types of sentences are claimed to occupy space in memory storage as a function of their transformational complexity, reflects retrieval rather than storage and comprehension processes.

There is also the possibility that there could be memories without comprehension, whatever comprehension may turn out to be. Marks and Jack (1952) give some data concerning immediate memory span for strings of various orders of "approximation to English," and although memory span increases with order of approximation, the results can be interpreted as suggesting that even when a sentence is not comprehended, rendition of at least a part of that sentence in immediate memory span can take place on the basis of pure memory. It is well known that with rehearsal and multiple trials, subjects can learn to reproduce much longer passages *verbatim* and without comprehension, e.g., materials in a foreign language.

It is curious, however, that, according to King and Russell (1966, p. 482), *S*s instructed to learn connected meaningful material for its substance and ideas "tend to recall proportionately more words, letters, sentences, etc., than ideas or sequences of words," whereas *S*s instructed to learn *verbatim* "recall proportionately fewer words, letters, sentences, etc., and more ideas."

Nevertheless, it is possible to take an entirely opposite view on the question of whether memory factors should be included in tests of comprehension. It can be argued that, at least in educational contexts, there is little use in comprehending a message unless the outcome of that comprehension is remembered and transferred to a long-term memory store. Certainly the evidence from a large number of studies employing memorial techniques is to the effect that material that is more "meaningful" and hence more easily comprehended is more likely to be retained. Thus, comprehension appears to facilitate memory even though it may be neither necessary nor sufficient for memory to occur.

Moreover, there is evidence to the effect that what is remembered from exposure to connected discourse tends to be its "meaning" content rather than the particular phraseology in which that meaning is couched. The work of Bartlett (1932), Gomulicki (1956), and Paul (1959), among others, shows that both in storage and retrieval processes subjects who are asked to learn connected discourse operate much more with "ideas" and basic meanings than with the *verbatim* phraseology. Sachs (1967a, 1967b) has shown that memory for syntactic and specific lexical content in prose fades very rapidly even when tested by recognition techniques, whereas memory for meaning persists much longer. What all this suggests is that the study of comprehension as such may profit from the judicious use of memorial techniques; with appropriate control of temporal factors one may largely eliminate the effect of quite superficial features of discourse, i.e., its surface structure in grammar and lexis, freeing one to deal only with deeper aspects of meaning. (Whether these deeper aspects of meaning are actually equivalent to the "deep structure" of transformational grammar is a question that I will not try to open at this point.) This conclusion actually has minimal conflict with the recommendations of Fillenbaum (1970) cited earlier, because Fillenbaum was concerned with the assessment of the understanding of syntactic features whose meaning components are relatively superficial, such as the difference between the sentences "Is the shop closed?" and "Isn't the shop closed?" that merely signals the speaker's expectation as to the answer.

Even though this discussion started with an argument against the use of memory techniques, we come out with a less trenchant attitude. On balance, we have to realize that memory factors can hardly be avoided, even when we try to restrict the testing of comprehension to an "immediate" test. For example, suppose we construct a typical reading comprehension test with paragraph stimuli and multiple-choice questions over the paragraphs. The test questions could be administered either with or without allowing the examinee to reexamine the paragraphs after he has had his initial opportunity to read and study them. If we do *not* permit reinspection of the paragraphs, we would certainly be emphasizing memory factors. The more typical manner of administering a reading comprehension test, however, is to allow inspection of the paragraphs along with the questions. Even this method does not completely eliminate memory because the examinee may still have to remember where in the paragraphs to look for a desired answer, and there is even the possibility of memory loss between the act of finding an answer and utilizing it in answering a question. Note that in the case of listening comprehension tests it is rarely possible for the examinee to rehear the initial material as he answers questions; in measuring listening comprehension we are virtually forced to allow memory factors to operate. Comparisons between reading and listening comprehension tests would have to control this factor.

Inference and related reasoning processes. I said above that we might want to consider eliminating inference and related reasoning processes from tests of comprehension. I had earlier suggested that many reading and listening comprehension ability tests may be for some purposes too heavily loaded with demands on the individual's reasoning processes, so that they tend to measure general verbal intelligence and reasoning skills rather than comprehension *per se.* Of course, it is possible that with the elimination of reasoning processes there would be nothing left, but I tend to doubt this in view of the factor analytic studies (e.g., Carroll, 1941) that have clearly separated inductive and deductive factors from "verbal ability." I would also appeal to the work of Davis (1968), who, at least according to my interpretation (Carroll, 1969), was able to separate several "pure" comprehension factors (depending, respectively, on lexical knowledge, grammatical knowledge, and an ability to "locate facts" in paragraphs) from an inferential factor requiring the examinee to go beyond the data given.

The problem of whether one wants to include "inference" in comprehension may be presented in a relatively simple form when we consider the three-term inference problem studied by Clark (1969), among others. That is, if we present a sentence like (2):

(2) John isn't as tall as Mary, but he is taller than Tom.

and then pose a question such as "Who is tallest?" or "Who is shortest?" or "Who is in-between?", producing the answer seems to require more than a simple "parsing" of the sentence. That is, a subject might fully "comprehend" the meanings of the two clauses without doing the additional processing of information required to answer such questions. The additional processing, perhaps, is dependent upon the question asked. Suppose one simply asked, "Who is shorter than Mary?" It seems likely (though I don't believe this experiment has been done) that the readiest answer would be "John," based solely on the first clause, thought "Tom" or "both John and Tom" would also be acceptable answers. Yet, even the processing of the first clause to yield the answer "John" intuitively requires a certain amount of intellectual effort that again goes beyond sheer comprehension, more effort, let us say, than answering the question, "Is John taller than Mary?" Clark's data suggest that there is a continuum ranging from comprehension of the simple surface structure in terms of what he calls its "functional relations" up through inferential processes of considerable complexity, whose stages can be identified by experimental techniques. (See Trabasso, this volume.) The problem we face is whether it is actually useful to draw a line between what I have called "simple comprehension," on the one hand, and "inferential processes," on the other, and if so, where on the continuum the line should be drawn. But even the three-term inference problem studied by Clark is by no means the most involved kind of inference required in standard reading comprehension tests. Consider the following item offered by Davis (1968) as measuring the skill of "making inferences about the content":

> The delight Tad had felt during his long hours in the glen faded as he drew near the cabin. The sun was nearly gone and Tad's father was at the woodpile. He was wearing the broadcloth suit that he wore to church and to town sometimes. Tad saw his father's hands close around a bundle of wood. He was doing Tad's work—and in his good clothes. Tad ran to him. "I'll git it, Pa."

> When Tad saw his father, he felt
> A disappointed
> B impatient
> C angry
> D guilty

It would seem extremely difficult (although conceivably it could be done) to specify any linguistic rules whereby the "correct" answer to this item could be predicted from the paragraph. Selecting the most likely correct answer seems to require, on the part of a test subject, not merely a literal comprehension of the paragraph and the question, but also an apprehension of the total situation described in the paragraph and a sensitivity to social relationships and expectations that are only hinted at in the paragraph. (In fact, the keyed answer, "*guilty*," is not the only answer that might conceivably be correct, given the statements in the paragraph. If Tad's father were a drunkard habitually given to acting on impulse and if Tad had promised his father that he would do his chores even if he were late, he might feel impatient, angry, or disappointed rather than guilty. This consideration adds weight to the assertion that an example of this sort suggests that inferential processing of information requires much more than literal comprehension.)

At least two important points emerge from this digression to explore processes that might accompany language comprehension:

(1) Language comprehension occurs in situational contexts whose characteristics may influence not only the degree to which comprehension processes operate but also the nature and extent of certain other processes that may accompany comprehension, usually as a consequence of it. The special arrangements that are frequently necessary to test comprehension constitute such situational contexts.

(2) Two processes often co-occurring with comprehension are memory and inference; while they are conceptually distinguishable from comprehension, their occurrence may make it difficult to assess the separate occurrence of the comprehension process itself.

Let us now address ourselves to attempting to make a preliminary characterization of language comprehension itself. I shall not attempt, however, to analyze the comprehension *process*, i.e., to specify *how* the individual arrives at a state of comprehension. This is a problem that has received much discussion, for example, in various papers presented at the Edinburgh University Conference on Psycholinguistics (Lyons & Wales, 1966), and it will undoubtedly be the concern of some of the other papers in this volume. For the purpose of providing a framework for assessing tests of comprehension, I am only interested in characterizing the end state of the comprehension process, that is, in specifying what the individual can be expected to have accomplished in comprehending a particular stretch of discourse.

To make the task somewhat less complicated than it might otherwise be, let us assume initially that the message is both "meaningful" and grammatically well-formed. Later we will consider cases in which there may be deviation from full meaningfulness and grammatical well-formedness.

The commonly accepted definition of comprehension is that it is the process of apprehending the "meaning" of something–the "meaning" of a word, of a phrase or idiom, of a sentence, or of a longer discourse. This implies that in order to assess the comprehension of a given segment of a verbal message, we must identify the "meaning" that is to be comprehended. The identification of meaning is a difficult and tangled problem, but I see no alternative to trying once more to explicate what is meant by meaning in the case of verbal discourse, at least to the extent of having a workable concept for use in assessing procedures for testing comprehension.

Discussions of meaning have often been encumbered by a failure to distinguish between the meaning of a given linguistic element that is implicit in the rules of its use in the speech-community and the total meaning of a discourse (of whatever length) composed of such elements. The kind of distinction I have in mind was referred to by Miller (1965, p. 18) when he urged that "the meaning of an utterance is not a linear sum of the meanings of the words that comprise it," but I feel that these different meanings of *meaning* need further explication.

First consider the "meaning of a given linguistic element." By "linguistic element" I mean any linguistic unit that has a meaning in the sense that one or more rules or conventions can be specified as to the relation of that unit with a concept or class of experiences as developed by members of the speech-community. The meaning of the linguistic unit would be incorporated in these rules or conventions. I do not wish to commit myself to any particular linguistic theory in saying this, nor to prompt a discussion of linguistic theories and techniques. I simply assume that however one analyzes a linguistic system, there are going to be certain units or elements whose correspondence with classes of speaker experiences can in theory be specified; examples of units might include, for example, what structural linguists have called morphemes and grammatical constructions, or what transformational linguists call formatives, base structures, etc., with meanings that could be quite concrete or quite abstract. A part of the "competence" of the language user is the "knowledge" of a large collection of these rules relating form and meaning. (I shall not try to specify how this "knowledge" should be characterized in psychological terms; it is not relevant here to discuss whether it is best conceptualized in terms of "cognitive structure," "habit," "response disposition," or whatever else might be proposed.)

We cannot, of course, expect every language user to have in his "competence" the sum total of the rules relating form and meaning in a given language, but it seems clear that the comprehension of any utterance or discourse would entail the knowledge of whatever rules are actually applied in that utterance or discourse. Thus, the comprehension of a sentence like (3):

(3) The Fundalan added an are to his plot.

would entail knowledge of such rules as the one whereby the suffix *-an* may imply "person originating from," the one indicating the possibility of the co-reference of *Fundalan* and *his*, the one whereby "are" is a noun denoting a unit of surface measure in the metric system, the rule specifying the meaning of the collocation "add" + "to," the rule specifying the meaning of "plot" as "a small piece of ground," and perhaps most important of all, the rules whereby the *Fundalan*, *added*, and *an are* stand in subject-verb-object relationship, with the meaning of that relationship.

A major contribution of contemporary linguistic developments has been to bring out the richness of the semantic and grammatical rules underlying linguistic elements. The rather primitive conceptions of word meanings exemplified in certain kinds of psycholinguistic investigations, such as studies of word association and of "semantic differential" ratings, fail to do justice to this richness. We now know that even single words like "add," "are," and "plot" entail elaborate lexicogrammatical information with respect to the classes of experience to which they relate along with the kinds of grammatical constructions in which they can participate. Thus, in tracing the development of an individual's competence in a language one must take account not only of frequently studied morphological and syntactical phenomena such as pluralization and passivization, but also of the detailed lexicogrammatical knowledge about individual elements that participate in these phenomena. For example, in a recent study I found that whereas most 6th graders know the meaning of *mill* (as a noun) in the sentence "The children walked to the mill," relatively few comprehend *mill* (as a verb) in the sentence, "Before class, the children mill in the halls" (Carroll, 1970).

Having tried to give some specification of what we mean by "the meaning of a linguistic element," we may turn our attention to trying to characterize the "total meaning of an utterance," whatever the length of that utterance. Clearly, as Miller noted, the total meaning is not the sum total of the meaning of the *words* in the utterance. But now that we have defined "linguistic element" in such a broad way as to include grammatical structures like the elements of phrase markers, it is tempting to conclude that the "total meaning" of an utterance is the sum total of the linguistic rules that have to be applied in the interpretation of the utterance, and that comprehension is therefore simply the application of these rules. Such a conclusion would correspond roughly to the proposal that has often been made that the comprehension of an utterance or discourse consists in the assignment of a "full structural description" to the message, if it is understood that such a structural description would have to include not only the ascription of a particular grammatical structure, but also the ascription of particular meanings to the constituents entering into that structure at various levels of analysis.

This solution does not seem completely satisfactory. One problem that arises is illustrated by the comprehender's task in assigning a meaning to "plot" in sentence (3). Suppose he knows that "plot" can mean either a "scheme, malicious plan" or "a small piece of ground." How does he know that in this sentence it means "small piece of ground"? That is, are there any linguistic rules that determine this? The kind of semantic theory developed by Katz and Fodor (1963) would probably answer that he knows it means "small piece of land" because both *are* and *plot* contain a common semantic feature of "surface area." In effect, the sentence signals that "the Fundalan added an area to his area," since a linguistic rule of interpretation would dictate that the meaning of "plot" should be selected in such a way as to accommodate its semantic features with those of other elements in the sentence. But such a rule may be gratuitous in the sense that it fails to honor the ability of the comprehender to "make sense" of the sentence "on his own," thus without applying such a rule. And in fact a context for sentence (3) is (rather remotely, one must admit) conceivable wherein "plot" is to be interpreted as "malicious scheme." Moreover, the sentence is ambiguous in a number of other ways: *Fundalan* and *his* may or may not be co-referential, and *Fundalan* may or may not denote a "person of Fundala," since this word might denote some person of authority like a *Nizam* or a *Mogul*—it might even denote a nonhuman entity, as some sort of decree like the Magna Carta. In actual use of the sentence in a discourse, these ambiguities could only be resolved by information given in some wider context, either preceding or following the sentence. It is possible that discourse rules could be devised and invoked to specify how the disambiguation would take place, and if so, one might say that the correct comprehension of the total meaning of the sentence would involve the correct application not only of rules applying narrowly within the sentence but also of rules relating the sentence to its wider context. It remains to be seen, however, whether discourse rules having the kinds of potentialities envisaged here can in fact be formulated.

What does, at any rate, seem to be suggested by this consideration of ambiguity is that the "total meaning" of an utterance has to do with the relation of a sentence or discourse to its total context. If we widen the context beyond a mere "verbal" context, that is, to include the total situation in which the message occurs, its "total meaning" may entail the point-to-point relations between the elements encoded in the sentence and the things, attributes, events, and relations existing in some actual or fictional reality. Comprehension of this "total meaning" would in this case imply awareness of these relationships. Thus, comprehension of sentence (3) would entail awareness of which Fundalan and which plot are referred to.

Suppose that sentence (3) occurs as the first sentence of a novel that is constructed in such a way that the full explanation of who or what the Fundalan was, and what was accomplished when an "are" was added to someone's plot, is disclosed only in the last chapter. If the "total meaning" of the sentence were held to be all these things, the gaining of that meaning is obviously a process that calls into play much more than a set of linguistic rules. This kind of "total meaning" would be best appreciated by a reader who returns to the first sentence after finishing the novel.

But what kind of comprehension could one expect when the reader reads the sentence for the first time? He could be expected at that point only to comprehend enough of it to get himself set to disambiguate the subsequent text at whatever pace the writer's design and the reader's patience would permit, and in this case we could say that comprehension entails the apprehension of just that amount of linguistic information that is "committed" to the sentence—information that could presumably be captured in a set of linguistic rules. Indeed, it might be part of the writer's design to leave the sentence ambiguous, allowing the reader to interpret it as he might. In such an interpretation, the predilection or disposition of the reader might be described probabilistically. For example, from past experience the reader would probably be more likely to infer the co-referentiality of *Fundalan* and *his* than the contrary. A joke-teller often deliberately leads a hearer into a misinterpretation of his opening narration so that the "punch line," requiring another interpretation, will have its humorous effect.

This line of argument suggests that an "adequate" comprehension of a message at the time of its reception may be achieved by the comprehension of just that linguistic information that is "committed" to the message in terms of its own structure and in terms of whatever information has been disclosed by virtue of previous context. Some of this information may be of an ambiguous character, to be disambiguated by later information, provided that memory for the former is adequate. At a later time, comprehension of "total meaning" becomes more complete.

Our preliminary characterization of language comprehension may be summarized by stating that comprehension of a message is adequate or satisfactory to the extent that the language receiver apprehends, at least provisionally, whatever linguistic information is present in the message and is able to relate that information to whatever context is available at a given time. This implies that comprehension may be regarded as a process that contains at least two stages: (a) apprehension of linguistic information, and (b) relating that information to wider context.

There is a kind of paradox or inconsistency in this that I cannot see how to resolve at the moment: I have tried to distinguish "literal" or "plain-sense" comprehension from processes of inference, yet the relating of linguistic information to a wider context may indeed require processes of inference. For example, "adequate" comprehension of the second clause of a sentence such as:

(4) John isn't as tall as Mary, but Mary is shorter than he.

would entail the detection of the logical contradiction contained there since the first clause provides the "wider context" to which the meaning of the second clause is to be related. Possibly one can resolve this contradiction by more closely identifying "literal" comprehension with the apprehension of linguistic information.

One may now ask what kind of comprehension can occur when messages are degraded in various ways. In natural situations, messages are often degraded by transmission failures, i.e., parts of the message do not reach the receiver. The concept of redundancy can and has been invoked to explain the fact that such a message can often be understood as well as, or nearly as well as, the original message; the redundancy may exist either purely among elements of linguistic information or between elements of linguistic information and some wider context. Nevertheless, redundancy is likely to involve probabilistic considerations in that a particular interpretation may become merely probable rather than certain.

Redundancy may also explain the fact that a subject in a psychological experiment such as the one conducted by Danks (1969) can claim to comprehend a scrambled, "ungrammatical" sentence such as (5):

(5) The helped nurse patient the.

even though interpretation may take somewhat longer, i.e., entail more processing of information, than it would if the sentence were unscrambled. The wider context contained in the subject's knowledge suggests, however, that the interpretation is more likely to be "The nurse helped the patient" than "The patient helped the nurse." Danks himself considers that the comprehension of deviant sentences of this type may be explained by an appeal to "Ziffian" rules (Ziff, 1964) whereby the "simplest route" from the deviant sentence to a nondeviant sentence would be found, but I feel that something more than these rules must be invoked. For example, the Ziffian "inversion" rule would not explain why the subject is more likely to select one interpretation than another in the sentence cited, because there are two possible inversions.

In naturalistic contexts, one would be interested in the case of comprehension of "unclear" or "poor" writing. In general, it would seem inappropriate to expect the individual to comprehend more information than has been "committed" to the message itself, yet we know that readers (and hearers) are often able to "make sense out of" unclear messages by some as yet unexplicated inferential processes.

There is also the obverse case, that is, the case in which a language receiver fails to comprehend a message, or misinterprets it. According to our analysis of the comprehension process, this could occur at either one or both of the two stages, apprehension of linguistic information, and relating this information to wider context. That is, either the individual does not have the knowledge of the linguistic rules required to form a proper reading of a message, or he fails in the processing of that information, or both kinds of failure occur.

Even more generally, the kind of problem posed by this analysis is the explanation of what processes occur in what we have called "relating linguistic information to a wider context." The study of linguistic rules whereby language receivers gain certain types of information from messages is important, but equally important— and probably independent of purely linguistic study—is the study of how the language user processes that information in order to assimilate or integrate it with his prior knowledge or cognitive structure.

THE TESTING OF COMPREHENSION

If the above analysis is correct, testing of comprehension involves consideration of the two conceptually separable stages of the comprehension process. That is, we would like to find out, in a given case, the extent to which the individual "correctly" apprehends the purely linguistic information that is "committed" to the message, and also the extent to which he "correctly" relates that information to some wider context.

There are several desiderata for tests of comprehension:

(1) *Validity*. An ideal test of comprehension should be valid in the sense that it reflects solely comprehension as defined here and not any other behavioral process such as memory, inference, guessing, or the like.

(2) *Reliability*. Ideally, a measure of comprehension should be reliable in the sense that it gives consistent outcomes on equivalent trials for a given individual.

(3) *Generality*. Ideally, a procedure for measuring comprehension should be applicable to (a) all types of verbal material, and (b) all classes of individuals. By "all types of verbal material," I have in mind variation in the quantity and complexity of the material—whether it be a single word, a single sentence, a paragraph, or a longer discourse, whether it be picturable or not, concrete or abstract, literary or technical in subject-matter, etc. By "all classes of individuals" I have in mind groups at different age levels, or with different degrees of competence in the language of the test.

(4) *Convenience and practicality*. The procedure should, ideally, be easy to prepare and easy to administer, and should yield outcomes that are easy to score or otherwise evaluate.

I have tried to develop a classification of procedures for testing comprehension on the basis of a survey of procedures followed either in psychometric devices or in experimental investigations. This proved to require a three-way classification in terms of (I) tasks, (II) types of measurements or observations taken, and (III) conditions of testing in terms of the temporal relations between presentation of the verbal stimulus and the taking of measurements or observations. Any given procedure can be classified as some combination of a particular task with a particular type of observational procedure with some particular arrangement of the temporal relationships involved. While the classifications of tasks, types of measurements, and conditions of measurement do not completely exclude overlap, the framework has been useful in organizing the subsequent discussion.

I. Tasks
  A. Subjective reports concerning:
    a. Comprehension vs. noncomprehension, degree of comprehension or comprehensibility
    b. Specific aspects of the message, e.g.:
      1. meaningfulness, analyticity, ambiguity, etc.
      2. grammaticality, "acceptability."
      3. "importance," "centrality," or "salience" of particular parts of the message.

  B. Reports of truth or falsity, or of equivalence (in some sense) with another stimulus
    a. Analytic judgments
    b. Verification with respect to another presentation
      1. With respect to another message (to determine equivalence of meaning)
      2. With respect to pictured referents
    c. Verification with respect to the individual's knowledge base

  C. Nonverbal response to the message: "following directions."

  D. Supplying missing elements in a message
    a. "Standard" cloze procedure (supplying missing words that have been deleted according to some rule)
    b. "Progressive" cloze procedure (progressive adding of words, with feedback)
    c. Sentence completions

    d. Supplying order (as in an anagram or sentence rearrangement task)

  E. Answering questions based on the message.
    a. Completion-type items
    b. Multiple-choice items

  F. Recognition of messages, or elements thereof, on subsequent presentation.

  G. Reproduction of the message, in whole or in part, in original form or in some transformation.
    a. Verbatim reproduction
    b. Paraphrase
    c. Translation into another language or symbolism
    d. The "probe latency" technique, e.g., reproduction of a given part of a message associated with a given cue
    e. Eye-voice span (in reading)

II. Measurements or observations
  A. Ratings or similar judgmental indices

  B. "Correctness" or response with respect to some criterion

  C. Time measurements
    a. Decision or response time
    b. Reading speed
    c. Learning time (or, number of trials)

  D. Physiological responses
    a. Overt: emotional responses such as laughter, fear, etc.; eye movements
    b. Covert: electromyography, GSR, etc.

III. Conditions of testing
  A. Responses elicited or observed simultaneously with message presentation
  B. Responses elicited or observed immediately following message presentation
  C. Responses elicited or observed after a delay.
    (In III B and III C the original message, in whole or in part, may or may not be physically available during elicitation of the response.)

The following discussion of the various procedures for testing comprehension will be arranged according to the tasks required of the individual whose comprehension is being tested.

1. *Subjective reports.* Some remarks on subjective reports of comprehension have already been made. If the subject's "honesty" and attention can be assured, and particularly if accompanying measurements such as decision time can be taken, subjective reports would seem to be valid and highly useful measurements of comprehension. They have been used only infrequently in psycholinguistic investigation however (Danks, 1969), and the full potentialities of the method have not been explored. For example, the method might be used to explore what particular elements of a message cause difficulty in comprehension, e.g., particular words, grammatical constructions, clauses, etc. By varying the nature of the message, as Danks did, it is possible to relate subjective ratings and decision times to message characteristics such as grammaticality, ambiguity, grammatical complexity, vocabulary

difficulty, etc. Kershner (1964) measured reading times for passages of different levels of difficulty, both before and after the subject learned that he was going to be required to answer questions on a passage. The amount of time taken by the subject to read a passage may be thought of as reflecting the judgment of the subject as to whether he understands it.

While subjective reports could easily yield false positive results when the individual believes himself to comprehend, but actually does not, it is unlikely that they would yield false negative results unless the individual is malingering. The presence of false positive results could be detected by use of certain other techniques, such as asking questions. If subjective reports of comprehension are taken simultaneously with, or immediately after, presentation of the message, memory factors will have little or no influence. The extent to which subjective reports of comprehension will reflect inferential processes would probably depend upon the degree to which the message requires the operation of such processes.

Unlike the remainder of the techniques, subjective reports of comprehension cannot be used in an adversary testing situation; the subject would be too likely to claim comprehension falsely.

2. *Reports of truth or falsity, or of equivalence (in some sense) with another presentation.* When verification of a message can be based either on the analyticity of the message or upon, say, a pictured referent, this technique has much to recommend it as a measurement of pure comprehension, because (if the subject is honest and attentive), a correct response is directly dependent upon comprehension. The technique has many of the features of the subjective report; in fact, it is a kind of subjective report of comprehension. On the other hand, when verification is against the knowledge base of the individual (e.g., "The capital of South Africa is Johannesburg: True or False?") it is more likely to measure that knowledge base than the presence of comprehension.

Because of the simplicity of the binary judgments required, the measurements may suffer from unreliability and therefore may have to be buttressed by additional measurements (replication, use of feedback and correction, and the like). Wason (1961) used this method in an experiment on the comprehension of negation; he measured the latency of judgments of the truth or falsity of analytic sentences like "88 is not an even number" and pooled the results over samples of such sentences. Nevertheless, Ss made relatively few errors. Extensive use of picture verification procedures has been made by Slobin (1966) and Gough (1965, 1966), with precautions similar to those taken by Wason. Gough experimentally varied the time relations between presentation of the verbal message and the picture.

An extension of this technique, particularly appropriate for listening comprehension, but also useful for reading comprehension, is to present a sentence and require S to choose which of several pictures best represents its meaning. Alternative choices can be designed to require S to make fine discriminations among linguistic elements. Its major disadvantages are its inconvenience (the difficulty of drawing satisfactory pictures) and the fact that there is probably a limit to what can be presented in pictorial form.

Another variant of this general technique would be to have S evaluate whether a given message is equivalent in some respect (e.g., meaning) to another message. A simple and common form of this procedure is to be found in vocabulary tests, where S is required to select a word similar in meaning to a key word. As applied to larger units such as sentences, the technique has received little use (unless one considers that certain types of multiple-choice comprehension tests are a variant of this technique).

3. *Nonverbal responses to a message: following directions.* Tests of S's ability to follow verbal directions by carrying out some performance have appeared in intelligence tests ever since the construction of the Army Alpha test in World War I, but have rarely been used in experimental studies of comprehension, despite the fact that such tests could be highly valid, reliable, and convenient measurements in many circumstances. Jones (1966) had children perform a cancellation task under instructions such as "Mark all the numbers [in a display] except 2, 5, 8." Shipley, Smith, and Gleitman (1969) tested children's comprehension by having them execute commands. Another variant of the technique has been effectively employed by Carol Chomsky (1969).

To insure validity, however, the task must be one that is not likely to be performed correctly unless S has understood the instructions. The procedure has the disadvantage that it may be applicable only to a certain limited set of verbal materials, and it may be subject to the influence of memory factors in that S may comprehend the instructions but forget them before he begins to perform the task.

4. *Supplying missing elements in messages.* The most typical and popular example of this technique is the "cloze" procedure introduced (or reintroduced) by Taylor (1953) initially as a measure of "readability" (the difficulty of a text). The procedure involves taking a passage of text and deleting words in it by some rule, e.g., every 5th word, every other noun, or every other "function" word. A subject is then presented with the passage and asked to guess the missing words. Usually the passage is presented in written form, in which case the missing words are indicated by blanks of a standard size, but techniques are also available for presenting the passage in auditory form (Peisach, 1965). The procedure has gained considerable acceptance as a measure of the *individual's* degree of comprehension of a given text (Bormuth, 1968; Greene, 1965; Taylor, 1957). Such measures are found to have substantial or even high correlations with more conventional tests of reading comprehension.

The validity of the "cloze" technique in measuring an individual's comprehension of a given text is open to some question. Weaver and Kingston (1963) performed a factor-analytic study that suggested that scores are affected by a special aptitude or ability for utilizing redundancy in a passage, and supplying missing elements, independent of verbal ability. Coleman and Miller (1968) tried to use the technique in measuring knowledge gained from prior inspection of the unmutilated passage but found that the scores were hardly higher, on the average, than those of Ss who had not been presented with the unmutilated passage. It would seem that cloze scores are dependent chiefly on what might be called the "local redundancy" of a passage, i.e., the extent to which linguistic cues in the immediate environment (generally, in the same sentence) of a missing word tend to supply it. Rankin (1958) found that cloze scores based on deletions of nouns and verbs seem to measure something other than what is measured by scores based on deletions of function words. There is no clear evidence that cloze scores can measure the ability to comprehend or learn the major ideas or concepts that run through a discourse. It is even possible to secure cloze scores on the basis of meaningless material so long as grammatical cues are present; thus, cloze scores are probably more dependent on detection of grammatical than of semantic cues. On the whole, the cloze technique in its usual form is too crude to permit measuring the degree to which the individual comprehends particular lexical or grammatical cues, or possesses a knowledge of specified linguistic rules. It probably depends to a considerable extent on inferential processes.

The "progressive cloze" technique requires the subject to guess each successive word of a passage. Rubenstein and Aborn (1958) allowed only one guess per word (but gave the correct word after each guess) and measured the difficulty of passages in terms of the percentage of words correctly guessed by a group of subjects. These scores were highly correlated with readability and learning scores obtained from other subjects. This illustrates use of the technique in scaling passage difficulty. Coleman and Miller (1968), however, used it in measuring an individual's ability to learn from a passage. Essentially, their procedure had the subject take two trials with the same passage. The gain in the percentage of correct guesses on the second trial was considered a measure of information gained through exposure on the first trial. Because of the interval between a guess on the first trial and a guess on the second trial their technique necessarily involves a memory factor and is thus not a pure measure of comprehension.

There are certain other forms of comprehension tests that require the supplying of missing elements from context and that are more highly focussed on testing the comprehension of particular types of cues. For example, a sentence may be given in which the supplying of the one missing word would be contingent (at least partly) on the detection of a particular grammatical or lexical cue. Sentence completion tests have been used in studies of grammatical ambiguity: the type of completion supplied by the subject indicates the particular interpretation he makes for an ambiguous expression (MacKay, 1966). When sentences are presented in a scrambled arrangement, the missing elements consist of the cues of word order that are present in normal text (Oléron, 1961); in reconstructing the text, the subject has to supply these elements from other types of cues.

5. *Answering questions based on the message.* One finds on nearly all standardized reading or listening comprehension tests the device of presenting a paragraph to read or listen to, with one or more questions to be answered over the content of the paragraph. Ordinarily, on reading tests this paragraph is available to the subject as he answers the questions; there is little control of the subject's strategy, and some subjects believe they will do better if they read the questions before they inspect the paragraph. In listening tests, the questions are usually given after the presentation of the message, and the subject has to depend on memory. Since the object is generally to measure comprehension *ability*, the selection of items is controlled by statistics concerning whether the correct answers on the individual items are correlated with scores on the test as a whole or with some external criterion such as

scholastic success. Scores on these tests are often highly correlated with measures of general verbal ability.

There is evidence that depending on the form and content of the questions, different kinds of reading or listening "skills" can be measured (Bateman, Frandsen, & Dedmon, 1964; Davis, 1968).

It is too often the case that the questions on reading and listening comprehension tests are not controlled for the ability of the subject to answer them above a chance level even if they are not exposed to the texts on which the questions are based. Often the questions can be answered on the basis of the subject's prior knowledge or on the basis of various incidental cues in the questions themselves. Sometimes the questions present difficulties that are extraneous to the comprehension of the text. A technique for controlling such factors has been presented by Marks and Noll (1967).

The construction of items for comprehension tests has traditionally been viewed as a matter requiring much ingenuity, creativity, and even artistry on the part of the item-writer. Bormuth (1970) has severely (and perhaps unjustly) criticized traditional test-construction procedures for their unsystematic, "unscientific" nature and suggests that a science of item-construction can be developed by using principles of transformational grammar. It remains to be seen whether such a suggestion can in fact lead to measurements of all the aspects of comprehension and learning that one might want to measure, but Bormuth's techniques have much promise for testing the individual's ability to apprehend the information provided by purely linguistic cues.

6. *Recognition of messages, or elements thereof, on subsequent presentation.* The recognition technique has been a traditional method of measuring learning and memory. The subject is presented with an array of material that he is asked to inspect or learn, after which (either immediately or after a delay) he is given elements of the original array together with new or modified elements and asked to indicate which elements are "old" and which are new. For example, Shepard (1967) asked college-age students to inspect, one by one, 612 short, unrelated sentences, after which they had to identify, in a series of 68 test pairs, which member of each pair had occurred in the previous series; they were 89% accurate in doing so (chance success being 50%). Since the sentences were all easily comprehensible on first presentation, the results undoubtedly reflect memory rather than comprehension processes.

Nevertheless, the recognition technique has been used by several investigators to examine detailed processes of comprehension. Clifton, Kurcz, and Jenkins (1965), and Clifton and Odom (1966) used a recognition task to index the grammatical similarity of sentences; after presentation of a series of sentences, these same sentences together with grammatical variants of them (involving negative, passive, and question transformations) were presented and the subject was asked to press a telegraph key whenever he thought he recognized one of the "old" sentences. Fillenbaum (1970), however, has shown that this technique was inadequate to capture subtle semantic differences among sentences. Lee (1965), Fillenbaum (1966), Newman and Saltz (1960), and Sachs (1967a, 1967b) have used the recognition task to determine the extent to which subjects remember the *verbatim* forms of words or sentences as opposed to their meanings. The evidence indicates, in general, that verbatim forms are remembered only for a relatively short time, if at all, whereas meanings are remembered much longer.

Another application of the recognition technique is the "chunked comprehension" test developed by Carver (1970). Carver presents a passage for reading, typically four or five paragraphs long. This is then immediately followed by a multiple-choice test that the examinee must complete without referring to the original passage. In each item of the multiple-choice test, each alternative consists of a "chunk" of the original—a clause, a phrase, or sometimes a single word; one "chunk," however, is changed in meaning by the substitution of a different word or phrase. The subject has to indicate which alternative does not convey the original meaning. An example will illustrate the technique. The first paragraph of one of Carver's selections is as follows:

> Voter apathy is almost a cliché in discussions of American politics. Yet, only a cursory look at voting and registration restrictions shows that many would-be voters do not cast ballots because they are prevented from doing so.

The test items covering this part of the selection are as follows:

1. (A)   Voter apathy
   (B)   is almost a cliché
   (C)   in discussions
   (D)   of American politics.
   (E)   A recent poll directed
2. (A)   at voting
   (B)   and registration restrictions
   (C)   shows that
   (D)   many would-be voters
   (E)   seldom protest or demonstrate
3. (A)   because they are prevented
   (B)   from doing so.
   (C) ⎫
   (D) ⎬ [The remaining alternatives cover the beginning of the next paragraph
   (E) ⎭ in the selection.]

The changed alternatives are constructed and item analyzed in such a way that individuals who have not read the original passage are unable to score much above chance; doubtless this process requires much ingenuity and experimentation.

By definition, the recognition technique reflects memory processes. Even if comprehension processes are involved, it is difficult to separate their effects from those of memory processes. Thus, Carver's "chunked comprehension" test cannot be regarded as a measure of comprehension as such; in fact, the manual for the published version of the test (Darby & Carver, 1970) states that it is designed to test "memory storage" for verbal content. It is a test of comprehension only to the extent that memory processes may be assumed to be solely a function of degree of comprehension, at least in the test situation. Some support for such an assumption can be found in Underwood's (1964) suggestion that amount of retention, when temporal factors are controlled, is chiefly a function of degree of original learning.

Even so, this would imply that the recognition technique can be used to index comprehension only when there is precise control of temporal factors.

7. *Reproduction of the message, in whole or in part, in original form or in some transformation.* An extraordinary variety of techniques for testing or investigating language comprehension or verbal learning involve tasks requiring reproduction of a message in some form. Depending on the nature of the task and the conditions of testing, memory processes may be involved, and thus, as in the case of the recognition task just discussed, the respective roles of comprehension and memory processes may be difficult to isolate.

For example, verbatim recall of single sentences immediately after visual or auditory presentation may depend either on pure memory span or upon comprehension, or some combination thereof. There is no systematic body of information about memory span for verbal material. Miller (1956) reports data from Hayes that indicate that the memory span for unrelated words is above 5 for mature speakers. As soon as there is any degree of semantic or syntactic organization in a series of words presented for immediate recall, the number of words that can be recalled increases beyond the span for unrelated, meaningless materials (Marks & Jack, 1952). This is not to say, however, that short-term memory factors cease to operate. Memory span for well-formed sentences has been considered an index of mental age (Terman, 1916, pp. 37-39). It has also been used in the study of the development of linguistic competence in young children (e.g., Slobin & Welsh, 1968).

The experimental study of verbatim reproduction of longer passages (Clark, 1940; Henderson, 1903; Lyon, 1917) has generally depended on a scoring procedure known as the "method of retained members." The stimulus passage is divided into a number of phrasal units of approximately equal size; the subject's response is then scored in terms of the number of these units that are reproduced. Levitt (1956) showed that different investigators are likely to make different divisions of a passage and these differences are likely to be reflected in recall scores. There seems to have been no application of strictly linguistic procedures to determine what units should be scored. King (1960, 1961) and his collaborators (King & Russell, 1966; King & Yu, 1962) have reported a series of studies showing that when judges are asked to scale written recalls for excellence, two factors influence their judgments: a "quantitative" factor having to do with the *amount* of recall (number of words, and the like), and an "organization" factor having to do with the quality and organization of the semantic content. This result implies, incidentally, that judges differ in the extent to which they are influenced by these factors.

One of the more perceptive studies of verbatim recall that I have found was by Gomulicki (1956), who presented his subjects with 37 prose passages, from 13 to 95 words in length. He studied the reproduction of each word, judging it as either "adequate" or "inadequate." Over the whole set of reproductions, 55.5% words were reproduced verbatim, 32.7% were omitted, 11.8% were changed, and 6.2% were added words or ideas. The frequency with which a given element was "adequately" represented was regarded as a measure of its "mnemic value." Mnemic value was then studied as a function of semantic content (action vs. description) and grammatical function. Recall was regarded as an "abstractive process." The best remembered materials described actor-action-effect sequences; there was even a tendency for Ss to turn descriptive passages into "quasi-narratives."

Immediate verbatim recall of verbal materials has been used to study many aspects of language behavior and learning: basic processes in recall (Bartlett, 1932; Paul, 1959); the effect of "order of approximation to English" (Miller & Selfridge, 1950; Tulving & Patkau, 1962); the effect of syntax and other grammatical factors (Miller, 1962; Slobin & Welsh, 1968); the effect of instructions as to what is to be recalled (King & Russell, 1966); the effect of associational factors (Rosenberg, 1968); and oral vs. printed stimuli (King & Madill, 1968).

Space does not permit discussion of the many variants of the recall task: delayed verbatim recall (Slamecka, 1959); recall after interpolated material (Savin & Perchonock, 1965); time for verbatim learning to a criterion (Follettie & Wesemann, 1967; Rubenstein & Aborn, 1958); paired-associate learning in which sentences are the responses (Martin & Jones, 1965); serial learning of sentences (Epstein, 1962); etc. Although the effects of various message characteristics (meaningfulness, grammatical structure, etc.) on the recalls can be studied by appropriate experimental controls, it remains difficult to differentiate comprehension, storage, and retrieval processes.

There are several special variants of the message-reproduction task that deserve consideration. One is the paraphrasing task, i.e., reproducing the message in the S's "own words." Generally it is required that this task be performed without S's being able to refer to the original message, but if memory processes are to be excluded, this need not necessarily be the case. If paraphrases can be objectively and validly scored, this task may be a useful technique for measuring comprehension. The catch is that it may be very difficult to score paraphrases for conformity of content to the original, as was noted for example by Downey and Hakes (1968). Moreover, telling the subject to use his "own words" may place an extra burden on him when he interprets this as meaning that he cannot use the words of the original message. And, of course, it is possible for paraphrases to be nothing more than grammatical transformations performed without full comprehension of semantic content.

The writer (Carroll, 1970) recently used a paraphrase task to study children's comprehension of single words used in unusual grammatical functions; the words in question were placed in imaginary "headlines" such as WHEN YOU ARE LOST, SOMEONE WILL *PAGE* YOUR MOTHER. High reliability in scoring the responses was achieved, but it was probably the case that some unsuccessful responses reflected simple inability to create a paraphrase even though the respondent actually comprehended the sense of the message; this would be an example of a false negative outcome.

Translating a message into another language is a traditional method of assessing comprehension in foreign-language learning, as where an English-speaking student is required to translate a French sentence or paragraph into English. Obviously, this method cannot be generally used in testing native-language comprehension, and even in foreign language instruction there is the problem of attaining adequate scorer reliability, not to mention the problem of defining what a truly adequate translation is.

The translation of verbal messages into mathematical or logical symbolism might appear to be an analogous possibility. I have in mind the kind of comprehension required, for example, in order to state an algebraic formula for the solution of a verbally-stated mathematical problem. I have not looked into the research literature concerning this problem, as there are obvious drawbacks to the generality of the procedure (the respondent's knowledge of the mathematical or logical symbolism involved would be a factor, certainly).

The "eye-voice span" in reading a text has been used by several investigators (e.g., Levin & Kaplan, 1970; Schlesinger, 1966) as an index of comprehension processes. It can be regarded as a variant of the reproduction task, in that the subject is required to reproduce that part of a printed message that is within his span of perception but not yet read aloud, in an oral reading task in which the subject's viewing of the stimulus is suddenly terminated at a particular moment. Presumably, the eye-voice span reflects the additional information processing that the subject is performing on material ahead of what he is reading aloud at that moment. While it may represent the operation of sentence-comprehension processes, it may also reflect certain inferential and guessing processes similar to those tapped in the "cloze" technique.

SUMMARY

This brief survey of techniques that have been used to test language comprehension points up the fact that there is no one technique that universally gives valid and reliable information. It is seldom the case that success or failure in any of these tests can unequivocally be traced to success or failure in language comprehension since there are other factors of guessing, inference, memory, reliance on prior knowledge, etc., that are operating. The influences of these other factors must be controlled as fully as possible by variation of message characteristics, control of temporal factors, and instructions to the subject.

In this discussion, not much has been said about the capability of the techniques to distinguish the two processes earlier identified as inherent in comprehension: apprehension of linguistic information, and relating that information to a wider context. Psycholinguistic investigations have, for the most part, ignored this problem. Little context is offered when single sentences are presented, and when the comprehension of longer discourse has been studied, there has been little attempt to explicate contextual elements or to vary them experimentally. Whether such an approach would be useful remains to be seen.

CONFERENCE DISCUSSION

A number of conferees expressed concern about the validity of using questions on a text to assess comprehension of it. It was pointed out, on the one hand, that sometimes questions can be answered quite well even without reading the text, and on the other hand, that the questions may be more difficult to understand than the text itself. Coleman felt, for example, that some of Bormuth's (1970; also Bormuth et al., 1970) questions were quite hard to understand, particularly when they tested for understanding of constraints between (as opposed to within) sentences. Carroll felt that there were indeed problems here, but that they could be minimized by performing suitable experimental research on the questions. He had mentioned in his paper the techniques developed by Marks and Noll (1967) and felt that these should be more widely known and employed. Essentially, these techniques compare performance of Ss on the questions as a function of whether or not they have read the text, and input the data into a statistical model to evaluate the adequacy of each item.

Scriven observed that sometimes the background knowledge required by a question (quite apart from the information provided by the text) may be very complicated, even though the question may look very simple.

Goodman pointed out that people can often devise strategies of responding to question formats that defeat the testing of comprehension *per se*. For example, in responding to Bormuth's transformed questions, a subject sometimes needs only to search for a sentence in the passage that contains the same elements; he can often answer the question on the basis of an "automatic" response to grammatical transformation, without necessarily paying attention to the total meaning of the question and the text. He is only manipulating syntactic forms, not the semantics. Carroll tended to agree with Goodman on this point, but felt that the solution would lie in the direction of trying to formulate the rules for *semantic* transformations, basing questions on the application of such rules. The examples of grammatical transformation Bormuth gives in his book are admittedly too simple, but the basic idea could be extended, Carroll thought.

Trabasso moved the discussion to a somewhat more theoretical plane by observing that while Carroll had classified the major methods used in the literature to measure "comprehension," hardly any of these had been devised on the basis of an explicit model of comprehension. It could at least be said that Bormuth had tried to state an explicit model (albeit primarily a syntactic one) which indicates the stages that one must go through (i.e., transformations) in order to reach a level at which a matching operation can be applied between question and text. But to do an adequate job of studying comprehension we must specify the operations underlying the "sheer" comprehension of the text as well as the operations underlying the comprehension of the questions used to assess degree of comprehension. There must be at least two sets of processes going on: one set deals with the analysis of the text as stimulus while the other deals with the analysis of questions which initiate the search for an appropriate response, if any, on the part of the subject.

This line of thinking led Trabasso to wonder, at this point, whether factor-analytic work on comprehension tests which have not been constructed according to an explicit comprehension model could be expected to yield any useful results. It seemed to him that one ends up merely classifying tests on the basis of their factor loadings, but in so doing one does not necessarily discover anything about the psychological processes that lie behind comprehension. Carroll granted that most factor-analytic work on comprehension tests has not yielded much information about *processes*, probably because there has generally been a failure to construct the tests on the basis of any clear theory. Nevertheless, he pointed out that the technique of factor analysis lends itself to the testing of hypotheses and theories. One can start with a set of initial hypotheses about factors, construct tests that presumably measure those factors, and then determine whether the tests load on factors as expected. If not, one can revise the hypotheses, construct new tests, and do a further analysis. This kind of cyclic testing of hypotheses has never been thoroughly carried out in the domain of comprehension tests, although it has been done in other domains (e.g., spatial abilities). Some of Guilford's (1967) work on "structure of intellect" factors may be applicable here; it may be said that Guilford starts from a kind of information-processing model concerning intellectual tasks, and comprehension is one such task.

Frederiksen expanded on this theme by mentioning that the assumptions underlying certain information-processing models could lead one to predict that certain patterns of correlations (covariances) would occur among a set of response measures obtained, for example, under different testing procedures. Such predictions could be tested by factor-analytic methods, and the results could allow one to decide whether or not the assumptions of the information-processing model needed to be revised or not.

Some of the difficulties posed by experimentation in sentence comprehension center on the problem of whether processes occurring in such experiments are truly similar to those occurring in natural situations. Carroll was reminded of an experiment he had recently come across (Feldman, 1971) which appeared to show that in natural conversations, people are not as much troubled by transformations and other sentence complexities as they are in experimental situations.

The discussion ended with a consideration of a point raised by Goodman. Goodman felt that there had not been adequate attention to two different aspects of language use: the acquisition of knowledge through language and the understanding of a message which is already within the conceptual grasp of the language user. For example, if someone says to you, "Close the door," or even, "The door is closed," this kind of message doesn't expand your knowledge domain in any real sense. But if someone says to you, "The door is made of mahogany," this may convey new knowledge to you. Chafe thought, however, there was no real distinction here: it was simply a matter of the relative transitoriness or permanence of the knowledge. Goodman's rejoinder was the observation that in any case, what one is capable of taking away from messages will depend upon the level of knowledge that the listener or reader already possesses. The depth to which one understands a passage may be intimately related to what one already knows.

REFERENCES

Bartlett, F. C. *Remembering*. Cambridge, England: Cambridge University Press, 1932.

Bateman, D., Frandsen, K., & Dedmon, D. Dimensions of "lecture comprehension": A factor analysis of listening test items. *Journal of Communication*, 1964, **14**, 183–189.

Blommers, P. J., & Lindquist, E. F. Rate of comprehension of reading: Its measurement and its relation to comprehension. *Journal of Educational Psychology*, 1944, **35**, 449–473.

Bormuth, J. R. Cloze test readability: Criterion reference scores. *Journal of Educational Measurement*, 1968, **5**, 189–196.

Bormuth, J. R. *On the theory of achievement test items. With an appendix by P. Menzel: On the linguistic bases of the theory of writing items*. Chicago: University of Chicago Press, 1970.

Bormuth, J. R., Manning, J., Carr, J., & Pearson, D. Children's comprehension of between- and within-sentence syntactic structures. *Journal of Educational Psychology*, 1970, **61**, 349–357.

Brown, J. I., & Carlsen, G. R. *Brown-Carlsen listening comprehension test*. New York: Harcourt, Brace & World, 1953.

Carroll, J. B. A factor analysis of verbal abilities. *Psychometrika*, 1941, **6**, 279–307.

Carroll, J. B. From comprehension to inference. In M. P. Douglas (Ed.), *Thirty-third yearbook, Claremont reading conference*. Claremont, Calif.: Claremont Graduate School, 1969.

Carroll, J. B. *Comprehension by 3rd, 6th, and 9th graders of words having multiple grammatical functions*. Final Report, Educational Testing Service, Princeton, N. J., December 1970. Project No. 9–0439, Grant No. OEG–2–9–400439–1059, U. S. Office of Education. (ERIC Document Reproduction Service, Document ED 048311.)

Carver, R. P. Analysis of "chunked" test items as measures of reading and listening comprehension. *Journal of Educational Measurement*, 1970, **7**, 141–150.

Chomsky, C. *The acquisition of syntax in children from 5 to 10*. Cambridge, Mass.: M. I. T. Press, 1969.

Clark, H. H. Linguistic processes in deductive reasoning. *Psychological Review*, 1969, **76**, 387–404.

Clark, K. B. Some factors influencing the remembering of prose materials. *Archives of Psychology*, No. 253, New York, 1940.

Clifton, C., Jr., Kurcz, I., & Jenkins, J. J. Grammatical relations as determinants of sentence similarity. *Journal of Verbal Learning and Verbal Behavior*, 1965, 4, 112–117.

Clifton, C., Jr., & Odom, P. Similarity relations among certain English sentence constructions. *Psychological Monographs: General and Applied*, 1966, 80(5).

Coleman, E. B., & Miller, G. R. A measure of information gained during prose learning. *Reading Research Quarterly*, 1968, 3, 369–386.

Danks, J. H. Some factors involved in the comprehension of deviant English sentences. (Doctoral dissertation, Princeton University) Ann Arbor, Mich.: University Microfilms, 1969. No. 69–2735.

Darby, C. A., Jr., & Carver, R. P. *Manual for the Carver-Darby chunked reading test.* Silver Spring, Md.: American Institutes for Research, 1970.

Davis, F. B. Fundamental factors of comprehension in reading. Unpublished doctoral dissertation, Harvard University, 1941.

Davis, F. B. Fundamental factors of comprehension in reading. *Psychometrika*, 1944, 9, 185–197.

Davis, F. B. Research in comprehension in reading. *Reading Research Quarterly*, 1968, 3, 499–545.

Downey, R. G., & Hakes, D. T. Some psychological effects of violating linguistic rules. *Journal of Verbal Learning and Verbal Behavior*, 1968, 7, 158–161.

Edfeldt, A. W. *Silent speech and silent reading.* Chicago: University of Chicago Press, 1960.

Educational Testing Service. *Sequential tests of educational progress: Listening.* Princeton, N. J.: ETS, 1956–1959.

Epstein, W. A further study of the influence of syntactic structure on learning. *American Journal of Psychology*, 1962, 75, 121–126.

Epstein, W. Recall of word lists following learning of sentences and of anomalous and random strings. *Journal of Verbal Learning and Verbal Behavior*, 1969, 8, 20–25.

Feldman, Carol F. The interaction of sentence characteristics and mode of presentation in recall. *Language and Speech*, 1971, 14, 18–25.

Fillenbaum, S. Memory for gist: Some relevant variables. *Language and Speech*, 1966, 9, 217–227.

Fillenbaum, S. On the use of memorial techniques to assess syntactic structures. *Psychological Bulletin*, 1970, 73, 231–237.

Follettie, J. F., & Wesemann, A. F. Effects of grammatical factors and amount of material on memorizing paragraphs, sentences and word lists. Human Resources Research Organization, No. 67–9, 1967. (Document AD 656 454, Clearinghouse for Federal Scientific and Technical Information.)

Freshley, D. L., & Anderson, H. E., Jr. A factor analytic study of listening. Paper presented at the meeting of the American Educational Research Association, Chicago, February 1968.

Gomulicki, B. R. Recall as an abstractive process. *Acta Psychologica*, 1956, 12, 77–94.

Gough, P. B. Grammatical transformations and speed of understanding. *Journal of Verbal Learning and Verbal Behavior*, 1965, 4, 107–111.

Gough, P. B. The verification of sentences: The effects of delay of evidence and sentence length. *Journal of Verbal Learning and Verbal Behavior*, 1966, 5, 492–496.

Greene, F. P. A modified cloze procedure for assessing adult reading comprehension. (Doctoral dissertation, University of Michigan) Ann Arbor, Mich.: University Microfilms, 1965. No. 65–5308.

Guilford, J. P. *The nature of human intelligence.* New York: McGraw-Hill, 1967.

Henderson, E. M. A study of memory for connected trains of thought. *Psychological Monographs*, 1903, 5 (6, Whole No. 23).

Jones, S. The effect of a negative qualifier in an instruction. *Journal of Verbal Learning and Verbal Behavior*, 1966, 5, 497–501.

Katz, J. J., & Fodor, J. A. The structure of a semantic theory. *Language*, 1963, 39, 170–210.

Kelly, C. M. An investigation of the construct validity of two commercially published listening tests. *Speech Monographs*, 1965, 32, 139–143.

Kershner, A. M. Speed of reading in an adult population under differential conditions. *Journal of Applied Psychology*, 1964, **48**, 25–28.

King, D. J. On the accuracy of written recall: A scaling and factor analysis study. *Psychological Record*, 1960, **10**, 113–122.

King, D. J. Scaling the accuracy of recall of stories in the absence of objective criteria. *Psychological Record*, 1961, **11**, 87–90.

King, D. J., & Madill, J. Complex methods of presentation, internal consistency of learning material, and accuracy of written recall. *Psychological Reports*, 1968, **22**, 777–782.

King, D. J., & Russell, G. W. A comparison of rote and meaningful learning of connected meaningful material. *Journal of Verbal Learning and Verbal Behavior*, 1966, **5**, 478–483.

King, D. J., & Yu, K. C. The effect of reducing the variability of length of written recalls on the rank order scale values of the recalls. *Psychological Record*, 1962, **12**, 39–44.

Lee, W. Supra-paragraph prose structure: Its specification, perception, and effects on learning. *Psychological Reports*, 1965, **17**, 135–144.

Levin, H., & Kaplan, E. Grammatical structure and reading. In H. Levin and J. P. Williams (Eds.), *Basic studies on reading*. New York: Basic Books, 1970.

Levitt, E. E. A methodological study of the preparation of connected verbal stimuli for quantitative memory experiments. *Journal of Experimental Psychology*, 1956, **52**, 33–38.

Lyon, D. O. *Memory and the learning process*. Baltimore: Warwick & York, 1917.

Lyons, J., & Wales, R. J. (Eds.) *Psycholinguistics papers: The proceedings of the 1966 Edinburgh conference*. Edinburgh: Edinburgh University Press, 1966.

MacKay, D. G. To end ambiguous sentences. *Perception and Psychophysics*, 1966, **1**, 426–436.

Marks, E., & Noll, G. A. Procedures and criteria for evaluating reading and listening comprehension tests. *Educational and Psychological Measurement*, 1967, **27**, 335–348.

Marks, M. R., & Jack, O. Verbal context and memory span for meaningful material. *American Journal of Psychology*, 1952, **65**, 298–300.

Martin, J. G., & Jones, R. L. Size and structure of grammatical units in paired-associate learning at two age levels. *Journal of Experimental Psychology*, 1965, **70**, 407–411.

McGuigan, F. J., Keller, B., & Stanton, E. Covert language responses during silent reading. *Journal of Educational Psychology*, 1964, **55**, 339–343.

Miller, G. A. The magical number seven plus or minus two: Some limits on our capacity for processing information. *Psychological Review*, 1956, **63**, 81–97.

Miller, G. A. Some psychological studies of grammar. *American Psychologist*, 1962, **17**, 748–762.

Miller, G. A. Some preliminaries to psycholinguistics. *American Psychologist*, 1965, **20**, 15–20.

Miller, G. A. & Selfridge, J. A. Verbal context and the recall of meaningful material. *American Journal of Psychology*, 1950, **63**, 176–185.

Newman, S. E., & Saltz, E. Effects of contextual cues on learning from connected discourse. *American Journal of Psychology*, 1960, **73**, 587–592.

Oléron, G. Compréhension d'un texte et liaisons entre les mots. *Année Psychologique*, 1961, **61**, 377–395.

Paul, I. H. Studies in remembering: The reproduction of connected and extended verbal material. In G. S. Klein (Ed.), *Psychological Issues*. New York: International Universities Press, 1959.

Peisach, E. C. Children's comprehension of teacher and peer speech. *Child Development*, 1965, **36**, 467–480.

Rankin, E. F., Jr. An evaluation of cloze procedure as a technique for measuring reading comprehension. (Doctoral dissertation, University of Michigan) Ann Arbor, Mich.: University Microfilms, 1958. No. 58–3722.

Rosenberg, S. Language habits and the recall of connected discourse. In E. M. Zale (Ed.), *Proceedings of the conference on language and language behavior*. New York: Appleton-Century-Crofts, 1968.

Rubenstein, H., & Aborn, M. Learning, prediction, and readability. *Journal of Applied Psychology*, 1958, **42**, 28–32.

Sachs, J. S. Recognition memory for syntactic and semantic aspects of connected discourse. *Perception and Psychophysics*, 1967, **2**, 437–442. (a)

Sachs, J. S. Recognition of semantic, syntactic and lexical changes in sentences. Paper presented at the meeting of the Psychonomic Society, Chicago, Illinois, October 1967. (b)

Savin, H. B., & Perchonock, E. Grammatical structure and the immediate recall of English sentences. *Journal of Verbal Learning and Verbal Behavior*, 1965, **4**, 348–353.

Schlesinger, I. M. The influence of sentence structure on the reading process. Technical Report No. 24, October 1966, The Hebrew University, Jerusalem, Contract No. N 62558–4695 NR 049–130, U. S. Office of Naval Research. (Document AD 653 263, Clearinghouse for Federal Scientific and Technical Information.)

Shepard, R. N. Recognition memory for words, sentences, and pictures. *Journal of Verbal Learning and Verbal Behavior*, 1967, 6, 156–163.

Shipley, E. F., Smith, C. S., & Gleitman, L. R. A study in the acquisition of language. *Language*, 1969, **45**, 322–342.

Slamecka, N. J. Studies of retention of connected discourse. *American Journal of Psychology*, 1959, 72, 409–416.

Slobin, D. I. Grammatical transformations and sentence comprehension in childhood and adulthood. *Journal of Verbal Learning and Verbal Behavior*, 1966, 5, 219–227.

Slobin, D. I., & Welsh, C. A. Elicited imitations as a research tool in developmental psycholinguistics. Working paper No. 10, May 1968. Berkeley, Calif.: Language Behavior Research Laboratory, University of California.

Spearritt, D. *Listening comprehension–a factorial analysis*. Melbourne: Australian Council for Educational Research, 1962.

Taylor, W. L. "Cloze procedure": A new tool for measuring readability. *Journalism Quarterly*, 1953, 30, 415–433.

Taylor, W. L. Cloze readability scores as indices of individual differences in comprehension and aptitude. *Journal of Applied Psychology*, 1957, 41, 12–26.

Terman, L. M. *The measurement of intelligence*. Boston: Houghton Mifflin, 1916.

Thurstone, L. L. Note on a reanalysis of Davis' reading tests. *Psychometrika*, 1946, **11**, 249–255.

Tulving, E., & Patkau, J. F. Concurrent effects of contextual constraint and word frequency on immediate recall and learning of verbal material. *Canadian Journal of Psychology*, 1962, **16**, 83–95.

Underwood, B. J. Degree of learning and the measurement of forgetting. *Journal of Verbal Learning and Verbal Behavior*, 1964, 3, 112–129.

Wason, P. C. Response to affirmative and negative binary statements. *British Journal of Psychology*, 1961, **52**, 133–142.

Weaver, W. W., & Kingston, A. J. A factor analysis of the cloze procedure and other measures of reading and language ability. *Journal of Communication*, 1963, 13, 252–261.

Ziff, P. On understanding "understanding utterances." In J. A. Fodor and J. J. Katz (Eds.), *The structure of language*. Englewood Cliffs, N. J.: Prentice-Hall, 1964.

2
THE CONCEPT OF COMPREHENSION: FROM SEMANTICS TO SOFTWARE[1]

Michael Scriven
University of California at Berkeley

INTRODUCTION

An argument is given that simple considerations of efficiency for an information acquisition-storage-retrieval-reaction device (IPD) interacting with a complex informationally rich environment will necessitate strategies that ensure meeting the criteria for comprehension. The first section analyzes "comprehension," the second deals with efficiency in IPDs, and in the third, implications of a comprehension theorem are briefly discussed.

Comprehension

The term "comprehension" appears to be essentially synonymous with "understanding" over its main range (although its range is desirably narrower, excluding the use of the latter in "*an* understanding" that is roughly equivalent to "an arrangement or agreement"). These concepts are intimately related to the concepts of explanation and knowledge, so the present result has some significance for explanation-theory and for epistemology. An explanation is a device or process for communicating comprehension and knowledge is the generic state under which fall the various species of comprehension, *inter alia*.

We can identify from previous discussions (Scriven, 1964) a positive and a negative way of precisifying the concept of comprehension. We may give (paradigm) *examples* of it or (paradigm) *contrasts* to it. Five 'types' of comprehension can be exemplified of which it is sometimes said that one or another of them is the 'real,' 'best,' 'fundamental,' or 'only scientific' sense. The present treatment analyzes all

[1] This work has been supported in part by an NSF Grant.

five as special cases of one concept, not as different senses or concepts. The same applies to the four main contrasts. (The phrasing is in terms of "understanding" because of its greater range of correlatives in English.)

Example 1. Understanding an event, phenomenon, or process, such as transistor deterioration or an error in reasoning.

Example 2. Understanding a theory, such as information theory.

Example 3. Understanding a natural language, such as English.

Example 4. Understanding an experience, such as the experience of divorce or childbirth.

Example 5. Understanding an entity or a class of entities, such as divorcees, children, sheep, or Chrysler hemi-V-8's.

Contrast 1. Understanding versus ignorance. This is the 'primary response' contrast for most native speakers.

Contrast 2. Understanding versus 'mere knowing,' as in knowing the time or knowing the age of the universe.

Contrast 3. Understanding versus misunderstanding, as in misunderstanding a flow chart.

Contrast 4. Understanding versus believing (or feeling) that one understands, a distinction commonly illustrated in the written answers to course examinations.

An analysis of "understanding" that fits these constraints is essential for any semantic program for outputting (or a disambiguation matrix for inputting) the term but it will not necessarily consist in a definition in the classical sense of a set of conditions that are necessary and jointly sufficient, this usually being impossible, other than trivially, with the important concepts of logic or science such as the so-called "open concepts" or "open-textured" concepts.

Various oversimplified analyses have been suggested which are obviously inconsistent with the above paradigms. For example, opponents of the scientific or logical legitimacy of the notion of understanding frequently attack it as if it were identical to felt understanding thereby violating Contrast 4.

Much better analyses center on such notions as "reduction to the familiar," "modelling," "semantic programming," "deduction from laws," etc. However, they all suffer from vagueness or from specific errors which have been extensively discussed in the literature. To avoid vagueness, some attempt at a more operational or behavioristic account is warranted.

Concentrating on Example 2 for a moment, we can ask how it is that we test comprehension or understanding of a theory? We ask the subject questions about it, questions of a particular kind. They must not merely request recovery of information that has been explicitly presented (that would test 'mere' knowledge, which must be excluded by contrast 2). They must instead test the capacity to answer 'new' questions. I shall suggest three criteria, not all always appropriate. The alpha criterion involves at least the following capacities which are not essentially distinct: (a) the capacity to make and recognize (what are currently held to be) obvious logical inferences from and translations of stored data; (b) the capacity to extrapolate or interpolate any general principles learned; and (c) the capacity to apply the theory to new problem cases to which it is relevant. A related test of comprehension, the beta criterion, seeks signs of organization of the material acquired, especially any sign of novel organization; we sometimes find a student's 'grasp' of the theory most impressively demonstrated by a novel axiomatizing or a new identification of fundamental concepts. The stress here, then, is on the capacity to *handle* novel problem situations and on the capacity to *produce* novel output (where 'novel' is subject-relative). But there is sometimes an emphasis on the gamma criterion: a good perspective or appraisal or evaluation of the theory, its components and its achievements, i.e., (roughly) its relations to other theories and the evidence.

Does this kind of analysis transfer to the other paradigms? There is a very close match with the requirements given by Chomsky and others for understanding a language (Example 3). Speaking precisely, one might be said to understand French even if one could not speak it. The proof would involve demonstrating that *novel* (French) input produced the appropriate non-verbal or non-French reactions; in particular, it would require the recognition of synonymous or equivalent passages as such, of true/false assertions and of inappropriate language as such ('ungrammatical' in the Chomskian sense). This is close to the alpha criterion. (We can say that the alpha criterion is the appropriate *reaction* criterion, the beta criterion refers to appropriate *reprocessing*, the gamma criterion to *meta-description* or data-comparison.) The apparently aberrant paradigms 4 and 5 present no difficulty if it is recognized that the notion of appropriate reaction (etc.) is not restricted to verbal performance. This is already clear in the case of understanding a language where obeying a command is the best proof of comprehension. We may say that a mechanic understands a certain family of engines, like the Chrysler hemi's, without any confidence in his capacity to tell us the theory on which the design is based, solely on the basis of his ability to fix them, improve them, and diagnose them. Similarly, a nurse need know nothing of academic psychology to understand children. She need only be good at "instinctive" diagnosis and treatment. Although the alpha criterion is the most important in these semi-linguistic areas, there is still a clear analogy to the beta and gamma criteria.

Understanding what it is like to have an experience like mortal fear or the urge to murder is almost synonymous with knowing what the experience is like, i.e., with having had it and being able to recall it. The use of the term "understand" in these cases is meant to stress the requirement that the knowledge 'goes deep,' is thoroughly integrated into the repertoire of the respondent, and in particular that it is tied to the correct reactions. The common remark "You can't possibly under-stand what it's like to _____ , if you haven't been through it yourself" is, on the present account, an empirical claim and not a definitional one. It stresses the similarity between an experience and a perception since, e.g., there are many people whom we would never recognize (know) from a description but would have to have seen. The situation is not unlike the problem of understanding an untranslatable French phrase or idiom; "You can't really understand that unless you speak collo-quial French," that is, unless you have all the syntactic and semantic connections hooked up. Interestingly, it is also like understanding a theoretical term such as the psi function. In all these cases, understanding is a cognitive state which generates certain S-R linkages, defined as producing appropriate responses to an open set of stimuli. It is natural for an ecologically oriented biologist to see this as an aspect of adaptation—we might call it cognitive adaptation. Notice that cognitive adaptability is different, being at the level of and connected with intelligence; and cognitive success (knowing an answer) is different in the other direction, being analogous to surviving for a period.

Turning to the understanding of a physical event or phenomenon, the paradigm almost all theory of explanation has been concerned with analyzing, we see an important difference between the phenomenon and the event. Understanding a phenomenon in the scientific sense requires a theory of it but the "it" means something which recurs in different forms and circumstances. For example, understanding the phenomenon of intermodulation distortion essentially means being able to place it in the framework of scientific knowledge which involves saying what its properties and causes are, knowing how to recognize it in all its manifestations, and this is very similar to understanding the pluperfect in Latin—the alpha, beta, and gamma criteria all apply. Understanding a particular event is a lower-level case corresponding to understanding a particular use of the pluperfect. Just as we can translate the latter description into "knowing what is meant by" a particular use of the pluperfect, so we can often translate "understanding a particular event" into "knowing what caused it" or "knowing its cause" or "knowing the reasons for it" or "knowing what kind of event it is." But we cannot as easily translate "understanding intermodulation distortion" into "knowing its cause" or anything else. The object of the understanding is much more complex, a set and not a point. It is variations in the kind of object that is said to be understood that control the interpretation of "appropriate" in the alpha criterion, and a large part of the work involved in getting computers up to the comprehension criteria has to be concerned with analysis of what understanding consists of in a given domain. A single context-free program for this can no more be given than it can for a computer intended to use the word "good" correctly, or—although this is a much simpler case—the word "large."

Efficiency in IPDs

We begin with a discussion of the usual basic IPDs, but artificial agents require other capacities than their storage, retrieval, and associated processing. An extra capacity must be tacked on at each end; information acquisition at the front and reaction at the back. The usual concept of artificial intelligence involves one or both of these capacities and for reasons that will not be discussed here, this is probably essential. Attempts have been made in the literature to reduce IPD efficiency measures to a single scale—time for retrieval is perhaps the best candidate—but we shall set out the desiderata somewhat more fully.

It is clear that maximizing storage capacity (1) is desirable although it is equally clear that it normally counts against cost (2), and recovery speed (3), and possibly storage speed (4), to move in this direction. Internal efficiency involves a great many factors of which the division of memory between short- and long-term (5), the division of processing capacity between central and peripheral processors (6), and the use of more than one simultaneous program (7) are three important variables to be optimized. Redundancy (8) and inconsistency (9) checks are likely to be necessary, as is fast feedback to indicate completion of storage (10). A general desideratum whose very presence indicates the necessity for compromise is reliability (11), in both the hardware and software sense, though the former will of course show up through any operational definition of the latter.

We now specify the task as any one of the set that involves handling more information, by orders of magnitude, than can be wholly stored in a usefully accessible way, where 'usefully' is defined by reference to the maximal reaction time consistent with the goals for the agent, e.g., survival in a fight with a predator, producing a book from the stack before a freshman gives up, etc. The description "informationally rich environment" in the introduction refers to this situation. It is possible that artificial intelligence, properly so-called, *logically* requires this condition but it is certain that most applications of it will involve this condition in fact.

In such situations, desperate measures are required that will, in addition to optimizing the above eleven parameters and others, acquire the relevant material from the environment (12) and effect the most apt amongst several relevant and valuable reactions (13).

Without, for the moment, considering the last two desiderata for an interactive agent, we can see that two keys to handling (over-) rich input are selectivity in allocating storage space and use of radically economical filing systems. The main trick consists in *creating* redundancies in the input. What can be counted as a redundancy obviously depends on the utility profile for the program/agent. What makes a datum redundant may be the trivial discovery of direct or approximate duplication of the datum—watching for this is what makes the ordinary redundancy check (8) useful. But this cannot cope with a rich informational environment. To do that we have to discover extrapolable regularities in the input. If there are none, the environment is totally chaotic and cannot be handled once capacity is reached (or before). But the slightest long-term deviation from randomness creates the possibility of using the (stochastic) pattern involved to render a large or infinite amount of input redundant since it can be generated internally from the stored pattern. So pattern-making and pattern-recognizing become the lifelines of the drowning IPD. The fundamental question for the evaluating routine is whether the mismatch between a new datum and what is already stored, or can be internally generated, is more serious than the use of resources involved in storing the exact datum. (The resources, of course, include the time and energy costs involved in storing, as well as the space.)

The use of the term 'patterns' covers what we refer to in various contexts as generalizations, rules, laws, tendencies, constancies, invariants, concepts, correlations, and properties. These are the life-lines that keep us, precariously, from drowning. But possession of these is *also* the skeleton of understanding, for they provide the capacity to answer new questions, to extrapolate and interpolate, and to identify equivalences. In short, the best way to handle a rich environment is to understand it. One real-time implication of this is truistic: The only way to predict in any environment is to discover underlying regularities. What we shall here call the comprehension theorem goes beyond this, however, by linking comprehension (which is both more and less than the power to predict) with efficiency in IPDs (which involves more than the use of regularities). In particular the comprehension theorem claims that comprehension is nothing more than a dispositional capacity side-effect of an effective information storage and retrieval system in a complex, open-ended environment. An environment is open-ended if its content increases with time or closer examination; it is complex if its features require more than a *few, simple, predictable* regularities to describe it completely.

The second storage trick is modelling. Modelling is a kind of second-order or analogical patterning which uses either a physical or a formal system as the pattern, plus a conversion rule, and usually a list of qualifications. For example, the atom's structure can be stored using the previously stored structure of the solar system as long as we remember the scale-transformation and a few non-equivalences. The simplest cases of modelling are the metaphor and the analogy itself. The most significant model is man, and anthropomorphic explanation its monument. Computers may be expected to develop a different repertoire of basic models from us although it will, by design, overlap. Thus they will correctly be said to comprehend things that we do not, or to comprehend in a radically different way some things we do understand. Correlatively, since humor is partly a useful tension-reduction device and is connected with mismatch recognition, computers are likely to have their own jokes.

The present approach might be thought instrumentalist or conventionalist. A critic might suggest that real understanding involves a *true* insight into, for example, nature and not just a convenient device for storing data about it. We may therefore inquire into the difficulty between a mnemonic and a model. The difference is depth. A model allows, indeed encourages, interpolation and extrapolation although it may prohibit *some* directions. A mnemonic is a convenient filing device for a finite set of facts and every extension of it is illicit. The value of a model, in IPD-efficiency terms alone, is not just to facilitate recall but to make future or past observations redundant, and this it can do only to the extent it reflects reality, since reality is the source of those observations. Thus models must be realistic to yield understanding rather than the illusion of understanding—so the equivalence implied by the comprehension theorem is upheld.

A theory may be anything from a naked law or analogy to a complex of existential and universal axioms together with their development into theorems and lemmas. In either case it is covered by the previous remarks.

It must be noted that the gains in efficiency from the use of these devices are put in jeopardy by any use of extremely complicated encoding or decoding rules, lists of exceptions, or lack of reliability in the model-manipulative rules. (Moving to the model from the law already represents a loss of simplicity because the transformation rules must be stored. In practice this is more than offset by the greater fertility of the model. Also the list of limitations on a model is usually offset in practice by the need to remember the degree of inaccuracy in almost all physical 'laws.' Finally the use of models for storage does not involve learning a new pattern, which distinguishes it from many new laws.) Aging physical theories often develop these symptoms and it is hard for those whose knowledge is built around them to notice the marginal cost point where the total cost of the complications makes them less valuable to the learner than a radically different approach. The comparative youth of the great innovators in science may be more a product of their lesser experience than their greater brilliance.

We should now note that an agent which interacts with the information environment will probably go beyond the preceding devices of pattern and model. It becomes necessary to use and refine peripheral processing systems. In the IPD this distinction is not necessarily a sharp one but for various reasons of internal economy it is likely to be so arranged as to make the distinction important. On the human side it is crucial since it is at the periphery that we use the most radical information-filter of all, the concept. The origin of this in perceptual constancies, its role in the phi-phenomenon and illusions would take us too far afield here. But it is clear that just as the development of logic and rules and analogs enables the central processor to define equivalences and generate infinities of output and thus cut great swathes of redundancy through the forest of facts, so the perceptual mechanisms—both hardware and software—do the same to the environment in converting it from energy to data, or from data to information, or from information to putatively useful and usable information. Corresponding to this pre-processing there will often be a need for post-processing—evaluation and simplification, for example.

Two concluding remarks about the affective side of comprehension. It seems plausible to suppose that the necessary feedback signal announcing successful discovery of a model/law/redundancy that takes care of a new datum corresponds to the flash of insight, the feeling of understanding. And it seems plausible to think that cases of understanding a moving experience are very like modelling in the sense that matching output will be exceedingly difficult in any way that does not involve having the model already in the memory. An analogous case is the challenge to phenomenologists to show how they can dispense with the concept of a material object in favor of a phenomenological description and still produce appropriate reactions.

Applications

Outside the computer field, the most interesting applications are possibly in the philosophy of science (explanation—theory), philosophy of history (the empathy theory), clinical psychology (theories of 'clinical insight'), and philosophy of mind where the consequences for the mind-body problem and the subjective-objective distinction are significant. The details of these applications have been or are being developed elsewhere.

CONFERENCE DISCUSSION

Scriven first wanted to point out that his particular view of comprehension necessarily implicates considerations of memory as well as of inference. In addition he felt that the concept of comprehension should include not only linguistic comprehension but also the comprehension of affective and motoric behavior. A complete model of comprehension, he thought, should also include provision for two kinds of "filters." One would be a "redundancy filter" that would operate on previously stored "templates" to find which one best matches a current problem situation; to the extent that the perceiver has found a template that provides a reasonable approximation to that situation, he can be said to understand the problem well enough to function correctly in that context, and he does not need to store further data. The other kind of filter would be an "inconsistency" or error-detecting filter that would prevent the storing of contradictions.

Goodman wondered, however, how one could explain the child's acquisition of "templates" and the ability to scan them for matches with current experience. Bever pointed out that it is a mystery how children are able to arrive at linguistic generalizations (which are special classes of "templates"), and how they are able to assign probabilities to the various possible ways of formulating generalizations from their finite set of experiences. He asked how Scriven viewed the problem of explaining the child's ability to discover which templates are relevant and fruitful, and which are irrelevant. Scriven cited the work of Minsky and Papert (1969) concerning the effect of differential reinforcement on Perceptrons, as a way to approach, through computer simulation, the problem of template acquisition. But upon Bever's further probing, Scriven acknowledged that one may have to adopt the nativist position that human beings have some built-in mechanism that makes them tend to favor some dimensions over others as relevant templates against which to assess future experience.

Goodman pointed out that Scriven's comprehension theorem (that comprehension is the disposition or capacity for effective information storage and retrieval under the constraint of the impossibility of total storage) was an interesting alternative to his own prior view that it is possible to have total storage. Simmons commented that an implication of the notion of total storage would be that in trying to find a template to match a new situation, one would have to plow through many more of the trivial details in memory than otherwise, with the result that it might take as long to retrieve the correct template as it took to experience the event in the first place. This would make for a very inefficient comprehension system. Scriven tended to agree, suggesting that what may happen is that when we first experience a situation, we store only its main template features, in order to economize on storage space; even if we had the capacity for total storage, we wouldn't store everything because that would slow us down when it came time to retrieve the memory.

Bever raised the issue of whether a theory of tasks (which would include language performances as a special case) wouldn't prove even more difficult to formalize than the more restricted theory of language has proven to be. Scriven thought that a good reason for going the "task" route, as opposed to narrowing attention to language comprehension alone, is the potential "social payoff" of doing so. One is more likely to be successful in training people if one does it in the framework of "tasks." You should ask not whether a person "comprehends," but what a person must *do* to *demonstrate* comprehension. If you then move in the direction of training the person to perform such demonstrations, you are dealing with a manageable situation inasmuch as there is only a small number of tasks that could be used to assess comprehension. In addition, one has developed a method of assessing broad comprehension that has sound training implications. This, Scriven said, was what he meant by "social payoff." He added that this is the direction that research should go; one should abandon looking into memory versus inference versus comprehension per se.

Trabasso didn't really see what this had to do with clarifying our special interest in understanding how language itself is comprehended. Scriven replied that when one narrows one's focus too radically, so that only a small sample of specially devised commands, questions, and syntactic forms are studied, this constrains the usefulness of the theories that lie behind comprehension when conceived in its broadest possible scope. Again he stated that the concept of comprehension must include not only its purely "linguistic" aspects but also the affective aspects, the comprehension of instructions, and the teaching of skills. One must devise tests that inquire into the subject's ability to do appropriate things with the material these tests contain. This may involve paying attention to the situational setting, which may be as important as the "linguistic" aspects. A satisfactory account of *real* linguistic performance will never be possible without attention to these other dimensions of comprehension which, at first sight, we *contrast* with linguistic comprehension.

Trabasso asked how Scriven would handle, within his system, the way inferences are carried out. Scriven outlined the following: the message comes in, it is 'unpacked' and something is stored depending upon its use at the moment. Behind the 'unpacking' and the storing is an analytic process which is the same device as that behind retrieval processes. Most of the future inferences that can be made depend upon how the item is stored (what templates it is stored on). As an example, suppose one is told that A is bigger than B, and B is bigger than C. This is likely to be stored as a visual model. Suppose it is. Then one is told in addition, or considers the possible conclusion, that A is bigger than C. This hits a *redundancy check* with the result that this additional piece of information is not stored—or is recognized as a valid inference—since it is already contained in the template (the visual template). Another way to state this is that the implication is stored along with the template representation. As another example, suppose you have read the five axioms of Euclid. Now should you conclude that you have stored all the theorems or not? Obviously not, but what may be stored is the general strategies that are learned concerning how to reconstruct or go about proving particular theorems. Freedle wondered how Scriven would handle the following difficulty with the two mathematical examples just mentioned. With the three-term problem, the required inference is but a *one-step* affair and the redundancy check principle is easily applied to rule out the storage of this final piece of information that A is bigger than C. However, with the Euclidean example, a problem arises when we attempt to apply the redundancy check principle. The problem is this. It is well known that the theorems of any mathematical system are tautologies consequent upon the axioms. Yet mathematicians go to a great deal of trouble to record their theorems and the proofs of the theorems even though, in a sense, the proofs are totally redundant given the set of axioms from which they stem. What does this do to the viability of the redundancy check principle? Scriven replied that while from a mathematical point of view the theorems are, truly, logically redundant, it is quite possible that we cannot claim that the theorems are psychologically redundant because redundancy in a psychological sense is a function of what one *can* read out as an immediate consequence of what you have stored. From the point of view of retrieval, it is more practical to remember (store) the theorems simply because it is faster than having to prove them from scratch (if indeed we can prove them from scratch). The whole structure of knowledge that we are operating with, which determines what we retain and what we discard as 'redundant,' is a function of how sophisticated our recovery mechanism is, and also a function of what we think the demands will be at the time retrieval is required.

Carroll asked whether the constraints due to the impossibility of total storage can be taken to imply that comprehension can never be complete. Scriven indicated that the notion of complete comprehension really is a function of contextual demands and can be likened to "complete" descriptions of a person, say. That is, if one's current purposes are motivated by just mild curiosity about someone, and one gets back a 45-minute description of who that new person is, what his interests are, etc., then one may say that this is a complete description of the new person with respect to one's current purposes. But a physician may say that this same description is quite inadequate and incomplete for his purposes. A similar point can be made about many scientific laws—they actually are only approximations to the real world (an idealization of it) which suit our current scientific needs and purposes.

REFERENCES

Minsky, M. L., & Papert, S. *Perceptrons: An introduction to computational geometry.* Cambridge, Mass.: M. I. T. Press, 1969.
Scriven, M. Dimensions of understanding. In M. Kochen, D. M. MacKay, M. E. Maron, M. Scriven, & L. Uhr, *Computers and comprehension.* Santa Monica, California: The Rand Corporation, Memorandum RM–4065–PR, April 1964.

3
DISCOURSE STRUCTURE AND HUMAN KNOWLEDGE

Wallace L. Chafe
Department of Linguistics
University of California at Berkeley

There are various kinds of questions which the field of linguistics has tended in the past to avoid and whose avoidance has, I think, seriously retarded progress toward a full understanding of what language is and how it works. For example, the question of what people mean when they say things has only recently become a central part of linguistic investigation and still, more often than not, seems to have a considerably lower priority than questions of "syntax." As another example, the question of "discourse" structure—of what goes on over stretches of speech larger than sentences—has received only sporadic or peripheral attention with by far the bulk of linguistic work being concentrated on the structure of sentences in isolation. It appears that an attempt to look deeply into one of these topics is sooner or later bound to lead into a concern for the other, or at least I can say that that has been my own experience. Although I was at first motivated chiefly by a desire to understand how language operates as an instrument for transmission of thoughts and ideas, I found myself unavoidably wanting to know more about semantic phenomena that cross the boundaries of sentences.

Above and beyond both these questions, however, lies the question of how what people say is related to what they know. For me it is the question of how linguistics is related to the study of human knowledge. It may again be unfortunate that linguistics has a tradition to the effect that certain issues can be avoided by attributing many facts to people's knowledge of the world and thus setting them outside the area of linguistic concern. It would, I suppose, be comforting to believe that language contained something—perhaps "grammar" would be the name for it—which was self-contained enough so that its workings could be understood without recourse to broader questions of human knowledge. A great deal of work on language has proceeded under the assumption that such is the case. My own opinion is that, in the end, it has proved impossible to avoid the conclusion that the assumption was wrong. It seems to me that if we really want to understand how language works, we have no choice but to launch an all-out attack on the question of how our knowledge of the world affects what we say about it.

In the discussion that follows there will be an interweaving of all three of these concerns: the question of how meanings can be formalized in a linguistically relevant theory of semantic structure, the question of how such a formalization can take account of semantic factors whose scope is greater than single sentences, and the question of the extent to which this formalization amounts to a formalization of human knowledge. The study is principally an attempt to introduce considerations of discourse structure into a semantic model more or less like that presented in Chafe (1970, henceforth referred to as MSL). Within that framework, the broad and challenging questions mentioned above will be brought to bear on a very simple formal device, which I will call a "contextual rule." The effect of such a rule will be to add and delete certain kinds of transitory constraints—constraints which come and go as a discourse proceeds. It will be seen that such constraints are equivalent to formalizations of various transitory things that a person "knows" during particular segments of a discourse. The particular constraints that will be discussed will involve past tense, foregrounding (related to the new vs. old information distinction discussed in MSL, pp. 210–233), the identity of the speaker, and definiteness. Particularly in connection with definiteness, we will be led to consider some important questions concerning the more permanent knowledge that a person holds, and we will see some evidence that a semantically oriented theory of language must contain some sort of formalization of such knowledge.[1]

SEMANTIC RESOURCES

Although the discussion will be based on a model of language—and particularly of semantic structure—that is much like that presented in MSL, I find it helpful to modify that model in a few respects. I will introduce a few simple changes in terminology, but more importantly, I will make use of an entirely different way of accounting for the well-formedness of semantic structures. Let me first of all outline briefly the kind of semantic structure I will be assuming for individual sentences. Reference can be made to the diagram in (1):

[1] Invaluable assistance in this study was provided by the members of a seminar in discourse structure held at Berkeley in the fall of 1970: Leonard Faltz, Leanna and Robert Gaskins, Hasmig Seropian, Masayoshi Shibatani, Ronald Sykora, and several auditors. Various versions of this paper were presented orally during late 1970 and early 1971 at Georgetown, Yale, Brown, the University of Michigan, the University of California at Santa Barbara, and the University of Southern California. I profited from and am grateful for suggestions received on all these occasions. As I reconsider this paper now (in early 1972) I can see that there is much that I would want to add or change. The revisions I have in mind are extensive enough that they will have to be accommodated in an entirely new work, or series of works. In the meantime I will let this paper stand as a statement of one stage of my thinking on these matters, hoping that it will have some value despite its imperfections.

(1)

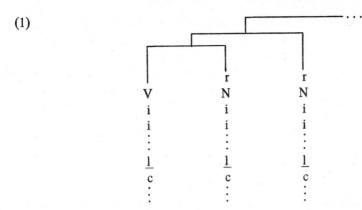

Basically, a simple sentence is thought to consist of a single semantic verb (V) to which (usually) one or more nouns (N) are attached, each standing in some relation (r) to the verb. [Noun-verb relations include *agent, patient, beneficiary*, and the like (c.f. MSL, pp. 144–166; Fillmore, 1968).] Each verb and each noun then contains within it, most importantly and above all, a lexical unit (l), which carries the main burden of the information conveyed by the verb or noun. I will continue the practice of referring to the lexical unit within a verb as the *verb root*; to that within a noun, as the *noun root*. Each lexical unit has associated with it certain inherent features (i), written above it, and certain contextual features (c), written below it. The names for these two kinds of semantic units constitute changes in terminology, since I formerly called inherent features "selectional units" and contextual features "inflectional units." The new labels seem to me somewhat preferable. Given a particular lexical unit, its inherent features are predictable; they are inherently associated with it. We might say that they correspond to pieces of knowledge necessarily associated with the knowledge conveyed by the lexical unit. The same is not true of the contextual features, which either are chosen freely by the speaker to communicate whatever he wishes to communicate or, probably more often, are determined by contextual or discourse factors of precisely the sort we will investigate here.

The semantic structure of an actual sentence, following (1), is (incompletely) diagrammed in (2):

(2)

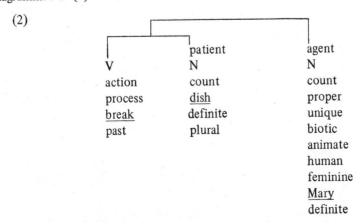

The surface form of this sentence is *Mary broke the dishes*. It consists semantically of a verb accompanied by two nouns, one the patient and one the agent of the verb. The lexical unit of the verb (the verb root) is *break*, that of the patient noun (the noun root) is *dish*, and that of the agent noun is *Mary*. Within the verb, the lexical unit *break* is inherently an *action* (something that someone does) and a *process* (something that happens to something). Within the patient noun, *dish* is inherently *count* (and certainly other things), while within the agent noun *Mary* is inherently *count, proper, unique, biotic, animate, human,* and *feminine*. (Most of these labels are self-explanatory. *Proper* and *unique* will be discussed below.) The framework given in (1) and exemplified in (2) is quite incomplete. For example, the phenomenon I have discussed under the heading derivation (MSL, pp. 119–43) has been ignored, as has the entire subject of embedding, by which simple sentences like (2) can be combined to form complex sentences. For our present purposes, however, the model sketched in (1) will be sufficient.

I mentioned above that I was going to make use of a way of accounting for the well-formedness of semantic structures that was different from that followed in MSL. Until recently I was willing to accept the Chomskian notion that deep structures (in my terms, semantic structures) are appropriately "generated" through the application of a series of "rewrite" processes. For reasons that are suggested in part in MSL (see pp. 350–351 as well as the footnotes on p. 142 and p. 298), I have more recently concluded that the well-formedness of semantic structures should be accounted for, not by rewrite rules, but by a large set of semantic constraints. Such constraints will account for the total range of possible semantic structures in a language. Each of them is essentially a statement that the presence of one item in a semantic structure requires, or entails, the presence of some other item or items. The majority of them are statable in approximately the format shown in (3):

(3)   X ⇒ Y

This formula can be read "the presence of semantic element X requires the accompaniment of semantic element Y," or, as I will say more often, "X entails Y." Statements of this sort will be of crucial interest below.

What I would now suggest is that the speaker of a language, when he says something, has available to him a large fund of semantic resources. These resources can be regarded in terms of three distinguishable components. The three components might be compared to the components of a game of some kind (although it would be dangerous to take the comparison too seriously). Let us say that a game has, first, a structured board on which it is played; second, a set of pieces which are arrayed on the board; and third, a set of rules which say how the pieces may be located with relation to the board and to each other. Semantic resources appear to consist of, first, a framework (analogous to the game board); second, a set of semantic units (analogous to the pieces); and third, a set of semantic constraints (in some ways similar to the rules of a game, in that they specify how the semantic units can be arranged within the semantic framework and with relation to each other).

The framework available for the semantic structures of single sentences may be approximately of the sort diagrammed in (1), supplemented with devices for derivation, embedding, and so on. Arrayed within this framework are the various semantic units, the total inventory of which is extremely large, though finite. Parts of the inventory vary with different speakers and at different times and places. Keeping in mind the functions of r, l, i, and c in (1), we can imagine the inventory of semantic units as being laid out in the fashion indicated in (4), with numerous subsets identifiable within the major sets of lexical units, inherent features, and contextual features:

(4) r = patient, agent, beneficiary, . . .
     l = break, dish, Mary, . . .
     i = action, process, count, human, . . .
     c = past, definite, plural, . . .

Finally, there is a large set of semantic constraints, a tiny and simplified sample of which [relevant to the sentence in (2)] is given in (5):

(5)

$$\text{break} \Rightarrow \begin{bmatrix} \text{action} \\ \text{process} \end{bmatrix} \qquad\qquad \text{dish} \Rightarrow \text{count}$$

$$\text{count} \Rightarrow \text{N}$$

$$\left\{ \begin{matrix} \text{action} \\ \text{process} \end{matrix} \right\} \Rightarrow \text{V}$$

$$\begin{matrix} \text{V} \\ \text{action} \end{matrix} \Rightarrow \begin{matrix} \text{agent} \\ \text{N} \end{matrix} \qquad\qquad \text{Mary} \Rightarrow \begin{bmatrix} \text{proper} \\ \text{unique} \\ \text{feminine} \end{bmatrix}$$

$$\begin{matrix} \text{V} \\ \text{process} \end{matrix} \Rightarrow \begin{matrix} \text{patient} \\ \text{N} \end{matrix} \qquad\qquad \begin{matrix} \text{feminine} \Rightarrow \text{human} \\ \text{human} \Rightarrow \text{animate} \\ \text{animate} \Rightarrow \text{biotic} \end{matrix}$$

That is, the lexical unit *break* entails the inherent features *action* and *process*, either *action* or *process* entails V, an action V entails an agent N, and so on.

In summary, as we proceed it will be useful to think of a speaker, whenever he says something, as having available to him a specific fund of semantic resources, and to picture these resources in terms of the three components just described: a semantic framework for individual sentences (1), a semantic inventory (4), and a set of semantic constraints (5). It is quite possible and quite justified, I think, to view these semantic resources as representing a significant part of a speaker's knowledge, and especially that part which is relevant to his use of language. In other words, if his semantic resources, formalized in the manner suggested and in other ways, were ever fully stated—a goal of huge proportions—we would have succeeded in stating a great deal of what a person knows.

VARIABILITY

It is important to emphasize that these semantic resources are far from being fixed and immutable. Indeed, if we identify them with a significant part of knowledge, we would certainly expect the knowledge of different individuals to differ. We would also expect the knowledge of a single individual to vary at different points in time. This latter kind of variation through time–particularly over short intervals of time within the confines of a discourse–will be our principal concern below. For a moment, however, we might reflect on the fact that differences in respect to both semantic inventory and semantic constraints are to be found among different subgroups of speakers of the same language. It is especially obvious that different speakers have different inventories of lexical units. Thus, for example, Iroquois Indians and a number of ethnologists who are familiar with Iroquois culture–but not very many other people–possess certain lexical units such as *longhouse, false face, Handsome Lake*, and *snowsnake* (c.f. MSL, pp. 272–273).

But people differ with respect to semantic constraints as well. One interesting kind of example involves the meaning conveyed by unstressed attributive adjectives, as in:

(6)   There's a big Cadillac out front.

in which the word *big* has low pitch and amplitude. A surface structure of this kind conveys the meaning that Cadillacs are regarded as inherently big, an observation that I would account for by assigning a semantic unit *big* as an inherent feature to the lexical unit *Cadillac*. In other words, I would posit the existence of a semantic constraint such as the following:

(7)   Cadillac ⇒ big

I would assume that this constraint is pretty generally present for speakers of the English language. That is, I would assume that English speakers with few exceptions *know* that Cadillacs are inherently big. On the other hand, I would suggest that the constraint:

(8)   professor ⇒ irresponsible

which allows one to utter a sentence such as:

(9)   He's an irresponsible professor.

with a weak pronunciation of *irresponsible*, is possessed only by a certain subgroup of English speakers–those who regard professors as inherently irresponsible (perhaps a majority of the California state legislature in 1970). Just as the lexical unit *longhouse* belongs to the semantic inventory of only certain speakers, the constraint in (8) belongs to the semantic resources of some people but not others.[2]

---

[2] It should be evident that some of the phenomena which some linguists have recently termed presuppositions can be accounted for in this way.

Here, however, we are less interested in the fact that the semantic resources of different individuals differ than in the fact that the semantic resources of a single individual change in certain ways over short time intervals. Although most of a person's semantic repertoire remains constant, some of it is constantly shifting, like the waters in a deep lake which are stirred on top by every passing breeze although the depths remain undisturbed. So far as the causes of this short term variability are concerned, we can distinguish two kinds: those which stem from the shifting extralinguistic environment in which discourse takes place, and those which stem from the discourse itself as it unfolds—from the linguistic environment. As an example of a temporary constraint that is extralinguistically established, we might consider circumstances under which I could begin a conversation by saying:

(10)   The antelope is lame.

Suppose, for example, you and I were standing outside a wire fence at the zoo, and a deer and an antelope were walking by on the other side. If I noticed that the antelope was limping, I might say (10). Under these circumstances you and I could be claimed to have in our common semantic repertoires the following constraint:

(11)   antelope $\Rightarrow$ definite

The subscript is meant to indicate that I have some particular antelope in mind. The constraint says that this lexical unit must be accompanied by the contextual feature *definite*. The meaning of definite will occupy us later, but for the moment it can be seen that I am able to say *the antelope*, as in (10), under the circumstances described, whereas I could not begin a conversation by saying *the antelope* under circumstances where I had no reason to think that you knew what antelope I was talking about. The presence of this antelope before our eyes, then, has created, extralinguistically, the constraint stated in (11). It is a temporary constraint which disappears when we no longer have this antelope before us or in our immediate memory.

From now on, however, we shall be principally concerned with temporary constraints that are introduced, not by the extralinguistic environment, but by language itself. We can visualize what happens in terms of the picture in (12):

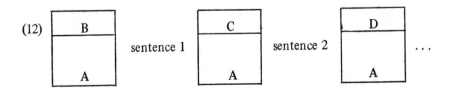

The first box is meant to contain the semantic resources present at the beginning of a discourse, resources which I have partitioned into a large subset A and a small subset B. Sentence 1, the initial sentence of the discourse, is then spoken. Its effect is to change the resources to those indicated in the second box. The presence of A in both boxes shows that some (in fact most) of the resources have remained constant—have not been affected by Sentence 1—but the presence of C in place of B shows that Sentence 1 has modified the resources to a certain extent. In other words, as a result of Sentence 1 the semantic resources present as a background for Sentence 2 are not identical with those that were present as a background for Sentence 1. Sentence 2, which follows, has the effect of changing the resources again, with D replacing C; and so on throughout the discourse—each succeeding sentence modifying the resources that are present as a semantic background for the next sentence. Here we will be particularly concerned with those resources that are formalizable in terms of semantic constraints. Our concern will be with the manner in which constraints that are present at the beginning of a discourse are continually modified by the succession of sentences in that discourse.

What happens can be formalized in terms of what can be called contextual rules, which can be given the following format:

(13) W : X ⇒ Y : Z

In the middle of this rule is the constraint $X \Rightarrow Y$. Suppose that this constraint is not present at the beginning of a discourse, but that it is introduced by something present, say, in Sentence 1. The particular element in Sentence 1 that results in the introduction of this constraint is indicated by W. W can be called the *initiator* of the constraint. That is, whenever W (whatever it is) occurs in the semantic structure of a certain sentence, it has the effect of introducing the temporary constraint $X \Rightarrow Y$ which then enters the semantic resources available at the beginning of the next sentence. In many cases, as we shall see, such a temporary constraint does not remain in effect indefinitely, but will disappear later in the discourse. Sometimes, at least, it will be possible for us to identify a semantic element which causes the constraint to disappear. This element is represented in (13) by Z, which we may call the *terminator* of the constraint. In short, the contextual rule in (13) says that the presence of the semantic element W introduces the constraint $X \Rightarrow Y$, which remains in force up to the point where Z appears, where it will then evaporate.

TENSE

To make all this more concrete, I have concocted the sequence of sentences given in (14), which may be regarded as spoken by one party at or near the beginning of a conversation:

(14) a. I went to a concert last night.
     b. They played Beethoven's Second.
     c. You don't hear that very often.
     d. I enjoyed it.
     e. Next Friday I'm going to another concert.
     f. They're playing something by Stravinsky.

What I am concerned with here are the semantic units—more specifically the contextual features—which might be called the *tenses* of these sentences. The features of this kind that are attached to the verbs in these sentences are as follows:

(15) a. past
      b. past
      c. generic
      d. past
      e. future
      f. future

The first two sentences are *past*. The third is what I have been calling *generic*: that is, it is a general, timeless statement. The fourth sentence is again *past*. The last two sentences are *future*. [There are several varieties of future in English; here we have that variety which I have labeled *anticipative* (MSL, pp. 177–178).] Now, I would like to suggest that the presence of these contextual features is governed by a contextual rule of the sort shown in (13). In particular, I would suggest that there is a constraint:

(16) V $\Rightarrow$ past

(discursively: a verb requires the accompaniment of the contextual feature *past*), whose domain is the first four sentences. More or less at any point, however, a generic sentence can be inserted, as is illustrated by (14c). That is, a speaker is relatively free to make a verb generic when it suits his purposes, and a generic verb is immune to the constraint stated in (16). We might then modify (16) as shown in (17), to show that it applies only to a nongeneric verb:

(17) V $\Rightarrow$ past
         ~generic

The initiator of this constraint is evidently the temporal adverb which appears in the surface structure of the sentence in (14a) as *last night*. The terminator of the constraint is another temporal adverb: that which appears in (14e) as *next Friday*. In general, we can say that a past adverb causes the sentence which it dominates as well as all following (nongeneric) sentences to be past, up to the point where a nonpast adverb is introduced. Following the format given in (13), we thus have the contextual rule:

(18) V   :   V $\Rightarrow$ past   :   V
        adverbial   ~generic   adverbial
        temporal   temporal
        past   ~past

(For the treatment of sentence adverbs as verbs which dominate other verbs, see MSL, pp. 303–307.) Aside from the immunity of generic verbs, there are doubtless further conditions which should be stated for (18), although I am not sure at the moment how they should be stated. It does seem, however, that (18) explains what happens in the majority of instances—that *past* has to be introduced by a temporal adverb and that it has to be maintained until some nonpast temporal adverb appears. It is odd, for example, to begin a conversation by saying simply *I went to a concert*, where the time of this event has not been made explicit through some adverb. One would only say such a thing if there were some extralinguistic reason to assume that the hearer knew when it happened.

It is easy to extend (18) to cover the fact that *next Friday* in the sentence (14e) is not only the terminator of the past constraint but also the initiator of another constraint:

(19) V ⇒ future

which might subsequently be terminated by some nonfuture temporal adverb. We could state another rule exactly like (18) except that *past* and *nonpast* were replaced by *future* and *nonfuture*, or we could conflate these two (and possibly other) parallel rules in the manner suggested in (20):

(20) V   :   V   ⇒   αtense   :   V
      adverbial   ~generic   adverbial
      temporal   temporal
      αtense   ~αtense

Here *tense* is a cover term for various contextual features such as *past* and *future*. The notation α*tense* means that the same feature (for example *past*) must appear throughout the rule. (This usage is a natural extension of the α convention employed in phonological rules.) Rule (20) says that a temporal adverb causes succeeding verbs to acquire its particular tense, up to the point where another temporal adverb introduces a different tense.

FOREGROUNDING

Let us now turn from this relatively straightforward example of how features of tense are introduced and maintained in a discourse, to a subject which is a bit more complex. It involves a semantic unit which I shall label *foregrounded*. The basic idea is that at any one point in a discourse there are certain concepts which are in the foreground of the minds of the participants in the discourse—concepts which are, so to speak, in sharp focus at that point. To use another metaphor, we might think of what is going on in a discourse as if it described states and events unfolding on a stage. We could then say that at any particular point in the discourse there are certain things which are "on stage." It is whatever is on stage that I am calling foregrounded.[3]

---

[3] More recently I have concluded that what is involved here is an assumption by the speaker that the material in question is presently in the consciousness of the hearer. *Foregrounded*, therefore, can be understood as an abbreviated label for *assumed to be in the hearer's consciousness*.

Again an example may be helpful. Suppose I begin a conversation with the sentences in (21):

(21) a. Yesterday I saw a little girl get bitten by a dog.
      b. I tried to catch the dog, but it ran away.
      c. The little girl was scared, but she wasn't really hurt.

I would suggest that what is foregrounded at the beginning of the first sentence is simply the fact that there is a speaker and, presumably, one or more hearers. Hence, the concept which underlies the surface pronoun *I* in the sentence (21a), the concept of the speaker, is the only foregrounded element in that sentence. This first sentence, however, has the effect of foregrounding various elements which are there introduced as new information. They include such items as *little girl, getting bitten*, and *dog*. All of these can then be regarded as foregrounded at the beginning of the sentence (21b). Of these several concepts brought on stage by (21a), only *dog* is actually included in (21b), where, in fact, it is included twice.

These first two sentences are enough to illustrate the surface structure treatment which is accorded foregrounded items. The principal surface manifestation of foregrounding is low pitch and amplitude. Thus, *I* has this weak pronunciation in (21a), and *I, the dog,* and *it* have it in (21b). It is consistently true that foregrounded items are weakly pronounced (although not all items so pronounced are foregrounded, a fact which need not detain us now), and it is obvious why they should be: they are already in the minds of the participants in the discourse, who are able to reserve louder and higher pitched pronunciations for the elements in the sentence which provide new information. It is also true that foregrounded items are often pronominalized, although they do not have to be, as the presence of the foregrounded but unpronominalized *dog* in (21b) illustrates. It may be noted that *the dog* here could have been replaced by *it*, and that, indeed, it is so replaced in the second clause. Pronominalization might be regarded as going one step beyond simply pronouncing the item with low pitch and amplitude. It amounts to actual deletion of the lexical unit, with certain inherent features left as remnants to form the surface pronoun. It can be said that foregrounding is a necessary but not sufficient condition for pronominalization, which depends on various other factors as well.

Since *dog* has been foregrounded by its occurrence in (21a), it must be pronounced with low pitch and amplitude in (21b). It must, that is, unless it is additionally accompanied by the semantic unit *contrastive*. To put it the other way around, if *dog* in (21b) is given greater amplitude and higher pitch, it can only convey a contrastive meaning. The meaning here would be that I tried to catch the *dog* rather than the *girl*, a rather improbable meaning under the circumstances. Contrastive meanings can be imagined for this and various of the following examples, where they will result in higher pitch being placed on foregrounded items that would otherwise have low pitch. I wish to ignore such meanings from now on; what I say will be restricted to noncontrastive sentences.

If we now look at (21c), we can consider the question whether *little girl* in that sentence is foregrounded or not. It may be noted that the little girl was introduced in (21a), and that if she had been mentioned in (21b) she would necessarily have been foregrounded there. It appears, however, that, because she was not mentioned in (21b), the speaker of (21c) may or may not treat her as foregrounded in that sentence. If he does treat her as foregrounded, he will pronounce *little girl* in (21c) with low pitch and amplitude. If, as he may, he treats her as no longer foregrounded, he will pronounce *little girl* in (21c) with greater amplitude and higher pitch. In the former case he is communicating the information that he assumes the little girl to be still in the foreground of the conversation—to be still on stage. In the latter case he is communicating the information that he assumes the little girl to have entered the wings when she was not mentioned in (21b). Either message is acceptable at this point; the speaker can have it either way.

In order to explain the introduction of foregrounding, we might posit a contextual rule of the following form:

(22) 1 : 1 ⇒ : ## ⋯

This rule says that the occurrence of a particular lexical unit, say *dog*, acts as the initiator of a constraint according to which that lexical unit is accompanied by the contextual feature foregrounded. We can consider, then, that at the time of its first occurrence in (21a) *dog* is not foregrounded, but that its presence in that sentence means that it functions as the initiator in an application of the rule (22), so that when it appears again in (21b) it is foregrounded.

The rule (22) also contains a terminator, given as "## . . . ", where # designates a sentence boundary. The idea is that the constraint may be terminated after two sentence boundaries have been crossed. That this is so is illustrated by the fact that *little girl* may be treated as not foregrounded in (21c). But the three dots in the terminator are meant to indicate that the constraint does not have to terminate at this point but may be retained up to some arbitrary limit. It is not clear that this limit can be pinned down in any satisfactory way. We do not seem to be able to say precisely when a speaker must henceforth treat a lexical unit as no longer foregrounded. The terminator in (22) simply says that he may do so after crossing two sentence boundaries. One has the impression that foregrounding tends to evaporate gradually as more and more sentences are uttered in which the foregrounded item does not appear. Seemingly, however, it is not just a matter of the number of sentences, but also of change of scene, the introduction of new events not involving the foregrounded items, and so on. The longer a concept is on stage without having any part in the action, the more likely it is to retreat into the wings. I would guess that in (23), where *Sally* is mentioned—and thereby foregrounded—in the first sentence but not mentioned again until (23f), and where various things not involving Sally happen in between, she is less likely to be still foregrounded in (23f) than was *little girl* in (21c):

(23) a. Sally came up to Jack's desk and set down a large box.
     b. It was tied with a blue ribbon.
     c. Jack untied it slowly.
     d. Then he reached inside.
     e. Suddenly the air was filled with music.
     f. Jack looked at Sally questioningly.

Sally may have high or low pitch in (23f), depending on whether the speaker wishes to communicate that she is or is not still foregrounded, but it seems to me that high pitch is perhaps more likely here than on *little girl* in (21c), indicating that the foregrounding has attenuated in the manner I have suggested.

There are cases where enough intervening events and changes of scene have taken place to make it seemingly obligatory to treat a once foregrounded item as foregrounded no longer. Remember, as an illustration, the story of Jack and the Beanstalk, in which Jack's mother plays a role at the beginning of the story. She sends Jack off to sell their cow, is disturbed when he comes home with only a few beans instead of money, and sends him to bed without any supper. After that, however, there is a long section of the narrative in which the mother plays no role. Jack awakens to find a huge beanstalk outside his window, climbs it, and has an adventure (or several adventures) with the giant at the top. Eventually he climbs back down the beanstalk. Suppose, at this point, where his mother had not been mentioned since she sent Jack to his room (and where nothing has been said about his home or the like), the next sentence is:

(24) His mother welcomed him.

I would assert that at this point, with all that had happened in between, the speaker is pretty well forced to treat *mother* as no longer foregrounded, and thus to pronounce her with higher pitch and amplitude. Between this situation, however, and the situation illustrated with *little girl* in (21), with *Sally* in (23) somewhere in the middle, it seems impossible to draw any firm boundary.

SPEAKER

The Jack and the Beanstalk situation just described can now be used to illustrate another interesting fact. Suppose, instead of (24), the next sentence in the narrative was (25):

(25) "Welcome," said his mother.

Under the circumstances described above, we would expect *mother* not to be foregrounded at this point in the story. Nevertheless, I think it is evident that *mother* in (25) would be pronounced with low pitch and amplitude. She appears, that is, to be foregrounded, contrary to our expectations. Why should that be? How can she be foregrounded—even obligatorily foregrounded—when she has not been mentioned over the course of important scene changes and a succession of important events in which she was not involved? What is evidently the case is that *mother* is brought on stage in (25) by the utterance which is attributed to her. As soon as the quotation "Welcome" appears, we know that someone is saying it, and the speaker of that quotation is automatically foregrounded at that point. In other words, whenever someone says something, that action necessarily puts him on stage.

In general, we can say that at any point in a discourse the speaker at that point is known. (We can extend this observation to say that the hearer is known as well, although there appear to be some cases in which only a rather vague or diffuse audience is understood.) We can thus posit a constraint like the following, which is always present among the semantic resources that form the background for a discourse:

(26) 1 ⇒ speaker

We may regard this as a semantic constraint which is always present, but which contains a variable term (the 1). It says that some lexical unit must always be identified as speaker, or must have *speaker* as one of its contextual features. Usually the identity of 1 is known from the environment of the discourse: it is simply the lexical unit whose meaning is the concept of whoever is speaking at the time (or the writer of a written text). Associated with the semantic unit *speaker* are several other semantic units. The speaker must be conceived of as *human* (having human qualities), for example. More important to us now is the fact that the speaker is always *foregrounded*, as may be expressed by the following additional constraint:

(27) speaker ⇒ foregrounded

(The same is true of the hearer as well.) This explains why the pronoun *I* (as well as *you*) is always pronounced with low pitch and amplitude, except in those sentences where it is contrastive. So long as 1 in (26) is the person actually speaking at the time, it will be converted by postsemantic processes into the first person pronoun, and the fact that it is foregrounded will lead to the weak pronunciation.

Quotations, however, whether direct or indirect, are a device by which the actual speaker may temporarily relinquish the role of speaker to someone else—by which, in other words, he may temporarily replace the 1 in 26, which normally represents the concept of himself, with the concept of some other person. We can, I think, imagine a quotation to be embedded in a discourse in approximately the following manner:

(28)
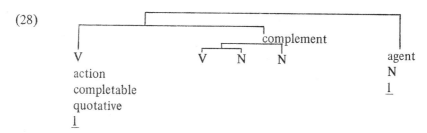

Here there is an outer sentence with a verb containing the inherent feature *quotative*; the lexical unit of this verb may be any one of a set including *say, assert, declare*, and so on. Two different kinds of elements are attached to this verb. One is an agent noun—the person who does the saying. The other is a complement sentence—the thing that is said—whose structure, of course, may be quite varied and may involve more than just a single sentence. What is important to us now is the fact that for the duration of this complement the speaker shifts its identity—the identity of 1 in (26) changes—from the person who is actually speaking to the person who is the agent of the quotative verb. That is, within the domain of this complement the 1 in (26) is identical with the 1 in the agent noun of (28). Since the 1 in (26), being the speaker, is also necessarily foregrounded, as stated in (27), the 1 in the agent of (28) will be foregrounded. That is precisely what we noticed was the case in the sentence (25).

The fact that one always knows the speaker (and usually the hearer) at any point in a discourse—and that the identity of the speaker may shift during a quotation— explains the various data noted by Ross (1970) in a way that seems to me more acceptable than Ross's explanation. To take only Ross's first example (everything else in his paper to the extent that his data are valid, is subject to the same kind of explanation):

(29) a. Tom says the paper was written by Ann and himself.
     b. *The paper was written by Ann and himself.
     c. The paper was written by Ann and myself.

We find that this "emphatic" use of reflexive pronouns (*himself, myself*) is for the most part restricted to embedded (indirect) quotations where (in my terms) the reflexive pronoun refers to the same person as the agent of the quotative verb. In (29a) *himself* refers to the same person as *Tom*, who is the agent of *says*. The only circumstance under which this condition need not be present is when the pronoun is first (or possibly second) person. Thus, (29c) with the first person reflexive pronoun *myself* is quite possible, but (29b), where the pronoun is not in a quotation and where it is not first person, is ruled out. Ross wants to explain these and many similar facts by positing the covert existence in (29c) of a quotative verb with a first person agent. In other words, the semantic structure of (29c) would be something like that of *I say (to you) that the paper was written by Ann and myself*, and the *I say (to you) that* portion would be postsemantically deleted.

I have always balked at the idea that every time we make a declarative statement we are semantically prefacing it with *I say (to you) that*, and it has seemed to me that Ross's observations can be better explained by saying somehow that the knowledge of a speaker (and hearer) are always "in the air." Ross himself suggests the possibility of such an explanation, which he labels the "pragmatic analysis," but he notes that "such a theory will have to be given a precise formulation, and that stylistic devices such as making use of colorful terms like 'in the air' do not ensure that such a theory exists" (Ross, 1970, p. 257). In fact, I think that the discussion above does provide us with a means of formalizing knowledge, relevant to a discourse, which is in the air. Given the constraint in (26), and the fact that the 1 must always be filled in, either by the actual speaker or the agent of a quotative verb, we can simply say of the sentences in (29) that this use of reflexive pronouns is limited to pronouns which refer to the speaker. In (29c) *myself* of course refers to the actual speaker. In (29a) *himself* refers to the quoted speaker, the agent of the quotative verb. This explanation is simple and straightforward, and applies to all examples of this sort that I am aware of.[4]

---

[4] In this discussion I have glossed over the differences between direct and indirect quotations, differences which complicate in interesting ways the picture just presented but do not invalidate it.

DEFINITENESS

So far I have discussed some fairly straightforward semantic constraints involved in the semantic presence of contextual features of tense, such as *past* and *future,* and I have tried to account for the slightly less straightforward matter of fore-grounding. The latter concern led us into a consideration of how knowledge of the identity of a speaker (and hearer) can be accounted for. In the final section of this paper I would like to turn to a matter which seems to exhibit considerably greater complexity, where I cannot promise to give anything like a complete and final solution, but where I do think the model I have described above presents a fruitful way of dealing with the intricacies involved. I refer to the occurrence of a semantic contextual feature which may be labelled *definite*. The appropriateness of this label stems from the fact that the presence of this feature is often, though by no means always, reflected in the surface structure presence of the "definite article," at least in English and some other languages. I will not have anything specific to say about languages—and they are many—which do not possess a surface structure definite article. It is my impression, however, that such languages possess the semantic unit *definite* just as English does, the only difference being that in English this unit does (often) receive a surface representation, whereas in those other languages it does not.[5]

The meaning of the semantic unit *definite* can be described as follows. A lexical unit like *cow* or *milk* has, in and of itself, a very general sort of meaning—one that extends over all conceivable cows and all conceivable instances of the substance milk. There are times when we do wish to communicate about these most general concepts, as when we say *Cows are docile* or *Milk is good for you,* but certainly in the majority of instances we need instead to communicate about some subset of all conceivable cows, or some milk that is less than all conceivable milk. When we do narrow down the lexical concept in this way, we may or may not assume that the hearer also knows about the same subset of cows, or the same instance of milk. Furthermore, we may or may not assume that the hearer knows that we are pres-ently talking about this subset, or this instance. Special communicative significance is evidently attached to the situation where (a) the speaker knows about a certain subset or instance, (b) he assumes that the hearer also has such knowledge, and (c) he assumes that the hearer knows that he is presently talking about this subset or instance. When these three conditions are present, the speaker adds to the noun in question the contextual feature *definite.*

The fact that interests us here is that the assumptions regarding the hearer's knowledge can be made on a variety of grounds. The speaker may have any one of a variety of reasons for thinking that the hearer already knows about a par-ticular subset or instance of the general concept, and that the hearer knows what

---

[5] There have been many discussions of definiteness in the literature. Christophersen (1939) is especially to be recommended, as is Karttunen (1968). Although I find it uncongenial to think that every occurrence of definiteness involves a deleted relative clause, the presentation in Vendler (1967, pp. 33–69) is lucid and relevant. My own earlier discussion in MSL (pp. 186–88) dealt with the meaning of definite and its relation to other semantic units in the same sentence, but failed to go into factors of the kind that will be treated here.

subset or instance he is presently talking about. To a large extent these reasons depend on factors which extend across the boundaries of sentences—although that is not always the case. Without attempting to provide an exhaustive formulation of how definiteness is established, I will try at least to touch on a variety of relevant considerations. It will be seen that some of them are of considerable interest when it comes to characterizing a speaker's (and a hearer's) knowledge.

It may be noted, first of all, that certain lexical units are *always* accompanied by the contextual feature definite. Clearly this must be so in those cases where the lexical unit has some inherent feature whose consequence is that the hearer can always be assumed to be familiar with the object being talked about. There are, I think, two inherent features of noun roots whose presence has this consequence. They may be labeled *proper* and *unique*.

We noted that a lexical unit like *cow* has a meaning which extends over all conceivable cows. For the members of a family that owns two or three cows, the concept of each of these cows is known and there may be frequent occasion to talk about one or the other of them. The concept of each cow is important for communication within this family. What people do in such cases is deliberately to provide the concepts with phonological symbolizations; in informal terms, they "give the concepts names." Thus, one particular cow may be called *Elsie*, and so on. The particular concept to which such a label has been given need not be knowledge that is limited to a small group of people, but may be quite generally known. A great many of us know about particular cities (*Chicago*), rivers (*the Missouri*), works of art (*War and Peace*, the *Eroica*), and the like. The concept may be one of a set of objects also (*the Aleutians*, *the Rockies*). A lexical unit of this kind can be said to be accompanied by the inherent feature *proper*. A lexical unit is proper, then, when its meaning involves a known subset of the objects involved in the meaning of some more general lexical unit (such as *cow* or *city*), a subset talked about frequently enough that it "has its own name". Such lexical units are definite by definition. They can be regarded as definite concepts which, because of their importance, have become institutionalized. Instead of talking about *the cow* or *the city*, under conditions where we can assume familiarity with the cow or city involved, we talk about *Elsie* or *Chicago* instead, and feel confident in assuming that our hearer is also already familiar with Elsie or Chicago. There is, then, a constraint to the effect that *proper* entails *definite*.

There appears to be another inherent feature, partially independent of proper, whose relation to definite is the same. We may call it *unique*. Some noun roots, such as *Elsie* or *sky*, always involve unique individuals. They can be regarded as known sets which have but one member. If, then, one knows the concept of (a certain) *Elsie* or the concept *sky*, one cannot help but know which member of the set is being talked about, since there is only one. We can say, therefore, that unique, as well as proper, entails definite, and we can formulate this constraint as follows:

$$(30) \quad \begin{Bmatrix} \text{proper} \\ \text{unique} \end{Bmatrix} \Rightarrow \text{definite}$$

Since both proper and unique are inherent features of certain lexical units (*the Aleutians* is proper, *sky* is unique, and *Elsie* is both), (30) means that all such lexical units will automatically receive the contextual feature definite.

The majority of noun roots, however, are neither proper nor unique, and are not automatically definite in all their occurrences. When they are definite, the definiteness is established by factors which may in the broadest sense be termed environmental. It is useful, as suggested earlier, to distinguish between between environmental factors which are extralinguistically established—established by circumstances surrounding a discourse but not by anything in the discourse itself—and environmental factors which are established by something that is said. The latter type will occupy us predominantly, but we can give passing attention to the former. It is also useful to distinguish further between extralinguistic factors that are real and those that are assumed. To illustrate the first, suppose you and I are in a room which has a prominent blackboard on one wall. If I want to talk about *the blackboard*, I am at liberty to assume you know what blackboard I mean. That is, I can treat *blackboard* as definite on the basis of the presence of this particular blackboard in the environment of our conversation. We might formalize the knowledge that is present in this situation in the manner shown in (31):

(31) blackboard ⇒ definite

That is, the lexical unit identifiable with the idea of this particular blackboard is accompanied by the contextual feature definite. This kind of environmental justification for treating something as definite is, of course, very common. Whenever you and I are in a room, for example, I can talk about *the ceiling, the floor, the walls*, and usually *the door, the windows*, and so on. Thus, just from being in a room, lexical units like ceiling, floor, walls, door, and windows enter the left side of rules like (31).

I mentioned that definiteness might also be established by extralinguistic factors which are not real, but assumed. I have in mind the fact that one often encounters stories which begin with definite nouns. The following, for example, would not be out of place as the opening sentence of a novel:

(32) The waitress brought him another cup of coffee.

There are actually two definite nouns in the semantic structure of this sentence: those that are reflected in the surface structure as *the waitress* and as *him*. Clearly we have no prior knowledge that enables us to know what waitress is meant, or who the person represented by *him* is. Evidently the novelist is assuming, as a literary device, that the reader does have such knowledge; that is, he is inventing certain semantic resources which are not present in actuality—resources such as:

(33) waitress ⇒ definite
     X ⇒ definite

where X is the noun root underlying *him*. He even treats the noun containing X (and probably that containing waitress also, although the absence of intonation markers in the orthography leaves that uncertain) as foregrounded, so that X can be pronominalized. The effect, of course, is to place the reader immediately within a context which, the author pretends, already exists. I suspect that this device is largely confined to imaginative literature, where its aesthetic value is apparent, and that it is seldom if ever used in sober expository writing. As for spoken language, it is not unusual for a speaker to assume knowledge of the same sort. He will not, however, do so in the typical case out of inventiveness, but rather on the grounds that certain special pieces of knowledge are indeed shared by him and the hearer (although they are not shared by a larger audience). For example, if I ask a member of my family *Did you feed the dog?*, we know without question what dog I mean. In general, then, certain information which can be formalized as in (34) is typically shared by small subgroups of speakers—often, it may be added, only when they are at a certain place, or only at a certain time:

(34) dog $\Rightarrow$ definite

We can now turn to the ways in which definiteness is established by something within the discourse itself. We will be concerned with the fact that the knowledge of particular objects or particular instances of a substance, and knowledge that they are at the moment being talked about, may be established neither by the inherent properties of a lexical unit nor by the environment of the discourse, real or assumed, but rather by things that are said within the discourse itself.

First of all, it is easy to see that once a particular object or set of objects has been mentioned in a discourse for the first time, the speaker can from then on assume that the hearer knows about it. For example, once *a cow* has been mentioned in (35a), the speaker can go on to talk about *the cow*:

(35) a. Once there was a widow who owned a cow.
      b. ... the cow ...

It is not enough, however, to say simply that the occurrence of a particular lexical unit acts as an initiator, so that from thenceforth the occurrences of that same lexical unit must be specified as definite, as suggested in (36).

(36) 1 : 1 $\Rightarrow$ definite

It is interesting to consider, for one thing, that not all occurrences of a particular lexical unit establish the knowledge of a particular object or set of objects. We can rephrase this observation in terms of (36) by saying that the initiator, given there as "1", is stated too broadly; that only under certain conditions does a lexical unit initiate the constraint there indicated. For example, a generic noun does not do so:

(37) a. Once there was a widow who was fond of cows.
      b. ...*the cows ...

In the first sentence the speaker was talking about cows in general, not any particular cows. He has no basis, therefore, for treating cows as definite in the next sentence. Genericness is a complex subject in itself, but let us simply assume here that there is a contextual feature *generic*, and that a noun which contains this feature does not qualify as an initiator of the constraint we are concerned with:

(38)　$\underline{1}$　　　:　　1　⇒　　definite
　　　　~generic

A rather similar phenomenon, sometimes confused with genericness, is that which I have labeled *randomness* (MSL, 199–200):

(39)　a. Once there was a widow who wanted a cow.
　　　b. ... (*)the cow ...

There are certain verb roots (*want* and *look for* are typical examples), as well as certain configurations involving "modals" and negation, which involve (or may involve) states or events that are random in nature. Certain nouns associated with such verb roots may have this random property also. The extension of randomness to the noun is actually not obligatory, a fact which explains why there is an ambiguity in (39a). It may have been some particular cow that the widow wanted, or it may have been any cow at all. It is in the latter case that the occurrence of the lexical unit *cow* does not justify its treatment as definite thereafter. We can thus expand (38) with a further condition:[6]

(40)　1　　　　　　　:　　1　⇒　　definite
　　　　~generic
　　　　~random

It is also worth noting that a singular noun may initiate definiteness for subsequent singular nouns, and a plural noun for subsequent plural nouns, but not singular for plural or plural for singular:

(41)　a. Once there was a widow who owned a cow.
　　　b. ... the cow ... (but not ... *the cows ...)
　　　c. Once there was a widow who owned some cows.
　　　d. ... the cows ... (but not ... *the cow ...)

Thus, we can make a further modification of the contextual rule, by which the plurality of the lexical unit which is the initiator and the plurality of that which is in the constraint must be the same:

---

[6] What I am calling *random* is related to the −specific designation discussed in Karttunen (1969, pp. 25–33). I would differ, however, in attributing random to *museum* in (one meaning of) *Bill intends to visit a museum* but not in *Bill visits a museum every day* (Karttunen's examples), where I suspect that a feature *iterative* spreads from the adverb *every day* into the verb *visit* and (optionally) into *museum*. The features random and iterative have some properties in common, but they also differ in some respects and certainly have different meanings.

(42) $\underline{1}$: $\underline{1}$ ⇒ definite
~generic
~random αplural
αplural

A fuller treatment would have to consider the question of whether there is a terminator for the constraint in (42); whether the definiteness of this lexical unit eventually evaporates or, at least, weakens. My suspicion at the moment is that definiteness (subject to the conditions mentioned above) remains obligatory as long as the lexical unit in question remains foregrounded, and that it becomes optional thereafter. Thus, it may persist much longer than foregrounding, but its obligatory retention depends on the retention of foregrounding as well. It would take some extended examples to illustrate this suggestion, which is only tentative in any case. Rather than dwell further on it here, I would like to turn to a different phenomenon—one that seems to me particularly intriguing when it comes to the formalization of semantic resources.

We can begin with certain facts that are illustrated in the following sentences:

(43) a. She decided to sell the cow and buy a shop with the money.
   b. The children came upon a little house. Entering it through an open door, they found themselves in the kitchen.

The question is why *money* in (43a) is treated as definite, and why definiteness is attributed to *kitchen* in (43b). A rough answer seems to be that the occurrence of *sell* in (43a) is enough to make *money* definite, and that the occurrence of *house* in (43b) is responsible for the definiteness of *kitchen*. In attempting to formulate this rough answer in more precise terms, we need to consider just what kind of knowledge it is that we associate with lexical units such as *sell* and *house*.

It seems that one knows, in effect, that selling involves money, and that a house has a kitchen; and it seems that it is this kind of knowledge which explains the definiteness of *money* and *kitchen* in (43). Such knowledge is most naturally formalized in terms of inherent features associated with lexical units, whether they be verb roots like *sell* or noun roots like *house*. In other words, we can posit that *involving money* (or something of the sort) is an inherent feature of *sell*, that *having a kitchen* is an inherent feature of *house*. It is interesting that the model pictured in (1) at the beginning of this paper must apparently be extended to allow inherent features that are more than unanalyzable semantic units—inherent features like *having a kitchen* which contain both a verb and a patient noun. Let us look more closely at this particular kind of inherent feature, which, it can be seen, involves the *parts* of objects.

It is evident that many noun roots involve objects which have parts, and that these parts are "known" to the speakers of a language in ways that are linguistically significant. Given the concept *bicycle*, for example, we know that a bicycle has a *frame*, a *seat*, *handlebars*, *wheels*, and so on. I am suggesting that such knowledge can be formalized in terms of inherent features of *bicycle*, and specifically that *bicycle* is accompanied by certain complex inherent features such as *having a frame*, *having a seat*, and so on. One observable consequence is that it is tautologous to say things like *My bicycle has a frame* or *My bicycle has a seat*. Given the concept *bicycle*, we already know these things. A second consequence—the one that led us into this subject—is that, once *bicycle* has been mentioned, *frame*, *seat*, and the like are as eligible to be treated as *definite* as is *bicycle* itself. Having mentioned a *bicycle*, the speaker can assume that the hearer knows what frame and what seat he is talking about if he goes on to use those lexical units:

(44) a. I bought a bicycle yesterday.
     b. The frame is extra large.
     c. The seat is unusual.

All of this follows naturally if we assume that not only the overtly expressed lexical unit, but also the lexical units present in its inherent features behave as initiators in the application of rule (42). Thus, when *bicycle* is mentioned in (44a), it is first of all itself subject to (42), so that subsequent occurrences of it (under certain conditions) must be definite. At the same time, however, all those lexical units like *frame*, *seat*, and so on, that are inherently associated with *bicycle* are subject to (42) also. Merely by mentioning *bicycle*, therefore, we establish a whole set of constraints of the following sort:

(45) bicycle   ⇒   definite
     frame   ⇒   definite
     seat   ⇒   definite

What we have been discussing so far have been the *obligatory* parts of objects. I noted that they are recognizable through two diagnostic criteria: first, that sentences such as *My bicycle has wheels* are tautologous; second, that, having mentioned *bicycle*, we can go on to say *the wheels* and the like. Apparently objects also have *optional* parts. For examples, we might say that *basket*, *light*, *bell*, and so on are optional parts of a bicycle. Most noticeably, optional parts are not tautologous in sentences like *My bicycle has a basket*. Just from hearing *bicycle* we don't know whether there is a basket or not, although we do know there is a frame, a seat, and wheels. In addition, I would suggest that the definiteness of *basket* in (46b) is slightly odd:

(46) a. I bought a bicycle yesterday.
     b. The basket is extra large.

The hearer might easily be prompted to say, "Oh, it has a basket?" whereas, clearly, he would not want to say, "Oh, it has a frame?" on hearing (44b). One feels, I think, that (46b) assumes slightly more knowledge on the part of the hearer than might be justified. It is nevertheless quite true that speakers do constantly overstep themselves in making assumptions about their hearers' knowledge, and that the definiteness of *basket* in (46b) is hardly very surprising. It does seem, in any case, that optional parts can be distinguished from obligatory ones by the absence of tautology in sentences of the type mentioned, and less definitely by the slight oddity (or "assuming too much" effect) of assigning definiteness to the optional part.

Obligatory and optional parts are subject to considerable variation in time and space. At one time a running board was an obligatory part of a car; now it is no longer even optional. Heaters and cigarette lighters seem to have moved from optional to obligatory in recent years. Evidently a basement is an obligatory part of a house in New England, for example, whereas in California it is decidedly optional. Thus, (47b) is tautologous if the house is in Massachusetts, but not if it is in California:

(47) a. I bought a new house yesterday.
      b. It has a basement.
      c. The basement is extra large.

Similarly, (47c), following directly after (47a), would be normal enough in Massachusetts, but in California might well elicit the question, "Oh, it has a basement?" All this is just to point out once again that semantic resources are far from being fixed for all speakers at all times and places.

We can say, then, that many noun roots have associated with them inherent features which are not simple semantic units (like *count* or *human*) but configurations relating the lexical unit in question, through a verb meaning *have as an obligatory (or optional) part*, to another noun root—as *bicycle*, for example, is obligatorily related to *frame* and optionally related to *basket*. The occurrence of an obligatory part as an inherent feature triggers the definiteness constraint expressed in (42) just as does the original lexical unit. The occurrence of an optional part may do so also, but in such a case we have at least a slight feeling that the speaker is skipping a step in his assumptions regarding the hearer's knowledge. I believe that the list of both obligatory and optional parts associated with any particular lexical unit is finite and manageable, even though in some instances it may be rather large. A worthwhile task would be to establish such lists for a large and representative sample of nouns. As was noted just above, the lists can be expected to vary somewhat with different speakers at different times and places.

I would assume that items which are not on such lists cannot be talked about as if they were parts of the objects concerned without creating sentences that are semantically anomalous. Thus, for example, since *glove compartment* is neither an obligatory nor an optional part of *bicycle*, it is at least as strange to say *My bicycle has a glove compartment* as it is to say *My bicycle has a frame*. The former is anomalous, while the latter is tautologous for reasons stated earlier. We do not need to worry about listing all the parts that a bicycle *cannot* have; anything not present on our lists of obligatory and optional parts is in this category. We do need to note, however, that we can say many other things, such as *My bicycle has foxtails attached to the ends of the handlebars*, which violate no semantic constraints. There would seem to be a limitless number of such possibilities, in fact, so that we are precluded from ever listing them all for any lexical unit. What is characteristic of such "parts" as *foxtails attached to the ends of the handlebars* is that they are complex semantic configurations–not single lexical units like *frame* or, at best, pluralized items like *wheels*. It may be, in fact, that all such ad hoc "parts" contain at least one verb in their semantic structure. In any case, the constraints involved in them go further than those we have been discussing. In the example just given, all that is relevant to our discussion so far is the fact that *handlebars* are an obligatory part of *bicycle*, a fact which explains why this noun is definite. That *handlebars* have *ends* is explainable in similar terms, but other kinds of constraints would have to be introduced to explain why the ends of handlebars can have *foxtails* (but not *refrigerators*) attached to them. All I am saying is that there may be a limitless number of things that a bicycle (or any other object) can be said to *have*, but that this is only true if we pass beyond the manageable lists of simple obligatory and optional parts into the area of complex semantic structures.

Objects, of course, have properties beyond those that fall in the category of *parts*. They may have size, weight, length, breadth, color, and so on. Two observations can be made regarding such properties. First, not all objects have all of them. A *table* has a *height* but a *ball* (in itself) does not; a *ball* has a *diameter* but a *book* does not, and so on. Evidently for any particular lexical unit like *table* or *ball* we can list which of these properties are relevant. Second, these properties are not single items but rather sets of possibilities–either points along a continuum, as with height and weight, or discrete sub-properties, as with color. To say any more than this would lead us far afield; it is enough here to point out that there are various things that are known about objects (and that may be formalizable as inherent features) beyond simply their parts, and that the nature of these other things may be somewhat different from the nature of parts.

We should, however, give at least brief attention to the manner in which verb roots, as well as noun roots, may establish the definiteness of subsequent nouns. An example of this phenomenon was given in (43a), where the occurrence of *sell* was responsible for the definiteness of *money*. If we were to attempt an explanation identical to that given above in connection with noun roots, we would have to say that verb roots (or what is meant by them) have parts. But that does not seem to be quite correct. The following sentences will, I think, help to clarify what is involved when the initiator of the definiteness constraint is contained within a verb:

(48) a. My neighbor's house burned down last night.
      b. The cause was some defective wiring.
      c. The flames could be seen for miles.
      d. The damage was extensive.

Imagine that (48a) is immediately followed by any one of the other sentences. We are interested, of course, in the fact that the occurrence of *burn down* in the first sentence allows us to use the definite nouns *the cause, the flames*, or *the damage* in the next sentence. It may be that an event or state, instead of having parts, as an object does, has (or may have) a *cause*, various *accompaniments*, and various *results*. So far as the cause is concerned, we seem to be able to make definite only the lexical unit *cause* itself (or sometimes *reason*), but not any specific cause. That is, while we can say *the cause* immediately after (48a), we cannot say *the defective wiring* or the like. Thus, it may be that the lexical unit *cause* is an inherent feature of most or all verb roots. On the other hand, it appears that a verb root is known to have various specific accompaniments, as *burn down* is accompanied by *flames*, *heat*, and so on. These lexical units too are eligible to be definite. Finally, there seem to be certain *results* or *effects* of a verb root which can be treated in the same way. Having said *burn down*, we can talk about *the damage* or *the insurance*. Evidently *money* was a result of *sell* in the example mentioned earlier. It would appear, in short, that while noun roots have parts inherently associated with them (as well as, often, dimensions and the like), verb roots have accompaniments, results, and the single item *cause*.

In closing this discussion I want to focus on one more way in which definiteness is established. I refer to the fact that definiteness may be brought to a noun by a relative clause attached to that noun. We will see that this phenomenon shows with special clarity the need to relate semantic resources to human knowledge, and consequently the need to admit that language structure and knowledge are inseparable parts of a single whole. We will also see more clearly here than in the preceding discussion the seriousness of the problems which this admission entails. What I have to say about definiteness and relative clauses will be brief and sketchy for two reasons. First, I do not at the moment pretend to understand everything that is relevant here. Second, I think I understand enough to realize that the subject is highly complex and that it calls for an extended treatment in its own right. It would be necessary, among other things, to spend some time discussing the general nature of relative clauses and their appropriate representation in semantic structures. Here I will gloss over such matters, and will only sketch what seem to be some of the considerations which are important from the standpoint of this paper.

Suppose I tell you that during a recent visit to Washington I was given a guided tour of the White House attic (or its equivalent in the Smithsonian Institution). Without any further context, it would not then be possible for me to go on to say:

(49) *I saw the golf clubs.

But I could, without any further context, say:

(50) I saw the golf clubs that were used by President Eisenhower.

The relative clause attached to *golf clubs* in (50) has served to narrow down the meaning of this lexical item in such a way that the speaker is able to assume that the hearer is familiar with these golf clubs, as he could not in (49). He is, therefore, able to treat the golf clubs as definite (although he is not obligated to do so; he could say *I saw some golf clubs that were used by President Eisenhower*).

It would be very easy to account for such instances if it were simply the case that all relative clauses narrowed down the meanings of noun roots in such a way that they could (optionally) be specified as definite. We could then simply add relative clauses to the list of other factors, sketched above, which permit the introduction of definiteness into a discourse. But that is not at all the way things are. For example, neither of the following sentences is possible in the context just described, even though each of them shows a relative clause attached to the definitized noun:

(51) a. *I saw the golf clubs that were covered with dust.
     b. *I saw the golf balls that were used by President Eisenhower.

The impossibility of (51a) in this context suggests that definitization of the type we are discussing is influenced by the content of the relative clause. Roughly speaking, to speak of golf clubs that were covered with dust does not particularize the meaning of *golf clubs* to the extent that the hearer can be assumed to know what golf clubs are involved, although to speak of those that were used by President Eisenhower does have such an effect. But the situation is complicated further by the kind of thing that is indicated in (51b), which contains exactly the same relative clause we found in the acceptable sentence (50). Here it is instead the modified lexical unit itself that has been changed. Apparently we have to accept the fact that one and the same relative clause is capable of definitizing *golf clubs* but not capable of definitizing *golf balls*. Speaking informally again, it is evident that we know different things about golf clubs and golf balls. We know that a single particular set of golf clubs may be used by one person over a long period of time, perhaps even over his entire golf-playing life, while the same is not true of golf balls, which are replaced at frequent intervals. (This piece of knowledge is not restricted to golf clubs vs. golf balls, but also applies to a tennis racket vs. tennis balls and other analogous equipment.)

But the definiteness—even the obligatory definiteness—of *golf balls* in (52), where it is modified by the same relative clause as in (51b), suggests that the matter is more complicated still:

(52) No building is big enough to house the golf balls that were used by President Eisenhower.

In particular, it suggests that it is necessary to take into account not only the content of the relative clause [as shown by (51a)], and not only, in addition, the nature of the modified lexical unit [as shown by (51b)], but also the nature of the higher sentence in which the relative clause is embedded. The difference between the single perceptual event involving *see* in (51b) and the generic condition involving *house* in (52) is evidently the determining factor behind the impossibility of the former (in the context described) and the possibility of (52) (in various imaginable contexts where the definiteness of *golf balls* has not otherwise been established).

What would we have to do to account for phenomena of this kind? The examples suggest that we would have to deal with triples of semantic properties: semantic properties (a) of the relative clause, (b) of the lexical unit to which the clause is attached, and (c) of the higher sentence in which the clause is embedded. If these semantic properties fit together in a certain way, the details of which are by no means clear to me at the moment, then the speaker would be able to assume that the hearer was familiar with the particular object(s) he was talking about and knew that he was talking about this object at the moment, and he could convey these assumptions by making the noun in question definite. The task of formalizing the relevant semantic properties and of stating the combinations which have this definitizing effect appears to be staggering. One reason is that the relative clause and the higher sentence are both likely to be themselves complex, so that the relevant semantic properties for each may depend on an interaction of a variety of factors. Another reason is that the semantic properties involved are likely to relate to very specific pieces of knowledge of a kind that could be dealt with only by some storage device of huge proportions. Thus, for example, the definiteness of *letter* in (53) depends on the speaker's assumption that the hearer knows about an incident during Truman's presidency in which Truman wrote a vigorous and subsequently well-publicized letter to Paul Hume, the music critic in question, reacting to Hume's criticism of a recital by his daughter:

(53) I saw the letter that Harry Truman wrote to the music critic of the Washington Post.

If the speaker did not assume such knowledge on the part of the hearer, this relative clause could not have the effect of definitizing *letter*, and the speaker would normally say *a letter*. In accounting for such definitizing, then, it would be necessary among other things to formalize such knowledge as that which distinguishes golf clubs from golf balls, as discussed earlier, and also knowledge of the kind exemplified by the facts about Harry Truman just mentioned. It is now clear that the semantic constraints which are relevant to the occurrence of *definite* require access to a vast store of information whose full systematization seems far beyond the powers of any practical linguistic description.

The task of formalizing human knowledge fully would evidently involve, among other things, an enormous extension of the inherent features associated with every lexical unit. Not only would there have to be an inherent feature for golf clubs which specified the continuing use of a particular set over a period of time by a single individual, but there would have to be inherent features associated with individual persons which specified every fact that was known about them. Thus, Truman's letter to Hume would have to be included in the inherent features associated with the lexical unit *Harry Truman* (and with the lexical unit *Paul Hume* also). The letter and the circumstances surrounding it constitute things that we know about Truman and Hume that are relevant to the way we talk. The point is that we do not use only part of what we know when we say something, we use all of it, and there is no way to divide knowledge that is linguistically relevant from knowledge that is not (excluding, to be sure, the likely possibility that there are some kinds of knowledge which are not readily communicated through language, and which are therefore not relevant to the semantic resources of a language).

It is easy to be discouraged by the vastness of knowledge, as well as by its variability (not everyone knows about the Truman-Hume letter). Nevertheless, the *principles* on which knowledge is organized seem much more likely to be within our grasp, as do the ways in which such principles influence the way we talk. We need not be put off by the apparent fact that definiteness cannot be fully accounted for without a complete formalization of everything everyone knows. It is still possible to investigate productively the principles which apply, some of which I tried to adumbrate above. Whether we will ever have a device so large and versatile that we can use it to store all the vast and variable pieces of knowledge that are ultimately relevant is not so much of theoretical interest as it is of practical importance in the development, for example, of machines for information retrieval or translation.

CONFERENCE DISCUSSION

Crothers wondered whether the concept of foregrounding couldn't also apply to units larger than individual lexical items. Chafe indicated that he didn't mean to give the impression, from the cited examples, that only nouns were relevant to the concept—entire propositions can also be foregrounded. In response to this, Bever indicated that he did not understand what it would mean for a whole clause to be in the foreground. Instead, wouldn't it be that each piece of the clause could be foregrounded? Chafe thought it may be more accurate to say that each piece of a whole clause can be in the foreground. For example, when one says "Mary hit John" all the parts (*John, hitting*, and *Mary*) are brought into the foreground—one has them in the forefront of one's mind, so to speak. One can then subsequently pronominalize any one or several parts of the sentence: for example, one can assert "Mary hit *him* again" or "Later *she* hit *him* again" or "*She* did *it* again and again."

Simmons inquired whether anything that is mentioned in noun or verb phrases becomes foregrounded at its first mention. Chafe indicated that, in general, that seems to be true.

Scriven suggested that the word *current* may be a more appropriate name than *foregrounding* because it introduces the notion of displacement. That is, in Chafe's example of suddenly referring to Jack's mother at the end of the Jack-and-the-beanstalk story, it isn't unusual to still think of her as foregrounded in spite of the long delay in mentioning her, primarily because there has been no *displacement* of her from the 'female' slot in the course of relating the story. Chafe welcomed the suggestion for finding a substitute for the foregrounding concept but disagreed with Scriven concerning the correctness of regarding Jack's mother as still in the foreground after so long a delay. Chafe did indicate, though, that competition for certain semantic slots (such as suggested above for the 'female' slot) is probably a relevant consideration.

Penny wondered why Chafe stuck to the notion that foregrounding is just an all-or-none kind of concept. That is, isn't it possible that foregrounding might exist in different degrees of strength? Chafe didn't think that admitting different degrees of strength would clarify matters.

Goodman indicated that most of the discussion had focused upon the presence or absence of foregrounding on the part of the speaker. But another distinction can be made; for example, we could maintain that some concept might be foregrounded as far as the speaker is concerned but may not be foregrounded from the point of view of the listener. Chafe thought that was quite true and cited as an example experiences where someone would come up to him and say something like "He did such and such today" without his knowing to whom the "he" referred.

Trabasso raised some questions concerning what the necessary conditions are for identification of foregrounding. He indicated that some of the examples seem to be describing foregrounded elements by referring to their pronominalization, whereas other examples describe foregrounding in terms of low pitch and stress. Chafe clarified this by indicating that one *always* gets low pitch associated with foregrounded elements except in contrastive cases. In addition, one usually or quite often will get pronominalization as well as low pitch.

Bever raised some issues regarding analytic versus synthetic truth. That is, in part of Chafe's paper concerning article definiteness, an example was given that once a car as a concept has been foregrounded, one can then go on to talk about its 'inherent' features using the definite article. For example, one might say "I bought a used car a year ago. *The* motor is still working just fine." In Chafe's terminology 'motor' is an obligatory part of the concept 'car' and so one is permitted to use the definite article without ambiguity about which motor one is referring to. Bever then inquired whether Chafe is suggesting that because 'motor' is presumably an obligatory part of the *definition* of 'car' that one is now dealing with something which has previously been called analytic (versus synthetic) truth value? In other words, is saying that the concept 'car' carries with it, by definition, the concept of 'motor' anything like saying that 'bachelor' carries with it, by definition, the concept of being 'unmarried'? If so, then the latter example, which has been used in discussions of analytic truth ("A bachelor is unmarried" is true by definition and so is analytic) would seem to imply that one must also regard saying "A car has a motor" is analytically true because 'motor' is part of the definition of 'car.' Chafe said that that was not quite what he meant to convey by the car-motor example. Instead, a more accurate characterization would be to say that in one's *normative* use of referring to 'cars' one tends to assume that the car has a motor. In other words, it is perhaps too strong a statement to insist that "A car has a motor" is a tautology.

REFERENCES

Chafe, W. L. *Meaning and the structure of language*. Chicago: University of Chicago Press, 1970.

Christophersen, P. *The articles: A study of their theory and use in English*. Copenhagen: Einar Munksgaard, 1939.

Fillmore, C. J. The case for case. In E. Bach & R. T. Harms (Eds.), *Universals in linguistic theory*. New York: Holt, Rinehart, & Winston, 1968.

Karttunen, L. *What makes definite noun phrases definite?* The Rand Corporation, Report P–3871. Santa Monica, 1968.

Karttunen, L. Discourse referents. *International Conference on Computational Linguistics*, Preprint No. 70. Stockholm, 1969.

Ross, J. R. On declarative sentences. In R. A. Jacobs & P. S. Rosenbaum (Eds.), *Readings in English transformational grammar*. Waltham: Ginn and Co., 1970.

Vendler, Z. *Linguistics in philosophy*. Ithaca: Cornell University Press, 1967.

4

SOME SEMANTIC STRUCTURES FOR REPRESENTING ENGLISH MEANINGS[1,2]

Robert F. Simmons
University of Texas at Austin

INTRODUCTION

The spoken or written representation of discourse in English has the explicit structure of a string. That is, the discourse is a sequence of spoken or written symbols—each symbol is followed by another symbol (including stops). Underlying this simple string structure, however, is a considerable depth of phonetic, morphological, syntactic, semantic, and pragmatic structure that is implied by the sequence of choices of symbols.

More than half a century of linguistic study has developed a fair understanding of how to derive and represent phonemic, morphemic, and syntactic structures implied by strings of natural language symbols—not that there is complete agreement in the choice of any one system. It is only in recent years, however, that the semantic structures of natural languages have become an important topic of linguistic consideration. Definitions of semantic structures and means for deriving and representing them had a limited place in Chomsky's (1965) transformational theory, while in newer versions of the theory (see Lakoff, 1969), the underlying semantic structures of language become a basic component.

Developments of semantic notions with particular regard to formal languages had previously been the province of logicians such as Tarski (1944) and Carnap (1946). Their influence on linguistics can be seen particularly in terms of the

[1] Supported by: The National Science Foundation, Grant GJ 509X.

[2] I am grateful to Marianne Celce, for helping me to understand better various forms of deep semantic structure, and to numerous other colleagues and students who continually tutor me in the finer points of the several disciplines of linguistics, psychology, logic, mathematics, and computer science, all of which seem to be deeply involved in computational linguistics.

methods and definitions of semantic analysis developed by Katz (1967), while, in computational linguistics, Thompson (Thompson & Gibbons, 1964), Woods (1968) and others developed semantic structures of natural language for question answering along lines suggested by these and other logicians. The way in which the levels of implicit structure of a natural language are obtained is outlined below.

The structures that are implicit in strings of linguistic symbols are made explicit with the aid of a lexicon and various grammars. Sequences of phonemes or graphemes are mapped by a system of rewrite rules into morphemes. Sequences of morpheme classes are mapped by a grammar of syntactic transformations into tree structures composed of syntactic transformations into tree structures composed of syntactic constituents. Syntactic constituents are mapped by a system of selection conditions and transformations into a semantic structure that unambiguously represents certain aspects of their meaning. There probably exist pragmatic conditions and transformations that map semantic structures into actions.

The syntactic structure of a statement explicitly shows the syntactic relations and their ordering, usually in a labelled tree structure that is implied by a choice of symbols and their ordering in a language string. The semantic analysis of the same statement is required to map the symbols into whatever represents their meanings in a given system and to transform syntactically related constituents into logically related meanings. Thus, a semantic structure for a statement is defined as *a system of unambiguous representations of meaning interconnected by defined logical relations*.

In a trivial example, the sentence "Apes have hair," a syntactic structure is as follows:

One method of representing the semantic structure is as follows:

$$\text{HASPART}(a, b) \ \& \ \text{MNG}(ape, a) \ \& \ \text{MNG}(hair, b)$$

The semantic system is required to map the ambiguous symbols "ape," "hair," and "have" onto a, b, and HASPART, respectively, as well as transforming them from the syntactic tree structure into this logical form. The symbols a and b must refer to particular meanings and the relations HASPART (for "Has this Part") and MNG (for "Meaning") must be explicitly defined as logical predicates in order for the semantic system to be useful in explicating meanings that are implied by the statement.

The predicate, MNG(ape,a), implies all that is known about apes, e.g., SUBSET (a, animal), HASPART(a, legs), etc. One semantic system is more powerful than another, to the extent that the first can obtain more implications than the second from a given statement. Two semantic systems can also differ in the type of inferences that they allow. One might be limited for some purpose to class membership and part-whole predicates while another might be specialized to numerical and directional relations. These differences are frequently seen in the semantics of experimental question-answering systems (See Simmons, 1970a).

One set of representation conventions—i.e., syntax—for semantic structure is given by various forms of predicate logic. Linguists such as McCawley (1968), Bach (1968), and Lakoff (1969) have so far preferred this form. On the other hand, computational linguists concerned with representing English textual meanings for question answering have often used attribute-value lists or semantic networks to represent semantic structure. These forms are alternate representational conventions, and the choice of conventions for semantic representation need have no relation to the resulting power of the system. A comparison of semantic network and predicate calculus representations is given in another paper (Simmons, 1970b).

Because of the simplicity of its syntax leading to easier readability and computational convenience, I have chosen to represent English discourse meanings in semantic networks closely related to those originally used by Quillian (1966), and further developed by Simmons, Burger, and Schwarcz (1968), Carbonnel (1970), Kay and Martins (1970), and others. This paper defines the structure of a semantic network for use in representing discourse and lexical meanings. It further attempts to develop a fragment of English semantics in showing some conventions for mapping certain syntactic constituents into semantic forms. Algorithms and transformational conventions for generating English sentences from such nets are the topic of another paper; additional papers are in preparation (Simmons & Slocum, in press) showing applications of semantic nets to computer-aided instruction, and computational methods for translating from English strings into the networks.

A SEMANTIC STRUCTURE FOR DISCOURSE

The structure for representing natural language meanings that will be developed here owes much to Quillian's original work in defining a structure of semantic memory. Unlike his structure, this one is linguistically motivated and indebted to discussions published by Fillmore (1968), McCawley (1968), Bach (1968), and Lakoff (1969). The structure is designed to conveniently represent underlying semantic meanings that, with a lexicon and a grammar, can generate natural language sentences in a linguistically justifiable manner.

In my opinion, a semantic representation should probably be completely free of its natural language representation. The correspondence between semantic structure and natural language representation should reside wholly in the grammar and lexicon. Such surface notions as tense and number, for example, should be represented semantically by relations such as Time of event and Quantity. The surface determiners, "a, an, the, some, all", and the null representation should be derived from values or interaction of values for Determination and Number relations in the semantic structure (e.g., DET definite NBR plural indicates "the".) The concepts which are the nodes of semantic structures should be representable by various lexical choices in such a manner that meaning-preserving paraphrases will be a natural consequence of repeated generations of sentences from the same semantic nets. Although these requirements are met in theory in this system, the reader will notice certain shortcomings in each of these areas in the present development.

General Structure

The primitives of the system are taken as word-sense meanings for concepts, and discourse relations for semantic relations. A given word such as "pitcher" usually has more than one sense meaning, e.g., "a person who throws a ball" and "a container for pouring fluids". Each such sense meaning is a concept that may be represented by subscripting as, for example, "$pitcher_1$" and "$pitcher_2$." (An unsubscripted word-sense will imply the subscript "1".) A concept, though taken as a discourse primitive, is actually defined by lexical relations with other concepts, thus forming its own concept structure, as will be seen in a discussion of the lexicon in the next section.

A semantic structure is a labelled list of pairs where a label is a concept designator and a pair is composed of a relation and a concept. An abstract attribute value representation of a semantic structure is as follows:

$$
\begin{array}{lll}
C_i & R_a & C_j \\
    & R_b & C_k \\
    & .. & .. \\
    & R_m & C_n
\end{array}
$$

This list can also be represented as a set of triples as follows:

$$
\begin{array}{lll}
C_i & R_a & C_j \\
C_i & R_b & C_k \\
.. & .. & .. \\
C_i & R_m & C_n
\end{array}
$$

or as the set of predicates,

$$
\begin{array}{ll}
R_a & (C_i \quad C_j) \\
R_b & (C_i \quad C_k) \\
\vdots & \\
R_m & (C_i \quad C_n)
\end{array}
$$

The corresponding graph representation is shown below:

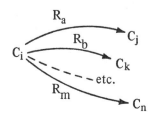

The relations in semantic structures for representing discourse are comprised of deep-case names such as AGT, OBJ, INST, SOURCE, GOAL, THEME, DATIVE, etc., each dominating a preposition and another concept. In addition, the intersentential connectors such as "because," "therefore," "thus," "since," "before," "during," "after," etc. are assumed to be semantic relations in the network. Each relation is presumed to be definable in terms of inferences to be made strictly as a result of that relation. AGT(a,b) for example, implies that a is animate, that b is a process, and that b has some effect on a. The case relations dominate prepositions which are also relational terms. For example, LOC may dominate a particular sense of "on," say ON7. LOC(a,b) implies that b has spatial coordinates and that these coordinates apply to the process symbolized by a (where a may be a verb or a noun). A more precise indication of how the spatial coordinates are to be applied is signified by the prepositional meaning that the case relation dominates. For the example of LOC dominating ON7, ON7(a,b) implies that a is in contact with b, a is above b, etc.

A similar situation applies to explicit sentential connectives. AFTER(a,b) implies that the event described by b occurs later than that of a. BECAUSE(a,b) means at least that the process of a occurs before that of b and that whenever a occurs, b must happen. THUS(a,b) means a implies b. Connectives like "however," "when," "whenever," etc., appear quite difficult to work out.

Determining precisely what is signified by each case relation, prepositional meaning, and intersentential connector is a task of linguistic-logic definition that has hardly yet begun, but one which promises great rewards in showing how natural languages represent the depths of meaning implied by such simple statements as "the book is on the table." So, in saying that a semantic relation is "definable," what is meant is that such implications, as in the above examples, can be derived as the meaning of the various relations. Once these are available, the semantic interpretation of a sentence is enriched by the explicit list of implications signified by such relations as AGT, OBJ, INST, LOC, TIM, etc., and by the particular prepositional relations they dominate. Such relations make clear and explicit the detailed features of interactions between pairs of concepts or processes in terms of space, time, effect, affect, causality, etc.

The use of case relations as semantic connecting links derives partly from work by Fillmore (1968) who has shown that verbs may be considered as n-ary predicates with labelled case relations indicating the role of each nominal argument. In this development Fillmore has also argued that every noun in an English sentence is in a particular case relation to the verb that dominates it and that the lexical structure for a verb must specify the case roles, prepositions, and priority rules for surface ordering of its nominal arguments. In considering that semantic relations have explicit implications, I am following Woods (1968) and Raphael (1964) who demonstrated the computational efficacy of treating relational words as LISP functions or predicates. If a case relation is considered as a function (or subroutine) when it is called, it will return the list of implications relevant to that relation and its two concept arguments.

From a case grammar point of view, the semantic structure representing a sentence is essentially a verb sense-meaning in case relations to its nominal arguments.

The notion of TOKen is introduced to indicate that a particular concept—i.e., word-sense reference—represents a particular occurrence of that concept limited by the choice of context. Thus, there is some set of "breakings" such that John did them, or Mary; that were done with hammers, with axes, with automobiles; that happened to various objects, at various times in various places. A particular "breaking" event—or notion or concept or process—is more or less precisely specified by the choice of its arguments. The semantic relation TOK(a,b) signifies that the event represented by a is a specified subclass of all the events signified by b. A subclass of "breakings" is specified in the following semantic structure for Fillmore's example sentence, "John broke the window with a hammer."

C1	TOK	break
	TIME	PAST
	AGENT	C2
	OBJECT	C3
	INST	C4
C2	TOK	John
	NBR	SING
	DET	DEF
C3	TOK	window
	NBR	SING
	DET	DEF
C4	TOK	hammer
	NBR	SING
	DET	INDEF

As in the use with "break," TOK(C3,window) signifies that subset of the concepts labelled "window" DETermined by the definite article in this context, and TOK(C4,hammer) is an indefinite member of the set of ideas that "hammer" refers to. If we suppose for the moment that the listener or reader is familiar with this particular event of breaking a window, he might be able to further specify "the window" as the "picture window in the house on Main Street," and the hammer as some particular entity as well. In an adequate communication procedure, the speaker has specified the particular event of "breaking" just well enough for the listener to identify exactly one of the many "breakings" he has remembered and the detailed conditions surrounding it.

Since each concept may be specified with numerous relations to other concepts, we need the indirection of reference exemplified in the concept name C3 referring to a particular token of "window" which is further specified by other relations of C3 to other concepts.

As the discourse is expanded with additional sentences such as "Its glass shattered, cutting his hand", the tree structure of the initial representation generalizes to a network in which "its" refers to C3 and "his" refers to C2. Other interconnections will become apparent later.

Representing English Content in Nets

The preceding example illustrated the manner in which verbs and nouns are represented in semantic networks, following case grammar ideas developed by Fillmore. The situation with modifiers, conjunctions, the various uses of "to be", "to have", etc. has not been as well worked out by linguists. Consequently the conventions suggested in this section are first approximations that are seeking correction and improvement.

1. Adjectival Modification. The semantic structure for adjectival modification must somehow take into account the relativity that this relation signifies. The phrases "small elephant" and "large ant" might be represented as the intersection of large things and ants, and of small things and elephants. If this approach were to be chosen, the relation SETX might be defined as that form of intersection. This is intuitively unsatisfying in that it simply ignores the relativity of the terms.

If we consider that SIZE is an attribute of physical objects such that each object has as a size value an appropriate range, then the relation SIZE(large, ant) would select the upper range of values for ants. In a similar fashion, COLOR(red, hair) and COLOR(red, firetruck) would select different values of the color, red. From a set theoretic viewpoint, the intersection of large things and ants, or red things and hair, is still being accomplished, but the second approach assumes that the noun already specifies a subset of each relevant attribute such as size, shape, color, etc., in the form of a range of measures. Recent psycholinguistic research reported by Olson (1970) supports this relative approach to adjectives.

The meaning of comparatives and superlatives as Celce (1970) is developing it also depends on such a relativistic approach to adjectives. The sentence, "John is taller than Mary" resolves to a logical structure such as the following:

$$\text{GREATER(SIZE(tall,John), SIZE(tall, Mary))}$$

This indicates that the SIZE measure associated with John is greater than that associated with Mary. Even such near-anomalies as: "the beer is colder than the coffee is hot" can be understood in terms of a relation that might be called GREATERDEV in the following:

$$\text{GREATERDEV(TEMP(cold,beer),TEMP(hot,coffee))}$$

This means the temperature of the beer deviates more from the average of beer in the cold direction than that of the coffee in the hot direction. This suggests that the measures might generally be in terms of deviations from averages. A sentence such as "The firetruck is redder than Mary's hair" suggests sets of ranges for each of the acceptable colors for firetrucks and hair.

In the semantic nets, the relation MOD is used to mean this relativistic interpretation of adjective meanings. MOD(large ant) is a relation that can eventually be defined as implying SIZE(large,ant) which in its turn can eventually be defined as a function that returns a measure in terms of average deviation units appropriate to its arguments. The comparative relation is signified in the network as GR for GREATER and it must have two arguments. In a sentence like: "John is taller, now", we must obtain the structure GR(MOD(tall, TIM(pres,John)), MOD(tall, TIM(past,John))).

2. Essive Relations. Four uses of the verb "to be" are considered. These are typified by the following examples:

> E1 The ape is happy.
> E2 The ape is an animal.
> E3 That ape is the animal.
> E4 The ape is in the tree.

In E1, there is simply an alternate form of the modification relation relationally represented by MOD(happy,ape) implying a positive measure on the ape's mood attribute. In semantic net form this would be shown approximately as follows (without back references or determiners):

E1	C1	TOK	ape
		MOD	C2
	C2	TOK	happy

Example E2 signifies the selection of a class of animals to be called apes. The cues that signify this usage are the choice of determiners showing that in the class of processes called animals there is a subset named apes. Relationally this is signified by SETX(ape, animal). In a semantic net it is shown as follows:

E2	C1	TOK	ape
		NBR	Sing
		DET	Def
		SETX	C2
	C2	TOK	animal
		NBR	sing
		DET	indef

The next case, E3, signifies an identity of two classes each containing a single member. It is signified relationally by SETID(ape, animal) and the relation SETID is used in the semantic net.

Example E4, "the ape is in the tree" is often seen in its transformational embedding as "...the ape in the tree". Relationally, both are expressed simply as IN(ape,tree). For semantic networks, it is expressed as follows:

E4	C1	TOK	ape
		LOC	C2
	C2	TOK	in
		−LOC	C1
		POBJ	C3
	C3	TOK	tree

This practice is equivalent to a relational representation such as the following:

$$LOC(ape, IN(ape, tree))$$

By introducing a case relation, the treatment of prepositions in modifying nouns becomes similar in form to their treatment as arguments of verbs.

3. The verb "have". This verb is understood in the following two senses:

E5   John has hair.
E6   John has money.

These two senses represent the HASPART and POSSession relations, respectively. Relationally, they appear as follows:

$$HASPART (John, hair)$$
$$POSS(John, money)$$

They are represented in semantic networks as follows:

E5	C1	TOK	John		E6	C1	TOK	John
		HASPART	C2				POSS	C2
	C2	TOK	hair			C2	TOK	money

The determination of which meaning is signified by the context can be accomplished with the aid of semantic markers and selection restrictions following Katz (1967). The apostrophe as in "John's hair" or "John's money" is the usual form of transformational embedding seen in discourse and is treated in the same fashion as the full sentence.

4. Conjunctions. The conjunctions "and" and "or" are treated identically as indirect references in semantic nets, while "but" is considered to be an intersentential connective. In a sentence such as "John and Mary ran," the relational structure might be expressed as follows:

$$AGT(run, AND(John, Mary))$$

The semantic net shows this as follows:

C1	TOK	run
	AGT	C2
C2	TOK	and
	1st	C3
	2nd	C4
C3	TOK	John
C4	TOK	Mary

The relations "1st", "2nd", etc., are arbitrary designators to separate the references to the arguments. The indirect reference of AGT to its arguments through the separating switch "and" is necessary to allow each member of the conjunction to be separately modified, as in "the spotted dog and the striped cat ran."

At first glance this treatment appears to be different from the usual deep structure approach which would represent two deep structure sentences as "John ran" and "Mary ran." Separating the elements of a conjunction with the indirection of an "and" and its series of arguments serves the same purpose by indicating that the relation AGT applies separately to each of the series.

Although the manner of signifying "or" is the same as that for "and," the meaning is obviously different in ways that will prove significant in attempting to apply paraphrase transformations to the structures. The effects of this difference are discussed in another paper (Simmons & Slocum, 1970).

5. *Adverbs.* Two major classes of adverbs are shown in the following examples:

> E7   John often/frequently ran to school.
> E8   John reluctantly ran to school.

Sentence E8 allows the paraphrase "John was reluctant in his running to school" while E7 does not allow "John was often/frequent in his running to school." One would be tempted to suppose that adverbs act on verbs in a manner analogous to the way adjectives do on nouns. Thus, the attribute "Frequency" might be supposed to characterize a verb and an adverb such as "often" might select a particular range of frequencies in the same manner that "large" selects from a noun's range of sizes. The manner class of adverbs, however, seem to be related in some fashion to the subject noun and "reluctantly" refers not only to the process "running" but specifically to "John's manner of running."

Lacking any deep understanding of adverbs, I have chosen to represent them in semantic nets with the relation VMOD which is taken in analogy to the adjectival relation, MOD. Thus the relational form

$$\text{VMOD(run, often)}$$

is expected to imply

$$\text{FREQUENCY(run, often)}$$

and to lend itself to the same relativistic interpretation that was used with adjectives. The similarity of comparative constructions between adverbs and adjectives may offer some support for this treatment. For example:

> E9   He ran more reluctantly than John.
> E10   He was more reluctant than John.
> E11   He ran more often than John.

6. Embedded Clauses. Deep structure sentences signified by adjectival modification, prepositional phrases, apostrophes, and conjunctions have been treated in previous subsections. This section considers relativization, some adverbial clauses, and apposition as exemplified below:

>E12   The man who caught the fish ate it.
>E13   Before the man ate the fish, he caught it.
>E14   Jones, the mayor, caught the fish.

The three examples are represented by the networks of Table 1.[3] In example E12 of Table 1, it can be seen that C2 (man) is the agent of both C1 and C4. This fact is reflected in C2 by the relation "-AGT" to C1 and C4. Similarly, C3 (fish) is the object of C1 and C4.

---

[3] Nothing is said there of the complexities of Voice, Mood, Tense, Aspect, Form, Mode, etc. A syntactic treatment of their use in semantically controlled generation is given in Simmons and Slocum (1970).

TABLE 1

Semantic Networks for Three Sentences

	E 12			E 13			E 14	
C1	TOK	eat	C1	TOK	catch	C1	TOK	catch
	TIM	Past		TIM	Past(0,1)		TIM	Past
	AGT	C2		AGT	C2		AGT	C2
	OBJ	C3		OBJ	C3		OBJ	C4
C2	TOK	man	C2	TOK	man	C2	TOK	Jones
	NBR	sing		NBR	sing		NBR	sing
	DET	Def		DET	Def		DET	null
	−AGT	C1,C4		−AGT	C1,C4		SETID	C3
							−AGT	C1
C3	TOK	fish	C3	TOK	fish	C3	TOK	mayor
	NBR	sing		NBR	sing		NBR	sing
	DET	Def		DET	Def		DET	Def
	−OBJ	C1,C4		−OBJ	C1,C4		−SETID	C2
C4	TOK	catch	C4	TOK	eat	C4	TOK	fish
	TIM	Past		TIM	Past(2,3)		NBR	sing
	AGT	C2		AGT	C2		DET	Def
	OBJ	C3		OBJ	C3		−OBJ	C1

In a simple sentence, "the man caught the fish," both man and fish would have a single backlink— -AGT and -OBJ respectively—to the verb structure for "catch". The presence of more than one backlink signifies some sort of embedding. In generating a sentence from a semantic structure, the recognition of additional backlinks offers an opportunity to embed a sentence modifying the structure in which it occurs. If we begin to generate from C4 (catch), we could produce the sentence, "the man who ate the fish caught it," which is not quite the same as E13. This is possible because both verbs are simply marked "TIM Past" and no importance seems to be attached to the order of the events described.

In E13, however, the situation is different in that the "catching" is marked as prior to the "eating" by the two-tuple value (0, 1) in contrast to the value (2, 3) on "eat". These numbers mean that the "catching" started at relative time 0, and was completed by time 1; and the eating occurred between times 2 and 3. Respecting these time values and explicitly representing them, we can generate:

E'13   After the man caught the fish, he ate it.
E"13   The man caught the fish before he ate it.
        etc.

The structure representing E14 shows that C2 (Jones) has only one backlink, "-AGT to C1 (catch)" but has the relation SETID connecting it to C3 (mayor). The relation SETID—for set equivalence—signifies that "Jones" and "the mayor" represent the identical concept. With this embedding relation we might generate the equivalent sentence:

D'14   Jones, who is the mayor, caught the fish.

The relation SETID is the signal of an embedded sentence and it is associated with transformations that allow the generation of either a relative clause or an apposition.

The relation MOD is treated in a similar fashion. Suppose in E14 of Table 1, that C4 (fish) had the relation "MOD C5 (old)." This would represent the deep structure sentence, "The fish is old" which could be generated either as an adjectival embedding, "old fish," or as a relative clause, "the fish that is old."

7. Determiner and Number. Two relations that have not so far been discussed, DET and NBR, also occur in Table 1. Values of DETerminer may be definite or indefinite, and exemplified by such words as "each", "every," "some," "all," etc. The values for NBR are Singular, Plural, and Indeterminate. The effect of these relations is to specify or determine some subset of the events, processes, or concepts named by a noun phrase. The complex manner in which they accomplish this feat has been the subject of numerous linguistic discussions summarized in Collinson (1937). For the present purpose it is sufficient to describe sketchily their effect in selecting—i.e. quantifying—a subset of the concept named by a noun phrase. The following list of examples and their relational equivalents are considered:

P1   some cup   Det(some, cup, Sing)
P2   some cups   Det(some, cup, P1)
P3   every cup   Det(every, cup, Sing)
P4   all cups   Det(all, cup, P1)

P5	a cup	Det(indef, cup, sing)
P6	the cup	Det(Def,cup,Sing)
P7	the cups	Det(Def, cup, P1)
P8	no cup	Det(Neg, cup, Sing)
P9	no cups	Det(Neg, cup, P1)
P10	some fish	Det(some, fish, Ind)

Examples P1 and P5 select any single event named "cup." P2 is an arbitrary selection of some subset of 2 or more cups. P10, in contrast, is ambiguous in that the NBR value of "fish" is indeterminate. P10 may indicate some one fish, some set of two or more fish, or some portion of one or more fish. P3 and P4 each specify the entire set but P3 considers the set one-by-one, while P4 takes the set as a class. P8 and P9 are the exact converses of P3 and P4. Finally P6 and P7 select a particular set of cups, P6 signifying a set of only one member or occasionally acting like the null determiner, indicating the class "cups." In order to discover the particular set specified by P6 and P7, further information is required from the context.

The purpose of this discussion of Determination and Number is only to show that the function of these relations is similar to that of all other semantic relations—to specify some subset of the event or process being described. Their difference from other means of specification is to be found in terms of their logical inter-relations, which as logicians have shown with respect to logical quantifiers, is a regular system that is often required for generating equivalent paraphrases.

LEXICAL STRUCTURES

In the previous section it was stated that word-sense meanings and semantic relations are the primitives of this semantic system. The lexicon is an inventory of the word-sense meanings available to the system. One of the tasks of a semantic analysis is to select a particular word-sense as the meaning of each word that occurs in a discourse string. The lexicon associates with each word and word-sense entry the morphological, syntactic, and semantic information required for this purpose. It also contains whatever additional information a particular semantic system requires in order to make explicit the meanings that are implied by the choice of words in the string.

Lexical structures are represented as a subset of the semantic network in exactly the same form as discourse nets. In this section they will be abstractly symbolized as a subscripted L-node associated with a list of attribute-value pairs, R_i-V_i, as follows:

$$
\begin{array}{lll}
L_i & R_a & V_j \\
& R_b & V_k \\
& \cdots & \cdots \\
& R_m & V_n
\end{array}
$$

V_i may refer to a constant, a lexical node, a discourse node, or an implicational structure. Discourse structures are directly related to lexical structures by the relation TOK. The relational representation:

$$TOK(C1, catch)$$

that has been used previously is more accurately represented as:

$$TOK(C1, L82)$$

where L82 is the lexical entry for the particular word-sense of $catch_1$. Thus the relation, TOK, connects an element of discourse with the word-sense concept to which it refers. The word-sense entry is defined in terms of syntactic features, semantic markers, selection restrictions, hyponyms, antonyms, and verbal and/or implicational definitions as required by the function of a particular semantic system.

Needless to say, the conventions developed in this section for representing lexical content are still highly tentative and are presented more for the sake of stimulating alternate considerations than for defining a semantics of the lexicon. Thus this section is to be taken as suggestive rather than definitive.

General Entry Form

There are two types of lexical nodes: words and word senses. A word node has the relations WDSN, PI, PIN, PIV, PIADV, PIADJ. The value of WDSN is a list of word-sense nodes. The other relations indicate the Print Images for printing the word. PI refers to the standard form; PIN, PIV, PADV, and PADJ indicate variations, respectively as a noun, a verb, an adverb, or an adjective. A word-sense node has an arbitrary number of relation-value pairs that must include -WDSN, the inverse relation referring back to the parent word node, -TOK, whose value is a list of the discourse structures in a TOK relation to that word sense, and WC, whose value is the syntactic word-class of that sense. Additional relations are such syntactic and semantic features as Gender, Mass-Count, HYPonym, ANTonym, Selection Restrictions, DEFinition, etc., as required by various syntactic and semantic operations.

Table 2 shows a fragmentary example of a lexical structure for the word "break" to illustrate the form of the structure and some of the relations. The actual content of a lexical structure will depend on the purpose of a semantic system that uses it.

In this figure we can see that the word has noun and verb print forms that are identical, that it has an adjective form that is the past participle of the verb, and no adverbial form. This is in contrast to a word such as "relate" whose noun form, PIN, would have the value "-ion" and whose adjective form, PADJ, might have the value "-or." The various print images of a word encode aspects of the morphological structure primarily at the word level. Assuming that the lexicon is alphabetically ordered by print form, the word "broke" is entry L90 which refers to "break" at L75 with the inflection "PAST." At L75, the PIV relation lists the present, past, and past participle forms for "break" as a verb. The entry L90 for

TABLE 2

Illustration of Lexical Structure

L75	WDSN	(L76 L77)
	PI	BREAK
	PIN	PI
	PIV	PI, BROKE, BROKEN
	PADJ	P PART
L76	WC	Noun
	PL	S
	GDR	N
	TYPE	Count
	DEF	(C21)
	−TOK	(C21 C52 . . .)
	−WDSN	L75
	HYP	(SEPARATION, STATE)
L77	WC	V
	PAST	BROKE
	PPART	BROKEN
	3PS	S
	AGT	(ANIMATE, ORGANISM)
	OBJ	(+, physical object)
	INST	(INSTRUMENT, PHYSOBJ)
	HYP	(SEPARATE, DIVIDE, DESTROY)
	DEF	C145
	−TOK	(C145 . . .)
	−WDSN	L75
L90	WDSN	L77
	PI	BROKE
	PIV	L75, PAST
L95	WDSN	L77
	PI	BROKEN
	PIV	L75, PPART

"broke" also refers directly to the relevant word-sense entry, L77, (and any other verb senses) eliminating consideration of sense L76, a noun sense. Additional discussion of morphological considerations in semantic nets can be found in Kay (Kay & Martins, 1970) and Chapin and Norton (1968). It is assumed in this discussion that the procedure for looking up words in a lexicon includes at least such morphological analysis functions as detecting regular inflections on words. Thus to look up "related," the morphological routines would analyze the word into "relate + PAST" and find the lexical entry for that form.

The example word-sense L77 for "break" also illustrates the conventions for identifying the arguments associated with the case relations "AGT," "INST," and

"OBJ." The value for the Agent relation is limited to concepts marked as (i.e., with HYP values of) "animate" or "organism." The object relation is marked as *required* (by the code +) and limited to concepts marked "physical object," and the relation "with" is limited to concepts marked "instrument" or "physical object." Since only the object relation is marked as *required*, the agent and instrument are taken as optional. The entry thus indicates that sentences such as the following are well-formed.

1. John broke the window with a hammer.
2. John broke the window.
3. The hammer broke the window.
4. The window broke.

and sentences such as these (as partial paraphrases of 1) are not:

*5. John broke.
*6. A hammer broke.
*7. John broke with a hammer.

This appears to be a satisfactory method for distinguishing *required* and optional arguments for verbs.

The semantic restrictions on the arguments follow Katz's (1967) system of selection restrictions. Restrictions such as "animate" and "organism" require that whatever noun phrase is the value of the argument "AGT" must have as one of the values of the HYP (HYPonym or Semantic Marker) relation exactly the marker "animate" or "organism". Thus if "John" has the markers "human," "organism," and "animate," while "hammer" has the list "instrument," "physical object," it can be seen that "John" can be in the AGT relation while "hammer" can be taken only in the INST or OBJ relations. If "window" is not characterized as "instrument" then it can only be taken in the object relation and the arguments of sentences 1, 2 and 3 can be correctly distinguished. In passing, it should be noted that the relation HYP is transitive. Thus if "John" has the HYP value "boy" which has the HYP value "male," "John" is also "male."

Although this Katzian approach to selecting word-senses and sorting arguments can be shown to work for simple texts, it is apparent that an additional semantic apparatus—still undiscovered—will be required for dealing with even such simple cases of metaphor as "John broke up the meeting with a joke."

The values of the DEF argument in L76 and L77 respectively are references to C121 and C145 whose content would be the discourse encoding of the following definitions:

C121   Space between two places or times
C145   Make into separate parts by force

It is probably these values that will eventually prove most useful for semantic analysis following methods suggested by Sparck-Jones (1965) and Quillian (1966) but so far not worked out in an adequate fashion.

Prepositions

An additional relation, ENTail, characterizes many sense meanings. ENT relates a word-sense to any implicational rules that refer to it. The definition of these rules and their use, although touched lightly in the following discussion of prepositions, is considered sufficiently important to warrant a section of its own following this one.

Some idea of the lexical structure for prepositional meanings is given by the examples of Table 3. In this table lexical structures for four of several meanings for the word "on" are outlined. The senses illustrated are taken from examples studied by White (1964) in the following abbreviated contexts:

L5   move on wires
      keys on the keyboard
      man on the street
      ports on the coast

L6   hear on the radio
      talk on the telephone
      see on television

L7   spend on advertising
      wasted on building

L8   push on pedal
      march on Rome
      force demands on people

The relations, HD and P OBJ are reserved for prepositional meanings and refer to the syntactic head and object of the preposition. Thus, for "move on wires," "move" is in the HD relation, and "wires" is in the OBJ relation to the preposition "on." In the discourse nets, the relation HD refers to that word-sense that dominates the Case Relation that dominates the prepositional phrase. In reference to a syntactic constituent, HD refers to the noun or verb that dominates a prepositional phrase.

These relations in the word-sense entry have as values selection restrictions on the concepts that can be taken as HD and OBJ arguments. The relation HYP indicates the hyponym or semantic marker that characterizes the meaning. The values of HYP in prepositional meanings are usually Case relations or other prepositional meanings. The relation IMPLY has a list of implication statements as values. Thus for L5, the locative sense of "on," I25 and I26 might have the following structures:

	TOK	touch
I25	DAT	HD
	OBJ	OBJ

	TOK	above
I26	HD	HD
	OBJ	OBJ

TABLE 3

Lexical Structures for Prepositional Meanings

L4	PI	ON
	WDSN	(L5, L6, L7, L8 . . .)

L5	W/C	PREP
	HD	(PHYS OBJ, ACTION)
	P OBJ	(PHYS OBJ)
	HYP	LOCATIVE
	IMPLY	(I25, 26 . . .)
	−WDSN	L4

L6	W/C	PREP
	HD	(Communicate)
	P OBJ	(Instrument)
	HYP	INSTRUMENT
	IMPLY	(I72, 73 . . .)
	−WDSN	L4

L7	W/C	PREP
	HD	(Expend)
	P OBJ	(Purpose)
	HYP	Goal
	IMPLY	(I35, 36 . . .)
	−WDSN	L4

L8	W/C	PREP
	HD	(Causal act)
	P OBJ	(PHYS OBJ, PLACE)
	IMPLY	(I35, 42 . . .)
	−WDSN	L4

It is intended that the meaning of each prepositional sense will be defined primarily by the implicational structures associated with it. To actually accomplish this for any number of prepositional meanings is a large task that has been studied to some extent by White (1964), and Glasersfeld (1965). In each case a few dozen prepositional meanings have been identified by context and specified as some combination of more elementary relations.

A similar form probably encompasses intersentential connectives such as "because," "since," "before," "if," etc., but examples of their content have not yet been studied in any depth.

Since the meaning of a prepositional word-sense is seen as primarily relational, no use has so far been found for a DEF relation with a verbal definition as its value. The relation -TOK is also not illustrated although it can be included if lists of contexts are desired for the study of prepositional meanings.

Lexical structures for adjectives include selection restrictions on their noun head and the noun must eventually include sufficient relational structure to account for the relativity of such meanings as "large ant," "small elephant," "oldest youth," etc. Conjunctions require agreement in syntactic class and semantic features among their arguments; pronouns specify agreement with their referent in terms of NBR, Gender, and Case; and function adverbs must also specify the nature of their arguments in their lexical structure. Most of this type of content structure is still to be worked out.

Implicational Structure

Several authors (notably Lyons, 1968; Woods, 1968; Fillmore, 1968) have attempted to explicate notions of implication, entailment, presupposition, etc., with regard to English word meanings. They have successfully demonstrated the importance of implicational structure as a part of the meanings. In this section, a semantic network and some examples of content are described to represent some of the implicational structure of sense meanings.

The simplest level of implicational structure occurs in the relations HYP and DEF. Generally, if a word-sense is used in a sentence or question, its hyponym or its definition can be substituted without changing its truth value. Thus if "a man ate a fish" is a true statement, the substitution of hyponyms and definitions results in another pair of true statements: "a human ingested an animal" and "a male adult human took in through his mouth as food an aquatic animal." This kind of substitution can be repeated to result in increasingly abstract statements on the hyponym level and ever more detailed specifications of word meaning at the definitional level. Question-answering research uses this technique as its first level of inference. (See Simmons et al., 1968; and Schwarz, Burger, & Simmons, 1970). It has probably been noticed that there is no explicit synonym relation in the lexical structure. This relation is accounted for by a word-sense mapping onto two or more different words that in their various contexts can refer to the same meaning. Thus it is expected that such words as "get" and "receive" would share a word-sense which in its turn would relate by the -WDSN back to the two print forms.

Another common form of inferential structure is the converse relation that holds between such pairs as "buy-sell" or "like-please," as illustrated in the following examples:

8a) John liked the play.
8b) The play pleased John.

9a.   John sold the boat to Mary.
9b.   Mary bought the boat from John.

These pairs of sentences are not considered to have the same semantic structure in this system in that they differ in terms of choice of verb token and in terms of case roles for the nouns. (For some purposes other semantic systems might choose to represent both members of the pairs identically as some deeper semantic structure such as "an exchange from John to Mary for value.") In each pair, the "b" sentence is related to the "a" sentence by a transformation on the semantic structure as shown in Table 4. The lexical entries for "like" and "please" each refer to the converse transformations by the relations ENT; and E1 and E2 can be seen to refer back to these lexical entries by the relation -ENT.

An Implication transformation is represented in the same net form as any other semantic structure with the expectation that V_i, the symbol for a variable, is allowed as an argument for relations. Implicational structures are characterized as numbered E-nodes associated with appropriate relations and their values. Every E-structure will have the relations −ENT and IMPLY as relations.

If it is desired to transform 8a into 8b, the lexical entry for "like" will have an ENT relation whose values will include E1. A straightforward algorithm is used to bind the variables V1, V2, and V3 to the appropriate arguments of the semantic structure to be transformed and to rewrite the structure into the form that is the value of the IMPLY relation. Thus, applying E1 to the discourse structure that represents "John liked the play" is illustrated as follows:

C1	TOK	like
	T	past
	DAT	C2 . . . (John)
	OBJ	C3 . . . (the play)

Further development of C2 and C3 are indicated in parentheses. In applying E1 to this structure, V1 is bound to C2, and V2 to C3. E1 and E2 now take on the following values:

TABLE 4

Converse Implicational Structures
for "like-please", "buy-sell"

1)	E1	−ENT	like
		DAT	V1
		OBJ	V2
		IMPLY	E2
	E2	−ENT	PLEASE
		OBJ	V2
		DAT	V1
		IMPLY	E1

TABLE 4 (Continued)

2)	E3	−ENT	SELL
		AGT	V1
		OBJ	V2
		GOAL	V3
		IMPLY	E4
	E4	−ENT	BUY
		AGT	V3
		OBJ	V2
		SOURCE	V1
		IMPLY	E3
	E1	−ENT	like
		DAT	C2
		OBJ	C3
		IMPLY	E2
	E2	−ENT	please
		OBJ	C3
		DAT	C2
		IMPLY	E1

C1 is now rewritten (by an IMPLY function) in the form of E2 to give:

C′1	TOK	please
	T	past
	Dat	C3 . . . (the play)
	OBJ	C2 . . . (John)

The pair, T-past, was not involved in the transformation so it was merely copied unchanged.

A sentence generator applied to C′1 will now generate "the play pleased John." The "buy-sell" transformation operates in a similar fashion with three arguments. It can be seen that the converse transformations are bi-implicational in that each verb meaning implies the other. For other types of implication exemplified by the pair:

10a. John killed Jim,
10b. Jim died,

sentence 10a) implies 10b) but 10b) does not imply 10a). Consequently, the E-structure referred to by "kill" implies "die" but not conversely, as shown below:

E5	−ENT	kill
	AGT	V1
	DAT	V2
	IMPLY	E6

E6   −ENT   die
        DAT   V2
        −IMPLY E5

Complex Relations

More complex relations, such as complex products, can be represented in a similar fashion. Consider the complex product of "lead" and "lose" (from Schwarcz *et al.*, 1970) in the example pair:

11a) Napoleon led the army that lost the battle.
11b) Napoleon lost the battle.

It is maintained that sentence 11b is implied or entailed by 11a in accordance with a complex product (with qualification to be mentioned later) such that: (lead C/P lose) IMPLY lose. This rule can be represented in semantic net form in accordance with Table 5. Table 5a is a semantic representation of sentence 11a while Table 5b shows the simplest form of the C/P rule. By binding V1, V2, and V3 to C2, C3, and C5 respectively, the rule E10 generates the structure of sentence 11b.

Additional restraints are often required in the applicability of complex products. For example "the lieutenant led the platoon that lost the football game" does not strongly imply that the lieutenant lost the football game. To accomplish any degree of restriction, the rule of 11b can be further specified as in Table 6, to limit the applicability of variables to lexical entries that have the features required. The use of the restriction requires a test of the proposed lexical entry, before binding it to the variable. Further extensions can be devised as needed for the complicated task of exploring the implicational relations of word meanings.

TABLE 5

Example of Complex Product Implication

A:	C1	TOK	lead
		T	PAST
		AGT	C2 . . . (Napoleon)
		DAT	C3
	C3	TOK	army
		NBR	sing
		DET	the
		−DAT	C1
		−DAT	C4
	C4	TOK	lose
		T	past
		DAT	C3
		OBJ	C5 . . . (battle)

Relevant Sentence Structure

TABLE 5 (Continued)

B:	E10	−ENT	lead, lose
		AND	(E11, E12)
		IMPLY	E13

	E11	TOK	lead
		AGT	V1
		DAT	V2
		−AND	E10

	E12	TOK	lose
		DAT	V2
		OBJ	V3
		−AND	E10

	E13	TOK	lose
		DAT	V1
		OBJ	V3
		−IMPLY	E10

Complex Product Rule

TABLE 6

Restricted Variables in Implication Rules

E10	TOK	C/P
	AND	E11, E12
	IMPLY	E13

E11	TOK	lead
	AGT	E14
	DAT	E15
	−AND	E10

E12	TOK	lose
	DAT	E15
	OBJ	E16
	−AND	E10

E13	TOK	lose
	DAT	E14
	OBJ	E16

E14	VAR	V1
	−HYP	leader
	−AGT	E11
	−DAT	E13

TABLE 6 (Continued)

E15	VAR	V2
	−HYP	military group
	−DAT	E11

E16	VAR	V3
	−HYP	battle
	−OBJ	E12, E13

DISCUSSION AND CONCLUSIONS

A network structure has been described to represent semantic forms and content of discourse, lexical entries, and implicational rules. Conventions have been suggested for representing meaning content of natural language statements and lexicon in this form. The semantics of natural English have been defined as a system of conditions and transformations applied to syntactic constituents to map them into semantic structures. A semantic structure is a system of unambiguous representations of meanings interconnected by logical relations. In this paper the discourse meanings have been taken as lexical word-senses and the logical relations are Fillmore's deep cases dominating prepositional meanings—such sentence connectives as "thus," "because," "before," etc., and certain other logical relations such as HASPART, SETX, etc.

It has been maintained that each semantic relation must be definable as a rule or function that takes a series of arguments and substitutes as its meaning another set of relations among the same or different meaning objects. Thus, part of the meaning of TOK(C1, L5) is that additional relations on C1 include all of the lexical and implicational relations associated with L5 including of course its print image. AGT(C1, C5) indicates that the action or process C5 was initiated by the organism, C1, while DAT(C2,C5) indicates that C2 is an organism that was affected by C5. No complete inventory of semantic relations is yet available and fully detailed definitions of those that have been recognized is still a matter for continued research along the lines of Leech (1970), Fillmore (1968), and Woods (1968).

The pragmatics of a language utterance is the effect that it has on the behavior of the listener (Morris, 1955). Some glimpse of a pragmatics of English is sensed in the implicational content associated with the lexical structure. If the system in question is one that tests truth values by comparing an input sentence such as "John liked the play" with one known to be true, as "The play pleased John," then the pragmatic structure would be those inference structures used to map the semantic form of the first sentence into that of the second. In such a formulation, pragmatic structures for paraphrase, question answering, and translation systems could each have similar forms but widely differing content. Further investigation of this hypothesis is also a matter for the future.

The potential value of explicating semantic, lexical, and implicational structures of natural language is amply demonstrated by the productive stimulation offered by recent work in linguistics and by the potential utility of computer-based language processing applications. This suggests that the detailed exploration and definition of these structures offers a highly rewarding research area for linguists whether their orientation is descriptive, structural, or computational.

CONFERENCE DISCUSSION

Crothers wondered, given the amount of controversy in linguistics over case grammars, why Simmons thought they were favored and why he has decided to adopt them so extensively in his analysis of discourse structure. Simmons said that a case grammar is particularly convenient for semantic net representation because it puts things in terms of node-relation-node. It also has the advantage that such relations as agent, object, and dative have definable meanings. That is, agent implies animate instigator or actant. Dative implies recipient and animate. Object implies recipient and inanimate, etc. The semantic-net representation is well suited to computational linguistics.

Carroll inquired whether Simmons was recommending this semantic net procedure as a basic method of representing meaning or simply as a convenient kind of note-taking system. Simmons thought it was more the former because there exist parsers and generators and question-answerers that work on these semantic nets. He indicated that what his paper does primarily is to show how to parse sentences on the semantic level, the semantic net being the format used to carry out the parsing.

A question was raised by Crothers as to just what the system is intended to accomplish, and if it tries to do it, how one evaluates and modifies it according to how well it has done its job. Simmons said that the semantic nets should do nothing but display logical relationships between unambiguous objects and by so doing represent an aspect of meaning. In order to find out whether these nets are any good or not you build parsers to see whether you can go from English into semantic nets. He has done that. The answer is, yes, you can, and it's a rather reasonable sort of thing to do. One can further inquire whether one can go from semantic nets back to English. The answer again is, yes. Also one can build question-answerers which are essentially theorem provers to see whether you can detect whether X is a paraphrase of Y or whether it is an answer to the question Z. He indicated that he has done such things and finds it quite convenient to do it with semantic nets.

Carroll wondered whether there are any alternatives to semantic networks. Chomsky's deep structure is such an alternative providing that each of the elements in that structure has an unambiguous sense, according to Simmons. Bever questions whether there is any formal difference between nets and deep structure. The notation is certainly different, but couldn't there be an algorithm that maps these semantic nets onto a deep structure? Simmons didn't know whether there was such an algorithm. He said he had the impression that the two systems are pretty much the same, differing only in arrangement. In this regard Chafe thought that things like Agent are more closely related to the meaning of the sentence than any part of Chomsky's tree representation. That is, one has to take an extra step, apparently, to get from Chomsky's deep structure to a notion like Agent. Bever countered, though, that it seems to be merely a difference in form because the notion of direct object is directly represented as the noun phrase that follows the verb. Chafe indicated that the notion of direct object is not a semantic notion, but a surface structure notion. Direct objects can be all sorts of things semantically. For example, take sentences like: "He received a letter." "He sang a song." "He broke the window." In these sentences the direct object has different semantic relations to the verb. Bever disagreed because these could be differently represented in the deep structure. Chafe acknowledged that that was probably true. In summary, it appears that the two systems differ primarily in notation.

Crothers ended the questioning by commenting that Simmons' theory seems more a linguistic than a psychological one. He wanted to know whether Simmons could predict the relative difficulty of different sentences. That is, is it possible for these semantic nets to predict something explicit about behavior? Simmons said that he realizes that there is a body of psychological theory which is concerned directly with communication and the mapping of cognitive structures onto language perception. But he added that he and his colleagues were a long way from showing how human behavior supports this particular semantic net theory. Theorists are still at the point of trying to establish what the important ingredients of the semantic net theory should be.

REFERENCES

Bach, E. Nouns and noun phrases. In E. Bach, and R. T. Harms (Eds.), *Universals in linguistic theory*. New York: Holt, Rinehart & Winston, Inc., 1968.

Carbonell, J. R. *Mixed-initiative man-computer instructional dialogues.* (BBN Report No. 1971) Cambridge, Mass., Bolt, Beranek & Newman, Inc., 1970.

Carnap, R. *Introduction to semantics.* Cambridge, Mass.: Harvard University Press, 1946.

Celce, M. A Recognition and reconstruction procedure for MORE/LESS comparatives. Santa Monica. System Development Corp. (Unpublished manuscript).

Chapin, P., & Norton, L. M. A procedure for morphological analysis. University of California at San Diego, 1968. (Unpublished manuscript)

Chomsky, N. *Aspects of the theory of syntax.* Cambridge, Mass.: M.I.T. Press, 1965.

Collinson, W. E. Indication: A study of demonstratives, articles and other indicators. *Language Monographs*, supplement to *Language*, 1937, No. 17.

Fillmore, C. J. The case for case. In E. Bach and R. T. Harms (Eds.), *Universals in linguistic theory*. New York: Holt, Rinehart & Winston, Inc., 1968.

Glaserfeld, E. Von. An approach to the semantics of prepositions. Symposium presented at the meeting of AMTCL, Las Vegas, Nevada, December 1965.

Katz, J. J. Recent issues in semantic theory. *Foundations of Language*, 1967, **3**, 124–194.

Kay, M., & Martins, G. R. *The MIND system: Structure of the semantic file.* (RM–6265/2 PR) Santa Monica, RAND Corp., 1970.

Lakoff, G. Generative semantics. In *An interdisciplinary reader in philosophy, linguistics, anthropology and psychology*. London: Cambridge University Press, 1969.

Leech, G. N. *Towards a semantic description of English.* Bloomington, Indiana: Indiana University Press, 1970.

Lyons, J. *Introduction to theoretical linguistics.* Cambridge, England: Cambridge University Press, 1968.

Morris, C. W. *Signs, language and behavior.* Englewood Cliffs, N.J.: Prentice-Hall, 1955.

McCawley, J. D. The role of semantics in a grammar. In E. Bach and R. T. Harms (Eds.), *Universals in linguistic theory*. New York: Holt, Rinehart & Winston, Inc., 1968.

Olson, D. R. Language and thought: Aspects of a cognitive theory of semantics. *Psychological Review*, 1970, 77, 257–273.

Quillian, M. R. The teachable language comprehender. *Comm. ACM* 1969, 8, 459–476.

Quillian, M.R. Semantic memory. (Doctoral dissertation, Carnegie-Mellon University) Pittsburgh, Pa., 1966.

Raphael, B. SIR: A computer program for semantic information retrieval. (Doctoral dissertation, Department of Mathematics, Massachusetts Institute of Technology) Cambridge, Mass., 1964.

Schwarcz, R. M., Burger, J. F., & Simmons, R. F. A deductive logic for answering English questions. *Comm. ACM*, 1970, 13, 167–184.

Simmons, R. F. Natural language question-answering systems: 1969. *Comm. ACM*, 1970, 13, 15–30.

Simmons, R. F. Some relations between predicate calculus and semantic net representations of discourse. Computer Sciences Department, University of Texas, Austin, 1970. (Unpublished manuscript)

Simmons, R. F., Burger, J. F., & Schwarcz, R. M. A computational model of verbal understanding, *Proc. AFIPS 1968 Fall Joint Computer Conf.*, Washington, D. C.: Thompson Book Co., 1968, **33**, 441–456.

Simmons, R. F., & Slocum, J. Generating English discourse from semantic networks. Comm. ACM (in press).

Sparck-Jones, K. Experiments in semantic classification. *Mechanical Translation*, 1965, 8, 97–112.

Tarski, A. The semantic conception of truth and the foundation of semantics. *Philosophy and Phenomenological Research*, 1944, 4, 341–376.

Thompson, F. B., & Gibbons, G. *DEACON breadboard summary*. (RM64TMP–9, TEMPO) Santa Barbara: General Electric, 1964.

White, J. H. The methodology of semantic analysis with special application to the English preposition. *Mechanical Translation*, 1964, 8, 110–117.

Woods, W. A. Procedural semantics for a question-answering machine. *Proc. AFIPS 1968 Fall Joint Comput. Conf.*, Washington, D. C.: Thompson Book Company, 33, 457–471.

Woods, W. A. *Semantic interpretation of English questions on a structured data base*. (Rep. NSF–17) Cambridge, Mass.: Harvard University Press, 1966.

Woods, W. A. Transition network grammars for natural language analysis. *Comm. ACM*, 1970, 13, 591–606.

5
PERCEPTIONS, THOUGHT, AND LANGUAGE

Thomas G. Bever
*Columbia University in
the City of New York*

"Thinking . . . follows a network of trails laid down in the given language . . . The individual is utterly unaware of this organization and is constrained completely within its unbreakable bonds."

Whorf, 1956 (p. 256)

"Sentences, not words, are the essence of speech just as equations and functions, and not bare numbers, are the real meat of mathematics . . . Reference of words is at the mercy of the sentences and grammatical patterns in which they occur."

Whorf, 1956 (p. 258–9)

"One whom some were certainly following was one who was completely charming. One whom some were certainly following was one who was charming. One whom some were following was one who was completely charming. One whom some were following was one who was certainly completely charming."

G. Stein (reprinted, 1946)

INTRODUCTION AND SUMMARY

Two complementary problems are involved in studying the acquisition of information through language, the influence of mind on language and vice versa. Previous studies have considered these problems in terms of the meaning and use of individual words and morphemes (Brown & Lenneberg, 1954; Carroll & Casagrande, 1958). This paper examines the relation between thought and language in the light of recent linguistic and psychological investigations of *sentences* and presents two complementary hypotheses; first, that cognitive and behavioral systems constrain certain linguistic structures and, second, that syntactic style (personal, ethnic, and linguistic) systematically modifies certain concepts.

99

It is axiomatic that the basic form of human thought at least partially determines the structure of all languages. That is, language structure is not completely *sui generis* in the mind but is molded by an interaction of the laws of thought, learning, speech perception, and speech production. Consequently, certain linguistic structures, both universal and language-specific, can be shown to be reflections of the structure of thought and speech behavior. The examples in this paper focus primarily on the influence on linguistic structures of the mechanism for speech perception.

The complementary hypothesis concerns the influence of linguistic structure on the availability of certain forms of thought. Syntactic order constraints determine the sequence of information in the presentation of complex concepts. Insofar as the presentation order itself interacts with the perceptual system, different presentation orders will result in different concepts. We know of stimulus order effects that occur in non-speech modalities with both faster and slower presentation rates than speech: hence, it is reasonable to expect that presentation order in speech also influences the percepts that are conveyed by determining the order in which they are constructed. Since languages and styles differ in syntactic orders they allow, they also differ in certain aspects of the concepts they can convey. This paper explores several examples in which components of linguistic concepts are determined by syntactic order constraints.

Personal, Cultural, and Linguistic Components of Concepts

The ordinary linguistic vehicle for reference is a *sentence*, not a word (cf. Whorf, 1956, p. 258 ff). Even single-word naming games presuppose an implicit "that is a _____." Thus, the study of the semantic and behavioral properties of individual words is premature, if not wholly futile. However, I shall present initially the basic distinctions of conceptual organization with respect to words, since they have usually been the focus of previous discussions. Later I shall turn to the parallel issues with respect to sentences.

The strongest form of the hypothesis that language influences thought is that associated with Whorf, claiming that language limits (and facilitates) particular concepts; consequently, if two languages differ, then the concepts available to monolingual speakers of those languages also differ. In this view the *kinds* of information we can process are constrained by the way we talk.

One source of clear evidence of the influence of language on thought would be comparison of thought processes in speakers of different languages. Speakers and writers often praise the unique virtue of their native language for the transmission of specific kinds of information; French is "logical," German "expressive," English "natural," and so on. The crucial test of such claims is whether fully accurate translations of conversation and prose from one language to another are possible. Skilled bilinguals appear to succeed, but often (anecdotally) complain about the inadequacy of even the best translations. It is usually the case that general basic concepts can be accurately translated from one language to another. But it is a common experience that "something is lost in the translation." Roughly, the "lost something" is described as specific emotional or other qualifying overtones that surround the concept in the original language, but are misrepresented in the translation.

These facts epitomize the puzzle that is one focus of this paper: If the structure of language does affect thought, then speakers of different languages with different structures must have different concepts. Nevertheless, it does not appear to be impossible to translate basic concepts from one language to another—there is only an occasional difference in the perceived completeness and directness of expression. But if language does *not* affect thought, why do bilingual speakers feel that true translation of concepts is impossible? A possible resolution of this puzzle lies in the distinction between two kinds of information contained within each concept shared by members of a culture, *semantic meaning* and *linguistic idea*. The linguistic structures of a particular language could determine certain features of the *linguistic ideas* embedded in concepts, without these features themselves being critical components of the semantic meanings of those concepts.

At any given moment, part of an individual's potential knowledge is the congeries of associated sensory, perceptual, and conceptual features, each such group associated by a linguistic label. It is useful to distinguish between the different kinds of knowledge that are components of every concept indicated by language. First, there is a *semantic meaning* which specifies the minimal information required to account for the synonymy, antonymy, and entailment relations with other concepts (cf. Katz, 1966, 1972). Second, there are *cultural ideas* which describe the nonsemantic aspects of a concept which may be a regular function of the role of the concept in the culture, but which are not critical to the semantic meaning. Of course, as one of the most highly regularized expressions of a culture, each particular language itself provides some of the most important *cultural ideas*, which I shall term *linguistic ideas*. Finally, *personal ideas* describe the penumbra of personal experience surrounding the cultural and semantic ideas in a concept.

Consider now the reflection of these distinctions in the description of the acquisition of concepts. A child learns what the meaning of the word "dog" is and presumably shares that meaning with other speakers of English: The child knows that dogs are domestic animals which have certain configurations and social functions. He may even know that the dog is (by definition) descended from the wolf or jackal, and that an animal not so descended would probably not count as a "dog" even though it might look like one (e.g., a domesticated racoon). The empirical test for whether a conceptual feature is critical to the semantic meaning is primarily in intuitions about synonymy, entailment, and contradiction (cf. Katz, 1972). For example, (a) is synonymous with (b), (a) entails (c), and (d) is self-contradictory.

(a) Max is a dog.
(b) Max is a member of the species of four-footed domestic animals descended from wolves.
(c) Max is an animal.
(d) Max is a dog that is not an animal.

Nothing is puzzling or obscure about the knowledge of the *semantic meaning* itself (although the formal representation of the facts like those in (a)–(d) is not automatically apparent). What *is* puzzling is that the child may never have been offered an explicit definition of "dog." The actual dogs the child has observed may differ from each other widely without any of them being a paradigmatic "dog." Thus the child's personal ideas about what a "dog" is are susceptible to the vagaries of his own individual experience. The problem for a theory of the acquisition of meaning is to determine how a child learns which parts of his personal ideas about referents are semantically critical and which are simply due to the vagaries of personal or cultural experience. For example, if all the dogs a particular child has seen are German Shepherds, how does the child learn that (g) does not linguistically entail (h)?

(g) Max has floppy ears.
(h) Max is not a dog.

One solution would be to argue that linguistic meanings are simply those individual ideas about the meaning of words which we *all* share. On this view it is our shared idiosyncratic experience that provides the basis for the uniformity of meanings; since we do not all see only German Shepherds, the meaning of "dog" is not limited only to them. This view, however, will not do. Consider for example the concept "stewardess."[1] In the 1950's it was common knowledge that stewardesses on airlines were female, young, adult, unmarried, conventionally attractive, and dressed to look like a cross between a cocktail waitress and a WAC. Although this was the shared knowledge about stewardesses, it did not constitute part of the shared semantic definition of "stewardess." For example, various airlines did modify the stewardess uniform to be exactly like cocktail dresses without changing the meaning of "stewardess." Furthermore, an airline that wished to discourage passengers from flying on a particular route could put ugly women with bad breath on that route and certainly continue to refer to such employees as "stewardesses." Neither of these changes from the norm would require us not to call such airline employees "stewardess"; accordingly, the changed features are not critical to the semantic meaning and (i) is not contradictory, while (j) is.

(i) Maxine is an ugly stewardess with bad breath.
(j) Maxine was hired as a stewardess to fly the plane.

Yet the change to ugly stewardess would modify our cultural ideas about the term "stewardess." Thus, certain of the features in our shared experience are critical to the meaning and others are critical only to our shared idea of what a stewardess is. (In some cases knowledge may be very vague on the subject of whether a particular feature is critical to the meaning or to the cultural idea. For example, it was necessary for "stewardess" to take both the notions of age and marital status to court in order to decide that both of these features were not critical to the legal definition of the term.)

"Stewardess" may seem to be an artificial example because of its commercial and legal overtones. However, the same distinction between shared meaning and

---

[1] The importance of such examples was called to my attention in conversations with J. Katz and H. Savin.

culturally shared features exists for common words such as "dog." For example, city children may share the idea that dogs are always housepets between 6″ and 4′ high, while a wild dog still satisfies the meaning of "dog," as would a 4-1/2′ dog. Conversely, a thoroughly domesticated wolf contrasts with our cultural idea about wolves, but not our definition.

The shared, nonsemantic linguistic ideas in these examples are themselves features that do not happen to be critical to the meanings but could become so. Culturally shared ideas can also themselves be affective components of concepts. For example, we all share the cultural idea about a roller coaster represented by a feeling of danger both in the mind and the pit of the stomach; it is hard to see how such a shared affective feeling could become part of a critical feature of meaning.

Standardized empirical tests for whether a conceptual feature is cultural or personal (given that it is not semantic) are much less clear than those for semantic features. In some cases (but not all) one can appeal to the cultural "purpose" implied in a cultural idea, that is, independent of the personal experience of the referent. Thus, I have never (consciously) tested the breath of a stewardess, nor have I discussed it with anybody, but I expect it to be (at least artificially) sweet, because of its consistency with the (semantically encoded) cultural purpose for which stewardesses are hired. Similarly, I have never been on a roller coaster but I know they are frightening, can simulate the intestinal feeling they would induce, and so on, simply because of my knowledge of their cultural role. That personal ideas are not merely a subset of cultural ideas is shown by the fact that they can come into direct conflict. Thus, it is possible for somebody to know that roller coasters are *supposed* to be frightening in the culture, but not be frightened by them personally.

These examples highlight the fact that shared experiences and semantic knowledge about words are quite different substances, even in a case like "stewardess" for which those experiences are conventionalized. This distinction between *semantic meanings*, *cultural ideas*, and *personal ideas* communicated by single words exists for *sentences* as well. If, in fact, sentences are the normal vehicle for reference, the effects of words on behavior can be understood only as a function of the behavioral properties of sentences. Accordingly, the following discussion explores ways in which the linguistic form of sentences can modify our cultural ideas about the concepts conveyed in those sentences. It involves a reformulation to the level of the sentence of the hypothesis that linguistic structure influences conceptual organization:

(1) The way we think partially determines the structure of speech perception.

(2) The mechanism for speech perception is also constrained by other variables, such as the fact that it must operate in real time.

(3) These properties of the perceptual mechanism restrict the kinds of linguistic sentences that can occur to those that are perceptually decodable.

(4) Part of what a sentence conveys by its cultural idea content is the emotional and perceptual operations occurring during its perception.

(5) If certain kinds of orders are unavailable in a particular language, then so are the corresponding ideas that would result from the perceptual operations applying to those orders. Hence,

(6) The linguistic structure puts some limits on easily coded cultural ideas which in turn

(7) Constrain the kind of concepts which we manipulate.

That is, there is a sense in which thought influences perception, that perception influences language and that in turn the structure of language influences the way we think about what we think about.

THE STRUCTURE OF SPEECH PERCEPTION

I shall make some elementary assumptions about the nature of thinking that are shared by many scholars. The basic distinction made is between those activities involved in thinking and those involved in the storage of previously acquired knowledge. The role of mental activities is to bring units into relation to each other. The role of a store is to retain plans and schemata for carrying out such activities.

Even such a general view has immediate implications for the nature of the mechanism of speech perception. This mechanism must both isolate *units* and construct *relations* between those units. The linguistic units in question are "designating phrases," while the relations include "semantic" concepts such as actor-action, action-object, modification, and so on. (It should be noted that these concepts are not unique to current transformational grammars, but have been accepted as central to the structure and use of language by almost every researcher into language. Theoretical differences have primarily concerned the structural role of such concepts.) This basic distinction of aspects of thought is reflected in the fact that the perceptual mechanism operates on actual sentences to extract the units of meaning in sentences and the relations between them.

If the mechanism for speech perception could operate without any time constraint, then a grammar would be the only computational device needed to comprehend sentences. One such "time-independent" mechanism would be an "analysis by synthesis" model of perception, in which the grammar is used to generate candidate sentences to "match" the input. When a candidate sentence is generated that does match the input (to some criterion) then the device assigns the particular structure that is generated to the input sequence. Given an unlimited amount of time to make false guesses as to what the input sequence is, such a device would ultimately assign all of the grammatical structures that a particular sequence should have assigned to it. However, real speakers and hearers do not have unlimited amounts of time in which to make incorrect guesses about the structure of what they hear. In recognizance of this fact, various researchers have proposed that the analysis by synthesis model include a "preprocessor," which makes gross assessments of the input sequence in order to guide the "guesses" that the grammar makes in the most efficient manner possible. Such a preprocessor can (by hypothesis) guide a grammar to guess about sentences according to particular properties, such as a certain length.

Current research has suggested three principal features of the speech perception carried out within the preprocessor: (1) the clause is the primary perceptual unit; (2) within each clause direct mapping rules assign semantic relations between major phrases; (3) after each clause is processed it is recoded into a relatively abstract form, thereby leaving immediate storage available for processing the next clause.

Responses to nonspeech stimuli presented during sentences demonstrate that closure occurs at clause boundaries and clicks are mislocated as occurring at such points (Fodor & Bever, 1965; Garrett, 1965; Garrett, Bever, & Fodor, 1966; Bever, Lackner, & Kirk, 1969)[2], but generally not at points of low transitional probability (Bever, Lackner & Stoltz, 1969), nor generally at all surface phrase structure breaks (Bever, Lackner, & Kirk, 1969). If speech is switched from one ear to the other, the point of switching is most accurately located if it occurs at a clause boundary. Reaction time to clicks between clauses is faster than to clicks far from such points (Holmes & Forster, 1970).

The second principle is that within each perceptual unit the deep structure relations are assigned by direct projection onto the deep structure of the apparent lexical sequences. Accordingly, sentences with explicit relative clause markers ("who," "when") are less complex than those without (Fodor & Garrett, 1966; Hakes & Cairns, 1970). Similarly, explicit marking of complement constructions (e.g., presence of "that") is facilitating (Hakes, 1971). Sentences with verbs having more *potential* deep structure roles are also relatively complex (Fodor, Garrett, and Bever, 1968; Hakes, 1972).

Both the clause segmentation and internal labelling processes place heavy emphasis on information inherent in individual lexical items as well as general properties of surface structures. Thus, sentence comprehension is the joint result of the segregation of clauses and phrases on the basis of specific external cues and *analysis* of grammatical relations between phrases within each clause (see Bever, 1968; Garrett, 1971; Fodor, Bever, & Garrett, in press, for reviews). On this view underlying structure relations are assigned by direct perceptual mapping rules, as sketched below.

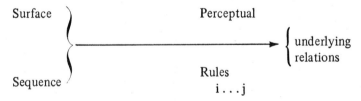

Such operations do not apply homogeneously throughout a sentence, and the effects of preliminary word- and phrase-processing are reflected in minor variations in attention to nonspeech stimuli during a clause (Garrett, 1965; Bever, Lackner, & Stoltz, 1969; Holmes & Forster, 1970; Garrett, 1971). The points of *maximum* sensory processing load are at the ends of clauses (Abrams & Bever, 1969; Bever, 1971b; Valian, 1971). This phenomenon has been interpreted in the following way: "During a clause we accumulate information and hypotheses concerning its potential deep structure; at the end of the clause, we decide on the structure of what we just heard" (Abrams & Bever, 1969). More recent research has suggested that once its internal structure is decided on, the external representation of a clause is erased from short-term storage. The surface structure of sentences in running text is forgotten after only a few clauses (Sachs, 1967). Moore (1971) has shown that the

[2] Various criticisms have been raised concerning whether this technique taps perceptual processes. These are reviewed and met in Fodor, Bever, and Garrett (in press).

time to judge the appropriateness of a noun to fill in a blank in an immediately preceding sentence is related to the *meaning* of the sentence and not the surface position of the blank. While immediate recall of the *meaning* of the first clause of a two-clause sentence is virtually perfect, free recall of the exact words in the first clause is distinctly worse than recall of the exact words in the second clause (Jarvella, 1970; Jarvella & Herman, 1972). Consistent with this is the fact that latencies to identify a probe word are faster if the word is drawn from the immediately preceding clause than if it is drawn from an earlier clause, regardless of the amount of interposed material (Caplan, 1971). Finally, the time to think up a completion of a stimulus sentence fragment is increased by ambiguity in the fragment only when the fragment is an incomplete clause (Bever, 1968; Bever, Garrett, & Hurtig, 1972). That is, the fact that a sequence is ambiguous is irrelevant once a clause boundary is passed, since one of the two meanings is already decided on.

The following picture of speech perception emerges from these studies. During a clause a listener isolates major phrases and projects a possible internal organization for the semantic relations between the phrases. At the end of each clause a structure is assigned, and the external form of the clause itself is erased from immediate memory.

The Influence of Speech Perception on Linguistic Universals

Recently we have been concerned with the extent to which certain universals of language are due to these perceptual principles rather than to universal grammatical principles (Bever, 1970, 1971b; Bever & Langendoen, 1971). There may be certain possible but nonoccurring kinds of languages which could be learned so far as their structure and rules are concerned, but which would generate sentences that cannot be understood. In a technical sense every actual language has this property. For example, in English it is probably the case that nobody can understand a sentence with five center embeddings or a sentence that is 100 words long with the subject at the beginning and its intransitive verb at the end. Nevertheless the grammar does generate such sentences; in these cases there is no restriction due to the rules in the language but it is rather due to their behavioral difficulty.

In certain cases it appears that the linguistic rules themselves are formed in accordance with the behavioral operations necessary in the use of sentences. The preceding section explained the behavioral importance of keeping clauses distinct and correctly assigning the relations between clauses. In many languages this requirement is reflected in a heterogeneous set of grammatical restrictions and rules, all of which have the cumulative effect of marking an initial subordinate clause as subordinate by the end of its verb phrase. In grammatical terms these rules include restriction on the deletion of relative pronouns and of complementizers as well as restrictions on movement transformations.

It is not difficult to understand the functional role of such constraints; they make it possible for the listener (and talker) to identify the main clause of each sentence, either by its initial position or by the fact that it is not marked as subordinate. While the usefulness of this property of performance constraints is clear, there is a further consequence that may seem trifling at first but is at the heart of the matter under discussion in this paper. By virtue of the grammatical rules, which themselves are the result of performance constraints on our interpretation, listeners are never presented with an initial clause without knowing whether it is the main or subordinate clause of the entire sentence. In this sense, speakers do not have the stylistic "option" of at first misleading listeners into thinking that the first clause is a main clause and then having it turn out to be a subordinate clause.

Before considering whether such stylistic limitations are important cognitively, let me also briefly present an example of the effect of perceptual constraints on linguistic structure that may be more restricted in its scope than the preceding. In English and many other languages (but not all) there is a set of restrictions on the ordering in prenominal adjectives. Three main theories have been proposed in recent years to account for the correct adjective ordering. Vendler (1963) suggests that the more "privileges of occurrence as a noun" that an adjective can have, the closer to the head noun it must be ordered. Thus we say "nice metal box" since "metal" has more uses as a noun than "nice." Martin (1968) proposes that the adjectives are ordered in terms of their intrinsic semantic relation to the noun, with the more intrinsic properties (e.g., "metal") ordered to be closer to the noun than the less intrinsic properties (e.g., "nice"). Finally, Ertel (1971) suggests that a supplementary set of constraints is sensitive to the implicative relations between the two adjectives. For example, we say "a long extensive discussion" not "an extensive long discussion" since if the "discussion" is "extensive," then it is *ipso facto* "long," but the reverse does not necessarily obtain.[3]

These three hypotheses share a common characteristic: The more specific an adjective is (where the term "specificity" can now refer to the dimension of nominalness or intrinsicness or uniqueness of designation), the closer to the head noun it must appear. I have argued elsewhere that this sort of restriction is a natural consequence of the operations that are carried out in the perceptual isolation of major noun phrases (Bever, 1970). As outlined above, one process involved in sentence perception is the segmentation of major designating phrases. If the phrase at issue is a noun phrase, as indicated by the presence of a determiner or by the preceding syntactic structure, then the listener is searching for the most precise referent in his conceptual repertoire to match that indicated by the external structure of the noun phrase; so long as the postulated noun-phrase referent continues to become increasingly specific the internal mapping processes are in accordance with the external order of the phrase. When the sequence becomes less specific, the preceding material is naturally segmented together. Thus, in a string of prenominal modifiers a decrease in "noun-likeness or specificity" that any two adjacent lexical items may exhibit constitutes a phrase boundary. When such a boundary occurs (as in the transition from the noun to a verb) then segmentation of the noun phrase occurs at that point. If the increasing specificity conventions were not met in prenominal modification, then premature perceptual segmentation would occur. For example, in the sequence "the metal nice box," segmentation would occur prematurely, following the word "metal."

Such a syntactic restriction example is presumably a case in which the "grammar" could allow either adjective ordering to occur, but extremely strong behavi-

---

[3] Notice that this constraint could be viewed as a special case of a "felicity constraint" on conversations: *Be informative.* (cf. Gvice, forthcoming).

oral constraints interpose themselves to force a particular ordering as normal. Of course, language order restrictions also differ in ways that are not obviously motivated by performance constraints. For example, there are such apparently arbitrary linguistic structures as subordinate clauses with verb-final position (German), postnominal position of adjective modifiers—not in a relative clause—(French), and so on.[4] In sum, for a variety of reasons, each language limits stylistic options available to speakers to vary the order in which concepts are presented and restrict the order in which the corresponding perceptual operations can apply.

The Influence of
Perceptual Order on Concepts

The important question is whether the psychological effects of carrying out perceptual activities in such constrained orders form part of the semantic meaning conveyed whether they form part of the cultural ideas about the concept perceived, or whether they are not part of the concept at all. I propose the middle position, that such perceptual activities are contained in concepts as part of our cultural ideas about linguistically defined meanings and consequently are one part of the concepts that contain the meanings. Thus, our cultural ideas are influenced by the structure of the language we speak, modifying the kinds of possible concepts but leaving unaffected the semantic meanings that can be conveyed.

There are at least three possible levels on which surface order can influence concepts, through stylistic options within a language, through differing availability of certain options in different languages, and through universal properties of surface structure/deep structure relations. (See Fishman, 1960, for an earlier discussion of different "levels" of the Whorfian hypothesis.)

First it has been acknowledged by most theorists that the surface order of constituents can affect the "meaning" of a sentence since it affects the "topicalization" or "focus." For example, "the boy hit the ball" and "the ball was hit by the boy" may share many elements of their meaning but they differ with respect to what each sentence is about. In such cases this difference may be argued to be more than "stylistic" if there are logical differences as a function of the construction used, for example in the interpretation of quantifiers (cf. Jackendoff, 1969). However, the two sentences below, which on any theoretical interpretation would be argued to have the same "meaning," have very different concepts.[5]

(1) John loves his mother, surprisingly.
(2) Surprisingly, John loves his mother.

Consider the affective difference between the perception of the two sentences on the initial assumption that "John" and "his mother" are normal. In the first, the

---

[4] Of course it is important for the generality of the considerations of prenominal adjective order that there be other languages in which prenominal adjective order is free, presumably because decrease of specificity is not used as a cue for a nounphrase boundary. Japanese may be such a language, since noun phrases characteristically end in unique particles (e.g., "wa," "ga"). I have been told by Japanese informants that prenominal coordinate adjective ordering is free, as predicted, but further investigations are needed. If this is true, comparative Japanese/English psycholinguistic research would be appropriate to test the empirical consequences of the differences in restrictions on prenominal adjective ordering.

[5] I am grateful to S. Fish for calling such examples to my attention.

listener is presented with a proposition which is intrinsically likely and is then told that that proposition was *in fact* unlikely presumably because of some special circumstances (in this case, the incapability of John to love anyone, or the unlovableness of his mother, etc.). Thus, we are not only told by the adverb that the proposition is surprising, but we are also surprised ourselves *at the same time*, thus lending a double force to the information that the main proposition is surprising. The second statement does not offer this resonance of perceptual sequence and meaning. Rather, the listener is first told that what is about to be heard is surprising, which dilutes the effect of the surprise itself. Since we have been told that it is surprising, we are no longer affectively surprised to be presented with the presumptive surprise. Similarly, if I tell you that I am going to scare you by going "boo" and then I go "boo," it will not scare you. In this way the conceptual communications of the two sentences above differ despite their semantic synonymy.

The preceding example demonstrates the potential effect on a concept of exercising a stylistic option within a language. The parallel effect may also occur between languages insofar as one allows orders that another does not.

If the standard order of clauses or prenominal modifiers is constrained in a particular language, then this in turn constrains the expected order of these constituents and the kinds of emotional tensions that can be created when that order is either followed or violated. For example, English speakers are limited to hearing the more specific adjectives later in a series of prenominal adjectives and thus are denied the ideas communicated by allowing the adjectives to appear in decreasing order of specificity.

It may seem at first that such a limitation is without any conceivable consequences. What difference does it make if prenominal adjectives are always in the order, "evaluative, size, material . . ."? What is lost to us by the fact that we cannot experience a phrase like "the metal nice red box. . . ," since that order of modifiers can occur postnominally, as in "the box that is metal and nice and red . . ."?

The psychological difference between the prenominal and post-nominal position of modifiers is demonstrated (informally) by the phenomenological difference in the apprehension of the following two sequences:

> I'm thinking of something. It's nice. It's red. It's large. It's a box.
> I'm thinking of a box. It's nice. It's red. It's large.

Clearly being presented with modifiers before the modified term has quite different effects from the reverse order.

Another question concerns the effect of a constrained order among the modifiers themselves. It is obvious that the order of presentation of the components of a cinema scene affects the concept that is conveyed (although not the logical content). For example, consider different effects of presenting a Dickensian feast scene in the order below, or in the reverse order.

(1) A shot of legs under a table, sounds of eating, food crumbs dropping to the floor (with at least two knees of opposite sexes, touching);

(2) A shot from above the table of 10 people gorging themselves;

(3) A shot from outside the dining room window at the dinner table scene, framed by the window;

(4) A shot of the house, neighborhood, and evening, revealing that the house is located on an isolated farm.

In both presentation orders the logical content of the scene is the same, but the dramatic concepts differ.

It might be argued that such examples do not bear on the question of order effects in speech, because the presentation of each modifier in a noun phrase is much faster than a film shot and, consequently, listeners could not perceive the different linguistic orders since they are aware only of the internal referent built up by the complete designating phrase, i.e., the difference between building up the internal referent in the order "evaluative color material" or "material color evaluative" is not perceptible because of its speed. This view is *prima facie* implausible since it suggests that listeners are not aware of differences in word orders within a phrase, which is not the case. Furthermore, the speed of presentation of parts of a stimulus is not incompatible with order effects. Imagine for example a figure with a dot surrounded by a circle. If the dot and the circle are flashed on in succession, the order of presentation determines what is perceived. If the circle precedes the dot, both appear. In the reverse order, only the circle appears. (See Kahneman, 1968, for a review of the temporal parameters determining this phenomenon, known as "metacontrast.")

Such examples show that there are psychological precedents for order effects occurring at slow rates of presentation (e.g., film shots) and at fast rates (metacontrast). Accordingly, it is reasonable to expect order effects at intermediate rates as well (adjective sequences), and to expect that the concepts conveyed by speakers of English are limited by the prenominal adjective order restrictions.

This is not to say that we cannot appreciate the impression which might be communicated by a stylistic device that would use ungrammatical order. Indeed, it is possible to discuss such impressions and to *imagine* ourselves as perceiving them, but it is difficult, and in some cases impossible, to construct actual linguistic situations in which they would be naturally received. This is analogous to the fact that we can talk about the nature and properties of visual illusions, but the illusions remain even though we may understand them.

A final possible example of the influence of syntactic structure on thought might be cases where there are linguistic properties that are themselves universal. For example the fact that a listener can rarely be in doubt as to whether an initial clause is main or subordinate means that it is rarely a surprise to discover a miscategorization by the time of the second clause. (Note that in a few cases in English such as "the horse raced past the barn fell but the horse pushed past the barn didn't" such an effect can occur.)

CODABILITY AND THOUGHT

The preceding discussion has outlined how syntactic order determines the order of perceptual and productive activities in the course of speech. The particular order of perceptual and productive operations determines some of the linguistically communicated cultural ideas within the concept conveyed by each sentence, without affecting the semantic meaning. If the syntactic structure of a language restricts in this way the kinds of linguistic concepts that can be communicated, then we can restate the Whorfian hypothesis to include the role of grammatical patterns in limiting thought: *the syntactic structure of a language partially determines the kinds of concepts available to speakers by limiting systematically the shared perceptual operations that can occur in the course of analysing the semantic meanings.*

A good deal of scientific effort has been devoted to investigating the Whorfian claim that language *determines* forms of thought (cf. Krauss, 1968). The upshot of this research is that meanings that are encoded within a language within a single word are more *easily* coded and retained in specific tasks, but there is no clear evidence that such influences determine momentary perceptions, or logical conceptual ability, as many have interpreted Whorf to have proposed. Thus, the ease with which we can process various meanings is influenced by the language that we use, but the possible occurrence of meanings is not necessarily limited by the language we use. Accordingly, the question of whether order constraints limit the kinds of sentence meanings that we can have is the same question that was raised earlier about words: Do the cultural and personal ideas that are included with meanings in concepts modify the meanings themselves? Just as the answer there was negative, the answer here too is negative. That is, meanings and cultural ideas intersect as components of concepts in independent domains. Each is the sea in which the other floats.

REFERENCES

Abrams, K., & Bever, T. G. Syntactic structure modifies attention during speech perception. *Quarterly Journal of Experimental Psychology*, 1969, **21**, 280–290.

Bever, T. G. A survey of some recent work in psycholinguistics. In W. J. Plath (Ed.), *Specification and utilization of a transformational grammar.* (Contract AF 19(628)–5127), Bedford, Mass.: I.B.M. Corp., 1968.

Bever, T. G. The cognitive basis for linguistic structures. In J. R. Hayes (Ed.), *Cognition and the development of language*, New York: Wiley & Sons, 1970.

Bever, T. G. The nature of cerebral dominance in the speech behavior of the child and adult. In R. Huxley and E. Ingram (Eds.) *Mechanisms of language development.* London: Academic Press, 1971. (a)

Bever, T. G. The integrated study of language behavior. In I. Morton (Ed.), *Biological and social factors in psycholinguistics.* Cambridge, Mass.: Logos Press, 1971. (b)

Bever, T. G., Garrett, M., & Hurtig, R. The interaction of speech perception and ambiguous sentences, unpublished manuscript, 1972.

Bever, T. G., Lackner, J. R., & Kirk, R. The underlying structures of sentences are the primary units of immediate speech processing. *Perception and Psychophysics*, 1969, **5**, 225–234.

Bever, T. G., Lackner, J. R., & Stoltz, W. Transitional probability is not a general mechanism for speech segmentation. *Journal of Experimental Psychology*, 1969, **79**, 387–397.

Bever, T. G., & Langendoen, D. T. A dynamic model of the evolution of language. *Linguistic Inquiry*, 1971, **2**(4), 432–463.

Brown, R., & Lenneberg, E. H. A study in language and cognition. *Journal of Abnormal and Social Psychology*, 1954, **49**, 454–462.

Caplan, D. Probe Tests and Sentence Perception. Unpublished doctoral dissertation, Massachusetts Institute of Technology, 1971.

Carroll, J. B., & Casagrande, J. B. The function of language classifications in behavior. In E. E. Maccoby, T. C. Newcomb, and E. L. Hartley (Eds.), *Readings in social psychology.* New York: Holt, 1958.

Ertel, S., unpublished manuscript, 1971.

Fishman, J. A. A systematization of the Whorfian hypotheses. *Behavioral Science*, 1960, **5**, 323–339.

Fodor, J. A., & Bever, T. G. The psychological reality of linguistic segments. *Journal of Verbal Learning and Verbal Behavior*, 1965, **4**, 414–420.

Fodor, J. A., & Garrett, M. Some reflections on competence and performance. In J. Lyons and R. Wales (Eds.), *Psycholinguistic Papers*. Edinburgh: Edinburgh University Press, 1966.

Fodor, J. A., Garrett, M., & Bever, T. G. Some Syntactic Determinants of Sentactical Complexity: II. Verb structure. *Perception and Psychophysics*, 1968, **3**, 453–461.

Fodor, J., Bever, T. G., & Garrett, M. *The psychology of language: psycholinguistics and generative grammar*, New York: McGraw-Hill, in press.

Garrett, M. Some experiments on the perception of sentences. Unpublished doctoral dissertation, University of Chicago, 1965.

Garrett, M. Does ambiguity complicate the perception of sentences? In G. B. Flores d'Arcais and W.J.M. Levelt (Eds.), *Advances in psycholinguistics*. New York: American Elsevier, 1971.

Garrett, M., Bever, T. G., & Fodor, J. A. The active use of grammar in speech perception. *Perception and psychophysics*, 1966, **1**, 30–32.

Gvice, H. William James Lectures (in preparation).

Hakes, D. T. Effects of reducing complement constructions on sentence comprehension. *Journal of Verbal Learning and Verbal Behavior*, 1972, **11**, 278–286.

Hakes, D. T. Does verb structure affect sentence comprehension? *Perception and Psychophysics*, 1971, **10**, 229–232.

Hakes, D. T., & Cairns, H. S. Sentence comprehension and relative pronouns. *Perception and Psychophysics*, 1970, **8**, 5–8.

Holmes, V. M., & Forster, K. I. Detection of extraneous signals during sentence recognition. *Perception and Psychophysics*, 1970, **7**, 297–301.

Jackendoff, R. An interpretive theory of pronominal reflexives. (PEGS Paper #27) Washington, D.C.: Center for Applied Linguistics, 1969.

Jarvella, R. J. Effects of syntax on running memory span for connected discourse. *Psychonomic Science*, 1970, **19**, 235–236.

Jarvella, R. J., & Herman, S. J. Clause structure of sentences and speech processing. *Perception and Psychophysics*, 1972, **11**, 381–384.

Kahneman, D. Method, findings, and theory in studies of visual masking. *Psychological Bulletin*. 1968, **70**, 404–425.

Katz, J. J. *The philosophy of language*, New York: Harper & Row, 1966.

Katz, J. J. *Semantic theory*, New York: Harper & Row, 1972.

Krauss, R. Language as a symbolic process in communication. *American Scientist*, 1968, **56**, 265–278.

Martin, J. E. A study of the determinants of preferred adjective order in English. Unpublished doctoral dissertation, University of Illinois, Illinois, 1968.

Moore, T. Unpublished doctoral dissertation, State University of New York at Buffalo, 1971.

Sachs, J. S. Recognition memory for syntactic and semantic aspects of connected discourse. *Dissertation Abstracts*, 1967, **27** (8-B), 2900.

Stein, G. Portrait of Pablo Picasso. *Selected writings of Gertrude Stein*. New York: Random House, 1946.

Valian, G. Talking, listening and linguistic structure. Unpublished doctoral dissertation, Northeastern University, Boston, Massachusetts, 1971.

Vendler, Z. The transformational grammar of English adjectives. *Transformations and discourse analysis papers*. Philadelphia: University of Pennsylvania, 1963.

Whorf, B. L. (Selected writings) In J. B. Carroll (Ed.), *Language, thought and reality: Selected writings of B. L. Whorf*. Cambridge, Mass.: M.I.T. Press, 1956.

6
MENTAL OPERATIONS IN LANGUAGE COMPREHENSION[1]

Tom Trabasso
Princeton University

How are we to understand how an utterance is understood? This question, faced by each of us in one form or another, explicitly relates the method of study with the process under study. That is, an empirical investigation of language comprehension is determined largely by our concept of comprehension.

Suppose we assume that the comprehending of linguistic information occurs in real time. Consider the situation where a person hears an utterance and then is tested for his "understanding" of it. For example, he may be asked to judge whether the number 7 is odd (Wason, 1961; Wason & Jones, 1963).

How might he go about processing this statement? Certain plausible mental operations are suggested. One strategy is to first classify and *encode* the subject, 7, as "odd." A second stage consists of *encoding* the predicate, "odd." A third stage involves the *comparison* of the two encodings. If the classification of the digit *matches* the predicate encoding, then the person can enter a fourth decision stage where the sentence is judged as true. If we assume that the stages are independent, serial, and require time, we can then design experiments to test this particular process model and estimate the time to complete each stage (Chase & Clark, 1972; Trabasso, 1970; Trabasso, Rollins, & Shaughnessy, 1971).

Comprehension, then, is viewed as a set of psychological processes consisting of a series of mental operations which process linguistic information from its receipt until an overt decision. Two main operations are noted: (1) *encoding* the information into internal representations and (2) *comparing* these representations. The

[1] This research was supported by United States Public Health Service, National Institutes of Health Grant MH 19223. I am indebted to Phil Gough for his consent to publish the concept learning experiments which we did together at the University of California, Los Angeles, 1963–64, and for stimulating my interest in language and thought. I also wish to thank Sam Glucksberg for his continued support and intellectual interest in my work.

results of the comparison process (a match or a mismatch of internal representations) determines the person's overt response (Chase & Clark, 1972; Trabasso, 1970). Comprehension may be said to occur when the internal representations are matched. The overt response ("True") is an end result of the act of comprehending.

The idea that the time between a stimulus (here, a sentence) and a response (here, the decision, "True") is occupied by a sequence of processes or stages is an old idea in experimental psychology, at least since the time of Donders, a century ago (cf., Sternberg, 1969). This stage theory implies that a person's reaction time (RT)—the time taken to respond given the sentence—is a sum of the durations of each of the stages. Thus, by suitable variations of the surface structure of the sentence and referential events one could determine the component times.

These time estimates might be used not only as a test of the theory describing the processes but in answering other interesting questions about the process. For example, Clark (1970) used time estimates on four kinds of negation: (1) explicit full negation, (2) explicit quantifier negation, (3) implicit full negation, and (4) implicit quantifier negation. Sentences (1)–(4) are examples of each of these kinds of negation.

(1)   Seven is not an even number.
(2)   None of the numbers is seven.
(3)   Seven is absent.
(4)   Seven is lower than eight.

Clark found that RTs for the negation component of these sentences order themselves $1 > 2 > 3 > 4$ and that the difficulty in processing negatives is in terms of what they presuppose and assert. I shall discuss this interpretation later.

Again, let me stress that the approach here is to view the person as an information processor in real time. Linguistic information is processed in ways similar to those for other perceptual inputs although internal linguistic structures (so-called "deep structure" and semantic memory) play a major role in determining how the input is represented (e.g., Bever, 1970) and on what basis the internal representations are compared (e.g., Collins & Quillian, 1969). An attempt is made to specify explicitly those stages or operations the person goes through in order to complete a comprehension task. This method can be shown to have a wide range of application, from simple problem solving to sentence verification (Chase & Clark, 1972; Clark, 1970; Trabasso, 1970; Trabasso et al., 1971).

In this paper, I shall first describe a general encoding and comparing model for comprehending sentences. This model has been concurrently developed by Bill Chase, Herb Clark and myself. Then, two alternative specific models are discussed. In one, called the Response Change model, the person does not process the sentence information beyond its internal representation prior to the comparison stage; in the other, called the Optional Recoding Model, transformations are made on the sentence constituents prior to and during the comparison stage. After discussing these alternatives and comparing them on various sets of data, I shall examine the relationship between encoding and processing operations in the comparison stage and report some new experiments on this relation.

Suppose we consider a sentence verification task where the person is asked to compare a sentence (or a description) against a picture. For example, the person is told:

(5) a. The ball is red.

Then, he is shown a picture of a round object which is either red or blue (or also green or yellow if more than two alternatives can occur). The person terminates the task by responding either "True" or "False" depending upon whether or not the sentence describes the picture.

The above example is probably one of the simplest sentence comprehension tasks. Syntactically and semantically more complex sentences have, of course, been used. You will recall the spate of sentence verification experiments (see Fodor & Garrett, 1966; Miller & McNeil, 1969) where an implicit process model was used. Here it was generally assumed that the number of transforms necessary to reduce the surface structure to some "kernel" form alone determined the number of RT components. However, as Fodor and Garrett have pointed out, when the formal linguistic theory motivating this research changed, interest by psycholinguists in these studies also dwindled. Presumably, the studies were rendered irrelevant on the basis of other than psychological considerations. However, the fact that these experiments exist, that their data are remarkably reliable and orderly, and that they are in some way concerned with language comprehension provides some compelling reasons for not dispensing with the considerable efforts of these first generation psycholinguists. I hope to show that the present stage model makes these studies "relevant."

In general, if we can explain these and other experiments by the encoding and comparing model, we then have some firm understanding of what mental operations occur in the comprehending of sentences. If the model is correct in such identifications, then the ease or difficulty in comprehending a particular utterance may be identified. That is, the prime source of a failure in comprehension may be identified as either in (a) the encoding of the material, e.g., as in concrete or abstract nouns (Paivio, 1969), (b) the finding of an internal representation, as in an embedded sentence (cf., Bever, 1970), (c) the differences between the internal representations as in comparisons of active and passive sentences, or (d) the nature of the recoding or transformation operations as in inverting an explicit negation into its complementary affirmative form (Wason, 1959). Thus one or another independent component links in our chain of thought may be missing, leading to a breakdown in comprehension. The stage model allows us to make these identifications and permits quantitative comparisons on different kinds of information as in Clark's (1970) study of negation.

Encoding Stage

How does one encode the sentence? Here, I will follow Clark's (1970) lead. Suppose we wish to negate explicitly the fact that the ball is red. We might use sentence (5)b.

(5) b. The ball is not red.

We might use this form if the listener had expected to see a red ball. According to Clark, the sentence expresses a presupposition and an assertion. The presupposition is that the speaker supposes that the listener believes that the ball is red and the assertion is that the belief is false. In Clark's notation, the sentence presented in (5)b then becomes what a person has understood approximately as in (5)c, a paraphrase of which is given in (5)d.

(5)   b. The ball is not red.
       c. (false (suppose (ball is red)))
       d. It is false (for the listener) to suppose that the ball is red.

Stage 1, then, is that stage of comprehension where the person achieves an internal representation of the sentence. Obviously, the example and representation chosen here are oversimplifications but they are sufficient for the model to work on a range of studies involving negation, passives, etc. The form of encoding is a problem for further linguistic and psychological analysis.

Response Change Model

We can now turn to what I shall call the Response Change Model of Chase and Clark (1972). A similar version of the model has been used by myself (Trabasso, 1970) in discussion of experiments by Gough (1965, 1966) and Slobin (1966) where sentences come before pictures but where the person *does not* transform the sentences prior to encoding the picture and comparing the internal representations. The Response Change Model is shown in Figure 1.

In the left-most column of Figure 1 are listed the stages in comprehension. The remaining four columns indicate the four information conditions obtained by including affirmative and negative sentences which are either confirmed as true or denied as false against the picture.

INFORMATION CONDITIONS

STAGE	TRUE AFFIRMATIVE	FALSE AFFIRMATIVE	TRUE NEGATIVE	FALSE NEGATIVE
1 ENCODE SENTENCE	(A IS RED)	(A IS RED)	(FALSE (A IS RED))	(FALSE (A IS RED))
2 ENCODE PICTURE	(A IS RED)	(A IS BLUE)	(A IS BLUE)	(A IS RED)
3 COMPARE INNER STRING	MATCH	MISMATCH CHANGE TRUTH INDEX	MISMATCH CHANGE TRUTH INDEX	MATCH
COMPARE OUTER STRING			MISMATCH CHANGE TRUTH INDEX	MISMATCH CHANGE TRUTH INDEX
4 RESPOND	"TRUE"	"FALSE"	"TRUE"	"FALSE"

FIG. 1. Mental operations and stages of the Response Change Model (modified from Chase and Clark, 1972).

In Stage 1, the person encodes the sentence in an internal representation described above. In Stage 2, the picture is encoded in a similar form. In Stage 3, the person compares the two representations to see whether or not they *match*. The order of comparison is inner string first, then the embedding or outer string. In Stage 4, he converts the result of the comparison into a response.

The first row of Figure 1 shows the representational forms (omitting the supposition for the affirmative sentences). In Stage 2, we shall assume that the person encodes those features of the picture which are listed in the internal representation of the sentence. Further, it is assumed that the representation has a true supposition and that the preferred order of representation is subject-verb-object (s-v-o) (*cf.*, Bever, 1970).

Within Stage 3, the comparison stage, there are a series of steps. The subject is set to match internal representations so that his "truth index" is set at "True." He first compares the content of the inner string. If there is a mismatch, he *changes* the truth index from **TRUE** to **FALSE**, hence the name, Response Change, for the model. Note, the content or internal representations are not changed, only the truth index. Should the outer strings mismatch, then the truth index may be changed back again. The index value at the end of Stage 3 is the overt response made in Stage 4.

To illustrate the operations, consider the True Negative (labelled TN) in Figure 1. In Stage 1, the person encodes the affirmative parts of the negative sentence as an embedded string. The outer, embedding string contains the negation. Thus "The ball is not red" is represented as (false (ball is red)). The picture of a blue ball is encoded in Stage 2 as (ball is blue). In the first part of Stage 3, the subject compares the inner, affirmative strings (ball is red) with (ball is blue). Since there is a mismatch on the color, the response index is changed TRUE→ FALSE. Next, the embedding strings are compared and the presence of a false changes the truth index back FALSE→ TRUE. Since TRUE is the final value, the response in Stage 4 is "True." If we assume that the component stages are independent, serial, and occur in real time, we can predict the RT latencies in verifying sentences. Essentially, component times are added in Stage 1 for representing negatives and in Stage 2 for detecting mismatches and changing truth indices. The important set of predictions is that the total processing times for the four conditions is ordered TA, FA, FN and TN and the differences are additive. That is the RT for TN's should be predicted from the other three conditions.

Evidence Favoring the Response Change Model. The bulk of the evidence favoring the Response Change Model comes from the research of Chase and Clark (1972; Clark, 1970). In all of their experiments, the person is presented *simultaneously* with a sentence on the left and a picture on the right side of a viewing screen. The sentences were of the form "A preposition B" and referred to a (star or cross) (above or below) (cross or star). The person had to respond "True" or "False." That is, for a TN condition, the sentence would be "Cross isn't above star" and the picture would be an asterisk (star) placed vertically over a plus sign (cross).

Figure 2 shows the mean RTs for the main study of Chase and Clark (1972). The times for the four information conditions are ordered TA < FA < FN < TN, as expected. Furthermore, the assumption of independence of serial stages is given

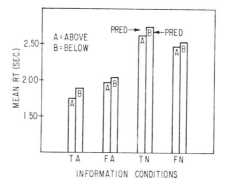

FIG. 2. Observed and predicted RTs to TRUE and FALSE, affirmative and negative sentences of the form Star is Above (or Below) Cross. The sentence and picture were presented together. Data from Exp. I by Chase and Clark, 1972.

strong support by the close additivity prediction of the TN RT from the remaining three conditions.

The Chase and Clark (1972) experiments are the only ones I know of where the sentence and the picture occur at the same time. Since the Response Change Model accounts so well for their data, we may conclude that the person begins the process by encoding first the sentence, then the picture without processing the negation beyond setting up the internal representation depicted in (5)c. In the comparison stage, the only changes which occur are on the truth index. Such a model involves no basic syntactic transformation of the encoded representations, contrary to what had been assumed by those researchers concerned with transformational grammar in the early and mid 1960's.

A second set of experiments which support the Response Change Model comes from studies where the sentence and picture were presented at different times. The data which favor the Response Change Model are those from experiments where the sentence came first but where the negative sentences could *not* be uniquely transformed prior to viewing the picture (Gough, 1965; 1966) or where the picture came first (McMahon, 1963, Exp. III; Trabasso *et al.*, 1971, Exp. IX). The data and predicted values for processing sentences for the four information conditions are shown for these experiments in Figures 3, 4 and 5.

In Figure 3, the results of Experiment III by Gough (1966) and an unpublished replication on one practiced subject by Sam Glucksberg are shown. In these experiments college students verified sentences and pictures of all combinations of (girl or boy) (hit or kick) (girl or boy). The sentence was read and then the picture was presented. For the negative sentence, "The girl didn't hit the boy," there are seven instances which confirm and only one (a girl hitting a boy) which disconfirms the sentence. Given the large number of alternatives, the subjects in these experiments could not transform the negatives uniquely and so the Response Change strategy seems plausible. The data in Figure 3 favor the Response Change Model in that TN's $\geq$ FN's. The predicted values of the TN sentences from the component times

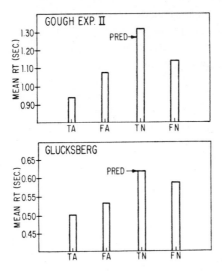

FIG. 3. Observed and predicted RTs for verifying sentences which precede the picture and whose transforms are not unique. Data from Gough (1966) and Glucksberg (personal communication).

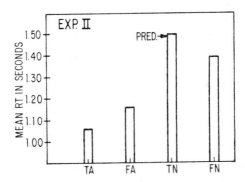

FIG. 4. Observed and predicted RTs for verifying sentences which come after the picture. Data from McMahon (1963).

are especially accurate. The fact that subjects did not process the sentences beyond their internal representations assumed by the model is lent further support by a comparison between Gough's results in his 1965 and 1966 experiments. In the latter, Gough introduced a longer (three second) delay between the sentence and the picture. The RTs for the two conditions, delay and no delay, were nearly identical.

Indirect evidence for the assumption that no processing beyond the initial internal representation comes from a study on comprehension by Wright (1969). In her experiment, subjects heard a simple affirmative sentence that was either active or passive. Then, after a five second delay, they were asked a question about the sentence in the active or passive voice. When the sentence and question were in the same voice, fewer errors were made, and in the matched conditions there was no difference between the active and passive voice. This indicates that the subjects did not transform the sentences after hearing them, for had they done so the passive questions should have been more difficult.

Returning to Chase and Clark's (1971) experiments, the failure to transform might well have to do with the fact that above and below are contraries rather than contradictories (Wales & Grieve, 1969). This means that it is uncertain what transform "not above" would have since there are many locations which are not above, such as, to the left and right, as well as below. Thus, one factor contributing to the Response Change Model is the uncertainty of which alternative form one may use to represent a negative sentence. In particular, explicit quantifier sentences have this property and only if they are treated as explicit full negation could they be transformed (see Chase & Clark, 1971, and Trabasso *et al.*, 1971, discussed below).

A second condition favoring the Response Change Model is where the picture precedes the sentence. Two experimental results on this are shown in Figures 4 and 5. Figure 4 gives the results of a sentence matching experiment by McMahon (1963). The model fits the data nearly perfectly. Figure 5 shows the data from one of my own experiments using only adjective descriptions. Again, the model fits the data reasonably well.

The Response Change Model also appears to hold for sentence-sentence comprehension. Figure 6 shows examples and data from two experiments by Greene (1968). In one (Exp. II) Greene had subjects judge the truth of affirmative or negative sentences given a preceding sentence as True. This procedure amounts to translating the "True" supposition of the internal representation for the Response Change Model into an operational definition. Thus subjects would go only through Stages 2, 3, and 4. Since Greene did not include affirmative sentences for Stage 2, only the TN and FN conditions were studied. The model predicts TN's to take longer than FN's and this was observed in both experiments. To see this, consider the FN for Exp. II. Since the first sentence is represented as (X exceeds Y) and

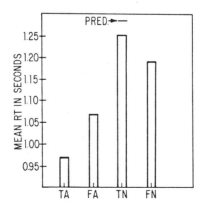

FIG. 5. Observed and predicted RTs for verifying adjective descriptions after viewing the objects. Data from Trabasso, Rollins, and Shaughnessy, 1971.

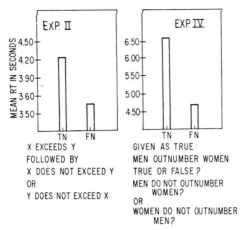

FIG. 6. RTs to verify negative sentences given an affirmative sentence as true. Data from Greene, 1968.

the second as (false (X exceeds Y)), then in Stage 3 the inner strings are matched and all the subject has to do is change his response to "False." for the TN's, however, the representations are (X exceeds Y) and (false (Y exceeds X)). There is a mismatch of the inner strings, leading to one change of the truth index and a subsequent change back to "True" since the outer strings mismatch. The same analysis applies to Greene's Exp. IV.

As far as I know, all experiments which have the sentence follow either an affirmative sentence or a picture [whose internal representation is assumed to be affirmative (s-v-o)] support the Response Change Model. Thus, subjects do not make syntactical transformations in comprehension where they are uncertain as to what the alternative representations might be, or after they have already encoded the referent.

An Optional Recoding Model

So far, we have seen that the Response Change Model accounts for several sets of results on sentence comprehension. However, there is also a considerable body of data that indicates the Response Change Model is either wrong or simply an optional strategy open to subjects. I prefer to think of the model as an alternative processing strategy for several reasons which I shall discuss below.

Before presenting an alternative recoding or transformation model (Clark, 1970, referred to this as a "conversion" model), let me illustrate what I mean by alternative processing strategies by use of some illustrations from experiments by Wason and Jones (Wason, 1961; Wason & Jones, 1963).

Wason (1961) and Wason and Jones (1963) asked subjects to verify sentences such as (6)a, (6)b, (6)c, and (6)d which correspond to the four respective information conditions: TA, FA, TN and FN.

(6)   a. TA: 7 is an odd number.
     b. FA: 7 is an even number.
     c. TN: 7 is not an even number.
     d. FN: 7 is not an odd number.

Let us consider the operations of the Response Change Model on these sentences. We can think of the digit, 7, as a "picture" which is represented not as a sentence but in terms of its classification, "odd." Thus in Stage 1, the subject encodes 7 as odd. (Wason called this subject decoding.) Then in Stage 2, he encodes the predicate, (digit is odd) or for negatives, (false (digit is odd)). In Stage 3 the inner and outer strings are compared and the truth index is changed as mismatches occur. The Response Change Model predicts, as before, TA < FA < FN < , TN. However, another strategy exists. If, in Stage 2, subjects invert negations, e.g., (not odd)→(even), then a different set of operations occur in Stage 3 for the TN and FN cases. Consider first (6)c, the TN: 7 is not an even number. If the predicate is transformed or recoded as (not even)→(odd), then in Stage 3 the inner strings would match so that only one additional operation (inverting the predicate) occurs for TN's. However, predicate recoding results in two operations for FN's. Consider (6)d, the FN: 7 is not an odd number. If (not odd)→(even), then in Stage 3, a mismatch will occur and one response change will be made. Thus FN's require two additional operations: recoding and a response change. The prediction from this Optional Recoding Model is that the TN's will be faster than FN's and the times will be additive for the conditions.

Wason (1961) and Wason and Jones (1963) report that slightly more than half of their subjects stated having used the subject decoding strategy. If so, then one would expect the additivity predictions to be off and the TN somewhat longer than the FN RTs. Figure 7 shows that the times for TN's were only slightly longer than those for FN's (the differences were not statistically reliable). If we added the (TA-FA) difference to the FN, we would underpredict Wason's (1961) results and overpredict by a wide margin the Wason and Jones (1963) results. Thus a mixture of optional processing strategies occurred, and no single model could be fit to these data. (Individual subject's results could, however, be fit if each subject were consistent in his strategy.)

Within Wason's (1961) study, there was another "construction" task in which subjects appeared to adopt the predicate recoding strategy. Figure 8 shows Wason's task and RT results on the four information conditions.

The subjects were asked to provide a digit that completed a sentence. An example is shown in Figure 8, "_____ is not an even number." They were asked to give a digit which confirmed or falsified the sentence, and since the sentences were affirmative or negative, the four information conditions held. The predicate recoding strategy involves three stages.

Stage 1. Encode predicate and recode if negative.
Stage 2. Search memory for a digit from the category in the internal representation.
Stage 3. If asked to confirm the sentence, output the digit found. If asked to falsify the sentence, add one to the digit found, then output.

You can see that this stage model predicts FN's to take longer than TN's since a FN sentence involves two operations (inverting the negation and adding one to the digit found) versus one operation for the TN (inverting the negation). By the

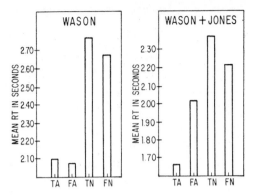

FIG. 7. RTs to verify sentences involving number classification and full explicit negation. Data from Wason (1961) and Wason and Jones (1963).

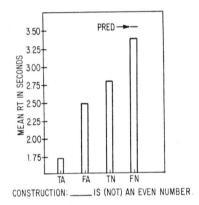

FIG. 8. RTs to provide a digit which confirms (T) or disconfirms (F) an affirmative (A) or negative (N) sentence. Data from Wason (1961).

subtraction method, we predict the value for the FN sentences shown in Figure 8. The prediction is quite good.

These experiments are the first which show negative evidence on the Response Change Model that does not admit transformations. Why should some subjects, at least, adopt a recoding strategy? We note that contradictories rather than contraries were used, i.e., the negation of odd is a full explicit negation or a contradictory since it directly implies even (*cf.*, Fillenbaum, 1966). Hence, given the context of digits which are either odd or even, the subjects would not be uncertain about the alternative, affirmative representation and could transform before the comparison or search stage.

Perhaps it is appropriate at this point to depict graphically what I shall call the Optional Recoding Model. Figure 9 outlines the model. In contrast to the Response Change Model of Figure 1, there are optional recoding operations in both the encoding and comparison stages. I have indicated the nature of the recoding in Stage 1 in the discussion of the Wason and Jones data. Here the explicit full

INFORMATION CONDITIONS

STAGE	TA	FA	TN	FN
1 ENCODE-RECODE	(A IS RED)	(A IS RED)	(FALSE (A IS RED)) ↑ (A IS BLUE)	(FALSE (A IS RED)) ↑ (A IS BLUE)
2 ENCODE	(A IS RED)	(A IS BLUE)	(A IS BLUE)	(A IS RED)
3 COMPARE	MATCH	MISMATCH	MATCH	MISMATCH
RECODE		(FALSE (A IS RED))		(FALSE (A IS BLUE))
4 RESPOND	"TRUE"	"FALSE"	"TRUE"	"FALSE"

FIG. 9. Mental operations and stages of the Optional Recoding Model (modified from Trabasso, 1970; Trabasso *et al.*, 1971).

negation is represented first as a false supposition of an affirmative assertion. This is transformed or recoded into an affirmative representation. The advantage of doing so is obvious since during Stage 3, one can match internal representations directly and avoid keeping one embedding string in memory. In Stage 2, pictures are also encoded affirmatively, as before. In Stage 3, comparisons are made between the internal representations from Stages 1 and 2. If a match occurs, the output in Stage 4 is "True." If a mismatch occurs, two things are possible, namely the subject recodes the sentence representation with a false supposition, or he changes the truth index and responds "False."

The recoding after a mismatch is like changing the truth index but suggests more than simply changing a response. We can illustrate what is meant here by a quotation from Bertrand Russell (1948, p. 39, cited by Miller & McNeil, 1969).

> "When I say truly, 'this is not blue,' there is on the subjective side, consideration of 'this is blue,' followed by rejection, while on the objective side there is some color differing from blue."

That is, if we asked for the subject to tell us what he was thinking as he went through the stages, he might say something very close to Russell's astute observation. If at the end of processing we asked him to explain his response, we might get something like the following:

For FA's: "I said 'false' since the circle was *not red*, it was blue." The "not red" corresponds to the (false (A is red)) representation in Figure 7. Likewise, for FN's the subject might say: "I said 'false' since the circle was *not* blue, it was red." If we had data such as these, the Optional Recoding Model would be favored over the Response Change Model.

There are two kinds of experiments we have thought of which bear on this issue. One is to simply ask subjects to explain their choice; the other is perhaps a stronger test since these operations happen so quickly. Suppose we had three inputs:

sentence–object–object. Suppose the description is "red," the first object is blue, and the second object is blue. A control condition is one where three objects are used: red, blue, and blue. The subject's task is to match pairs, inputs one and two; inputs two and three. Of critical interest is the last comparison. If subjects recode as we say they do, they should take longer to match the two blue objects when the verbal description "red" precedes than when the visual red object comes first. We have yet to test this conjecture but it indicates how one might begin to assess in more detail the linguistic and perceptual recoding that occurs or is assumed to occur by the model.

If we apply the same assumptions of stage independence, serial processing and real time, the Optional Recoding Model predicts the order to be TA faster than FA as before, but now TN is faster than FN. This key prediction is opposite to that for the Response Change Model.

Let us now examine the data which appear to favor the Optional Recoding Model. The first set of data come from experiments on explicit quantifier negation in our laboratory (Trabasso *et al.*, 1971). We had subjects first read descriptions with zero or one or two negations, e.g., one object is (is not) orange and the other is (is not) large, and then they had to verify the sentence against a picture of the objects. We separated the process into two stages: (1) storage, where the subject encoded the sentence, and (2) verification, where the subject encoded the picture,

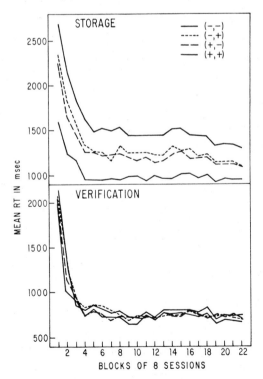

FIG. 10. RTs to store (Stage 1) and verify (Stages 2–4) statements with 0, 1 or 2 negations. Data from Trabasso *et al.*, Exp. II.

compared representations, and responded "True" or "False." If the subject recoded during Stage 1 (storage) then negations should have no effect on verification time. Figure 10 shows this to be the case for a highly practiced subject.

Since, in Figure 10, negations affected RTs in only Stage 1 and not in the remaining stages, these data favor the Optional Recoding Model. Secondly, the effect of negation on one stage and not the other supports the idea of stage independence (Sternberg, 1969).

Figure 10 is, however, atypical. Most subjects in these tasks do not complete their transformations before they ask to see the objects. However, their data uniformly show FN's to take longer than TN's and favor the Optional Recoding Strategy. Table 1 shows the storage (Stage 1) and verification (Stages 2, 3, and 4) results from four experiments in our laboratory (Trabasso et al., 1971). You will note that for the verification RTs, all four cases show the FN times to be longer. Furthermore, the nonsignificant interactions of truth and negation in Table 1 show that the effects of these variables were additive, as expected by the Optional Recoding Stage Model. Some other results are of interest here. Experiment VI was on a highly practiced single subject. Note that negation affected her storage (Stage 1) time but had no effect in verification (Stages 2, 3, 4). These data show no effects due to changes in the truth index. Experiments VII, VIII, and X are on groups of subjects who verified single adjective descriptions. All conditions show effects of negation in storage (Stage 1) and, more importantly, FN times to be longer. Finally, Experiment X examined response bias *per se* by asking subjects in the Agree condition whether the description "agreed" with the picture and in the Conflict condition whether it "conflicted." Thus, response (Yes or No) was crossed with truth (True or False). In these groups, there is an effect of Truth, despite the response differences. These data favor the idea that in the comparison stage, the subjects are set to match what is represented internally rather than set to respond True or False. If the latter were the case, Conflict subjects should have taken longer

TABLE 1

Mean RT (in sec.) to Process Truth and Form[a]

			Conditions		
Experiment	TA	FA	TN	FN	Truth S Form Interaction F
VI (Store)	.56	.56	.72	.71	< 1
(Verify)	.45	.44	.45	.46	1.48
VII (Store)	1.13	1.17	1.24	1.28	< 1
(Verify)	.91	1.00	1.14	1.24	< 1
VIII (Verify)	.65	.71	.77	.88	< 1
X (Agree)	.08	.09	.23	.25	< 1
(Conflict)	.09	.12	.14	.27	< 1

[a]Data from Trabasso, Rollins, and Shaughnessy, 1971.

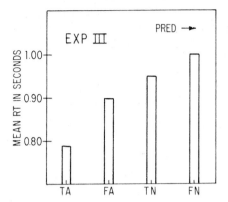

FIG. 11. Observed and predicted RTs for verifying sentences that come before the picture and whose transforms are known. Data from McMahon (1963).

since they would have one more response to cancel for each information condition. The idea that subjects seek identity matches is also supported in a recent study by Blake, Fox, and Lappin (1970) who found that matching pictures were responded to faster than when they mismatched and the overt response was the same (e.g., lifting one's finger).

As should be clear from Figure 9, the Optional Recoding Strategy can operate where the alternatives are certain and where the sentence precedes the picture. Again, if the subject recodes the sentence, then FN times are longest. This prediction is supported by the data of McMahon (1963, Exp. III) which are shown in Figure 11.

In discussing the data of Wason and Jones (Wason, 1961; Wason & Jones, 1963), I indicated that both models might operate since the recoding is an optional strategy and thus, subject controlled. Two experiments support this assertion. The first, by Slobin (1966) shows that adults (college students) invert explicit negations while children do not. Figure 12 shows Slobin's results.

Slobin's subjects first heard the sentence and then viewed the picture. All subjects were presumably treated alike so that differences in RTs for the four information conditions would indicate different processing strategies. Figure 12 shows this to be clearly the case. The data of the adult subjects conform to the Optional Recoding Model while that for the children is predicted by the Response Change Model. Thus, in Stage 1, adults process the sentence beyond the initial internal representation assumed by the Response Change Model; children do not. To show that this age difference in processing is consistent for all children, I have tabled Slobin's data by age groups in Table 2. Again you can see that for all age groups, 6, 8, 10, and 12, and independent of sentence type (Reversible or Non-Reversible subject-object), the children's data correspond to the expectations of the Response Change Model, i.e., the TN sentences take longer and the TN times are accurately predicted by the model. The adult data, however, show FN's to be longer and these times are predicted by the Optional Recoding Model.

The nature of the recoding strategies would have to differ for the Reversible (R) and Non-Reversible (NR) subject-object relations. For an R type, the negative inversion involves a rearrangement of subject and object as in (7a) and (7b),

(7)   a. (false (cat chase dog))
       b. (dog chase cat)

whereas for NR sentences, the verb is changed as in (8a) and (8b).

(8)   a. (false (girl is watering))
       b. (girl is standing still)

The longer RTs for R sentences could come about because of more operations in the encoding stage for the adults, i.e., interchanging of subject-object versus inverting the verb. Note that there are no consistent differences for the children on R and NR sentences, a result supporting this interpretation. The reasons why adults recode probably has to do with their knowledge of what the alternatives are as well as the binary logic underlying inversions.

Strong evidence that recoding is a subject control process comes from a study by Young and Chase (cited by Chase & Clark, 1972). Young and Chase instructed their subjects to convert negative sentences in one of two ways: by changing the preposition, as in (9a) and (9b),

(9)   a. (false (A above B))
       b. (A below B)

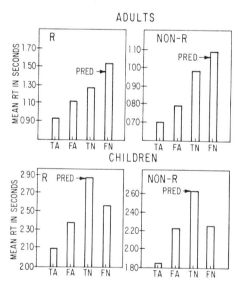

FIG. 12. Observed and predicted RTs to affirmative and negative sentences which came before the picture. The predicted values for children are by the Response Change Model and for adults by the Optional Recoding Model. The sentences had Reversible (R) or Non-Reversible (NR) subject-object relations. Data from Slobin (1966).

TABLE 2

Mean RTs (in sec.) for Children and Adults to Verify Sentences
(Data from Slobin, 1966)[a]

| Type | Age | Conditions | | | |
		TA	FA	TN	FN
R	6	2.96	3.21	3.74(3.85)	3.60
	8	2.17	2.61	3.15(3.23)	2.79
	10	1.71	1.98	2.30(2.30)	2.03
	12	1.58	1.70	2.28(1.98)	1.86
	Adult	.93	1.12	1.27	1.54(1.46)
NR	6	2.59	3.23	3.82(3.80)	3.06
	8	1.78	2.19	2.54(2.83)	2.43
	10	1.65	1.88	2.06(2.09)	1.86
	12	1.39	1.63	2.10(1.89)	1.65
	Adult	.70	.79	.98	1.09(1.07)

[a]Additive predictions are in parentheses.

and by changing the subject as in (10a) and (10b),

(10) a. (false (A above B))
      b. (B above A)

Given a negation, either recoding is possible, and the question was whether subjects did these transformations. If subjects do recode, then FN sentences should take longer than TN sentences. Figure 13 shows the data for Young and Chase.

One can see that in Figure 13, the recoding model fits the data remarkably well for all four conditions studied. The fact that subjects were able to do the appropriate inversions is indicated by the interaction of the Above and Below results and the TN and FN conditions under each instruction. (Earlier, in Figure 1, Chase and Clark had found Below to be harder to process than Above. This is because the subjects tend to encode the pictures as (star above cross), necessitating a mismatch with Below sentences.) If subjects invert the preposition, then Above (A) becomes harder than Below (B). This is shown in the upper figure. If they invert subjects, then Above (A) is easier than Below (B). This is shown in the lower figure. In this way, one can thus assess a source of difficulty in comprehension as well as showing that certain recoding operations are under the control of the subject.

This concludes my comparison of the stage models. It is clear that either processing strategy may operate. The experiments indicate that recoding occurs when the person knows the alternative form and hears the sentence prior to seeing the referent. If the alternatives are other than binary, and if the sentence occurs either simultaneously or after the referential event, then no further processing is done beyond representing the negative sentence as an embedded affirmative sentence with a negative embedding clause. What recoding that takes place after a mismatch is an open question. However, the logic of the match–mismatch comparison process and decision rule for responding suggests that some kind of new internal representations are made during the third, comparison stage.

We can think of a representation not only as paraphrased by Clark (1970) [as in sentence (5d); It is false to suppose that the ball is red] but as a conditional decision rule in the sense of Hunt, Marin, and Stone (1966). That is, prior to encoding the referential event, the person formulates a rule something like (11a).

(11)   a.   If (ball is red) is true (that is, the picture is encoded as (ball is red)), then respond "True"; respond "False" otherwise.

The rule in (11a) expresses a response rule equivalent to Clark's paraphrase of the representation in (5c). Our subjects frequently report such decision rules. Glucksberg (personal communication) has protocol data on a single subject who adopted the decision rule in (12b) for the TN sentence in (12b).

(12)   a.   The girl is not hitting the boy.
       b.   If (girl hit boy) in picture, respond "False."

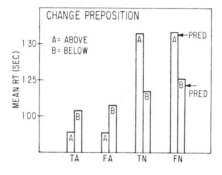

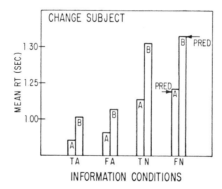

FIG. 13. Observed and predicted RTs where subjects were instructed to recode the preposition or subject of sentences (Star above (A) or below (B) cross) prior to verification. Data from Young and Chase, cited by Chase and Clark, 1972.

This rule gives the same results as the Response Change Model and suggests that the internal representation is not just a supposition on the part of the listener but a decision rule on how to behave.

The point of this discussion is that although the models have been successful in identifying at least two independent stages of processing, encoding and comparison, much work needs to be done on identifying the nature of the encodings. My discussion on recoding options also indicates the need for further linguistic analysis of where these might occur. These problems of form of encoding and which process model operates for various cases would appear to cast some doubt on the usefulness of Clark's (1970) comparative study of negation using component RTs. If different processes are involved, some requiring more stages than others, then estimating component times with one model would give misleading estimates.

To What Extent Does the Encoding Affect Processing?

In the second half of this paper, I would like to examine the above question. Here we are asking, in effect, that if we know the form of the subject's initial encoding, can we determine the way in which the information in the internal representation is processed? For example, if we know that a person has encoded the event of a boy hitting a girl as (boy hits girl), how does the subject—verb—object order of encoding affect his processing during the comparison stage? Other questions arise. Are the constituent members of the internal representation processed in the order in which they are encoded or are they checked all at once? Is the comparison process stopped after the first mismatch is found or are all comparisons made? These questions will be recognized by those who are familiar with visual or memory search and perception as issues of serial versus parallel processing and self-terminating or exhaustive search, respectively (Egeth, 1966). They are of some importance to the use of the model in estimating component RTs since different estimates arise for the different kinds of processing.

Classification and Encoding Order. In collaboration with Phil Gough some years ago (in 1963–64) I carried out a series of unpublished experiments on concept learning and internal representation which I would like to report here since they now have some new theoretical relevance not fully recognized then.

In one kind of concept learning experiment, called the reception paradigm, the subject is first shown an instance of a concept (typically, a picture). Then he is asked to classify the picture into one of two categories according to some rule. After he makes his classification, he is told the correct category. Then he is shown another instance to be classified. If you think of the inductive reasoning process as beginning with evidence (an instance) which leads to a hypothesis (a rule for classification) which is then tested against new evidence (another instance), you can see how this concept learning task is an analogue of inductive reasoning.

Gough and I reasoned that the subject would encode the instances in some form which would then influence the order in which he would consider attributes for testing. Suppose we use as instances the eight pictures that result from combining (boy or girl) as subject with (hit or kick) as verb with (boy or girl) as object. We could then choose to make the sex of the subject, or of the object, or the verb form, the basis for classification. That is, if the picture contained a boy as the subject, its classification would always be in category A; if a girl was doing the action, then it is always in category B. In this case, it would not make any difference what was the action or who was the object. In the terminology of those who study such problems, we would say that the sex of subject is the *relevant* feature while the verb and object are irrelevant. If the encoding is as in (13),

(13)   (boy hit girl)

that is (subject-verb-object), and if the person considers each constituent in turn as a series of hypotheses (e.g., boy—A, girl—B; hit—A, kick—B; boy—A, girl—B), then the rate at which these concepts are identified should correspond to the same order.

How are Pictures Encoded? In our first experiment, Gough and I wished to obtain some preliminary data on how the subjects would represent the instances used in the concept learning experiment. We used the 16 slides Gough had used in his sentence verification studies (Gough, 1965, 1966). (There are 16 slides since the position of the actor is varied.)

To a group of 70 introductory psychology students at the University of California, Los Angeles, we showed the slides and asked the students to write a sentence for each slide. We showed the slides for 30 seconds each, in a random order. After the subjects were through describing the slides, we instructed them to imagine that they were in an experiment where if they were asked to learn a rule to classify the slides into two categories, A and B, what rule they would use to classify a particular instance? We then showed them one classified slide and had them write down as many "hunches" (rules for classifying) as possible, in their order of importance.

Sixty subjects wrote sentence descriptions; the other ten gave the characters in the slide utterances, etc. The descriptions were predominantly in the active voice. Of the 960 descriptions, 90% were active, 4.2% were passive, and the remainder were not classified as either (e.g., "there are two boys fighting"). Thus subjects preferred the (subject-verb-object) form of description assumed by the encoding-comparing models during the encoding of pictures.

The hypotheses offered as possible rules for categorizing showed that for the 60 subjects, the probability of at least one hypothesis relating to the actor in the slide was a .70; to the object, the probability was .33. Thus we found a strong correlation between the encoding order and likelihood of consideration of the constituent as a hypothesis for classification.

Encoding Order and Classification Learning. We then performed a concept learning experiment that was concerned with two questions: (1) Would the actor (sex of the subject) be learned more quickly than the victim (sex of the object) when each were respectively relevant? and (2) Could we influence the rate of learning of the actor-victim concepts by encoding the pictures for the subject prior to classification learning?

There were 300 introductory psychology students from UCLA in this experiment. They were run in groups of 15 subjects each. These subgroups were necessary to counterbalance all the experimental variables. Half of the subjects learned a problem with the actor (logical subject) relevant; the other half learned with the

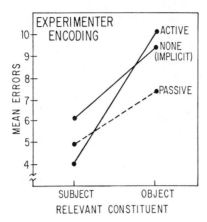

FIG. 14. Mean number of errors in 32 trials of concept identification where the experimenter encodes the pictures prior to training.

victim (logical object) relevant. There were three encoding conditions. In one, called None (or Implicit) the students learned to classify the slides without any prior familiarization of the slides. In a second, called the Active condition, the experimenter first described each of the 16 slides in the active voice. For example, "In this slide, a girl is kicking a boy." In a third, Passive condition, the experimenter again described each of the 16 slides but used the passive voice. For example, "In this slide a boy is being kicked by a girl." So there were three kinds of encodings: subject, experimenter-active and experimenter-passive. Then, the subjects learned to classify the slides. The experimenter announced a slide number, showed the slide, gave the subjects 10 seconds to write the classification of the slide, and then gave them the correct classification. After 5 seconds, he announced the next slide and a new trial began. All subjects had 32 trials.

The main results are shown in Figure 14. In Figure 14 are shown the mean number of errors made in 32 trials by each of the six subgroups. It can be seen that the subject of the sentence is learned faster than the object, regardless of the encoding condition. This result is clearly in line with the idea that the subject prefers the (s-v-o) encoding and considers the constituents, in turn, when deriving hypotheses for classification rules. The experimenter encoding had the main effect of reducing errors overall, probably by drawing the subjects attention, and hence restricting the content of their internal representations only to the (s-v-o) characteristics. Encoding in the Active voice enhanced the subject-object differences; encoding in the passive voice reduced these differences but did not make the object easier to learn than the subject. Despite our efforts, it is apparent that the students preferred the active (s-v-o) representation.

In a third experiment, we asked what the order of learning would be if we used sentences rather than pictures as instances? Since the active sentence is the preferred representation, this question asks whether or not passive sentences would be transformed prior to consideration of the constituent members for classification.

Sentences and Classification Learning. In the third experiment, 240 introductory psychology students at UCLA were run in eight different groups of 60 subjects each. Half of them learned concepts with the sex of subject of the sentence as the relevant feature; the other half had the sex of the object as the relevant feature. We varied the modality in which the sentences were presented: half of the subjects heard the sentences via a tape recorder (Auditory) and the other half saw them projected on slides (Visual). Finally, half of the subjects were given sentences in the Active voice and the other half had sentences in the Passive voice. The orthogonal combinations of which constituent was relevant (Subject or Object), the modality in which sentences were presented (Auditory or Visual) and the syntactical form which the sentence had (Active or Passive) resulted in eight different groups. The procedure was identical to that used in the second, concept identification experiment.

Figure 15 shows the data of main interest, namely, the mean number of errors in learning the concepts.

In comparison with the second experiment, here the surface structure of the sentences influenced the order of learning concepts based upon the constituents more than when pictures were used.

In Figure 15, one can see clearly the interaction between the surface structure and learning rate: the subject concepts are identified more readily (fewer errors) when the active voice is used but the object concepts are learned almost as readily

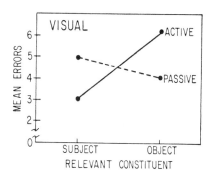

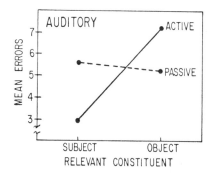

FIG. 15. Mean number of errors in 32 trials of concept identification where active or passive sentences serve as instances.

when the passive form is used. To some large degree, these results are very much like those obtained by Wright (1969) in her active-passive sentence and question study.

One might conclude that no recoding took place prior to classification, i.e., the subjects processed the characteristics of the constituents in the surface order. Two facts argue against this conclusion. Within the Passive condition, the subject was identified nearly as fast as the object, particularly when the sentences were heard. Second, the object is still learned more slowly than the subject even though both occur first in the surface structure. These data support the assumption that listeners recode or transform passives prior to searching the internal representation for a basis of classifying events.

In overview, these experiments on concept learning are consistent with the hypothesis that the listener prefers the (s-v-o) internal representation and that this is also the order of comparison or testing of the constituent members.

Our first experiment showed that the dominant description of events was in the active voice (i.e., the order of encoding corresponded to the order in which the events happen). The second experiment showed that the subject of the action was identified more readily than the subject of the action in a classification task. This was true, regardless of whether the subjects encoded the pictures or whether the experimenter encoded the pictures in either voice. However, experimenter encoding helped identification and passive encoding facilitated identification of the object. These results are also consistent with prior findings on preferred representation (Clark & Begun, 1968; Bever, 1970) and the function of the passive in directing attention to the object (Johnson-Laird, 1968). Finally, when we used sentences rather than pictures, surface order effects were more marked on subject-object identification, i.e., surface order interacted with which constituent was relevant. However, the subject was still identified more rapidly, suggesting that the passive sentences were recoded, especially when they were heard rather than read.

In conclusion, I have tried to describe a general encoding-comparing model for sentence comprehension. The model takes on two specific forms—one for recoding or transforming where such transforms are possible, and the other which does not transform but changes a "truth" index as contradictions are detected. Both models describe a considerable range of data from experiments on sentence verification, negation, memory search, and problem solving. The processing which depends upon the encoding and comparison stages was examined in experiments on concept learning. These experiments suggest that the order of encoding is related to the order of comparison or testing. The order appears to be serial and left-to-right within the internal representation. A question for future research is whether information is processed from the embedded representation outward through the outer embeddings. The success of the Response Change Model indicates that this is a real possibility. It is in this sense that "deep" structure may have a psychological reality in our comprehension of language.

CONFERENCE DISCUSSION

Frederiksen inquired whether the example Trabasso gave early in his paper in illustration of the verification process model, namely "7 is an odd number," was meant to implicate a class-inclusion type of evaluation to get at the truth or falsity of such statements. Trabasso said he was not necessarily ruling out such additional semantic analyses of the sentences, but that such approaches as class-inclusion concepts represented a more detailed analysis of each step in the comparison process than he was willing to make at the present time.

Bever inquired whether Trabasso's models were different from McMahon's (1963). Trabasso said that McMahon's approach was never quite as explicit as these current models; he also indicated that he was more indebted to Wason (1961) than to McMahon for his models. He stressed that the main virtue of what he (Trabasso) has proposed is that the main steps and their sequencing in the verification process are clearly stated so as to yield quantitative assessment.

Scriven raised the possibility that what may be compared in the Trabasso models may not necessarily be the linguistic representation of the percepts but rather the percepts themselves. For example, he said, this might be the case when names are not readily assigned to the pictured objects. Another question he raised was whether the subject, when he does use linguistic representation, formulates perhaps *two* linguistically equivalent (or semantically equivalent) expressions. For example, when only a red or blue object can occur and, say, the red one occurs, why wouldn't the subject keep in mind two linguistic representations of this, namely, "Not blue" as well as "Red"? Trabasso answered the second part of Scriven's inquiry by indicating that some of his subjects reported that they did generate both linguistic alternatives. To test that possibility more thoroughly, however, requires an alternative model of recoding; he indicated that an experiment is currently in progress to do this.

Bever raised some problems about the form of the process models. He suggested that for reasons of clarity, one should add an outer string to represent more explicitly the subject's presupposition that, for example, "A is red" should be represented "True, A is red." Also one should add the codicil that in the comparison process subjects do not explicitly process this outer string when it has the form "true" in both linguistic representations but *will* process it when *one or both* of the linguistic cognitive representations of the picture and sentence have "false" in the outer string. Trabasso agreed that it may be advisable to avoid ambiguities in the model by making these additions.

General discussion concerned the possible artificiality of these operations since the particular operations seemed to be induced by the nature of the experiment with its many trials and restricted set of stimulus combinations and (restricted set) of response options. Trabasso agreed that this was a difficulty, but pointed out that if one accepts this line of argument, one would necessarily have to doubt the usefulness of a great many other psychological studies. He also indicated that in spite of the fact that these experiments have a certain artificial aura surrounding them, nevertheless one would like to explain the consistencies found to hold among them and this was the purpose of devising the explicit processing models.

REFERENCES

Bever, T.G. The cognitive basis for linguistic structures. In J. R. Hayes (Ed.), *Cognition and the development of language.* New York: Wiley, 1970.

Blake, R. R., Fox, R., & Lappin, J. R. Invariance in the reaction time classification of same and different letter pairs. *Journal of Experimental Psychology,* 1970, **85,** 133–137.

Chase, W. G., & Clark, H. H. Mental operations in the comparison of sentences and pictures. In L. Gregg (Ed.), *Cognition in learning and memory.* New York: Wiley, 1972.

Clark, H. H. How we understand negation. Paper presented at Workshop on Cognitive Organization and Psychological Processes, University of California, Irvine, August 1970.

Clark, H. H., & Begun, J. S. The use of syntax in understanding sentences. *British Journal of Psychology,* 1968, **59,** 219–229.

Collins, A. M., & Quillian, M. R. Retrieval time from semantic memory. *Journal of Verbal Learning and Verbal Behavior*, 1969, 8, 240–247.

Egeth, H. E. Parallel versus serial processes in multidimensional stimulus discrimination. *Perception and Psychophysics*, 1966, 1, 245–252.

Fillenbaum, S. Memory for gist: Some relevant variables, *Language & Speech*, 1966, 9, 217–227.

Fodor, J. A., & Garrett, M. Some reflections on competence and performance. In J. Lyons and R. J. Wales (Eds.), *Psycholinguistic papers: The proceedings of the 1966 Edinburgh conference*. Edinburgh: Edinburgh University Press, 1966.

Gough, P. B. Grammatical transformations and speed of understanding. *Journal of Verbal Learning and Verbal Behavior*, 1965, 4, 107–112.

Gough P. B. The verification of sentences: the effects of delay of evidence and sentence length. *Journal of Verbal Learning and Verbal Behavior*, 1966, 5, 429–496.

Greene, J. M. The relation between syntax and semantics in the psychological study of grammar. Unpublished doctoral dissertation, University College London, 1968.

Hunt, E., Marin, J., & Stone, P. *Experiments in induction*. New York: Academic Press, 1966.

Johnson-Laird, P.N. The choice of the passive voice in a communicative task. *British Journal of Psychology*, 1968, 59, 7–15.

McMahon, L. E. Grammatical analysis as part of understanding a sentence. Unpublished doctoral dissertation, Harvard University, 1963.

Miller, G. A., & McNeil, D. Psycholinguistics. In G. Lindzey and E. Aronson, (Eds.), *The handbook of social psychology*. Vol. III. Reading: Addison-Wesley, 1969.

Paivio, A. Mental imagery in associative learning and memory. *Psychological Review*, 1969, 76, 241–263.

Russell, B. *Human knowledge: Its scope and limits*. London: Allen and Unwin, 1948.

Slobin, D. I. Grammatical transformations and sentence comprehension in childhood and adults. *Journal of Verbal Learning and Verbal Behavior*, 1966, 5, 219–27.

Sternberg, S. Memory-scanning: Mental processes revealed by reaction-time experiments. *American Scientist*, 1969, 57, 421–57.

Trabasso, T. Reasoning and the processing of negative information. Invited Address, Division 3, 78th Annual Convention, American Psychological Association, Miami Beach, September, 1970.

Trabasso, T., Rollins, H., & Shaughnessy, E. Storage and verification stages in processing concepts. *Cognitive Psychology*, 1971, 2, 239–289.

Wales, R. J., & Grieve, R. What is so difficult about negation? *Perception and Psychophysics*, 1969, 6, 327–332.

Wason, P. C. The processing of positive and negative information. *Quarterly Journal of Experimental Psychology*, 1959, 11, 92–107.

Wason, P. C. Response to affirmative and negative binary statements. *British Journal of Psychology*, 1961, 52, 133–142.

Wason, P. C., & Jones, S. Negatives: denotation and connotation. *British Journal of Psychology*, 1963, 54, 299–307.

Wright, P. Transformations and the understanding of sentences. *Language and Speech*, 1969, 12, 156–166.

7
LANGUAGE USE FOR COMMUNICATING, INSTRUCTING, AND THINKING[1]

David R. Olson
The Ontario Institute for
Studies in Education

In this paper, a rough characterization of two quite different uses of language will be made; for convenience they may be described as "sentences as descriptions" and "sentences as propositions." I will try to show that the former is developmentally prior and that it underlies the ordinary use of language for communicating and instructing. The second is developmentally late and it underlies such verbal activities as justifying (Reichenbach, 1938) and propositional thinking (Tarski, 1969). It is primarily this second use of language that gives language its formal properties, including its base grammatical structure and its formalized lexicon.

SENTENCES AS DESCRIPTIONS: MAPPING SENTENCES ONTO PERCEPTION

In an earlier paper I discussed some aspects of the way in which sentences map onto perceptual contexts (Olson, 1970). For example, in a communication context, a speaker chooses words and expands his utterance to the point that is required to differentiate an object or event from the set of perceived or inferred alternatives. Thus, in the context of a black block, a large white block will be described as "The white one," while in the context of a small white block, the same block will be described as "The large one." By looking at sentences in this way it became apparent that several problems about the referential basis of meaning could be resolved. Two may be mentioned—it showed that a theory of reference could not be excluded as a theory of meaning simply because something was left over after

[1] The research reported in this paper is part of a project "The instructional potential of language and other media" supported by the Research and Development Review Board of the Ontario Institute for Studies in Education. I am greatly indebted to Angela Hildyard and Carolyn Dundas for their assistance in the preparation of this manuscript.

reference was accounted for. In Frege's (1892) example, the Morning Star and the Evening Star have the same referent, the planet Venus, yet they do not have the same meaning, therefore an account of reference is not an account of meaning. This argument has been repeated and expanded by Quine (1953) and Miller (1965). If the referential basis of meaning is approached, not as labelling, as the previous theories imply, but as specifying a referent relative to a set of alternatives, then one may explain "What is left over" simply by pointing out that the Morning Star and Evening Star differ only in the excluded alternatives; the meaning of a word is determined by what is partitioned in each case. Alternatively, the meaning of a word may be considered as that feature or set of features which permits that partitioning. Semantic features are, presumably, the substantives inferred from the effect or "use" in partitioning alternatives, only some of these features are explicitly marked in a language.

A second problem, the nature of ostensive definitions, could be modified from saying that "in some cases the meaning of a word is provided by pointing to an object" (Wittgenstein, 1958) to saying that in some cases the meaning of a word is provided by indicating an object relative to some context of alternatives.

There are a number of important ways in which language maps on to the perceptual world, many of which are relevant to instruction. The first, related to the problem of ostensive definitions, concerns the ways in which perceived events are tied into the meaning of a sentence and its ease of comprehension. In some way, the sentence "A zebra is a striped, horse-like animal" is equivalent to pointing to a zebra (in the appropriate context of alternatives) and saying, "That is a zebra." Notice that in this latter case, a perceptual feature, "striped," comes to be part of the meaning of "zebra" just as much as the named feature, "striped," did in the first case. That is, semantic features are sometimes and perhaps always perceptual features (or bundles of such features). Generalizing from this case, we may suggest that semantic features are perceptual features that have been selected for the purpose of guiding semantic decisions. That is, they are a subset of perceptual features.

A second implication is that the meaning of a word is provided or taught by making unambiguous what is partitioned by a word or utterance. If a learner does not "see" what alternatives are being partitioned by a word, he doesn't know the meaning. As most words in any language differentiate large sets of alternatives, that is, possess many semantic features, the meaning of a word is provided originally by means of large numbers of such contrasting cases. This technique is most explicit in Harlow's (1949) learning set experiment in which some event is differentiated from increasingly large sets of alternatives until only the critical features are attended. A second means is the use of cleverly arranged visual depictions. Thus Richards (1968) has shown how a series of pronouns and adjectives can be differentiated through visual depictions (see Figure 1). This illustrates an important relation between perception and language to which we shall return. A more frequent alternative for ordinary language learning utilizes an extended memory system in which these critical partitionings or features are recalled through cuing with the word. Thus, when an adult says to a child, "cat," he is not labelling a concrete event; rather, the word *cat* serves as a retrieval cue for those previous occasions on which

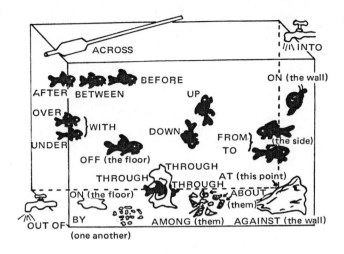

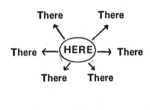

FIG. 1. Pictorial representations of lexical items (adapted from I. A. Richards, 1968, pp. 75, 96).

cat was differentiated from some other alternative. On one occasion, for example, a cat may be differentiated from a doll in the context of a sentence *cat*; on another occasion a cat may be differentiated from a dog. The meaning of *cat* is thus the sum of the features that have been used for these various differentiations at different points in time. Language therefore is a means of telescoping experience; another way to say this is that language drags a context with it that forms the frame of reference for subsequent experience. This is apparently what Bruner (1966) had in mind when he indicated that words are invitations to form concepts.

Several implications follow from the view that the meaning of a word is its use in partitioning sets of alternatives. One may be mentioned. Children who fail Piaget's conservation task apparently fail to see what an adult partitions by the words "same quantity"—not knowing, they seize on the most salient perceptual feature, that of relative height. Thus, in Halford's (1970) recent experiment, when "same quantity" has been taught to the child as a term or event to contrast with "either added to or subtracted from," young children learn to conserve. Similarly in Gelman's (1969) study, young children were taught quantitative concepts, "same number," "same length," by differentiating them from "different number," "different length" by means of a learning set technique. By means of large numbers of partitionings, the children came to attend to the features critical for the partitioning involved in the adult's use of "same." Even more impressive was the fact that after such perceptual training and without E's suggestion, children gave such explanations for their judgments as "you haven't taken any away."

The first problem then in language learning is for the child to arrive at a knowledge of what adults partition by the use of a word, that is, what features are relevant to that differentiation. Minimally, higher order partitioning involving higher order invariants (Gibson, 1970) requires more of such differentiation to arrive at the critical feature list than do lower order partitionings.

Once acquired, language is a highly effective means of communication and instruction. It has striking advantages over immediate perception and such media as representational drawing in that it is, at least for ordinary purposes, less ambiguous. Thus, for example, a picture of a cat is ambiguous between the readings or codings "cat" and "animal" and "Felix" whereas the word or utterance is not. Similarly, Figure 2 is ambiguous between the codings "The car is hitting the truck" and "The truck is hit by the car." The corresponding sentences do not have that degree of ambiguity, a fact to which we shall return in the consideration of the comprehension of passive sentences. Further, in my earlier discussion of meaning I argued that this uncertainty in pictures may account for some of the experimentally found differences between learning from words and from pictures. Note, too, that this

FIG. 2. Sample picture used in verifying active and passive sentences
(Olson & Filby, 1972).

difference occurs only in communication and instruction contexts where there is an asymmetry in the information possessed by the speaker and listener. That is, to the artist, the drawing is not ambiguous. It is the listener who benefits from the non-ambiguity of words relative to some other media. This speaker-listener asymmetry, coupled with the fact that language obviously influences the learner, may explain the popular assumption that language influences thinking.

Some of the ways in which language depends on perceptual information have been indicated but it may be worth making this relation more general and more explicit. Language is a social or shared system for marking or differentiating objects and events. Perceptual events which are private are not easily, perhaps never, marked in the language—it is impossible to indicate to the listener what perceptual events are being partitioned by the utterance. Perhaps that is why it is very difficult to discuss psychological issues or communicate about them. Further, such objects or events are differentiated only to the level of usual utility (Brown, 1958). That is, descriptions are elaborated only to the level required to make oneself clear to some listener. If the listener doesn't "know" what you are talking about you have limited linguistic resources to make yourself known. McLuhan (1964, p. 146) has an appropriate remark: "All the words in the world cannot describe an object like a bucket, although it is possible to tell in a few words how to make a bucket. This [is an] inadequacy of words to convey visual information." Not only is language highly dependent upon shared knowledge of the symbol system and upon common experience that can serve as the ground of comprehension, but in some fields of study it is highly dependent upon the structure of information provided by other media. Ivins (1953) has shown how the development of botany was dependent upon the invention of repeatable prints; copies of drawings quickly lost the distinguishing features of the plants. Ivins further shows how inadequate language is to replace a concrete visual image. It is simply impossible, for example, for an illustrator to make a drawing of such a creature as a barnacle from correct and elaborate verbal descriptions. Richards (1968), too, has shown how inadequate prepositions such as "in" or "out" are relative to a photograph or drawing. His example is shown in Figure 3. The roughness of the fit of the sentence to the picture can be seen by imaging the wide range of pictures that could be drawn and still be compatible with the description. Language can partition and reorganize only the information that one has

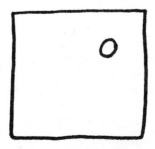

FIG. 3. The circle is inside the square (adapted from I. A. Richards, 1968).

available from other sources and then only to a limited degree of precision. This lack of precision is the price to be paid for the high degree of selectivity or "abstraction" that gives language the advantages indicated earlier.

The manner in which words and sentences derive their meaning from perception and the ways in which perceived context determines both the production and comprehension of utterances are aspects of the primary use of language for communication and instruction, a use which may be characterized as "sentences as descriptions," the enterprise of mapping sentences on to reality. I now believe there is another quite different and developmentally later use of language and that may be characterized as "sentences as propositions," the enterprise of mapping sentences on to other sentences. But that is to get ahead of the story.

Consider now the development of this language system, that is, the manner in which the child comes to map his sentences on to his perceptions of situations. An example and a generalization. A 4-year-old recently said "My hot boiling water is cold"—surely a formally anomalous sentence—however, in the context of a hot-water bottle in hand, the meaning was clear. The generalization is from Grace de Laguna (1927): "Just because the terms of the child's language are in themselves so indefinite, it is left to the particular context to determine the specific meaning for each occasion. In order to understand what the baby is saying, you must see what the baby is doing" (pp. 90—91).

De Laguna's point was that this perceptual or contextual dependency of speech decreases with age. While it appears to do so in our culture, there is considerable evidence that in nonindustrialized cultures, speech remains in context (Bruner, 1966; Mundy-Castle, 1967), and hence, formally, somewhat anomalous. Even ordinary language in our culture may retain this informality. Weinreich (1963, p. 150) points out that: "The unspecialized, laymen's sectors of language simply do not have the depth of structure of scientific zoological or botanical taxonomy."

Some recent evidence collected in collaboration with William Ford and B. Randhawa bears more specifically on intellectual limits and contextual determinants of children's speech.

Ford (1971) presented to 4- and 7-year-old children a gold star which was then hidden under a wooden block. The first child who saw where the star was hidden was then asked to tell a second child where to look for the block. For several of the problems the star was hidden under the same object; all that differed was the context of alternatives. Problems differed both in terms of which adjective was critical and in the number of critical adjectives (bits) required. The critical block and the context of alternatives for three of these problems are shown in Figure 4.

We had expected that the child's utterance would reflect the contrasting alternative and it does, but to an unimpressive degree. When different children are given the tasks at each level of complexity, 4-year-olds in the one-bit tasks (tasks requiring only one adjective, but a different one each time) did in fact put the critical adjective first in their description (p. < .05). Further, children in the 3-bit task (description requiring three adjectives, e.g., "The gold star is under the small, black, round one.") gave somewhat longer descriptions than the children in the one-bit condition. The fragility of this effect is shown by the fact that when the one, two, and three bit tasks were mixed together for a fourth group of children, both the

	Event	Alternative	Utterance
Case 1	o	●	. . . the white one
Case 2	o	□	. . . the round one
Case 3	o	□ ● ■	. . . the round, white one
Case 4	o		. . . (look under) the round, white, wooden block that is about one inch across . . .

FIG. 4. Contrast sets (from Olson, D. R., 1970).

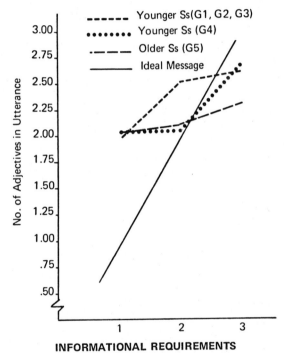

FIG. 5. Length of children's utterances as a function of the information requirement of the task (Ford, 1971).

differential length of the messages disappears and the tendency to put the critical, informative adjective first disappears. These data are shown in Figure 5.

What is going on here is more clearly shown in Ford's second experiment. In this experiment, sets of stimuli differing on five binary features: color, size, shape, lined, and starred were employed. As in Experiment 1, the number of alternatives presented to the child varied from two—one adjective would serve to differentiate them—to eight alternatives—five adjectives were required to differentiate them. The one to five feature tasks were presented in random order to 4- and 7-year-old children. Data on the total number of adjectives in their descriptions and the informativeness of these descriptions are presented in Figure 6. For both 4- and 7-year-olds, the descriptions are just as long for messages requiring one adjective as for those requiring five adjectives. Notice too that they hit on the critical ones only part of the time—some features were consistently overlooked and some were consistently given regardless of their informative value. Note also the fact that the 4-year-olds' messages tend to level off at about two adjectives (two bits of information) while 7-year-olds' tend to level off at about three bits of information. These ceilings on the amount of information that children can put into their descriptions is corroborated by a separate experiment conducted by Randhawa (in press) in which either visually presented or verbally described objects differing on any one or more of eight binary features were presented to 5-, 8-, and 12-year-old *S*s who were to either select the object out of a display or describe the object seen. Their descriptions were limited in much the same way as Ford's *S*s were. Randhawa's analogous data for 5-, 8-, and 12-year-old *S*s asked to describe a visually presented object are shown in Figure 7. Note that these data correspond to those for the small circles (critical adjectives) in Ford's experiment. As may be seen from this figure, 5-year-old *S*s' descriptions levelled off at a little over two bits (two adjectives), 8-year-olds at about five bits, and 12-year-olds appear to be levelling off at about seven bits of information.

Even more interesting than the limitations on the length of young children's descriptions was the fact that Ford's 4-year-olds structured the information in their utterances quite differently than did the 7-year-olds. Children's descriptions were classified into the categories of lists of adjectives, "big, white, round"; sentences,

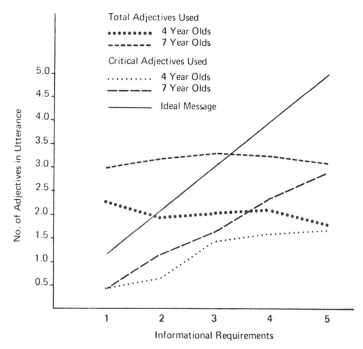

FIG. 6. Number of adjectives given relative to the number of critical adjectives required.

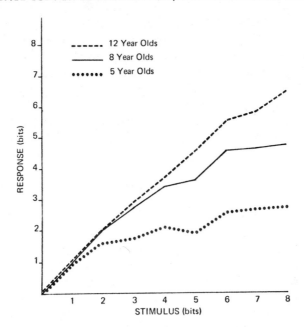

FIG. 7. The amount of information in children's description
of an event (Randhawa, 1969).

"It's the big, round one"; conjunctive constructions, "It's big *and* it's round *and* white"; and complex descriptions, "The big one, it's white . . . " While the older Ss tended to use more conjunctive constructions and younger Ss more lists, the interesting finding occurred when utterances were cross-classified in terms of their obeying or violating adjective ordering rules in English (Martin, 1969). In English, adjectives are always ordered "The large black circle" and never "The black large circle," for example. While both older and younger Ss violated this expected ordering in about 50% of their utterances, young children simply violated the order rules while the older Ss, when forced to violate the ordering, inserted the conjunction "and" between the disordered adjectives, thereby preserving those grammatical rules. Thus, the use of conjunctive clauses appears to serve a double function of providing a pause for the Ss' further processing of the critical features and a means of permissibly altering the ordering of adjectives in the utterance.

As to the relation between perception and language it is clear that for both age groups the selection of adjectives is strongly determined by the perceptual features that are salient. When it comes to a conflict between what is perceptually salient and what is informative to the listener, the perceptual saliency is dominant (Glucksberg & Krauss, 1967).

However, the sentences children use are not tied to the immediately perceived cues. The sentences for subjects in both age groups quickly come to reflect the alternatives *in the context as a whole*, up to the maximum the child is able to process. Thus the description of an object is determined not by the immediate context but by the range of alternatives to the object in the total context. This would seem to be the explanation of the observation that utterance length was constant over the whole set of experimental tasks. This, then, is evidence for the assertion I made earlier, namely, that descriptions are cumulative. The use of any word quickly comes to reflect not just the immediately present context of alternatives, but the cumulative range of alternatives from which the event is being differentiated. As Grace de Laguna (1927) stated it, "the evolution of language [is] characterized by a progressive freeing of speech from its dependence on the perceived conditions under which it is uttered and heard, and from the behavior which accompanies it." However, it is not *free* from the perceived context; it comes to reflect a wider and wider context; the context is now the present plus the historical context, not just the immediate one.

The processes of mapping sentences on to perceptions is thus complicated by at least two factors. Since perceptual processes occur in the service of many performatory activities other than speaking (Olson, 1970), the perceptual world comes to be much more differentiated than the linguistic world would indicate. This is further complicated by the fact that because sentences come to reflect the accumulated context, a minimum number of sentences come to be mapped on to a maximum number of perceived contexts. Situations change more so than do sentences. The sentence elaboration that does occur will depend on the speaker's intention, the listener-speaker shared knowledge of the symbolic system, the assumptions the speaker makes about the listener's background knowledge, and the differentiations the culture has found to be important.

Given this general characterization of the relation between perception and language it is possible to make some more analytic statements about the ways in which sentences are comprehended in various contexts. Five preliminary hypotheses may be specified:

1. A sentence is comprehended (or miscomprehended) relative to a context. This context is specified either by a perceptual situation or by preceding sentences. These contextual events may be considered as the presuppositions of an utterance in that they determine the form of utterance that will be permissible.

2. Sentences compatible with their contexts, that is, sentences which do not violate their presuppositions, are more easily processed than those that are not.

3. Sentences which are not compatible with their contexts must be brought into such a correspondence either by recoding the context or recoding the sentence.

4. In the case of an incompatibility of an utterance and its context, the perceptual or contextual events are more readily recoded than are the sentences.

5. Ease of comprehension depends upon the number of alternatives among which the reader must choose.

Because they are not specified in any of the above hypotheses, it may be worth indicating the assumptions about the role of grammatical factors in comprehension. In my estimation, the grammar is merely one, albeit an important one, among several semantic devices. Information is coded in the surface structure in much the same way that it is coded in the lexical system. The information coded in the grammar is well reflected in Fillmore's (1968) analysis of a case grammar. That is, the surface structure codes the grammatical relations between primary sentence constituents. It is an easy matter to illustrate that these grammatical factors are crucial for extracting the information appropriate to a context. If, for example, a minimally required utterance began with "The small circle is . . .," a person listening only in terms of semantic substantives would, upon hearing an utterance "The circle is . . . ," treat the third word as another adjective or noun (which he requires informationally). That is undoubtedly an infrequent error. Hence, the contextual expectancies do not substitute for an appropriate parsing of the sentence. Similarly, tense and plural markers differentiate alternatives in a way parallel to semantic features; it seems possible to me that some information which is handled semantically in one language is handled syntactically in another.

In line with the above hypotheses regarding the processes of comprehension, a series of studies on the verification of active and passive sentences were carried out by N. Filby of Stanford and myself (Olson & Filby, 1972). These studies involve a sentence verification task in which Ss were shown a picture of an event such as a car hitting a truck and then, after a brief delay, shown a sentence such as "The truck was hit by a car" which they were to judge as true or false. Reaction times (RT) were recorded from the onset of the sentence until the S's judgment. The usual findings in related experiments (Gough, 1965; Slobin, 1966) are that passive sentences are more difficult to verify than active sentences. Assuming that pictures are ambiguous, for example, whereby Figure 2 could be coded actively, "The car hit the truck" or passively, "The truck was hit by the car," we reasoned that the coding given to the preceding picture, the context, would determine the ease of processing a subsequent sentence. That is, if S codes the picture in terms of the actor (*car hit truck*) an active sentence would be most easily verified while if he codes the picture in terms of the receiver of the action (*Truck hit by car*) then the passive sentence would be most easily verified. One of the techniques by which Ss were induced to give passive codings (see Figure 2), was by giving the two pictures in succession and asking Ss to look at the second picture in terms of the first as if to find out what happened to the car (truck). Three separate experiments confirmed that the hypothesis was true; passive sentences were processed more quickly than actives when the preceding picture was coded in terms of the receiver of the action. To account for these results we proposed a model for the comprehension and verification of active and passive sentences in the spirit of models developed by Clark (1970) and Trabasso (1970) for the comprehension of negation. This model, shown in Figure 8, assumes that the task is solved in three phrases, encoding, comparison, and response output, which involve a series of binary decisions each of which takes time. In the encoding phase, it is assumed that S begins by giving the first event, the picture, a propositional coding which is marked as "true" (the truth index). This "reading" of the picture is not immediate and some ways of reading the picture appear to be more complex than others. In a related experiment (see Experiment 5 in Olson and Filby) it was found that it took adult Ss longer to answer the question "What was hit?" in reference to a subsequent picture than it took to answer "What hit?" This finding, which we interpret to mean that it is more difficult to extract information about the recipient of a specified act than about the actor, would appear to account for Gough's (1965) finding that passives were more difficult to verify than active sentences. In the model, the greater difficulty of assigning a passive coding to a picture is reflected in the variable latency

150

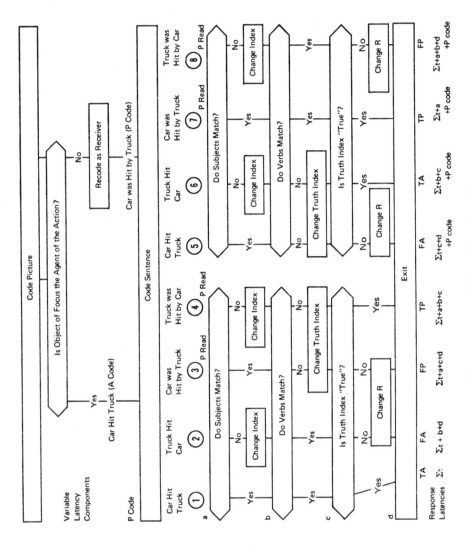

FIG. 8. Processing model for active and passive sentences.

component code. Just how this picture coding process proceeds is not known. In the present experiment sufficient time was allowed for Ss to produce either an active coding or a passive coding of the picture in response to the experimental contexts in which the picture was presented. Next it is assumed that Ss give the second event, the sentence, a parallel propositional coding in terms of the surface grammatical structure of the sentence (that is, they simply read and store the sentence); English passive sentences take longer to read than do active sentences.

The verification phase involves the process of sequentially comparing the two propositions in a series of binary decisions. In the case of a match of the grammatical subjects of the two codes the comparison process goes on to the next decision; in the case of a mismatch, the truth index is changed to false, thereby adding an increment of time. A similar comparison is carried out for the grammatical verb.

In the response phase, it is assumed that a decision of the form "Is the index set at 'true'?" is made. If it is, the "True" response is output; if it is not, the response is changed to "False" and then output, thereby adding an extra operation. This operation, which did not appear in the Clark and Trabasso models, was added because of the consistently longer reaction times to false sentences. The total RT, therefore, is a function of the number of operations involved in the coding, comparison, and output phases of the verification process.

Given this general form of the model, it is possible to estimate the parameters by averaging the difference in reaction times to sentences including or not including a particular factor. The components contained in each sentence are indicated at the

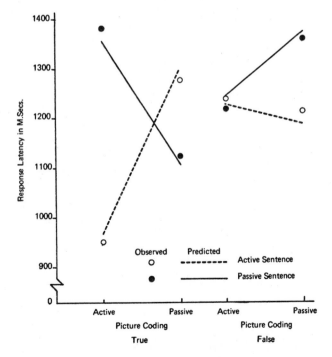

FIG. 9. Response times to active and passive sentences given active and passive coding of a picture.

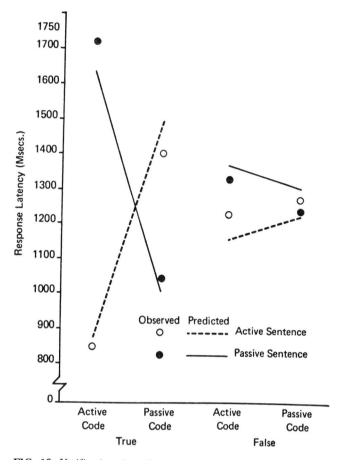

FIG. 10. Verification times for active and passive sentences after reading either an active or passive sentence.

bottom of the model in Figure 8. Using these estimates the reaction times to each of the sentences in each of the experimental sentences were predicted. Predicted and observed values are shown in Figure 9. This figure indicates that the model provides a good fit to the data obtained. Angela Hildyard and I at OISE (Olson & Hildyard, in preparation) have just completed a replication of this experiment using, this time, active and passive sentences which were compared to subsequently presented active and passive sentences. Again it was found that the model provided a good fit to the data and the only alteration in the model required was the deletion of the check on the false items (the 'd' latency component in the model). This evidence also confirms the fact that our Ss in the earlier experiments were giving the pictures active and passive codings as we had assumed. The values predicted from the model and those actually obtained in the sentence-sentence verification task are shown in Figure 10.

Note three things about this model. First, the ease of comprehension of any sentence depends on the perceptual coding of any preceding event; this was shown in the first interaction between the codings of the event and the grammatical form

of the sentences. Secondly, comprehension or verification proceeds on the basis of
the surface structure of the sentences. This is most readily shown by a comparison
of sentences 3 and 4, the true and false passives in the active coding condition. If
passive sentences took longer to process (latency component 'a') but were resolved
into an underlying coding of actor-action-object prior to the comparison process,
then the false passive should take longer than the true passive. In fact, the true
passive takes longer than the false passive, a finding which suggests that the short
term memory representation of the passive sentence retained its surface grammatical form and this surface form was involved in the verification process.

This analysis is appropriate, not only for the verification task data collected by
Gough and Slobin (their tasks are sentences 1 to 4 in the above model) but also for
tasks such as answering questions about passive and active sentences. We recently
completed a study (Experiment 4, Olson & Filby, in press) in which Ss were asked
to answer the questions "Who hit?" or "Who was hit?" on the basis of a subsequently presented sentence. The findings were that Ss could more quickly answer
an active question on the basis of an active sentence and a passive question on the
basis of a passive sentence. This is essentially a replication of Wright's (1969) study
of errors made in answering such questions. McMahon, Correil, and Smith (personal
communication) have more thoroughly examined and replicated this finding with
the added factor of asking about both the subject and object of both active and
passive sentences, including, for example, such questions as "What was something
hit by?". In general, it is easier to answer questions that correspond to the surface
grammatical structure of the sentence asked about, or more generally, to the coding
of the preceding information. A rough model of this process is shown in Figure 11.
The predicted and obtained RT's for these questions from our study are shown in

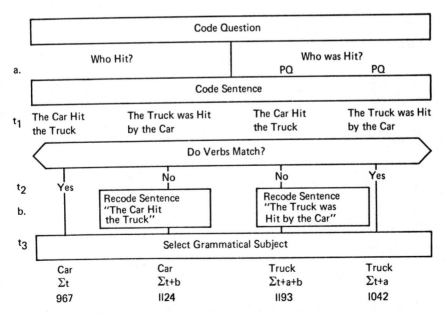

FIG. 11. Processing model for answering active and passive questions.

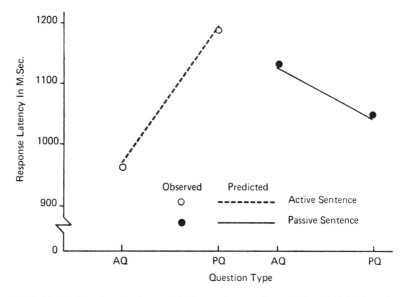

FIG. 12. Predicted and observed RT's to the questions "What hit" (A_Q) and "What was hit" (P_Q) as a function of sentence type.

Figure 12. Why in this case the passive question added an increment of time while the passive sentence did not cannot be explained.

Another aspect of our most recent study examined the effect of the number of alternatives on the verification process. As mentioned above, the hypothesis here was that the "depth" of processing is determined by the size of the sets of alternatives among which the listener-reader must choose. In the present experiment, in one case, a sentence (e.g., The car hit the truck) was verified against either of two sentences (e.g., The car hit the truck; The truck hit the car) while in the other case it was verified against any of four sentences (e.g., The car hit the truck; The truck hit the car; The car was hit by the truck; The truck was hit by the car). Predictably, verification times were much faster in the two-alternative conditions (570 milliseconds) than in the four-alternative sentence conditions (930 milliseconds; $t = 8.27$, $p < .001$). From this it may be concluded that the comprehension process for any sentence is not invariant but reflects both the structure of the information in the context and the number of alternatives among which Ss must choose. The depth of processing depends on both of these factors. The sentence, like other events, is perceived selectively, with attention being directed to those cues which the listener or reader requires for his purpose. The comprehension models discussed in this paper have to be elaborated or simplified to reflect these sets of alternatives.

The conclusion that the complexity of the comprehension process reflects the number of alternatives among which Ss must choose is compatible with some other lines of evidence. Slobin (1966) and Herriot (1969) examined the effects of sentence reversibility on the comprehension process. For reversible sentences, as the above model would predict, passives would found to take longer to comprehend than active sentences. For nonreversible sentences and those sentences which if reversed would run counter to expectations (e.g., "The flowers were watered by the girl"), the difference between active and passive sentences disappeared. For the reversible sentences there are two credible alternatives or sets of alternatives to look for; for the nonreversible there is only one, one which is as easily specified by the passive sentence as the active one. Specifically, in Slobin's case, after hearing either the sentence "The girl is watering the flowers" or "The flowers are being watered by the girl" there is only one picture to verify the sentences; the direction of the action is unambiguous. After hearing the reversible sentence "The cat is chased by the dog" or "The dog is being chased by the cat" there are two possible pictures to verify or refute the sentences, the direction of the action is ambiguous, and one additional decision is required to specify it.

The size of the sets of alternatives bears interestingly on the acquisition of grammatical structures. While the addition of one new lexical item to a language of n units yields one of $n + 1$ units, the addition of one new syntactic device, for example, negation, to that language yields a language with $2n$ units. Hence it is understandable that grammatical development is more orderly than lexical development.

Further, the role of the number of alternatives considered by the reader appears to be involved in Frase's (this volume) studies of the ways that Ss examine and remember aspects of propositions in attempting to answer questions about them. Information irrelevant to the question tends to be overlooked or quickly forgotten. Students and their teachers are notorious for their selectivity in reading the writings of others.

A caveat regarding the generality of this model of sentence comprehension should be mentioned. The model was developed to account for the immediate verification of sentences. As was pointed out earlier, the verification process reflects the surface structure coding stored in short term memory (STM). Following the interesting leads of Garrett, Bever, and Fodor (1966) and Bever (1970) regarding the role of grammar in sentence perception, Jarvella (1971) showed that in connected discourse sentences are stored in STM only until a grammatical constituent is assembled and analyzed. Recall from a prompt within the last constituent boundary resulted in complete, verbatim recall; recall from outside that phrase boundary was essentially a paraphrase. From this it follows that question-answering or verification tasks may involve quite different mental operations when the information to be examined must be retrieved from long term memory, as opposed to information that is in STM, as has been the case in all of the studies addressed to this point. It would seem to be a relatively direct matter to do the required experiments. Ss could, for example, read an entire paragraph before verifying the sentences employed in these studies.

In this way it may be possible to develop comprehensive models that would account for, or at least include, the interesting findings in sentence recall reported by Slobin (1966), Turner and Rommetveit (1968), Fillenbaum (1966), Sachs (1967), and others on the form of information stored and recalled following comprehension (see also Fillenbaum, 1970).

Finally, notice from the model that Ss are capable of recoding the passive sentence into an active sentence and vice versa in the case of a double mismatch, as in sentences 4 and 6. This is not merely a matter of mapping sentences on to perceptions but rather the apparent derivation of some new knowledge from another sentence. In our experiment the picture had disappeared so there was no possibility that Ss could be recoding the picture. It seems necessary to postulate another use of language beyond mapping sentences on to perceptions, namely, mapping sentences on to other sentences. The remainder of this paper will be concerned with the development of this ability and the corresponding implications of using sentences as propositions.

SENTENCES AS PROPOSITIONS:
MAPPING SENTENCES ONTO SENTENCES

There are a large variety of sentences that map on to other sentences, the most common being those involving grammatical transformations such as passives, negatives, and questions, as well as a variety of semantic relations such as inclusion, opposition, etc. that make up the structure of subjective lexicon (Miller, 1970).

Consider first the relations that hold among various grammatical forms. Adult Ss given the sentence "The car hit the truck" can infer "The truck was hit by the car"; one sentence implies the other. Similarly, "A is more than B" implies "B is less than A." Frequently, negative sentences imply their contradictions, as in Trabasso's study where "not green" implies "orange." A similar equivalence may be found between questions, such as "Did the boy hit the ball?" and their declarative answers "The boy did hit the ball." It is the basic equivalence among sentences that leads to the assumption that these sentences share a common underlying or base structure (Chomsky, 1957; Katz & Fodor, 1963). The hypothesis to be developed in this section is that the recognition of this equivalence among sentences: (1) is more complex than that involved in using language for ordinary communication about the world; (2) is developmentally late in appearing; (3) provides a new basis for language use, a use that may be roughly characterized as a logical use, a use of language for theorizing, justifying and thinking; and (4) is a candidate for a revised conception of base structures—base structures are those structural invariants, or implicational relations among sentences.

First consider the possibility that sentences may be verified in two quite different ways; by recoding one's perceptions of the event and by recoding the information in the sentence. It has already been shown that any event or pictorial representation of that event is ambiguous in that, for example, it could be coded in terms of the actor or in terms of the object. This ambiguity was exploited in the Olson and Filby studies so that the form of coding given the picture determined the difficulty of verifying the subsequent sentences. When the picture coding corresponded to the surface grammatical coding of either the active or passive sentence, the sentence was more easily processed than when there was a mismatch between those codings.

This ambiguity in pictures and in situations is the primary basis for the assertion that the perceptual codings are revised on the hearing of sentences. It remains hypothetical that in the event of a mismatch between the structure of the perceptual coding and the sentence coding, either the perceptual code can be altered (by looking at the picture again) or the sentence code can be transformed. Evidence that the ability to transform sentences develops later in children than the ability to transform perceptions is indicated by only a few lines of evidence.

That children do somewhat different things in sentence verification tasks than adults, has been shown in Trabasso's (1970) reinterpretation of Slobin's (1966) data on negation. Trabasso proposed two models for verification, depending on whether the sentence was given prior to or after the perceived event. The difference in these models provides for the fact that Ss given the sentence first (e.g., "not green") transform the sentence into its affirmative equivalent ("orange") before they look at the verifying event. This fact could be determined by noting that if Ss transform the negative "not green" to "orange" the true condition (TN) would be easier than the false condition (FN); if it was left untransformed the FN would be easier. While adults do in fact make this transformation, thus making the TN easier, Trabasso suggested that children did not. The data are shown on the left half of Figure 13. That is, adults given the sentence "The cat is not chasing the dog" transformed it to "The dog is chasing the cat" and then looked at the picture, thus making the TN easier than the FN. Glucksberg (referred to in Trabasso, 1970) confirmed that this transformation occurs for adults. Young children, on the other hand, found the FN easier than the TN, from which it may be concluded that young Ss cannot recode or transform negative sentences into affirmative ones.

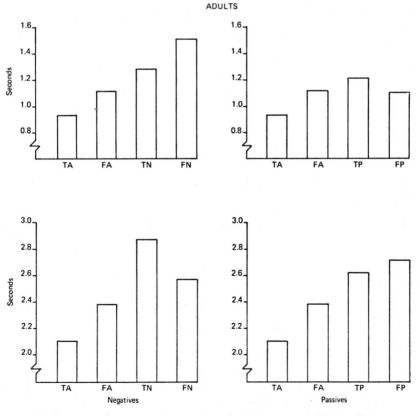

FIG. 13. Verification times for negative and passive sentences (Slobin, 1966).

The case is less clear in regard to passive sentences. For Slobin's (1966) data the same pattern of interaction between age and ease of verifying true and false passive sentences may be observed, but the interaction runs in the opposite direction; it is the adults who find the false passives (FP) easier. This fact is shown in the right half of Figure 13. Although some guesswork is involved in interpreting this interaction, the first thing to note is that adult Ss appear not to recode passive sentences into active ones. In Gough's (1965, 1966) studies on passives, Ss did not carry out such a recoding even when given a 3-second delay. If Ss had carried out such a recoding, they should have found the TP easier than the FP. Both Gough's and Slobin's results are just the reverse; TP is more difficult for adults than FP.

If adult Ss had been given enough trials they would undoubtedly come to recode the passive sentence just as they came to do with the negatives in Glucksberg's replication of Gough. That is, most adults can recode a passive sentence into an active one but they usually do not bother to. It may be worth collecting data parallel to those of Glucksberg to demonstrate this point with certainty.

That explanation, however, fails to account for the relative ease 6- to 10-year-old Ss have with the TP relative to FP. If adults fail to recode the passive to the active, it is unlikely that younger Ss do, particularly in view of their inability to transform negative sentences. Rather it seems necessary to consider the interaction between age level and true and false passives in other terms, specifically, in terms of picture recoding. It may be assumed that the picture is not given a standard coding on all trials. Rather, for young children, the picture is coded in terms of the sentence; if the sentence is active, the picture is coded in terms of the actor, and if it is passive, it is coded in terms of the receiver of the action. That is, younger Ss recode the picture; older Ss recode the sentence. These models for verifying TP and FP for younger and older Ss, are shown in Figure 14. This figure shows that if it is assumed that young Ss recode the picture, that is, look at the picture in terms of the sentence thereby coding a picture after a passive sentence in a passive code, the predictions correspond to Slobin's results. Older Ss, on the other hand, appear to give the picture a standard active coding and then compare sentences and pictures.

This interpretation of Slobin's data must remain tentative. However, there is evidence from Beilin and Spontak (1969) that supports both aspects of this interpretation: Older Ss can recode sentences, younger Ss can recode pictures. Beilin tested the ability of children 4 to 9 and 7 to 11 years old to comprehend active and passive sentences by having them select a picture corresponding to a sentence, e.g., "Susan is hit by Mark." About 75% of the youngest children could comprehend the active sentences and by first grade about 75% of the children could comprehend the passive sentences. However, it was not until the second grade that Ss performed above chance in their judgments of the equivalence between the active and passive sentences. This equivalence was tested in two ways; first, by having S repeat the sentences to himself and then judging if they meant the same thing and second, by having S select the picture(s) which showed "Mark hits Susan" and "Susan is hit by Mark." Both lines of evidence showed that passives may be both comprehended and produced before Ss see how they are related to active sentences. If passives were learned as a transformed active, this equivalence should be learned prior to the effective use of passives; however, it was found to be acquired later.

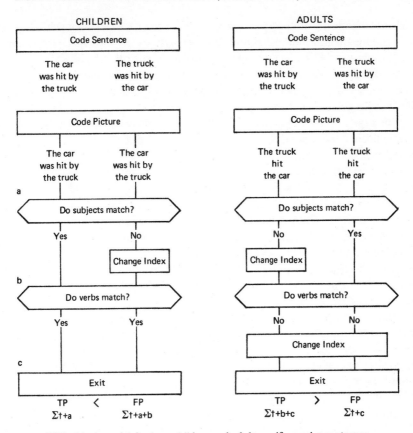

FIG. 14. A model for how children and adults verify passive sentences.

Two implications follow. The first is that the surface structure of passive sentences may not be learned as a transformation of the base structure shared by the active sentence. Rather it may be learned as a new surface grammatical device appropriate for handling certain kinds of information. It is only later that its relation to and equivalence with the surface structure of active sentences is learned. Thus, the base structure may be considered as the set of structural invariants or implicational relations among sentences and these base structure relations represent the end product of development, not the beginning. Braine (1963, 1965) was the first to make this suggestion. This is to do to Chomsky's (1965) and McNeil's (1970) assumption about innate base structures what Piaget did to Kant's assumption about innate ideas. The reasons children come to note these equivalences and the utility of these "base structure relations" in logical thinking will be considered presently.

Secondly, since young children cannot recode active and passive sentences into their common base structure and hence judge their equivalence, they must be able to verify or comprehend these sentences by recoding the pictures. That is, both the active and the passive sentences can be verified against a common event, the picture; since the sentences cannot be recoded, the picture must have been. This claim should not appear to be strange, as it is well known from Luria's (1961) work that from approximately four years of age, a spoken sentence can alter a child's perceptual coding of an event. Sentences and perceptions are closely tied together, as Ford's data on children's descriptions showed. On the other hand, older Ss, second grade and over, can see the equivalence between the active and passive sentences. Hence, older Ss can transform or recode sentences whereas the younger Ss can recode only perceptual events.

This type of account may explain the current controversy between Huttenlocher (Huttenlocher, Eisenberg, & Strauss, 1968) and Bem (1967) as to how Ss follow verbal instructions. When the grammatical subject of the sentence corresponds to the object in the listener's hand, the sentence is easily followed. However, when the grammatical subject does not correspond to the object in S's hand, as for example, when S has a red block in his hand and he is asked to "Make it so that the green block is on top of the red block" it is much more difficult. Huttenlocher suggests that when the sentence does not match the situation, Ss recode the sentence into "The red block is under the green block" so as to achieve a correspondence between the object in hand and the subject of the sentence. Bem argues that Ss do not recode the sentence but rather visualize the end-state given by the description and then carry out the act to achieve that end-state. In that line, Bem taught Ss to visualize the end-states implied by the sentences and found that young Ss improved their solutions markedly. Thus it appears that Bem is correct; younger Ss cannot recode the sentence prior to following it; for them it is easier to recode or visualize the perceptual end-state specified by the sentence. Subjects trained to imagine the perceptual end-state specified by the sentence continued to use this strategy for other related problems. This was shown by the fact that, following the instructional sessions, when asked to describe what they had produced, Ss replied with the untransformed sentence 77% of the time. It may be concluded that they did not transform their sentences; rather, they transformed their perceptions. Older Ss, on the other hand, could recode either the sentence or the perceived situation, and presumably they frequently do as Huttenlocher suggested, namely, recode the sentence into its formal equivalent. It should be pointed out, however, that Bem did not include the critical control of teaching Ss to recode sentences to see if that improved their performance in a way comparable to that achieved by teaching them to recode their perceptions.

Robbie Case, Ruth Pike, Angela Hildyard, and I have several experiments underway that will test somewhat more directly both the hypothesis that either sentences or events may be recoded and that the latter is simpler and hence developmentally earlier. It appears to be the case that young Ss can verify both active and passive sentences against a picture earlier than they can verify them against each other, as Beilin found. It may be that common perceived events of this sort mediate or establish the equivalence of these different grammatical forms. Further, it appears that it is easier to verify a sentence-picture pair when the sentence is presented prior to the picture than when the picture is presented prior to (and disappears before) the sentence. This is expected because it is easier to recode the picture to the sentence than vice versa.

A similar pattern is emerging for the comprehension of the relational terms "more" and "less" (Donaldson & Wales, 1970). Young Ss appear to be able to verify "A has more than B" against a picture and "B has less than A" against the same picture long before they realize that the sentences imply each other. That is, they fail to realize the "deep" structure relationship that $A > B$ implies $B < A$.

As the same picture is used to verify two dissimilar true sentences, which children fail to see as equivalent, it follows that Ss could code or read the event or picture in more than one way, that is, young Ss can recode pictures. If they had recoded the two sentences into a common base code, it would be hard to explain why they did not see the two sentences as equivalent. This, together with the data from the Filby and Olson study mentioned above, on the role of surface grammatical structure in the comprehension of passives, leads to the conclusion that these same young Ss who could recode pictures could not yet recode sentences.

This proposal may also be related to the controversy between Clark (1969) and Huttenlocher et al. (1968) and Jones (1970) as to how three-term series problems are solved. The question as to whether spatial or linguistic processes are involved may depend on the age of the subject and the medium in which the problem is presented. Arnheim (1969) illustrated how different the process of reading comparative information off a visual diagram is from making the equivalent set of inferences from a set of propositions; yet, either process may lead to a solution. However, the critical difference between the two types of theories rests on the inferences from negative equative sentences such as "A is not as bad as B; B is not as bad as C." Note two facts about this problem. First, unlike the case for analogous problems, the *question* for negative equatives does not match the comparative term. Thus, other problems express the relation as "better" and question "Who is best?", whereas for the negative equative, the comparative terms are never directly questioned, e.g., "Who is not as bad. . .?" When the sentence does not match the question the sentences may have to be recoded, usually to match the question. However, "A is not as bad as B" could be recoded either as (1) A is better than B or as (2) B is worse than A. But (2) is a recoding of the negation while (1) is a recoding of the semantic relation. While both are correct and possible, Clark's (1969) data indicate that (2) is easier and usually chosen by Ss, but this idea could be tested more directly. Once recoded to (2) Huttenlocher's spatial predictions appear to be valid. In any case, the ability to extract such a relation depends on S's knowing what sentences are implied by other sentences.

As the model presented in this paper was based on the negation models of Clark (1970) and Trabasso (1970) it may be important to point out one point of divergence. Clark has emphasized that the coding given sentences is a base structure representation whereas the present model assumes they are given a surface structure representation. The present model has emphasized that the base structure representations are ordinarily or primarily involved only when the surface codings are incongruent. This incongruence may be either grammatical, as when an active is compared or related to a passive or an affirmative to a negative sentence, or lexical as when "better" is to be related to "worse" or "heavier" to "lighter." They may also be involved when long term memory codes are compared.

Another, more minor divergence is the assumption of the present model that the number of mental operations is determined by the set of alternatives considered by the listener-reader. This assumption was made in the current model because of the importance of these sets of alternatives differentiated by a speaker.

That assumption may provide an alternative explanation for Clark and Young's (reported in Clark, 1970) finding that the comprehension of the implicit negative "absent" differed from the explicit negative "not present" primarily in their presuppositions, resulting in a much longer RT for the latter. In terms of the size of the set of alternatives, it could be pointed out that the sentence "star not present" would require three comparisons, one for each relevant component of the surface structure, while "star absent" would require only two. The sets could be made comparable by expanding the latter set of sentences to include such sentences as "star not absent." These are minor questions relative to the important contribution to our understanding of comprehension made by Clark and Trabasso.

It remains to suggest the nature and implications of this late-developing ability to recode sentences. In general it is proposed that language serves at least two quite different purposes. The simplest and earliest developing use of language is for communication, the aim of which is to specify a referent relative to a set of alternatives. To this end sentences are comprehended, generated, and verified in terms of the perceived or inferred context in which they are uttered. The normal consequence of hearing a sentence in such a context is to alter the listener's perceptions of that context; language restructures the perceptions of the listener (Olson, 1970).

The second, more complex and developmentally late use of language is involved when a speaker reflects on the implications of his own or other's sentences. Not only does the sentence map on to a revised perceived context, but the sentence maps on to or implies other sentences. When a child comes to see that one sentence entails another, he can recode sentences into other sentences. Sentences which have implicational relations with other sentences may suitably be called *propositions*. And the relations among propositions constitute at least a part of what is called logic. Equipped with these implicational structures (as, for example, in Trabasso's experiment where "not green" implies "orange"), Ss no longer have to wait for the perceived event to carry out their matching operations; they can operate on the proposition, derive a second proposition, and then verify this derived one against the event. As we have pointed out, adults can both recode perceptual situations and recode sentences. Once a child knows these implicational structures among propositions, language can indeed, contrary to my earlier argument (Olson, 1970), restructure the perceptions of the speaker himself. Such thinking, following out the implications of the original assertion or premise, is called *deductive* thinking and it has some of the properties of operations in any formal symbolic system such as geometry or logic. Piaget (1950) calls this type of thinking "formal operational thought." If, for example, you know that whales are mammals and further that all mammals have fur, you can infer the further new information that whales must have fur, something you may not have known before. These implicational structures are then used as tools of thought. Yet these implicational structures are not intrinsic to ordinary language in ordinary communication contexts such as those described by Wittgenstein. Simmons (present volume) has discussed how these implicational relations may operate. Further, Bormuth's (1970) recent attempt to develop a theory of achievement test items appears to be based on these implicational or transformational relations among sentences.

Two points may be suggested as to the origin of these implicational relations among sentences. While these implicational relations are implicit in ordinary language, they appear not to be noticed or exploited in either the language of children or in the ordinary language usage of adults. This may be the case because such implicational relations derive from a different point of focus than that involved in ordinary conversational use of language. In the first use of language, the language is completely transparent to the reality that lies behind it; one focuses on the world through the language. In the second use of language, the focus is on the propositions themselves and their relation to other propositions rather than to the reality specified by the sentences; this latter requires a divorce of language from reality. What originally provided the occasion for this attention to the implications of propositions themselves can only be guessed. My preference is to believe that it originated with the "new" medium of written language, a hypothesis suggested by McLuhan's (1962) writings. The difference I have been sketching is roughly analogous to the difference between looking at nature and looking at art. Art requires a new pictorial attitude (Gibson, 1970); quite different features appear to be involved in perceiving a picture of a horse from those involved in perceiving actual horses. Attention to these features or perhaps inventing features that produce an appropriate representation is the problem faced by artists (Gombrich, 1960).

Secondly, it appears that the equivalence among sentences is established originally by their overlapping extension or compliance classes (Goodman, 1968, p. 144). That is, if two sentences correspond to some invariant in a situation, they come to be equivalent to each other. Thus, "A is more than B" and "B is less than A" have the same extension, or share the same perceived event, hence, they come to be regarded as equivalent. Arnheim (1969) has made a strong case for the visual basis of "propositional" thinking.

It may be noted that these implicational relations among grammatical structures are also closely tied to corresponding structures among lexical items. As was suggested earlier, grammatical structures are only one, however important, semantic device. Just as a passive sentence logically implies an active one, so lexical items imply other lexical items; if it is a cat, it must be an animal. Young children appear not to recognize these implicational systems, so that if asked "Is this an animal?" they may reply "No, it is a cat." Similarly, in my earlier example, the child said, "My hot, boiling water is cold," thus failing to notice that if it was hot, that excluded the possibility that it could be cold. Either through sorting out the extensions or referential range of terms or through focusing on the implicational relations among terms, the semantic system comes to have the quasi-formal properties of superordination, inclusion, polar-opposition, etc., that characterize the "intrinsic meanings" of subjective lexicon of adults (Miller, 1970). How far a language can be pushed towards a fully formal system depends on one's willingness to sacrifice its adequacy for ordinary discourse. As Tarski (1969) pointed out, "A natural language is not a formalized one."

In summary, I have been examining language both as a means of communication or instruction and as one means of being intelligent. As to the latter, the relations among propositions provide a generalized means of solving a wide array of verbal, logical problems. Clark (1969), for example, has shown how adult Ss solve three-term series problems by transforming the propositions involved into some sort of congruence from which a conclusion can be derived. Wason and Johnson-Laird (in press) have examined the processes involved in solving other logical problems. These language skills, quite different from those involved in ordinary use of language for communication purposes, therefore, provide one means of being intelligent. As to the former, language for communication and instruction involves the use of language for restructuring the listener's perceptions; the teacher knows something the child does not and he directs his attention, or otherwise restructures the child's perceptions to lead to some new knowledge in the child. Education involves both uses of language. Language in instruction is primarily a matter of showing the child how to map his language on to subtle perceptual situations and to elaborate his perceptions to match that language. The ease of comprehending such an instructional sentence will depend on the congruence between the sentence and its presuppositions as specified either by the perceptual or linguistic context and the number of mental operations involved in arriving at that congruence. Language in thinking is concerned more with the child's coming to realize that any proposition has implications. New knowledge can be derived from old by reading off the implications of a proposition. Once acquired, these skills are important tools for the child's further self-education.

CONFERENCE DISCUSSION

A number of questions arose concerning the number of parameters needed to fit the data points that appeared in Olson's Figure 9, for example. Frederiksen indicated that with a large number of parameters to be estimated and with only a few degrees of freedom left, one should stress more the value and meaning of the parameters as interpreted by the model and give less stress to the goodness of fit.

Discussion then turned to some of Olson's studies on passive sentences. Olson elaborated on an idea suggested earlier by Chafe. Chafe had said that even though a child can't give a passive sentence description, this doesn't mean that his internal representation of it couldn't be in terms of the recipient of the action. For example, if children use a pronoun as in "The car hit *it*" then they are indicating that the recipient of the action has been foregrounded. Presumably the child didn't use the passive form as in "It was hit by the car" because he may not have known that particular grammatical device for expressing it.

Herriot inquired whether foregrounding was the usual reason for using the passive. Chafe responded that a passive is usually employed when the recipient of the action is foregrounded and it is put in the subject position of the sentence. Olson suggested that a possible conclusion to be drawn from the above examples was that children are capable of having a perceptual code prior to the time that they know the linguistic device for specifying that information. Chafe agreed with this and went on to say that whatever semantic structure one has, the active and passive are going to be very similar—the main difference will be in the distribution of what is foregrounded in the two cases. That is, there are more things that one has to do to this semantic representation to get to a surface representation if the object is foregrounded than if the agent is foregrounded. Chafe indicated that this seems to mean that for some reason the normal situation is for us to have a foregrounded agent rather than a foregrounded object.

Bever then raised a general problem concerning Olson's stage models for dealing with isolated experimental problems as well as Olson's remarks about the problem of reference and meaning. Bever thought that Olson's arguments regarding reference were wrong and he furthermore indicated that he didn't think that they were pertinent to the types of studies that Olson reported on. He granted the value of building mathematical models for special types of experimental situations but thought such an enterprise should be shaprly distinguished from the broader issues involved in the problem of reference and meaning. He then gave an example of why he thought the latter problem had not been adequately dealt with by Olson. The meaning of a word such as "large" has to be stated in such a way that when it is used to select from real-world alternatives its use is relative to some standard that is available from the world. But the meaning of the word "large" remains *constant* over and above the particular sets of alternatives to which it has been applied.

Olson granted that there was an element of truth in what Bever said but indicated that focusing solely upon the 'formal' analysis of words and sentences went beyond his main concern, which is with *how* sentences and words are processed. With that emphasis on behavioral consequences of sentence and word usage, he suggested that the set of alternatives which are present (either implicitly or explicitly) in some situation are the key to understanding the observed relative difficulty of sentences which are asserted or produced in those contexts. Olson also mentioned that he had not totally ignored what may be called the 'formal' aspect of words and sentences since his paper had contrasted two uses of language: language used for communication and instruction and secondly, language used as propositions. In this second aspect of language usage one begins to hit upon these more formal kinds of constraints, but he again emphasized that for both uses of language his focus was always on the real-world consequences of language use.

Bever agreed that one can study many interesting rules about language usage but he still maintained that this did not solve nor did it effectively skirt the main issues in the problem of reference and meaning. He then gave another example by way of illustration. The phrase "The tallest building in the world" has a meaning over and above any particular situation in which it is applied. Naturally, the *use* of that phrase will change according to an individual's beliefs and motives such as (a) what he thinks the tallest building in the world actually is and (b) whether he wants to become known as a liar or not, etc. Olson responded that if one believes that sentences do have fixed meanings, then he would agree with what Bever said. However, he didn't think that sentences do have fixed meanings; instead he indicated that the meaning of a sentence is always intertwined with the speaker's intention in uttering it.

This interchange between Bever and Olson continued at great length with essentially the same arguments being restated.

REFERENCES

Arnheim, R. *Visual thinking.* Berkeley: University of California Press, 1969.

Beilin, H., & Spontak, G. Active-passive transformations and operational reversibility. Paper presented at the Biennial Meeting of the Society for Research in Child Development, Santa Monica, March 1969.

Bem, S. L. Verbal self-control: The establishment of effective self-instruction. *Journal of Experimental Psychology*, 1967, 74, 485–491.

Bever, T. G. The cognitive basis for linguistic structures. In J. R. Hayes (Ed.), *Cognition and the development of language.* New York: Wiley, 1970.

Bormuth, J. R. *On the theory of achievement test items. With an appendix by P. Menzel: On the linguistic bases of the theory of writing items.* Chicago: University of Chicago Press, 1970.

Braine, M. D. S. On learning the grammatical order of words. *Psychological Review*, 1963, **70**, 323–348.

Braine, M. D. S. On the basis of phrase structure. A reply to Bever, Fodor, and Weksel. *Psychological Review*, 1965, **72**, 483–492.

Brown, R. *Words and things*. Glencoe, Illinois: Free Press, 1958.

Bruner, J. S. On cognitive growth; I and II. In J. S. Bruner, R. R. Olver, P. M. Greenfield, *et al.* (Eds.), *Studies in cognitive growth*. New York: Wiley, 1966.

Chomsky, N. *Syntactic structures*. The Hague: Mouton, 1957.

Chomsky, N. *Aspects of the theory of syntax*. Cambridge, Mass.: M.I.T. Press, 1965.

Clark, H. H. How we understand negation. Department of Psychology, Stanford University, August, 1970. (Unpublished manuscript).

Clark, H. H. Linguistic processes in deductive reasoning. *Psychological Review*, 1969, **76**, 387–404.

Collins, A. M., & Quillian, M. R. Retrieval time from semantic memory. *Journal of Verbal Learning and Verbal Behavior*, 1969, **8**, 240–247.

Donaldson, Margaret, & Wales, R. On the acquisition of some relational terms. In J. R. Hayes (Ed.), *Cognition and the development of language*. New York: Wiley, 1970.

Fillmore, C. J. The case for case. In E. Bach, & R. T. Harmes (Eds.), *Universals in linguistic theory*. New York: Holt, Rinehart & Winston, 1968.

Fillenbaum, S. Memory for gist: Some relevant variables. *Language and Speech*, 1966, **9**, 217–227.

Fillenbaum, S. On the use of memorial techniques to assess syntactic structures. *Psychological Bulletin*, 1970, **73**, 231–237.

Ford, W. Information and communication in child's language. (Masters dissertation, University of Toronto) 1971.

Frege, G. Über Sinn und Bedeutung. (1892) Translated as *On sense and reference* in Peter Geach and Marx Black. Translations from the philosophical writings of Gottlob Frege, Oxford, 1952.

Garrett, M., Bever, T.G., & Fodor. J. The active use of grammar in speech perception. *Perception and Psychophysics*, 1966, **1**, 30–32.

Gelman, R. Conservation acquisition: A problem of learning to attend to relevant attributes. *Journal of Experimental Child Psychology*, 1969, **7**, 167–187.

Gibson, J. J. The psychology of representation. Cornell University, 1970. (Unpublished manuscript).

Glucksberg, S., & Krauss, R. What do people say after they have learned to talk? Studies of the development of referential communication. *Merrill-Palmer Quarterly*, 1967, **13**, 309–316.

Gombrich, E. *Art and illusion*. New York: Bollinger Foundation, 1960.

Goodman, N. *Languages of art*. Indianapolis, Ind.: Bobbs-Merrill, 1968.

Gough, P. B. Grammatical transformations and speed of understanding. *Journal of Verbal Learning and Verbal Behavior*, 1965, **5**, 107–111.

Gough, P. B. The verification of sentences: the effects of delay of evidence and sentence length. *Journal of Verbal Learning and Verbal Behavior*, 1966, **5**, 492–496.

Halford, G. S. A theory of the acquisition of conservation. *Psychological Review*, 1970, **77**, 302–316.

Harlow, H. F. The formation of learning sets. *Psychological Review*, 1949, **56**, 51–65.

Herriot, P. The comprehension of active and passive sentences as a function of pragmatic expectations. *Journal of Verbal Learning and Verbal Behavior*, 1969, **8**, 166–169.

Huttenlocher, J., Eisenberg, K., & Strauss, S. Comprehension: Relation between perceived actor and logical subject. *Journal of Verbal Learning and Verbal Behavior*, 1968, **7**, 300–304.

Ivins, W. M. *Prints and visual communication*. Cambridge: M.I.T. Press, 1953.

Jarvella, R. J. Syntactic processing of connected speech. *Journal of Verbal Learning and Verbal Behavior*, 1971, **10**, 409–416.

Johnson-Laird, P. N. The interpretation of the passive voice. *Quarterly Journal of Experimental Psychology*, 1968, **20**, 69–73.

Jones, S. Visual and verbal processes in problem-solving. *Cognitive Psychology*, 1970, **1**, 201–214.

Katz, J. J., & Fodor, J. A. The structure of semantic theory. *Language*, 1963, **38**, 170–210.

de Laguna, G. A. *Speech: Its function and development.* New Haven: Yale University Press, 1927.

Luria, A. R. *The role of speech in the regulation of normal and abnormal behavior.* New York: Liveright, 1961.

Martin, J. E. Some competence-process relationships in noun phrases with prenominal and post-nominal adjectives. *Journal of Verbal Learning and Verbal Behavior*, 1969, **8**, 471–480.

McLuhan, M. *The Guttenberg galaxy.* Toronto: University of Toronto Press, 1962.

McLuhan, M. *Understanding media.* New York: The New American Library, 1964.

McNeill, D. *The acquisition of language: The study of developmental psycholinguistics.* New York: Harper and Row, 1970.

Meyer, D. E. On the representation and retrieval of stored semantic information. *Cognitive Psychology*, 1970, **1** 242–300.

Miller, G. A. Some preliminaries to psycholinguistics. *American Psychologist*, 1965, **20**, 15–20.

Miller, G. A. Subjective lexicon. Paper presented at the 78th Annual Convention of the American Psychological Association, Miami Beach, September, 1970.

Mundy-Castle, A. C. Culture, communication and social change. Paper presented at the 11th Interamerican Congress of Psychology, Mexico City, December, 1967.

Olson, D. R. Language and thought: Aspects of a cognitive theory of semantics. *Psychological Review*, 1970, **4**, 257–273.

Olson, D. R., & Filby, N. On the comprehension of active and passive sentences. *Cognitive Psychology*, 1972, in press.

Olson, D. R., & Hildyard, A. The role of long and short term memory in the verification of active and passive sentences. In preparation.

Piaget, J. *The psychology of intelligence.* New York: Harcourt and Brace, 1950.

Quine, W. V. *From a logical point of view.* Cambridge, Mass.: Harvard University Press, 1953.

Randhawa, B. S. Non-verbal information storage in humans and developmental information processing channel capacity. *Journal of Experimental Child Psychology*, in press.

Reichenbach, H. *Experience and prediction.* Chicago: University of Chicago Press, 1938.

Richards, I. A. *Design for escape.* New York: Harcourt, 1968.

Sachs, J. S. Recognition memory for syntactic and semantic aspects of connected discourse. *Perception and Psychophysics*, 1967, **2**, 437–442.

Slobin, D. I. Grammatical transformations and sentence comprehension in childhood and adulthood. *Journal of Verbal Learning and Verbal Behavior*, 1966, **5**, 219–227.

Tarski, A. Truth and proof. *Scientific American*, 1969, **220**, 63–77.

Trabasso, T. Reasoning and the processing of information. Invited address, 78th Annual Convention of the American Psychological Association, Miami, September, 1970.

Turner, E. A., & Rommetveit, R. Focus of attention in recall of active and passive sentences. *Journal of Verbal Learning and Verbal Behavior*, 1968, **7**, 543–548.

Wason, P. C. The context of plausible denial. *Journal of Verbal Learning and Verbal Behavior*, 1965, **4**, 7–11.

Wason, P. C., & Johnson-Laird, P. N. The other side of the card. *Quarterly Journal of Experimental Psychology*, in press.

Weinreich, U. On the semantic structure of language. In J. Greenberg (Ed.), *Universals of language.* Cambridge: M.I.T. Press, 1963.

Wittgenstein, L. *Philosophical investigations.* Oxford: Basil, Blackwell and Mott, 1958.

Wright, Patricia. Transformations and the understanding of sentences. *Language and Speech*, 1969, **12**, 156–166.

8

LANGUAGE USERS AS FALLIBLE INFORMATION-PROCESSORS: IMPLICATIONS FOR MEASURING AND MODELING COMPREHENSION[1]

Roy Freedle
Educational Testing Service,
Princeton, New Jersey

INTRODUCTION

The plan of this paper is as follows. First, I will outline Olson's (1970) cognitive theory of semantics. One of Olson's key concepts is that the set of explicit (or implicit) alternatives strongly influences the types of messages that are constructed for a receiver (listener); this concept is critically examined for purposes of specifying what additional factors may influence the degree to which the conjecture holds or fails to hold. I then summarize a number of empirical investigations that examine the effect of some of these factors on message structure. Following the construction of a more general probabilistic model, which includes Olson's hypotheses as special cases, I then outline how the set of stimulus alternatives can lead us to study a somewhat broader problem: How we as listeners determine from the flow of speech the nature of the general *topic* that the speaker is discussing. It is argued that the set of explicit (or implicit) alternative topics will strongly influence our ability to isolate the correct topic of the discourse to which we are listening. Several models are suggested as possibly appropriate descriptions of how we decide what the topic is in the absence of clear information about the topic. This latter situation could occur, for example, if the speaker has either failed to make mention of his topic (that is, the speaker has failed to appreciate the ambiguity of what he is saying) or it could occur if we as listeners have appeared in the middle of some speech or have simply failed to pay sufficient attention to important topical cues that the speaker has already provided.

Next, I summarize the import of the studies cited above for what they can tell us about how we as language users are able to detect semantic errors and on some occasions are able to correct these errors.

[1] The research reported in this chapter was supported in part by the National Institute of Child Health and Human Development under Research Grant 1–PO1–HDO1762.

The next topic to be considered in an ever-broadening scope of topics is a critical examination of Dawes' (1964; 1966) conception of story comprehension as a network of relational concepts. An experiment is presented to provide a test of some of the critical points raised. A model is then presented in order to illustrate a measurement problem connected with the recall of explicitly given information in the story. Some problems associated with our ability to draw inferences from the explicitly given information are briefly outlined.

Following a summary of what direction these quantitative models have taken us in and whether they can tell us anything new and useful about the comprehension process, a final section broaches a very large problem—the effect of cultural knowledge and cultural goals on the problem of what we learn from being told. Anthropologists have a special name for this discipline: ethnoscience.

OLSON'S COGNITIVE THEORY OF REFERENCE

One of the most persuasive theories of reference to emerge in recent years is, in my opinion, that put forth by Olson (1970). While many aspects of the effect of perception and cognition on our use of language have been illuminated by Olson, we are here interested in inquiring further into his paradigm cases which attempt to clarify how some explicit or implicit set of alternatives affect the way we construct messages in communication situations.

It will be necessary to summarize Olson's paradigm cases and the postulates that he draws from them in order to submit these ideas to further analysis. I have adapted many of the ideas which follow from a forthcoming report by Freedle and Kingsley (1972).

In the paradigm cases considered by Olson, the following format is assumed. A subject is presented with a particular stimulus array—a set of potential referents. One item from this set is to be designated as the target item. The task of the subject is to construct a message which will uniquely specify the target item so that a recipient of the message will be able to pick the target item out of the same array. Only the first three of Olson's cases will concern us here. Case 1 consists of two alternative referents—two small, round, wooden blocks which are identical except that one is white and one black. The target item will be the white block. In Case 2 the *same* target item is used but now the alternative item is a small, white, *square,* wooden block. In Case 3 the same target item is again used but there are three additional alternatives present—a round, black block; a square, black one; and a square, white one. Olson hypothesized that even though the *same* item (the white, round one) is the target in each case, nevertheless, the messages which are used to designate it will differ in the following ways. For Case 1 the message will be essentially of the form "It's the *white* one;" for Case 2, "It's the *round* one;" and for Case 3, "It's the *round, white* one."

From these reasonable inferences about the message content, Olson drew the following conclusions concerning word-referent relations. (a) Words do not invariably name things; for each of the paradigm cases, the target object is a block, yet few, if any, of the messages will name the specific class of objects because all the items in the array are blocks. Hence the word "block" conveys no useful information for such an array. We shall refer to this hypothesis as the *pronominal usage hypothesis*. It tells us what level of noun/pronoun specificity to expect to occur in messages. All the messages given above would be scored as using a low-specific pronominal because they all used the word "one"; however, if any message included words such as "block" to designate the target, then this would be an example of high-specific pronominal usage. (b) Words do not name the particular target items. In each of the three cases, the same item is to be designated, yet the messages will differ. Hence words here serve to designate a particular referent with respect to the set of alternatives from which it is to be differentiated. (c) A message will not exhaust the potential list of features of the target. For the above cases, none of the messages will indicate that the target is also a wooden or physical object, none will mention that the material is porous, etc. Instead, the messages will specify the item only to the *minimum* level required in order to distinguish it from the remaining alternatives in the set. We shall call this the *minimum feature usage hypothesis* or, equivalently, the *minimum redundancy hypothesis*. For the first two cases, the minimum number of features required was '1' while for Case 3 the minimum was '2'.

Olson realized that these hypotheses may not always hold under all conditions; that is, it may not always be the case that the minimum number of features will be used—some settings may lead to a certain degree of redundancy in the messages. A similar qualification of the pronominal usage hypothesis was made [see Olson (1970, p. 266) for further details].

One of our concerns in this section will be to attempt to characterize some of those variables that may affect the degree of redundancy in messages and those variables that may affect the pronominal usage hypothesis. Thus, while an initial reading of Olson's paradigm cases is intuitively compelling, nevertheless some questions about their completeness can be raised when one attempts to characterize *how* one processes the information in a set of alternatives in order to construct messages.

We shall raise five problems concerning message content; for three of them, some empirical evidence will provide us with some answers to these problems.

1. The first question centers around the possible effect that the *number of dimensions* used to construct the set of items will have on the message. Suppose that a set of five alternatives were constructed using two perfectly correlated dimensions. That is, suppose we had five distinct levels of height (and called it dimension-1) and suppose we had five distinct levels of shading (and called this dimension-2). There are two ways to produce a perfect correlation between these two dimensions. Let one alternative be a combination of the tallest level along with the darkest shade, let another alternative be the second tallest along with the second darkest shade, and so on. (The other way to produce a perfect correlation is to let one alternative be the tallest in combination with the lightest shade, the next alternative to be the second tallest along with the second lightest shade, and so on.) Now, any one of these levels from just *one* of these dimensions can be selected to designate in a nonredundant way an intended referent. But because either one of these dimensions is equally appropriate, there is the possibility that the message writer may well be prone to choose to include both dimensions in his message,

especially since he may fail to realize that the dimensions are perfectly correlated. The recognition that the dimensions are correlated or not would seem to be a purely cognitive problem-solving concern and hence relevant in constructing an information-processing approach of communication via messages.

2. A second question that one can raise is whether the *number of alternatives* will affect the degree of redundancy in a message. Again, one can postulate in an information-processing sense that a subject evaluates the adequacy of what he has already included in his message in an attempt to decide whether the receiver will find it adequate. It is not too difficult to imagine that the message writer (who here is functioning as an implicit message receiver—he evaluates his message as he writes it from the point of view of a potential receiver) will tend to write a more redundant message if many alternatives have to be processed, especially so if these alternatives happen to be constructed using perfectly correlated dimensions. That is, if more items have to be processed before the message is written, this should make it even more difficult to detect the nature of the correlation among the dimensions (given that they are correlated). Since we have already characterized such a decision as a cognitive problem-solving one, the number of alternatives in the set is, by the above argument, going to be implicated as an important factor in affecting the degree of redundancy that a message may have.

3. A third question that can be raised concerning Olson's paradigm cases is the overall familiarity or codability of the objects that have been constructed using n-dimensions. Suppose that we have used dimensions which form very familiar types of objects—for example, height and width combinations (drawn at 90 degree angles) form a familiar object, a rectangle. But if the lines had not been connected at the corners, it would be a less easily coded object; given that it is less codable, this surely should affect the number of features that the subject will use because he may decide that the receiver will need all the extra information he can get in order to deal effectively with these unfamiliar objects. Thus, one can give at least an intuitive argument about a possible relationship between object familiarity and degree of redundancy. This same aspect of object familiarity might also affect the extent to which the message will contain an overly-specific pronominal. That is, instead of just referring to the unfamiliar object by the nonspecific term "one," as in "It's the tallest one," he may feel the need to be more explicit, such as "It's the tallest object that almost looks like a rectangle." This would be an example of an overly specific pronominal because all the items in this unfamiliar set could be designated as "objects that almost look like rectangles."

4. Another concern is whether the *number of items that are to be designated as target items* will influence the degree of redundancy. However, here it is not quite clear how to apply the redundancy concept. For example, if there are five alternatives and *four* of them are designated as *targets*, then is it necessarily redundant to list each of the designated alternatives? Or should we interpret the redundancy concept as one which designates this subset of target items by *exclusion*, as in the following way: "Pick all of them except the third tallest."? This message is to be contrasted with saying, "Pick the shortest, second shortest, second tallest, and the tallest ones." Or equivalently, "Pick the two shortest and two tallest ones." While it is

clear that designating the target subset by a process of exclusion is definitely a more efficient way to write messages, it is not completely clear whether the other messages should be considered redundant.

5. A fifth question is the following. Suppose we have four objects in an explicitly given set of alternatives. Let these objects be constructed from two dimensions: dimension-1 consists of two sub-classes of animals (dogs versus cats) while dimension-2 consists of four levels of darkness (white, light-gray, dark-gray, and black). Suppose that the first item is a white cat, the next a light-gray cat, the third a dark-gray dog, and the fourth a black dog. If the first item is the target, then a literal reading of Olson's redundancy concept would require a message of the following type: "It's the white one." To say "It's the white *cat*" would be redundant. If the fourth item were the target, a nonredundant message would be "It's the black one" and a redundant message would be "It's a black *dog*." (Here the noun class of dog versus cat acts like a feature, since it can operate to reduce uncertainty as in examples where multiple targets divide the set of objects into just cats versus dogs.) Yet I believe everyone will agree that it sounds *more natural* to use the redundant message form whereas there is something unsettling about the use of the purely nonredundant form (which requires *only* the use of the brightness dimension to completely designate the target item).

Can we account for this intuitive judgment in a more formal way? I believe we can. The crux of the matter is that we *first* seem to process the set of four alternatives in terms of the most *salient* dimension available (the dog versus cat dimension, or species dimension). We need not inquire as to how it is that some dimensions can become more salient (more attention capturing) than others; we simply assume that dimensions can differ in this respect. If we further assume that this species dimension *strictly dominates* the effect of the second dimension (the darkness dimension), then this would account for why we feel compelled always to include the species name in writing messages in this context. First, we scan the available set of alternatives; the feature we notice first is from the most salient (dominant) dimension—in this case, the species dimension. Then, because this feature (dog versus cat) does not completely designate the desired target, we *add* the qualifying information about darkness. While this explanation is completely ad hoc, it *does* account for our intuition that it is more natural to use the redundant form over the nonredundant one. The fact that we can be forced to admit that only the brightness dimension need be used to write these messages, though, means that, under special conditions of instruction, we can override the strict dominance of one dimension over the other.

6. A final question concerns what effect varying the minimum number of features needed to designate an item will have on the degree of redundancy that is obtained. Suppose that the minimum number of features required by a strict observance of the redundancy concept is two or more. Is it any more likely that the degree of redundancy (with respect to this minimum level) will be any greater than the degree of redundancy obtained when the minimum is just one feature?

Empirical information regarding some of these questions is now available. Specifically, the first four problems raised have received some tentative empirical answers based upon some studies conducted by myself and Philip Kingsley. I shall now describe some of these findings.

EXPERIMENTAL STUDIES OF MESSAGE CONSTRUCTION

First Experiment

The first experiment varied the number of dimensions (three and five dimension arrays) and the type of instructions (so as to induce differential codability of the figures used in each stimulus array). Examples of the five dimensional stimulus arrays (five items in each array) are shown in Figure 1. In this figure, four different correlation patterns are illustrated among the five underlying dimensions (the five dimensions being height, width, and darkness of the rectangular parts, and height and darkness of the triangular parts of the figure). Regardless which of the correlational patterns one examines, it is clear that only *one* feature (one dimension) of the target figure (the target for which a message is to be written has an "x" below it in each array) need be mentioned to completely designate which item in the array is being described; however, the choice of *which* feature is to be selected for writing the message depends completely upon the subject.

The four correlational patterns were selected somewhat arbitrarily (there are others that could be constructed from these five dimensions); the main reason for choosing several correlational patterns was to introduce variety in the stimulus arrays presented over successive trials. Another way in which variety was introduced was to alter the *order* in which the five items in each array were arranged; none of the five item arrays were presented in exactly the order shown in Figure 1. Instead, the order was randomly determined with the restriction that no items which are *adjacent* in Figure 1 arrays would be permitted to occur in the stimulus arrays. Also, the figure which was selected as a target in each five-item array was randomly determined, with the restriction that over all trials, all five possible positions would be equally represented.

Three dimensional figures were constructed by deleting the triangular parts of the items shown in Figure 1 (thus the three dimensions of the resulting figures would consist of just the height, width, and darkness dimensions of the rectangular part).

Forty subjects were tested (ten in each of four conditions). In Condition 1, the subjects were given the three dimensional figures. The instructions for this condition designated the items as "geometric forms." The three remaining conditions used the five dimensional figures; they differed in the type of instructions given. For example, subjects in Condition 2 were told that the figures represented "buildings casting shadows" (henceforth called the "buildings" condition); in Condition 3, the figures were called "bookends"; and in Condition 4, the figures were referred to as "geometric forms." Thus, Conditions 1 and 4 have the same instructions but differ in number of dimensions used to construct the figures. Conditions 2, 3, and 4 present the same stimulus figures but differ in the way in which the stimulus figures are designated; this latter variation was intended to induce differentiable codability such that figures designated as "bookends" or as "buildings" should be readily coded (and this might affect the pronominal hypothesis and/or the redundancy

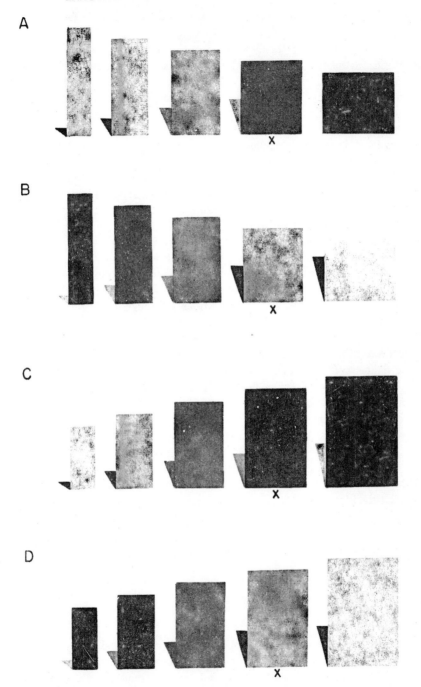

FIG. 1. Examples of the four types of perfectly correlated feature patterns which were used to construct the five-item stimulus arrays used in the first experiment. The "x" which occurs in each five-item array shows how the subjects identified which item in the array was the target item for which a message was to be written.

hypothesis), whereas the figures in Condition 4 should be less readily coded.

The mean number of features that were encoded per message for the three dimensional geometric forms, "buildings," "bookends," and five dimensional geometric forms conditions was 1.54, 1.56, 1.16, and 1.98, respectively. Analysis of variance revealed that the instructional variable significantly affected the degree of redundancy present in the last three conditions such that the arrays which were presumably easily coded (the "buildings" and "bookends") were significantly lower in redundancy than the unfamiliar or hard to code figures in Condition 4 ($p < .01$). Thus, differential codability induced by the instructions for the *identical* stimulus arrays significantly alters the degree of redundancy present in messages. A comparison of Condition 1 with Condition 4 suggested only a marginal level of significance ($p > .10$) was produced by varying the number of dimensions used to construct the stimulus figures (later studies to be reported below, though, indicate that the number of dimensions used does significantly affect redundancy).

The test of the pronominal hypothesis for this experiment also indicates significant differences among these four conditions. The proportion of low-specific pronominal usage (use of "it," "one," or no noun at all) to designate the target item was .625, .290, .760, and .370 for Conditions 1 through 4, respectively. The most interesting significant difference obtained here was between the "buildings" and "bookends" conditions ($p < .05$). This was an unexpected result, inasmuch as the instructions given in both conditions were expected to make the subjects see that all the figures were easily coded. A possible *post hoc* explanation for this difference may be that the figures designated as "bookends" were viewed as single objects which could be unambiguously referred to by use of the low-specific pronominal, whereas the "buildings casting shadows" may have been viewed as figures having *two* separable "parts" (building; shadow), thereby leading to an ambiguous referent when a low-specific pronominal was used. To avoid this ambiguity, the subject more often chose to use a high-specific pronominal.

The effect of the number of dimensions on pronominal usage was again of marginal significance ($p > .10$). This was obtained by contrasting the three-dimensional "geometric forms" condition with the five-dimensional "geometric forms" condition.

I shall return to this first experiment, for purposes of constructing an information-processing model of the message-writer's covert decisions, after I have summarized the results of two additional experiments concerned with messages written in a communication-type setting.

Second Experiment

This second experiment was conducted by myself and Philip Kingsley in order to examine whether the number of alternatives present in an array as well as the number of dimensions used to construct the alternatives would significantly affect the degree of redundancy and the number of low-specific pronominals used. In each experimental condition only *one* feature was necessary to designate the target item and only a low-specific pronominal was needed.

(a) The first condition contrasted two similar shapes (circles) which differed only in size. Thus, the salient aspect of this condition is that it presented *two* alternatives which varied in *one* dimension. (b) The second condition contrasted two alternatives which, like the first condition, were constructed using only one dimension. However, in this condition the dimension consisted of *shape* contrasts (triangle versus square, for example). Thus, the salient aspect of this condition is that it presented two alternatives which varied in one dimension. By contrasting the first and second condition, one could determine whether the choice of dimension used to construct the figures would make any difference in the degree to which the minimum redundancy principle held. (c) The third condition contrasted *two* alternatives of rectangular shape. *Three* dimensions were used to construct the figures: height, width, and darkness. (d) In the fourth condition, *five* alternatives were present in the array. *Three* dimensions were used to construct the rectangular figures (height, width, and darkness). (e) In the fifth condition, *two* alternatives were present in the array. *Five* dimensions were used to construct the alternatives (these figures were identical to the types shown in Figure 1 above). (f) In the last condition, *five* alternatives were present in the array and *five* dimensions were used to construct the figures (these figures were identical also to those found in Figure 1).

All subjects received exemplars from each of the six conditions; the order of presentation of these six conditions was randomized for every subject. In all, 26 subjects were tested.

Friedman analyses of variance were conducted for both feature and pronominal usage (the Friedman test was used because one or more of the conditions resulted in highly skewed distributions). Both tests resulted in an overall significant effect across conditions ($p < .001$ in both cases).

The mean number of features used in Conditions 1 through 6, respectively, was 1.10, 1.17, 1.58, 1.71, 1.73, and 1.88. For pronominal usage, the proportion of low-specific pronominals ("it," "one," or no noun) was .12, .20, .29, .31, .64, and .65 for Conditions 1 through 6, respectively. Comparisons among the conditions with respect to feature usage indicated that, as the number of alternatives in the array increased, the degree of redundancy increased. Also, as the dimensions used to construct the figures increased, the degree of redundancy increased. With regard to pronominal usage, it was found that as the number of alternatives increased, the pronominal hypothesis was *more* likely to be satisfied; similarly, as the number of dimensions used to construct the figures increased, the pronominal hypothesis was again more likely to be satisfied! This result was somewhat surprising inasmuch as it suggests that the feature usage postulate is more adversely affected by increases in the number of alternatives and dimensionality of the stimulus arrays, whereas the pronominal usage postulate is more nearly satisfied by increases in the number of alternatives and dimensionality.

Third Experiment

The third study attempted to determine whether the number of target items would increase the tendency of subjects to use what we have called efficient messages (here the most efficient way to specify multiple targets is by the process of *exclusion,* as in "Pick all of them except the tallest" in the case of four items being designated as targets out of a five-item array). A full analysis of this study has not yet been completed, but a bird's-eye view of the data suggests that people tend to designate multiple targets by a process of exclusion (but not invariably). A further effect appears to be that people tend to be less redundant with the five-dimensional figures used here (the stimuli were identical to those used in Condition 6 of the second experiment). Apparently, when subjects are forced to make a choice between being highly redundant (and inefficient) versus being nonredundant and efficient (using messages of exclusion), they tend to choose the latter.

A Probabilistic Model for Message Construction

Now we shall return to the data collected in the first experiment for purposes of illustrating how a mathematical analysis of the data might illuminate some of the cognitive decisions that a subject makes when he constructs messages. Our main motivation for constructing a mathematical model is that we have already seen that the algebraic (all-or-none) hypotheses of Olson concerning feature and pronominal usage are not fulfilled. Yet the *majority* of the messages written for each of the four conditions did satisfy the minimum redundancy hypothesis. How then do we try to account for those trials where the subject decides to use more than the minimum? What is the subject *doing* that leads him on some trials to use the minimum and on other trials to violate the minimum needed? A further question can be raised concerning a new finding that was not given earlier; it concerns the fact that a *steady increase* in the number of low-specific pronominals occurs over trials within each of the four conditions. What is the explanation for this increase? Can one adequately predict the course of this practice effect? (The reader may be interested to learn that a similar practice effect was not found for feature usage; only pronominal usage showed a significant practice effect over trials.)

A Model for Feature Usage

Suppose the subject scans the array of alternatives and decides that he must use a minimum of m features (this m may or may not coincide with the true minimum number of features M required by the minimum redundancy hypothesis). It is assumed that he writes down these m features with probability P (and with probability $1-P$ he decides that no more features need be added). Given that the subject decides to write down yet another feature, he does so with probability P; given that he has written down this additional feature, he again examines what he has written so far and decides again whether to add yet another feature, (one is added with probability P), etc. In this way, a subject can build up a number of such features before he finishes a particular message.

Since the figures were composed using only a finite number of dimensions, it seems natural that there should be only a finite number of features that the subject could reasonably include in his message. Because of this, we need another parameter x which will indicate for each subject what the maximum number of features is that he can find to encode in message form; or, alternatively, we shall consider x to be the maximum number of features that a subject thinks might be necessary for a recipient of the message to have given a large number of alternatives in the set and a large number of dimensions used to construct the figures. In other words, each subject sets up two internal criteria which guide his decision to use features: He sets up a lower limit m and an upper limit x. The probability distribution that will tell us how often he actually uses each number of features between and including these two values is governed by the parameter P. Clearly, in outlining the above, we did not have to consider what the "real" minimum M was, nor did we have to consider how this "real" minimum might affect the value x or P. (The influence of M on m, x, or P could, of course, be studied *after* these parameters have been estimated by examining the distributions of each of these parameters across subjects, but that need not concern us here.)

The above model leads to what we shall call a Generalized Truncated Geometric Distribution (a separate such distribution is estimated for each subject). If m is always set at '1' and if x is allowed to become arbitrarily large, then this Generalized Truncated Distribution becomes the classical Geometric Distribution. It also deserves comment that if $m = M$ and if $1\text{-}P = 0.0$, we then get Olson's minimum feature postulate as a special case of this more general probabilistic model.

Appendix A presents some results on how to calculate the means and variances for up to the first five terms of this new distribution (only the first five terms sufficed for our present purposes). Appendix A also shows how to compute the maximum likelihood estimate of P, given that m and x are known.

Table 1 presents the observed and predicted means and variances for each of the forty subjects in the first experiment for feature usage. The fit seems reasonably accurate. This table also shows us that most subjects set m equal to '1' regardless of which experimental condition they were in; however, we note, too, that the upper criterion x did appear to be strongly influenced by the experimental conditions. Similarly, the P values for the five-dimensional "geometric forms" condition appear to be lower in magnitude than for the other conditions. (The fact that m varies so little suggests that future applications of this model can probably fix the value of m at '1' and still adequately fit the data with fewer free parameters to be estimated.)

Model for Pronominal Usage

We shall use a linear probability "learning" model to account for the increase in probability of using a low-specific pronominal as trials progress. This linear model, due to its combining-of-classes assumption, is ideal for our present purposes, inasmuch as we clearly find it meaningful to *combine* a variety of responses (such as "it," "one," or no noun at all) into a single class of responses called low-specific pronominals.

Two versions of this linear model were explored. The first assumed that all subjects shared the same 'sampling' proportion Θ (theta) but could differ in their probability of emitting a low-specific response in trial 1 (designated by p_1 where the subscript '1' designates the trial number). The change that occurs from one trial to the next is assumed to be governed solely by the following equation (see Estes, 1959):

$$p_{n+1} = p_n + \Theta (1\text{-}p_n) \tag{1}$$

TABLE 1

Observed and Predicted Means and Variances for Feature Usage

Subject I.D. and Experimental Conditions	Obs. Mean	Pred. Mean	Obs. Variance about Mean	Pred. Variance about Mean	Values taken on by the 3-parameter model for each subject		
					m	x	P
3-dimensional							
1.	1.00	1.00	0.00	0.00	1	1	1.000
2.	1.10	1.10	0.09	0.09	1	2	0.900
3.	2.45	2.53	0.37	0.25	2	3	0.473
4.	1.05	1.05	0.05	0.05	1	2	0.950
5.	1.00	1.00	0.00	0.00	1	1	1.000
6.	1.00	1.00	0.00	0.00	1	1	1.000
7.	3.00	2.87	0.42	0.73	2	4	0.444
8.	1.25	1.25	0.20	0.19	1	2	0.750
9.	2.20	2.16	0.69	0.76	1	3	0.314
10.	1.40	1.46	0.25	0.25	1	2	0.555
"buildings"							
11.	1.00	1.00	0.00	0.00	1	1	1.000
12.	2.20	2.33	0.38	0.22	2	3	0.666
13.	2.50	2.67	0.47	0.22	2	3	0.333
14.	2.00	2.00	0.00	0.00	2	2	1.000
15.	1.00	1.00	0.00	0.00	1	1	1.000
16.	1.85	1.80	0.87	1.00	1	4	0.528
17.	1.10	1.10	0.09	0.09	1	2	0.900
18.	1.10	1.10	0.09	0.09	1	2	0.900
19.	1.00	1.00	0.00	0.00	1	1	1.000
20.	1.25	1.25	0.30	0.29	1	3	0.792
"bookends"							
21.	1.10	1.10	0.09	0.09	1	2	0.900
22.	1.10	1.10	0.09	0.09	1	2	0.900
23.	1.05	1.05	0.05	0.05	1	2	0.950
24.	1.20	1.20	0.27	0.22	1	3	0.826
25.	1.00	1.00	0.00	0.00	1	1	1.000
26.	1.00	1.00	0.00	0.00	1	1	1.000
27.	1.25	1.25	0.20	0.19	1	2	0.750
28.	1.00	1.00	0.00	0.00	1	1	1.000
29.	1.00	1.00	0.00	0.00	1	1	1.000
30.	1.85	1.78	0.56	0.70	1	3	0.485
5-dimensional "geometric forms"							
31.	1.75	1.72	0.62	0.67	1	3	0.516
32.	2.90	2.84	0.83	1.08	2	5	0.514
33.	1.45	1.42	0.37	0.45	1	3	0.679
34.	2.90	2.91	1.04	1.16	2	5	0.486
35.	2.45	2.32	1.42	1.86	1	5	0.396
36.	1.40	1.46	0.25	0.25	1	2	0.555
37.	1.30	1.30	0.22	0.21	1	2	0.700
38.	1.05	1.05	0.05	0.05	1	2	0.950
39.	1.95	1.91	1.10	1.16	1	4	0.486
40.	2.60	2.68	0.67	0.44	1	3	0.111

Equation 1 can be manipulated so as to estimate the Θ parameter which all subjects (in all four conditions) are assumed to have in common. A bit of algebra gives:

$$\Theta = (p_{n+1} - p_n)/(1-p_n) \qquad (2)$$

If we take grouped data (which it is permissable to do because of the linearity of the model), we can then use all adjacent trial proportions of low-specific usage in order to esimate Θ. Once Θ is estimated, we can then work through Eq. (1) to get an estimate of p_1 for each subject.

A second model was also tested because, as we shall see, the overall fit of the first model was quite inadequate in terms of fitting the runs statistics. (Both models, though, did about equally well in fitting the overall 'practice' curve.) This second model assumed that Eq. (1) was still appropriate, but now it was assumed that each subject differed in both his p_1 value as well as Θ value. Since the runs test was a good discriminator between these two models, only this has been presented in Table 2. A Monte Carlo simulation of each subject was carried out in order to determine the 'predicted' run lengths. (Although run statistics are available for each subject, for convenience I have combined over subjects for purposes of presenting a concise overall fit of the two models in comparison with the data).

Comment on Quantitative Approaches to Reference

A question which some may raise about the above models is whether they really tell us anything new about the communication process, and by implication, about a cognitive theory of reference. Furthermore, what do they tell us about the measurement of message content? Taking the second question first, it is my belief that simply observing a mean feature usage score for each subject and using this to reflect the subject's performance is a naive and inadquate way to understand the complexities of the data actually collected in the communication task. According to the model sketched above, it is possible for two subjects to both have the same mean feature usage scores but to differ in the information-processing steps by which each arrived at that score. Only by stating a clear model of what these steps are, and by fitting a model which is sensitive to all aspects of the data and not just the mean, can we hope to *measure* the ways in which these two subjects actually differ. Regarding the first question, I believe that the models suggested above do actually tell us something new about a theory of reference. In the first place, it suggests that a probabilistic information-processing model possesses the desired degree of generality which will yield adequate fits in a variety of experimental settings, but, in addition, it is capable of handling those special situations which may be in complete accord with what we have called the algebraic (all-or-none) hypotheses of Olson regarding feature and pronominal usage. That is, under appropriate restrictions of the parameters of this probabilistic model, one can obtain Olson's model as a special case of the more general one. In this way, we manage to retain much of the power of Olson's analysis but extend it in the sense that now we can also offer an account of why it is that subjects may depart from these postulates in some experimental settings.

TABLE 2

Observed and Predicted Frequencies of Run Lengths of Low-Specific and
High-Specific Pronominals

Run Length	Predicted (simulated) Frequency using 2-parameter Linear Model[a]	Observed Frequency for each Run Length[b]	Predicted (simulated) Frequency using 1-parameter Linear Model
1	38	24	93
2	19	14	42
3	14	6	17
4	1	6	11
5	7	5	4
6	2	4	5
7	2	0	4
8	2	2	2
9	0	1	4
10	0	5	1
11	2	0	1
12	0	1	3
13	2	1	3
14	0	0	2
15	0	2	0
16	0	1	1
17	1	0	0
18	0	4	1
19	4	1	0
20	23	21	12

[a] For the two parameter linear learning mode the p_1 and Θ (theta) values for every subject were allowed to differ; for the one-parameter model all subjects shared the same Θ value but were allowed to differ in their p_1 value. See text for further discussion.

[b] Data from all four experimental conditions combined.

FACTORS IN COMPREHENSION

Identification of Subject Matter

One aspect of comprehension that has not received much attention is that in addition to assigning semantic interpretations to individual sentences we are also attempting to understand a larger issue: What the speaker is driving at. That is, part of saying that we comprehend what the speaker has said or is saying is that we know what his main *topic* is. I shall attempt to investigate in this section a few of the factors that influence our ability to isolate what the relevant topic of conversation is.

Naively, one might suppose that the main topic is always conveyed by the utterance of a few key words in the speaker's introductory statements. While key words undoubtedly do play an important role here, I shall argue that an additional factor which alters the effectiveness of these key words is the *implicit or explicit set of topical alternatives* that might be talked about in special situations.

When we listen to prolonged discourse (say on some lecture concerning art history) we could take the text of the talk after having read it several times and break it up into sections, where some sections emphasized perhaps the esthetic aspects of the key artists of various periods while other sections placed the listener in proper historical perspective for each such period. Finally, there might be a third gross division for those parts which showed how the esthetics of the period were tied to the historical trends. (There would be many other subsections to each of these main sections, of course.) The point of this rather obvious sectioning is that one could regard this set of topics to be the implied set of cognitive alternatives (subject matters) of differing levels of refinement which we expect to hear the speaker comment on when we listen to his talk for the first time.

As the speaker shifts from one key section to another, and back again, he will often clue us in to this topical shift by special devices (such as topic sentences of paragraphs) which attempt to inform us that he will next concentrate on, say, primarily esthetic problems—in other words, if he is a "good" speaker and is sensitive to the point of view of the listener, he will reduce the uncertainty of what the next topic will be by trying to announce it by some special introductory sentence.

Since humans are fallible creatures, he will presumably not always set aside such special topical cues (he especially won't announce *each* subtle shift in his talk by a special topic sentence). But as we listen, we do at some point notice that he has shifted the emphasis of the main momentary topic from, say, the purely historical concerns to the esthetic concerns. Also, it is likely that not all topic sentences that he might insert to reduce our uncertainty at points in his talk will necessarily remove all our uncertainty as to just what he is driving at; yet we presumably do eventually come around to grasp his special point of view if we listen long enough.

At a more mundane level, all of us have probably walked in on a group that was in the process of discussing some topic while eating lunch. After sitting down and listening for awhile, we usually can decipher just what it is they are talking about and begin to offer comments of our own.

With these preliminary observations, let me explain what I am about in this section. It seems reasonable to expect that the relative difficulty we have in isolating the relevant topic of conversation (or the topic of some talk) is related to the *size of the set of possible alternatives* that we believe might be discussed under a given set of circumstances. That is, it should be easier to identify the topic if only two different topics form the set of possibilities than if, say, eight different possible topics formed the set of possibilities. How might this be studied so as to show beyond a reasonable doubt that the set of cognitive alternatives (the set of possible topics and subtopics that a speaker may touch upon) does influence our ability to isolate the correct? One way is to select an explicit set of alternatives and give this list to the listener. Then we select one of these topics from the list at random and begin reading until the listener stops us and says that he has identified the correct topic. We are interested in *how much* we had to read to him before he could identify it; further, we are interested in how the amount we had to read is related to the *number* of alternative subject matters from which his choice was to be made. Another way to evaluate this idea is exactly like the first method except that the experimenter controls the maximum number of words that will be presented to the subject. For example, the experimenter may read only eight successive words from one of the randomly chosen subject matters and require that the listener make his identification on the basis of just these eight words. In the experiment to be reported below, this second approach was used since it lends itself to group testing; the first method necessarily requires individual testing.

Let us hypothesize that as the number of alternatives increases the subject becomes increasingly less *efficient* (with respect to some baseline, to be described below) in utilizing the semantic information in the message that the experimenter presents him with (the message here is that successive string of *n* words which have been taken from some particular subject matter). As an example of what is meant by efficiency in identifying subject matters, let us consider the following word string: "Women have . . . ." Suppose that the set of alternative subject matters consisted of "physics" and "anthropology." We would be *completely certain* that this string of words must have come from the subject matter of anthropology. Thus, for this set of alternatives we would experience no uncertainty whatever in our decision. Now suppose that for the same word string "Women have . . . " we present the following set of alternatives: "physics," "anthropology," "history," and "physiology." We see that we now experience relatively great confusion about what *may* be the topic of discussion (and hence experience confusion as to what subject matter it may have come from). We might reason that the speaker may be about to tell us about the physiology of women, or that the speaker is about to tell us about some famous women in history, etc. The point of this example is that the number of alternatives can influence our ability to decide which subject matter is the correct ource for the same word string. It also suggests that there is no simple one-to-one corresondence between key vocabulary words (such as the word "women") and subject matters; if there were a simple correspondence between content words and subject matters, we would always be able correctly to identify the subject matter source regardless of how many other alternative choices were made available. Clearly, the above example shows that this cannot be the case and hence key content words do not invariably signal a unique subject matter. As a final point, the above example illustrates that the exact subject matters which have been included in the set of possible alternatives will influence our ability to be correct.

Let's concern ourselves now with measuring efficiency in the identification of subject matters. In the above example "Women have . . . ." we said that everyone would select anthropology over physics as the appropriate subject matter—100% would choose anthropology. If the string of words provides no useful information (such as "It is . . . ." or "also the . . . ," and so on), then only 50% of the people would guess anthropology as the correct subject matter. Let *r* be the observed proportion correct, let *g* be the probability of being correct by chance alone, and let *a* be some number between zero and one. We wish to express how much above chance the observed proportion correct is. Equation 3 will allow us to calculate this efficiency parameter *a*:

$$r = g + a(1-g) \tag{3}$$

Since we are going to interpret the parameter a as a measure of efficiency in identifying subject matters, we want to be sure that this parameter does what it is intended to do. A desirable property that we expect of a is that if all the subjects are correct, then a should take on its maximum value of 1.00 regardless of what the guessing baseline is. It is easy to see that Eq. 3 has this property. Also we want the parameter a always to assume its lowest value of zero if every subject is guessing, and we want this to be independent of what the guessing baseline happens to be. Again, Eq. 3 possesses the desired property, providing that r is never less than g.

A numerical example will help to demonstrate what we are trying to establish. In the above example, where "physics" and "anthropology" alone were the alternative subject matters, we decided that everyone would correctly choose anthropology as the source of "Women have . . . ." Since the guessing baseline for this number of alternatives is .50 and since $r = 1.00$, we estimate a to be 1.00 (its maximum value). Now, when four alternative subject matters are available, let's assume that $r = .60$. The guessing parameter is .25 since there were four alternatives present. This gives us $a = .47$. Comparing the value of a from the two alternative case ($a = 1.00$) with the a value from the four alternative case ($a = .47$) tells us that the efficiency of identifying the correct subject matter was greater for the two alternative case in comparison with the four alternative case. We shall now demonstrate the same effect with real data.

Experiment Four

A number of years ago, I demonstrated that the identification of subject matters improves as the number of words presented in a word string increased (Freedle, 1965); that study also showed that as the number of alternative subject matters increased, the ability of the subjects to correctly guess the source subject matter decreased. For a number of reasons a partial replication of that study will be presented here. Each of 30 subjects responded to each of nine main conditions. (A total of 208 observations were collected from each subject.) A maximum of eight subject matters were chosen from which word strings were sampled (these samples were then presented as stimuli to the subjects): "history," "linguistics," "anthropology," "psychology," "botany," "physiology," "physics," and "geology." The word strings that were sampled always began a sentence from the text from which it was taken. When eight alternatives were available to choose from, the word strings varied in length from only two words, then four words, and finally eight successive words. (Each of these different strings of words, though, were different; that is, none of the longer strings were continuations of the shorter strings.) Another three conditions provided the subjects with four alternative subject matters (three different combinations of the eight subject matters were chosen to represent the four-alternative condition). For each of these four alternatives, two successive words, four, and eight successive words were presented as stimuli. Finally, the last three conditions presented three main combinations of the eight categories to represent the two-alternative subject matter sets; for each of these two, four, and eight successive words were presented as stimuli. Figure 2 presents the proportion correct for each of these nine conditions.

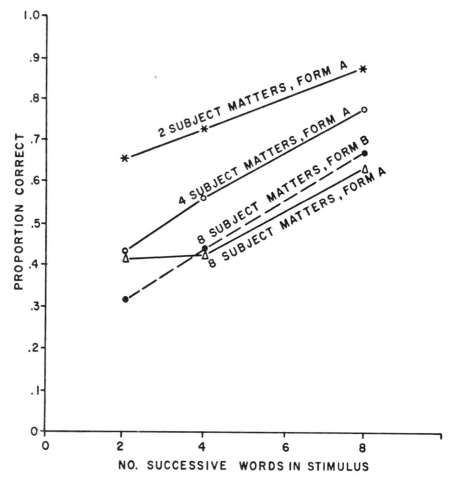

FIG. 2. The proportion of correct identifications of subject-matters for each of the nine experimental conditions (form A) and a replication of three conditions for the eight alternative subject-matters condition (form B).

Because one of the points (the eight alternative case with two words as stimuli) was dramatically out of line with my earlier findings, an additional 27 subjects were run using a different random sample of stimuli (two, four, and eight words) for the eight alternative condition alone. This is also shown in Figure 2.

The efficiency parameter a was calculated for each of these nine conditions (and for the smaller study using 27 subjects as well). These are given in Table 3. We see that as the number of alternatives in the set increases for the two-word stimulus strings, the efficiency decreases. This is true as well for the four-word strings and eight-word strings. In addition this table tells us that the efficiency increases as the number of words presented as stimuli increases for the eight-alternative condition; a similar effect is noted for the four-alternative and two-alternative conditions.

We shall now attempt to probe deeper into this data in order to clarify what decision processes are influencing our experimental subjects. That is, we seek answers to such questions as: "When a subject is *not* completely certain of the subject-matter which acted as the source for a particular word string, does he simply guess at random?" Or to put it another way, "If a subject is known to have made an error on some item that came from anthropology, is he more likely to have made his error by guessing that it came from just certain subject-matters such as psychology or history than he is to have guessed it came from physics?" These questions can be answered by examining what is called the confusion matrix. Suppose we take just one of the nine conditions, say, the one involving eight subject-matters and eight stimulus words. Whenever a particular string of words is known (by the experimenter) to have come from, say, anthropology he can examine the proportion of these guesses which were correct, and the proportion who mistakenly choose each of the other alternatives as their response. These proportions would form one row of the confusion matrix. Since there are eight subject-matters there would be a total of eight such rows in the confusion matrix.

Multidimensional Analysis of Confusion Matrix

Following the application of a correction for bias, and after testing the form of the matrix to see how well it satisfied the three distance axioms (some theoretical work of Luce, 1963, was used here to evaluate these axioms) the matrix was submitted to a multidimensional analysis program (Kruskal, 1964). The results for both a one-dimensional and two-dimensional space is given in Table 4.

The first dimension was interpreted as representing a social versus non-social emphasis underlying the different subject-matters. A two-dimensional analysis gave a much better fit in terms of the Stress index but it appears to defy a clear interpretation. In my opinion, this dimensional analysis, which assigns scale values to each subject-matter, sheds some additional light on the processes underlying comprehension. This analysis informs us that the types of confusions that occurred among the different subject-matters was a highly predictable and regular process. That is, given that one of the 'social' subject-matters such as anthropology was the correct alternative and given that an error was made, the above analyses clearly indicated that this error was not distributed at random among the remaining alternatives; rather the errors tended to be restricted to the three remaining 'social' alternatives.

The identification design used above need not be confined to the particular choice of method employed. A slight variation on this design could lead one to study the factors that affect our ability to detect that a *shift* in subject matter has occurred. This could be done by selecting three kinds of paired sentences: (1) a sentence which ends a paragraph followed by another sentence which begins a new paragraph, (2) a sentence which begins a paragraph followed by the next sentence which occurred in the same paragraph, and (3) two sentences which are selected at random from anywhere within a text or across different texts. By varying the perceived set of possibilities for each of these three conditions one could study the ability of subjects to decide whether the two sentences represent a continuation of the same topic or represent a shift in topical emphasis (as in selecting two sentences from widely different places in the same text) or represent radically different ideas, as in the case of sampling from two different texts each on different topics. For example, one might inform the subject that sometimes the two sentences that he

TABLE 3

Estimates of an Efficiency parameter a for each of Nine Conditions

Number of Alternative Subject-Matters	Value of Efficiency a Per Number of Stimulus Words				Number Observations for each Condition		
	2 words	4 words	8 words	No. Subjects	2 words	4 words	8 words
2	.650	.726	.865[b]	30	720	720	720
4	.426	.558	.771	30	720	720	720
8	.415	.425	.631	30	480	480	480
8	.315	.433	.667	27[a]	448	448	448

[a]This last row represents the efficiency parameter estimates for the smaller group of 27 Ss who were given only the eight subject-matters as alternatives.

[b]It is important to note the implication, that as the number of stimulus words increases without bound the data suggest that the efficiency parameter a will approach its upper limit of 1.00. This means that if a sufficiently large string of words is provided some subject that he will be able to reduce all of his uncertainty as to which topic (subject-matter) of the set of possible topics is being discussed.

TABLE 4

Results of the One-Dimensional and Two-Dimensional
Analyses for the Eight Subject Matters' Confusion Matrix
(Using 8 Successive Words as Stimuli)

Subject Matter	Scale Value for the One-Dimensional Solution (stress = .218) Dimension I
1. history	1.502
2. linguistics	1.139
3. anthropology	0.726
4. psychology	0.300
5. botany	−0.578
6. physiology	−0.618
7. physics	−1.060
8. geology	−1.410

	Scale Values for the Two-Dimensional Solution (stress = .099)	
	Dimension I	Dimension II
1. history	1.222	−0.301
2. linguistics	1.112	0.236
3. anthropolgy	0.335	0.819
4. psychology	0.180	−0.035
5. botany	−0.700	0.818
6. physiology	−0.871	0.115
7. physics	−0.757	−0.536
8. geology	−0.521	−1.115

examines will both be from the same text (on, say, anthropology), but when the two sentences are from different texts the alternative is always a shift from anthropology to only *two* other texts—physics or physiology. Clearly by varying how many different options can occur in this last list we can expect to alter the ability of the subject to discriminate the topic similarity of the two sentences which he sees on any given trial.

Some Similarities between Message
Writing and Topic Identification

What is the relationship between the first group of message-writing tasks and the task on topic identification? First of all, they both illustrate that the size of the stimulus set of alternatives (number of distinct items in the stimulus array for the message-writing studies and the number of alternative subject-matters in the topic identification study) significantly influences response output (it alters feature redundancy and pronominal usage in message-writing and it alters the probability of being 'efficient' in choosing a correct topic to match the stimulus word string). There is a further similarity. We argued that the message-writer can function as an implicit message receiver. That is, as he writes the message he attempts to decide whether he should add more features to the message on the basis of whether he thinks the message receiver can make good use of this additional information. We suggested that if many alternatives are present in the stimulus array, the writer is more likely to believe that additional features (albeit sometimes redundant information) will prove useful to the message receiver. Assuming that he is correct in judging that the receiver *can* make good use of the additional features (presumably because it prevents him from making errors in identifying the target item) we see that this provides us with a link across the studies; It is harder to be correct when many alternative subject matters are to be scanned in searching for the correct topic (i.e., searching for a match between word string reference and the semantic structure of knowledge implicit in a topic label) just as it is presumably harder for the message receiver to scan large arrays when searching for a match between the linguistic content of the message and the linguistically encoded representation of each visually perceived item in the stimulus array. Somehow scanning more information via the set of alternatives interfers with efficiency in both cases.[2]

---

[2] Trabasso as well as Olson (see this volume) have suggested chronometric models which deal with the information-processing steps underlying the comparison of sentential content and pictorial information which either does or does not match the sentential information. We see here the possibility of an exciting extension of their chronometric approach to the problem of modeling the mental operations involved in a message receiver's comparison of the message content with each figure in the stimulus array. That is, one should be able to model the *time* it takes for a subject to perceptually scan the stimulus alternatives all the while converting each dimensional feature of each figure into a linguistic representation so as to match these features against the featural information in the message; the subject is assumed to keep testing each figure (by some fixed serial strategy, such as left-to-right) until one of the stimulus figures produces a perfect *match* with all aspects of the message.

Some Speculations on Semantic Error Detection and Correction

What we have already said about message content and subject matters and the constraints exerted upon them by the set of perceived alternatives provides us with a framework to 'explain' how it is that we as language receivers can *detect* semantic errors, or how we can be lead, under certain circumstances, to believe that an error has been committed. Suppose a speaker is going on at length about the virtues of being a boy scout. If we have had any experience with the activities engaged in by scouts—their outings, summer camps, etc.—then we will formulate a set of likely alternatives that will be linked together by the speaker. In each 'part' of the speaker's talk there is assumed to be some implicit or explicit set of alternatives that the speaker may be discussing. Suppose the speaker suddenly begins to discuss an interesting movie that he has seen. This topic of movies does *not match* any element of the implicit set that we as listeners may have been considering. Many listeners will conclude that an error has been committed. This suggests that we detect topical errors when we can find no match between the classification of this new assertion and the set of items that are in our inferred or explicit set of possibilities.

The speaker may of course have intended to relate how the boy scouts reacted to this particular movie but had neglected to properly cue his listeners to this sudden shift in emphasis. Had he done so, no semantic error would have been detected. Again the reason no error would have been detected is that a match between the topic of movies and some element in the set of possibilities *would* be possible because the speaker has caused this item to be added to our set of possibilities.

Now once an error has been detected, we as listeners may interrupt the speaker and suggest to him that what he really meant to say was such-and-such. That is, occasionally we both detect and correct semantic errors. Presumably we make the correction by choosing that element in our inferred set which most nearly matches what has already been said. This again suggests the influence that the set-of-possibilities has upon our ability to offer corrections. If the speaker has been speaking only a short while and if our set of possible topics is still very large (because the speaker hasn't had a chance to narrow it down for us as yet), under these circumstances we may not feel that we can offer a correction given that we believe an error has been made. The reason that we don't offer a correction here is that no single element stands out as the most likely element.

By hypothesizing that some experimental subjects may differ in what elements are included in their inferred set of subtopics, we could account for the presumed 'fact' that individuals differ in their ability to detect and correct errors. Suppose some subjects typically infer a *larger set* than is necessary regardless of what they are listening to (they are in some sense always prepared for the speaker to present a more general and far-reaching talk than is usually warranted). Suppose there is another group of subjects who typically underestimate the complexity of formal speeches. Then this difference in their cognitive set of possibilities should produce a difference in their ability to comprehend what the speaker is saying and, in addition, should lead to differences in their ability to detect and correct true semantic errors made by the speaker.

If the inferred set is too small (allows for too few possibilities) then the listener will find that he must continually revise to himself what the speaker is talking about—he must continually revise because what is said does not match what is in his inferred set of possibilities. This person should find it very difficult to follow what the speaker is saying because he has so much trouble settling on a reasonable set of possibilities. This listener may also have the feeling that what the speaker has said is full of contradictions. He would conclude this because he detected so many mismatches due to the paucity of his set of topical possibilities. By supposition though, we have placed the blame on the listener and not on the quality of the speaker's presentation. The subject who slightly overestimates the range of subtopics should have no difficulty understanding this same speaker. This same individual should be able to choose a reasonable match of what the speaker intended to say given that he detects an error, whereas the person with a very small set of possibilities should more often choose (if he chooses at all) an unreasonable alternative given that he thinks an error has occurred.

We shall have more to say about individual differences in the next section which deals in part with the comprehension of stories.

Story Comprehension and Relational Networks

Several researchers have shown renewed interest in studying the comprehension process from the point of view of examining the relational concepts which hold among key elements in some discourse. (Dawes, 1964, 1966; Frase, 1971). Dawes' approach is closest to what we shall have to say about the broader issues of comprehension so I shall summarize some of his ideas. "In our literate society, a primary means of acquiring knowledge is reading. The memory of what we read, and our distortion of it, is therefore a major determinant of what we know, think we know, and don't know." (Dawes, 1966, p. 77). He goes on to consider an appropriate way to measure and characterize what it is that is understood in the reading process. "The measurement method is based on the fact that *meaningful declarative statements assert set relations* . . . . The central thesis is that memory and distortion of meaningful material may be measured by the memory and distortion of the set relations asserted in that material. Set relations embody 'what is said' in a passage." (Dawes, 1966, p. 77).

Before we go further, let us attempt to relate this conception of Dawes with what we have already considered. Presumably in certain types of discourse (Longacre, 1970, has identified five types of discourse) such as Expository Discourse, the listener uses the various topical cues provided by the speaker in order to form an implicit set of subtopics that could be the focus of the talk. Or it may be some *combination* of these subtopics that the speaker wishes to interrelate. While we listen to more and more of what the speaker has to say we gradually narrow down what it is the speaker is driving at. (This bears a clear relationship to the gradual improvement in identifying subject-matters as the number of stimulus words increases.) If Dawes is correct, then not only have we a clearer idea of some overall topic that the speaker was driving at but, in addition, we have stored up a number of relations which tied together key concepts that were discussed by the speaker at various points in his presentation (perhaps the key concepts occurred in what we previously called the various subsections of a talk). By understanding the particular set of relational assertions made by the speaker we feel that we have understood his speech. Presumably, in remembering these various relational links between key concepts we have learned something; that is, we have formed new ideas between concepts (topics or subtopics) that we might not have hit upon by ourselves.

Now let's continue with Dawes' conception of comprehension and the measurement problems associated with set relations. Dawes distinguished four types of set relations for purposes of experimental study. (1) Identity—here all of x are y, and all of y are x. (2) Exclusion—here none of x is y; by Aristotelian logic this implies that none of y is x. (3) Inclusion—all of x is y, but not all of y is x. (4) Disjunction—some of x is y, and some of y is x.

The kinds of set relation errors that Dawes concentrated on were called overgeneralization and pseudo-discrimination. In order to understand these concepts we must define a nested relation. The relations of identity, exclusion, and inclusion all are related in the sense that one set is entirely *nested* in the other or in the complement of the other. However if two sets are related by disjunction then neither is completely nested in the other or the complement of the other. Dawes used this distinction between disjunctive relations and nested relations as the basis for what he calls a measure of *simplification*. He suggested that prose material has been overgeneralized whenever the subject remembers a disjunctive relation as a nested one (that is, the subject errors in recall or in identifying the correct relations between concepts would be called an error of overgeneralization if the story asserted a disjunctive relation between x and y but the subject mistakenly recalled the relation as either an identity, exclusion, or inclusion relation). If the obverse error occurred (a nested relation was remembered as a disjunctive one) this would be an error of pseudo-discrimination. Dawes then defines a simplification measure by examining whether overgeneralized errors occur more often than pseudo-discriminated ones: The degree to which this occurs provides one with a measure of simplification of the story content.

I propose to provide a more general measurement scheme which will allow us to measure the proportion of confusions that occur between any two of the Gergonne set relation (there are 17 types of confusion that can occur some of which will be described later). Dawes' measure of 'simplication' as defined above collapses many of these possible 17 types into just *two* types (overgeneralization versus pseudo-discrimination). Once this larger matrix of possible confusions has been determined, it is then possible to collapse over several entries in this larger matrix to obtain just the two types of Dawes' errors. The virtue of constructing this larger matrix is that it provides us with a more detailed examination of the types of cognitive distortions that occur in our memory for asserted (or inferred) relations between elements in some discourse. The Dawes measures necessarily discard much of this additional information.

In order to identify the set relation that a subject may have remembered it is necessary to obtain two judgments from him. If a story asserts an inclusion relation between two social groups such as "All of the farmers are voters but only some of the voters are farmers" then we shall ask the subject to indicate whether "All, some, or none of the farmers were voters" and also ask him whether "All, some, or none of the voters were farmers." Only by obtaining both judgments is it possible to uniquely identify the set relation that the subject 'remembered'.

By giving such questions one might object that I must necessarily be testing only the logical ability of subjects and cannot be testing the memory that subjects have for relations asserted in the story. While I do not deny that there is a strong aura of logic surrounding questions formulated in this way, one can provide several reasons why these questions do not provide a strict test of logical abilities. At the simplest level, if the story asserts that "some x are y" and later I ask the subject "Did the story assert that some of x are y?"—this certainly is not a test of logic. When an inference has to be made to get a test question correct though, this certainly looks like it may be closer to logic—yet it can be shown that some of the conclusions that we reach (legitimate conclusions, I believe) 'have' a truth value not by any logical deductions but because of the nature of the presuppositions that go into our language. To give an example, if I tell you that George Smith and Harry Smith are both over six feet tall while Tim is five feet tall, you are able to make the legitimate deduction that Tim is shorter than George or Harry. However if I told you instead that George and Harry are adults while Tim is a newborn infant (all human) you would still be able to reach the legitimate conclusion that Tim is shorter than George or Harry. But you have done this by a process that lies outside of traditional logic (or at least outside the kind of logic I am familiar with).

There is another reason why I decided to ask the converse of each test questions (if the explicitly given relation is of the form xRy, the converse would be to evaluate the relation T holding for yTx). There is the possibility that one can form all of the combinations of the key elements asserted in the story (taken two at a time) so as to evaluate how the subject perceived, in set relational terms, all of the concepts considered as a single pattern. This could be done using Venn diagrams. Since every subject responded to all these test items, one could presumably draw a separate Venn diagram for each subject. Also one could redraw the Venn diagram each time the subject heard the story (and answered the questions) and so provide a way to 'visualize' the way in which the subject's perceptions of the story have changed from one exposure to the next. While this is in part a legitimate expectation, it turns out that it cannot be fulfilled. One difficulty stems from the fact that not every Venn diagram is *uniquely* determined by knowing the relations which hold among every two elements. For example if x, y, and z are three elements in a set and every pair of them is evaluated, then it would be impossible to decide whether to draw the Venn diagram such that z may equal x or y (this last 'or' is to be interpreted as a set operation) or whether the set x or y is a strict subset of z. Because of this we shall not claim that any Venn diagram which we may choose to draw is necessarily unique. A second difficulty stems from the possibility that logical contradictions can occur when subjects evaluate set relations. For example, if a subject responds that some of x is y, but later, in evaluating its corverse decides to say that none of y is x, this yields a contradiction. Whenever this occurs it prevents drawing a complete Venn diagram.

Before we get into the experiment proper, consider the following possibilities concerning individual differences. In the previous sections we raised the possibility that if some individuals have too narrow a set of alternative subtopics in mind, they will find a particular speech difficult to follow; but if they have a 'sufficiently' large set of subtopics in mind, then they should find this same speech relatively easy to grasp. We are going to consider an analogous idea for the present section. Suppose that we give the test questions to some of our subjects prior to their hearing the actual story. Of these subjects, some will guess many questions correctly even before they hear the story, and others will guess less well. Will the number of questions guessed correctly influence how easily they will comprehend (grasp the set relations) the story once they finally hear it? To put it another way, suppose we use their guesses to the test questions as a way to *define what their inferred set of subtopics is* prior to hearing the story. Some of these guesses (some of these subtopics) will match what will in fact be said in the story, and some of these guesses will not match what will be said. Will we find a significant correlation between the number correct on prior guessing and the number correct after first hearing the story? Another way to approach individual differences is to consider the following. Suppose some individuals in their prior guesses use the quantifier "some" much more often than they use "all" or "none". Here we disregard whether the actual use of "some" correctly matches or not what will be asserted in the story; we simply count the number of guesses which use the quantifier "some" and use this as an index of *the degree to which the subject is ready to hear a very complex and highly interconnected story*. If, on the other hand, other individuals use a large number of extreme responses such as "all" or "none" then we shall use this count as an index of the degree to which they are set to hear a relatively simple story of extreme relations holding among the key elements in the story.

Experiment Five

One of Dawes' original stories (1964) was used. This was done primarily because information on the story is already available and it is known to produce the simplification phenomenon which was referred to above. Fifty-one subjects were tested. In the experimental group, 33 subjects guessed the answers to the test questions prior to hearing the story. The 18 subjects in the control group responded to the questions only after hearing the story. (In addition the control group did not know what type of questions would be asked.) The experimental group responded to the test questions three times—the prior guessing session, followed immediately by the first listening, and then, a second guessing session immediately thereafter; after a second listening, they responded a third time. The control group responded only twice—once after first listening, and again after a second listening to the story.

The Pearson product moment correlation between the number of items guessed as extreme quantities (use of "all" and "none") and the number of items correct after first listening was $-.59$ ($p < .01$). A similar correlation between initial guesses and number correct after a second exposure to the story was $-.34$ ($p < .05$). This suggests that those subjects who were set to hear a *simple* story did worse than those who were set to hear a complex story (a plot of this correlation indicated a linear trend.)

On the other hand, a Pearson correlation between number of items actually guessed correctly prior to hearing story and the number correct after first exposure to the story was only −.002 (not significant). This is quite surprising, since one might think that the difficulty in remembering what a story says should be greater if one has incorrectly guessed many items. That is, if we guess poorly then we have to *alter* all these 'memories' as we listen to the story; the fact that this is not so indicates that our previous argument concerning the possible relationship between the inferred set of possibilities and the subjects' prior guesses must be wrong—at least it appears to be wrong for story comprehension; it may not be wrong for comprehension of other kinds of discourse.

Confusions among Set Relations Asserted in Story

Table 5 shows the types and frequencies of confusions that occurred among different types of relations. The reader should note that there are only three rows of the confusion (labelled 'exclusion,' 'inclusion,' and 'disjunction'). The reason there is no row for the 'identity' relation is that the story did not assert any such relation.

The first row of Table 5 shows the confusions that occurred when the story asserted a disjunctive relation between any two social groups mentioned in the story. (There were five social groups: farmers, ranchers, senators, people who were members of a canal association, and people who voted in favor of canal construction.) We notice that most of the disjunctive relations were responded to correctly by both the experimental and control groups (108 for the experimental and 70 for the control subjects). The most frequent confusion error made when a disjunctive relation was asserted in the story was to confuse it with an inclusion relation (experimentals made 24 such errors, and controls made 10 such errors). In the second row, when an inclusion relation was asserted, most subjects in both groups got it correct (experimentals got 71 correct, and control got 43 correct); the most frequent confusion errors involved confusing an inclusive relation with an identity relation (experimentals made 20 while controls made 7 such errors). And for the third row, when an exclusion relation was asserted most subjects again got this relation correct. A moment's reflection on the relative magnitudes of these errors reveals that there is a smaller chance that errors will occur when a nested relation is asserted in the story (inclusion or exclusion relation) than when a disjunctive relation is asserted. The proportion of errors for the first is .06 versus .24 for the proportion of errors made when a disjunctive relation is asserted. Hence, we find something similar to what Dawes found—there is a greater tendency towards what he called 'overgeneralization' type errors than towards 'pseudo-discrimination' errors. Because Table 5 separates each possible type of confusion, it allows us a more detailed look into 'memory' for set relations.

Actually Dawes has mislead us here in regarding all such errors as 'memory' errors; such a confusion table could reflect pure memory errors if all relations (and their converses) were explicitly stated in the story. However, for the stories that Dawes constructed, only some of the relations were explicitly stated and the remaining items had to be inferred. (Recall again that when I say an item is 'inferred'

TABLE 5

Confusions Among Frequencies of Different Types of Set Relations Which Were Asserted in the Dawes Story After First Exposure to the Story

		Responses Given by Subjects[a]				
Type of Set Relations Asserted in Story	Disjunction $S_{i,j}$ $S_{j,i}$	Inclusion A_{ij} $S_{j,i}$ $\quad$ S_{ij} $A_{j,i}$	Exclusion N_{ij} $N_{j,i}$	Identity A_{ij} $A_{j,i}$	Contradiction [A_{ij} (or) S_{ij}] $N_{j,i}$	Row Total
Disjunction $\quad$ $S_{i,j}$ $S_{j,i}$	108/70	24/10 $\quad$ 0/1	21/2	3/2	9/6	165/90
Inclusion $\quad$ A_{ij} $S_{j,i}$	7/2	71/43 $\quad$ —	0/0	20/7	1/1	99/54
Exclusion $\quad$ N_{ij} $N_{j,i}$	5/1	1/0 $\quad$ —	55/31	0/1	5/3	66/36
					Overall Total	330/180

[a]The symbols are to be read in the following way: $S_{i,j}$ means "some of i is j," A_{ij} means "all of i is j," while N_{ij} means "none of i is j." The conjoining of any such assertion along with its converse (if A_{ij} is some assertion, then its converse would be either $A_{j,i}$ or $S_{j,i}$) defines one of the four Gergonne Set Relations: Disjunction, Inclusion, Exclusion, or Identity. Since not all subjects follow the constraints of logic, we also include a fifth category for Contradictions. A special type of confusion can occur when Inclusive relationship is asserted in some story: if the relation asserted is that A_{ij} and $S_{j,i}$, then this can be identified correctly by the subject (which accounts for the column labeled A_{ij} and $S_{j,i}$) or the subject can *confuse* this Inclusion relationship by asserting $A_{j,i}$ and $S_{i,j}$ (this accounts for the other column labeled under the Inclusion relationship. This special type of confusion does not occur for the other set relations and this is signified by placing dashes in some cells. The entries above the slash mark apply to the tallies made using the experimental subjects' responses after first exposure to the story. Below the slash mark are the corresponding entries using the data from the control group after their first exposure to the story.

from explicitly given relations, this does *not* necessarily mean that strict logical operations must be at work which lead to these inferences.)

Another way to examine these data on set relations is to separate those test items which refer to explicitly stated relations in the story. Since all the inferred items follow from this explicit information, it is reasonable to assume that the more explicit items that a subject gets correct, the more likely he is to be *able* to get the inferred items correct. In other words, if the subject hasn't remembered the explicit information correctly, then we should expect him to be around chance level in getting the inferred items correct. Table 6 presents some evidence for this point of view. The results seem fairly clear. For both the experimental and control subjects (and for both exposures to the story) the mean number of inferred items that the subjects got correct increased as the number of explicit items that were correct

TABLE 6

The Mean Number of Inferred Items that were Correct as
a Function of the Number of Explicit Items that were Correct

Condition	No. Explicits Correct (max. = 6)	No. *S*s Having This Many Explicits Correct	Total Mean Inferred Correct (max. = 14.0)
Experimental:			
(first	6	9	12.4
exposure	5	19	11.3
to story)	4 or less	5	8.6
		33*S*s	
Experimental:			
(second	6	27	13.7
exposure)	5	3	11.7
	4 or less	3	9.0
		33*S*s	
Experimental:			
(guessing	6	0	—
prior to	5	3	10.0
exposure)[a]	4 or less	30	9.7
		33*S*s	
Control:			
(first	6	7	13.7
exposure	5	6	13.0
to story)	4 or less	5	10.2
		18*S*s	
Control:			
(second	6	11	13.6
exposure)	5	5	13.6
	4 or less	2	10.5
		18*S*s	

[a]The entries in this condition isolated those test items which later would be given explicitly in the story (here of course the subjects were strictly guessing at the correct answers throughout the test).

guesses indicates that the most likely number of 'explicits' that are correct through guessing alone is four or less. Also, that same condition indicates that the mean number of inferred items that will be correct by guessing alone is about 9.7. It is interesting to note that those few subjects in the remaining four conditions who also got four or less explicit items correct also got approximately 9 or 10 inferred items correct. Thus, this guessing data establishes for us a kind of threshold or baseline against which to assess the effect of successive exposures to the story on the subjects' memory for explicit items and the influence this has on their ability to draw inferences.

A Model for Some Aspects of Story Comprehension

What do we want to predict with a model? For one thing we would like to predict the overall frequency of correct responses to items given explicitly in the story. Also we would like to say how often these correct items involved the use of the quantifiers "all," "some," and "none." Further, when subjects make errors on this explicitly given information, we want to predict how frequently this will occur and again we want to predict how many of these errors involved the use of the quantifiers "all," "some," and "none." If we are really ambitious we would also like the model to tell us how many inferred items the subjects will get correct and the relative frequency with which they will use the quantifiers, and to have the model predict the kinds of errors that will be made on the inferred items. Clearly if the model does not do well in accounting for the explicitly given information, then there is little point in asking how well it accounts for the inferred information. Hence our first concern is to construct a workable model for the explicitly given information.

Let's consider the simplest possible model for explaining how and why we make errors for the explicit information given in stories. We shall assume that when a subject listens to the story he hears everything that is said and understands the meaning of each sentence. However, in order to be able to properly retrieve this explicit information, he must encode it properly and store it in his long-term memory. Furthermore, for simplicity, let's assume that the subject has no trouble retrieving the few pieces of explicit information stored in his memory (obviously if the story were very long we may want to abandon this particular assumption).

Suppose there is a fixed probability e that he will properly encode each item after he hears it. This probability is assumed to be the same regardless of whether the explicit information is of the form "all of x is y," or of the form "some of x is y," or of the form "none of x is y." Given that the item has been properly encoded, the subject will be in a *non-guessing state* when he evaluates this particular item on a test. If the item has not been properly encoded, then he will be in a *guessing state* when evaluating this item on a test.

The observed number of explicit items that a subject gets correct is arrived at in two ways: For each item, the subject was correct either by a lucky guess or because the item was properly encoded in his memory.

All of this seems quite simple, and indeed it is up to a certain point. The problem begins to look difficult when we realize that what the subject will do when he is in a guessing state will depend upon what the *particular item is* that he is attempting to answer at the moment. Simply assuming that he guesses each of the three options (all, some, or none) equally often when in a guessing state is known to be wrong. We know it is wrong because the guessing data collected from the experimental subjects tell us that each item evokes a slightly different pattern of guessing depending upon what the content of the item is. Our prior experience with the semantic categories (farmers, ranchers, senators, etc.) leads to different guessing patterns for each item. However, the fact that we already possess this information about guessing behaviors for each item suggests that we can put this information to work in improving our predictions about what subjects do when they are in a guessing state. This is precisely what was done.

It is worth point out that, if the above simple model is correct, one should not use the observed proportion of correct explicit items as the index of memory ability. Instead the appropriate index of memory ability is the parameter e which tells us the actual proportion of items that were properly encoded. This point should now be quite familiar but it bears repetition: In order to properly measure aspects of comprehension one must first be willing to state an explicit model of the comprehension process. Only when this model is made explicit can one arrive at an appropriate procedure for estimating the relevant parameters of comprehension—just observing raw scores will not usually suffice. The further virtues of stating explicit models is that they often can tell us how one experimental condition relates to another condition. Both these points will be illustrated below.

When a group of subjects first listens to the story (we do not have enough data on each subject to fit a separate model to each subject) we determine the proportion e of explicit items that they properly encoded. Now when these same subjects hear the story again, what might one assume about the proportion of items that will be encoded? Surely it will increase with respect to the e estimated after their first exposure. We shall assume that the same proportion e of the explicit items that were *not* properly encoded after the initial exposure (proportion 1-e) will be encoded after a second exposure. For example, if e on first exposure was estimated to be .685 then one would estimate the proportion properly encoded after a second listening to be: $e = .685 + .685(.315) = .901$. Such an approach was applied to both the experimental and control subjects (grouped data in both cases). It is worth noting that in order to estimate the e parameter for the control subjects it was necessary to use the prior guessing data of the experimental subjects in order to improve the prediction of what these subjects were doing when they were in a guessing state. Hence all five experimental conditions have been interlinked by the above model.

Table 7 indicates how well the model fits the data. We see that on first exposure to the story the control subjects did somewhat better than the experimental subjects (.720 versus .685). After a second exposure both groups got nearly all the explicit items correct (this is also reflected in the large e parameter estimates for experimental and control subjects—.901 versus .922, respectively). There is some indication in Table 7 though that the model is not fitting the experimental subjects' data on their first exposure to the story. We note that there is a tendency to underestimate the use of correct "all" responses (78.7 versus 91.0) and to over-

TABLE 7

Observed and Predicted Frequencies of Usage of "All," "Some," and
"None" for Explicitly Given Relations in Dawes' Story

Experimental Group (guessed first)

| | First Exposure to Story[a] | | | | Second Exposure to Story[b] | | | |
| | corrects | | errors | | corrects | | errors | |
	obs.	pred.	obs.	pred.	obs.	pred.	obs.	pred.
"all"	91.0	78.7	8.0	2.4	95.0	91.6	4.0	0.8
"some"	45.0	61.7	21.0	26.3	61.0	64.6	5.0	8.4
"none"	30.0	24.5	3.0	4.3	33.0	30.0	0.0	1.4

Control Group (did not guess prior to hearing story)

| | First Exposure to Story[c] | | | | Second Exposure to Story[d] | | | |
| | corrects | | errors | | corrects | | errors | |
	obs.	pred.	obs.	pred.	obs.	pred.	obs.	pred.
"all"	50.0	44.2	4.0	12.8	50.0	51.3	4.0	0.3
"some"	25.0	33.9	11.0	12.8	30.0	35.4	6.0	3.5
"none"	17.0	13.9	1.0	2.1	17.0	16.8	1.0	0.6

[a]The encoding parameter e was estimated to be $e = .685$.

[b]The encoding parameter of .685 was applied twice to yield the estimate for the proportion of explicitly given relations which were correctly encoded after the second exposure. Thus e here was as follows: $e = .685 + .685 (.315) = .901$.

[c]The encoding parameter e was estimated to be $e = .720$.

[d]The encoding parameter was estimated by using the e value from the first exposure $(e = .720)$ and applying it twice: thus $e = .720 + .720 (.280) = .922$.

estimate the use of correct "some" responses (61.7 versus 45.0). Oddly enough this discrepancy is not as pronounced for the control subjects in spite of the fact that data from the experimental subjects (prior guessing data) were used to predict their responses (the *only* extra parameter needed to make the predictions for the control subjects' data was the e parameter).

It might be that considerable improvement in predicted values could be effected by collecting more data for the prior guessing condition (that is, the guessing data is subject to sampling fluctuations, and this may be the source of the somewhat poor fit). Should this fail to be the case there are other alternatives to be considered in attempting to fit the data for the explicitly given information. One might hypothesize that the e parameter is dependent upon what quantifier is used in the story; thus e may be larger if an extreme quantifier is used ("all" or "none"). However, this route should not be explored until one has tested the possibility that the guessing data fluctuations may be the true source of the discrepancy between observed and predicted values. Until a more adequate model for the explicit items is found it would be unwarranted to attempt to fit a model for the more-difficult process of inference. But it may be worthwhile here to suggest what some of the anticipated difficulties may be in modeling the inferred items.

Tentative Model for Inferred Items

One approach is to ask ourselves the following. Of the *particular* explicit items that the subject got correct, what is the maximum number of inferred items (and which ones are they) that this subject could get correct if he experienced no information-processing problems? For those inferred items which he could possibly get correct, we ask what proportion f of these he actually did infere correctly (this is analogous to our encoding parameter e used above). We would then procede much as before by allowing the subject to be in two possible states when responding to an inferred item on the test—a non-guessing state and a guessing state. To account for what the subject does when he is in a guessing state we again would use the prior guessing data for each relevant inferred item. The reason this model is so difficult is that we have to take into account the exact pattern of explicit items which the subject happened to get correct and ask ourselves what limit this places on how many inferred items he could possibly get correct. Once this is known we then have to decide whether we want to assume that the same parameter f applies regardless of the exact pattern of explicit items that were correct or not. In order to get some leverage on this difficult problem it will probably be necessary to test several hundred subjects in order to subdivide them into groups who happened to get the same pattern of explicit items correct after at least the first exposure to the story and then to study how the parameter f appears to be influenced by each of these patterns of explicit items.

Implications of Quantitative Models of Comprehension

In many ways one can make a case for the influence of an explicit or implicit set of cognitive alternatives at almost every step of the comprehension process. We are influenced by the set of possibilities when we function as implicit language receivers in the writing of messages. The quantitative probabilistic model which was constructed allowed us to measure particular aspects of the decision process; again, this measurement was only possible once the explicit model had been constructed. The model was general enough so that when questions were raised about other factors that might influence the content of messages we were still able to use the model to study the effect of several experimental conditions on the distribution of individual parameters that resulted from the fitting process.

We are influenced by the set of possibilities when we attempt to identify which of several subject matters is currently being discussed. Efficiency analysis allowed us to decide whether the increase in the number of correct identifications as the number of alternatives decreased was due solely to the change in the guessing baseline or whether it was due to a decrease in the cognitive uncertainty experienced by the subjects (incidentally, instead of an efficiency parameter we could have used a measure of transmitted information in Garner's, 1962, sense).

It was further argued that the set of possibilities is one way to characterize individual differences among subjects' in their ability to identify and correct semantic errors that are made. Another way to study individual differences that arise in story comprehension is to consider identifying the initial guesses that subjects make as one way to make explicit what the set of possibilities are that the subjects expect to be considered when the story is finally heard. The results there suggested that it was not so much which items had been correctly or incorrectly guessed but rather the degree to which subjects were set to hear a simple or complex story. The quantitative model suggested for the retention of explicitly given story information was found to give only a moderately successful fit to the data. However, the issue was raised that the exact set of explicit items that were gotten correct would have to be taken into account in constructing an adequate theory of the processes that language users engage in when making inferences based on the explicit information. That is, the set of possibilities in making correct inferences is quite naturally connected to the memory of what explicit information was presented. The point again was raised that if one wanted to measure something specific about the story comprehension process then one way to do it (at least for the explicitly given information) is to construct a clear model of the processes that affect what we remember (the encoding parameter concept). Just observing the raw proportion of explicit items that were correct is not an adequate way to measure this aspect of comprehension.

Although it was not discussed above, the possibility that some of the questions raised concerning additional factors that might affect the degree of redundancy and the pronominal usage hypotheses of Olson can also be raised for some of the other models constructed. That is, in identifying subject matters, isn't it possible that the familiarity or codability of the subject matters may well affect the magnitude of the efficiency parameter within each of the experimental conditions? In similar fashion, isn't it also possible that *the number of dimensions* that interrelate the subject matters in the subject-matter identification task will affect the efficiency parameter? In story comprehension we can raise similar questions. If the story seems to be of a familiar type (say a 'murder' story, or a high-seas adventure story, etc.) we may very well dispense with certain descriptive information in the telling of the story (or as listeners we may fill in such details that are not explicitly given us simply because the familiarity of the tale leads us to believe that these inferred details are appropriate). Thus, familiarity may very well alter the magnitude of the encoding parameter for explicit information (which just happens to be highly redundant from the point of view of the overall familiarity of the type of story). Familiarity may also alter, as suggested above, the kinds of inferences that are made; if this is so it will greatly complicate any quantitative model of the inference process.

Be this as it may, the models outlined above attempt to capitalize on the fact that language users are fallible information processors, and highly variable processors (from the point of view of variance statistics of errors). The models attempt to explain why it is that errors occur and attempt to explain the pattern of errors that result. In this way the fallible nature of the language user allows us to make use of the errors to gain insight into what the information-processing steps are which underlie what is called comprehension.

THE ANTHROPOLOGIST'S CONTRIBUTION
TO COMPREHENSION

Although it has been popular to talk about linguistic universals we find that the anthropologist has usually taken a back seat to the linguist in suggesting what these universals are. What is rather encouraging to note is that a new band of anthropologists are about (they call themselves ethnoscientists) and they are saying some highly relevant things about knowledge structures which have some bearing on what we learn from listening. Since this volume is devoted in part to explicating this question, it behooves us to attempt to outline what ethnoscience has uncovered and how this might relate to what has already been discussed above.

Let me select a few key statements from Werner (1966) to illustrate what domain of language the ethnoscientists attempt to clarify. "The ability of a native speaker of a language to distinguish culturally true from culturally false sentences is not part of his linguistic competence but part of his cultural competence. In other words, cultural competence . . . is the native speaker's ability to use language appropriately within the context of his culture. The study of culturally appropriate sentences is the domain of ethnoscience. Thus ethnoscience *ipso facto* concerns language use, i.e., how language is used to talk about cultural things." (Werner, 1966, p. 44). He goes on to classify two types of cultural competences which are reflected in sentence use. First he considers sentences which are statements about the socio-physical universe and hence deals with knowledge systems embraced by the majority in a cultural system (in our own Western culture it presumably would embrace what the *layman* thinks are the relevant workings of the socio-physical universe—as such it would emphasize proto-scientific belief systems). A second part of cultural competence is a native hearer-speaker's knowledge of Plans which represent a particular culture's way to *manipulate* the socio-physical universe—it would embody a set of beliefs and actions that must be engaged in, in order to accomplish a particular cultural goal (such as what do you do when you celebrate a particular religious ceremony; what do you do when you want to marry someone; how do you build a hut, etc.) This emphasis on the pragmatic aspects of language use takes as given that the sentences used to describe Plans already have a semantic interpretation. But knowledge systems and pragmatic know-how are not independent competences. It takes knowledge to appreciate how, when, where, and why Plans are executed.

At this point I am tempted to embellish Werner's theory by pointing out that the *set of possible Plans* that could be executed in some given cultural situation will place constraints on how the members of the culture talk about these Plans (especially the target Plan or some subset of Plans). This is exactly analogous to Olson's paradigm cases where the perceived set of explicitly given alternatives (or implicit alternatives) influences the way we talk about a target item (or multiple targets) in the set. In this regard Werner does discuss the fact that the amount of *detail* that we use in discussing Plans will be related to such presuppositions as whether all the members of our audience are familiar with the details of some particular target Plan. If they are familiar with it, this may 'explain' why many of the details that could be discussed about the Plan are omitted—we assume as speakers that our listeners already know this and so can fill in the missing details for themselves. If the situational setting is instructional (as in speaking to children in the culture) then the speaker may very well increase the amount of detail he uses in referring to a Plan of activity since he realizes that his listeners have not yet acquired full competence with the necessary details in executing this particular Plan.

Werner maintains that there are three main aspects of extralinguistic competence that native speakers use in the interpretation of sentences. The speaker knows that Plans consist of several ingredients: They have *actors* (someone does something to something or someone); they involve *artifacts* (we need such-and-such implements to carry out this Plan); they consist of sequences of *activities* (actions) which may or may not be carried out in particular prearranged orders. Also the speaker in the culture knows that some Plans require special preconditions for their execution, such as proper time, place, etc. Furthermore, the speaker knows why some Plans have to be executed: He can provide a cultural rationalization of why such-and-such a Plan must be executed. Presumably all of these elements of Plans and the ways in which they can be organized into permissable, culturally-patterned sequences of activities, as well as the way they can be discussed so as to offer choice among alternative Plans of actions for a given problem, are some of the things that can be *learned from being told.* (Of course, not all of this knowledge is necessarily acquired from verbal communication—some parts undoubtedly require perceptual and motor learning—but we do assume that some aspects of these Plans have been imparted by discourse.

Werner's ideas are certainly stimulating inasmuch as he places the problem of language use into the broadest possible perspective—that of cultural knowledge and cultural goals. But this in itself, while interesting, does not clarify the psychological processes and psychological states which lead to learning through discourse. To deal with this problem let us contrast two kinds of semantic learning—the 'elementary' learning of simple facts, such as "Washington was the first President of the United States," versus the learning of complex systems of ideas such as learning about the theory of relativity.

It seems likely to me that a precondition for the second type of learning to occur would be to assume that the subject has a representation of the 'raw' or elementary assertions made in the discourse (this is akin to the idea of the encoding formulation of explicit information which I sketched earlier in this paper). Granted that the raw information is present and that the elementary *inferences* which stem from the explicit relations have been carried out (this would represent a somewhat intermediate level of learning which is somewhere between the elementary type and the complex type) we also will need two additional steps of processing before the complex type of learning can occur. First, we must engage the subject's knowledge of the world to such a degree that he is compelled to *evaluate the believability* of the raw assertions (and the elementary inferences) vis-a-vis his knowledge of the physical world and his knowledge of the culture. Secondly, after he has evaluated whether the assertions are acceptable (believable) statements, he must further evaluate whether the particular set of assertions are more *valuable* or *useful* than other statements which could be made. If the subject decides that the set of statements are believable and highly valuable, then he may incorporate this knowledge into his internal representations of the real-world. But having once decided to merge this new information, our subject has taken on a very great task since the new knowledge may require one of several possible reorderings or restructuring of his internal knowledge: It may require the *replacement* of old knowledge by the new more valued knowledge; or it may require just the *addition* of this new knowledge alongside the old; or it may require forming new *hierarchical* links to supplement those semantic links already existing among a set of concepts; or it may require a total reworking of the hierarchical links among a set of concepts such that some links are deleted, others remain intact, while other links require additional branchings, etc.

We see that this conception of the conditions that must be met for the more complex type of learning to take place after exposure to discourse cannot be handled by such limited conceptions as short- and long-term memory, nor by such concepts as multiple copies of memory traces versus single traces, nor by a variable strength idea for traces, etc. Instead what is needed is some evaluative apparatus that makes decisions concerning semantic believability and pragmatic importance and that *matches* the results of these decisions against the hierarchical system of knowledge that existed prior to exposure to the discourse. In addition, one needs some apparatus which will select those parts of the old knowledge system which need alteration (substitution, addition, or subtraction of semantic relations) in the light of the semantic and pragmatic decisions and which will also carry out the necessary changes. To do less than this is to do a disservice to the complexity of our knowledge and the complexity of the internal representations of that knowledge. I readily admit, though, that the adequate modeling of such a complex mechanism is a forbiddingly difficult enterprise. To do a thorough job of the modeling one would also have to consider the fallibility of the subject and somehow represent the sources of error at each step of the decision process. Consistent with the theme of this chapter, one would also have to show how it is that the set of implicit or explicit semantic alternatives evoked by the discourse passage will influence each stage of the decision mechanism that evaluates the believability and value of the semantic assertions in the passage. Once such a model is constructed one presumably would be in the ideal position of being able to *measure* the degree of complex learning that a given subject has achieved after exposure to some discourse passage or passages and to pinpoint, hopefully, the stages in the process wherein the subject may require additional special training.

APPENDIX A

Table 8 presents the theoretical means and variances for the Generalized Truncated Geometric Distribution as a function of the number of terms in the distribution. Up to five terms sufficed for our present purposes.

Maximum Likelihood for the Generalized
Truncated Geometric Distribution

Suppose that m and x are known (in terms of our model m is the minimum number of features that will be used, and x is the maximum number that will be used). Let a be the number of data trials which apply to the theoretical first term of

TABLE 8

Theoretical Means and Variances for the Generalized Truncated Geometric Distribution

Number of Terms (n) Allowed in the Truncated Geometric Series[a]	Mean of Generalized Truncated Geometric	Variance about mean of the Generalized Truncated Geometric
$n = x-m+1$		
1	$[m]$	$[0]$
2	$[(1-p) + m]$	$[p - p^2]$
3	$[(1-p)^2 + (1-p) + m]$	$[5p-10p^2+6p^3-p^4]$
4	$[(1-p)^3 + (1-p)^2 + (1-p) + m]$	$[-p^6+8p^5-28p^4+49p^3-42p^2+14p]$
5	$[(1-p)^4 + (1-p)^3 + (1-p)^2 + (1-p) + m]$	$[30p-120p^2+207p^3-202p^4+120p^5$ $-45p^6+10p^7-p^8]$

[a]The symbol m refers to the minimum number of features that a particular subject will encode in message form (typically $m=1$, but for some subjects a larger value gives a better fit to their data). The symbol x refers to the maximum number of features which a subject will encode. For a given p, $0 \leqslant p \leqslant 1$, with $m=1$ and with $x = \infty$ we get the *classical* geometric distribution where the mean equals $1/p$ and the variance about the mean equals $(1-p)/p^2$. We notice that the number of terms n in this Generalized Truncated Geometric Distribution can be found by the formula $n = x-m+1$. For example, in the *classical* distribution there would be an infinite series—an infinite number of terms.

the distribution, let b be the data trials which apply to the second term, let c be the number of data trials which apply to the third term, d to the fourth, and e to the fifth term.

Then for a two-term distribution (i.e., $x-m=2$) we have the following maximum likelihood estimate for P: $L(\text{data};P) = P^a(1-P^b)$. Taking logs of both sides and differentiating with respect to P and setting the result equal to zero yields $P = a/(a+b)$ as our maximum likelihood estimate for P for a two-term distribution.

For a three-term distribution (i.e., $x-m=3$) we have the following result: $P = (a+b)/(a+2b+2c)$.

For four terms we have $P = (a+b+c)/(a+2b+3c+3d)$.

For five terms we have $P = (a+b+c+d)/(a+2b+3c+4d+4e)$.

For a particular subject, depending upon the minimum number of features that he used (his m value) and depending upon the maximum number of features he used (his x value), exactly one of the above maximum likelihood formulas was used to estimate his P value.

CONFERENCE DISCUSSION

In the three-parameter model which Freedle used to fit his test of Olson's minimum redundancy hypothesis, Trabasso inquired whether the P parameter should be interpreted as a 'learning' parameter. Freedle indicated that feature usage did not show any 'learning' or practice changes over trials (only pronominal usage showed such a practice effect). What the P parameter referred to was a property of the sequential decisions that a subject made *while* he was writing any given message. He would write the minimum number of features (designated by the parameter m) with probability P and then decided whether to add another feature to his message or not before going on to the next trial. With probability P he did add another feature to that same message (and with probability $1-P$ he terminated the message); this sequential decision about whether to add yet one more feature to what he had already written was continued until he terminated the sequence either due to the probabilistic occurrence of a stopping decision $(1-P)$ or because the subject had already reached his maximum number of features that he had set as an *upper limit* on what he would write (this was the third parameter x). Trabasso thought that the different kinds of frequency distributions which could result from this feature usage model which Freedle had used to account for individual differences deserved greater emphasis than was given in the paper.

Carroll mentioned a study by Maclay and Newman (1960) that was quite similar to Freedle's. It attempted to investigate some of the factors that influence such message characteristics as length (in morphemes) and type-token ratio. In this experiment, the subject had to describe, orally, a single item from a known set in such a way that a hearer of the message could identify it from a larger set of alternatives. The hearer was physically present but was actually an experimental "stooge." One of the independent variables studied was feedback. In the "positive feedback" condition, the speaker was led to believe, on every trial except the last, that the recipient of his message was successful in picking the correct item. In the "negative feedback" condition, the speaker was led to believe, again on every trial except the last, that the recipient was unsuccessful in picking the correct item. In the "no feedback" condition, no information was provided the speaker as to the success or failure of the recipient. A second factor studied was the effect of homogeneous vs. heterogeneous sets of alternatives on messages. A homogeneous set might consist, for example, only of rectangles in different orientations, some composed of dashed lines and others composed of unbroken lines; a heterogeneous set would consist, say, of a triangle, a rectangle, an oval, and a straight line. The results indicated that negative feedback significantly increased the number of morphemes used in successive messages. (There was no scoring for features, as in Freedle's experiment.) Positive feedback and absence of feedback both resulted in a decrease of message length over trials. Homogeneous sets were described with significantly more message morphemes than heterogeneous sets. Carroll inquired what problems this earlier study might pose for some of the models that Freedle constructed.

Freedle responded by saying that there were several possibilities, but first he thought it worth mentioning that a morpheme count alone clearly would not allow one to test Olson's two hypotheses. However, even if one assumes that the number of features used is to some extent indexed by the number of morphemes in the message, one would need a much more complex model to account for the effects of the three feedback conditions in the Maclay and Newman experiment. For example, with the three-parameter model (P, m, and x) for feature usage it may be that only P undergoes a change in strength as a function of the feedback conditions, and in this case one would have to decide also what function relates the prior P value to the new value after a particular feedback outcome. But it may be that feedback also effects changes in the integer values taken on by x and m. Thus, one might hypothesize a Markovian transition matrix that would indicate the transitional probabilities of, say, the maximum parameter x going to other integer values as a function of which feedback condition occurred. This would certainly constitute a broader model than Freedle's present model, and would encompass many more factors affecting message characteristics. Nevertheless, Freedle thought that working out such a complex model would pose grave difficulties.

Trabasso made the further comment that the fact that one gets violations of the minimum redundancy hypothesis seems to be related to results in other areas such as discrimination learning; that is, this literature shows that adding redundant features to stimuli retards learning a discrimination. This is quite similar to what Freedle reported in his first two experiments—that as the number of correlated dimensions used to construct the stimulus figures increases, the degree of redundancy which subjects introduce into their messages increases. Thus, both tasks show that subjects are unable to filter out completely from their responses the irrelevant (or redundant) aspects of the stimuli, with the consequence that these irrelevant features show up in the messages written (in Freedle's task) or retard learning (as in discrimination learning).

Carroll inquired whether the second experiment, which dealt with the ability of subjects to recognize (identify) a particular subject matter or 'topic' given a randomly chosen string of connected words from some text, couldn't be extended into other domains as well, such as studying the number of words that a subject needs to identify from a newspaper editorial whether an author is a 'hawk' or a 'dove' on some particular issue; another extension might involve testing the subject's ability to identify which of several opposing theories a particular author is in favor of, and so on. Freedle agreed and commented that when he first ran the experiment, he had briefly considered extending the technique to get at the subject's ability to identify which of several literary authors was being quoted, but this particular variation was abandoned for a host of reasons. Crothers wondered what role rare content words played in a subject's ability to identify the correct subject matter from a fixed list of possible alternatives. While acknowledging that 'key' words that happen to occur in a sample string probably play an important role in the probability with which a correct response is made, Freedle believed one can argue that there is no simple one-to-one connection between a particular rare word and a particular subject matter; the ability to correctly identify subject matters is a function of the *set* of particular alternative subject-matters which he is allowed to choose from. It would be interesting to know, of course, the extent of vocabulary overlap for every pair of subject matters used in the experiment, but in a practical sense the sample sizes that one would need to provide a measure of this overlap would prove to be an overwhelming task.

Rothkopf suggested yet another extension of the subject-matter experiment. One might study the effect, on 'shaping' the reader's response to some prose passage, of telling him that he is about to read something that conveys any one of six ideas. The person reads the text and has to say which of the six ideas he thinks is the correct one. He presumably does this by caryrying out higher-level inferences while reading the text. The question then is, will this procedure affect *how* the subject processes the text and *what* he remembers when given a recall test at some subsequent time? (The control condition would involve no explicit mention of the alternative ideas—the subjects simply recall the text at some subsequent time.) This suggestion of Rothkopf's is somewhat related to work already conducted by Carl Frederiksen. (The reader is referred to the latter's chapter in this book.)

REFERENCES

Dawes, R. M. Cognitive distortion. *Psychological Reports*, 1964, Monograph Supplement 4–VI4.

Dawes, R. M. Memory and distortion of meaningful written material. *British Journal of Psychology*, 1966, 57, 77–86.

Estes, W. K. The statistical approach to learning theory. In S. Koch (Ed.), *Psychology: A study of a science*. Vol. 2. New York: McGraw-Hill, 1959.

Frase, L. T. Influence of sentence order and amount of higher level text processing upon reproductive and productive memory. *American Educational Research Journal*. 1971, 7(3), 307–319.

Freedle, R. O. Investigations in the human limitations of semantic decoding of information and its application to automatic information retrieval systems. Manuscript submitted to Office of Science Information Service, National Science Foundation, Washington, D.C., May 11, 1965.

Freedle, R. O., & Kingsley, P. On a cognitive theory of reference: An empirical evaluation. Educational Testing Service Research Bulletin, Princeton, N.J., 1972, in preparation.

Garner, W. R. *Uncertainty and structure as psychological concepts*. New York: Wiley, 1962.

Kruskal, J. B. Multidimensional scaling by optimizing goodness of fit to a nonmetric hypothesis. *Psychometrika*, 1964, 29, 1–28.

Longacre, R. E. Sentence structure as a statement calculus. *Language*, 1970, 46, 783–815.

Luce, R. D. Detection and recognition. In R. D. Luce, R. R. Bush, & E. Galanter (Eds.), *Handbook of mathematical psychology*. Vol. 1. New York: Wiley, 1963.

Maclay, H., & Newman, S. Two variables affecting the message in communication. In Dorothy K. Wilner (Ed.), *Decisions, values, and groups*. New York: Pergamon, 1960.

Olson, D. R. Language and thought: Aspects of a cognitive theory of semantics. *Psychological Review*, 1970, 77, 257–273.

Werner, O. Pragmatics and ethnoscience. *Anthropological Linguistics*, 1966, 8(8), 42–65.

9
EFFECTS OF TASK-INDUCED COGNITIVE OPERATIONS ON COMPREHENSION AND MEMORY PROCESSES[1]

Carl H. Frederiksen
University of California at Berkeley

The research to be described in this paper began as a project concerned with investigating cognitive processes involved in "complex ideational learning." Since results previously obtained with rote learning tasks had indicated that learning processes may be rather more specific to a given task than has generally been supposed (Frederiksen, 1969; 1970), it was decided to investigate processes governing the acquisition of knowledge in different learning *contexts*. In particular, two sorts of contexts were to be considered: arbitrary contexts in which a set of stimulus elements are to be remembered and reconstructed; and nonarbitrary contexts in which, in addition to remembering and reconstructing the elements to be learned, these elements are to be the object of some other stipulated cognitive activity such as applying inductive or deductive reasoning to solve a problem involving the elements, or relating a set of ideas to other knowledge in a nonarbitrary manner. It was supposed that processes involved in acquiring knowledge from connected, logical arguments would be dependent on the nature of "superordinate" processing operations on the semantic content of the essay. Thus, the experimental strategy adopted involved "manipulating" through task conditions the likelihood and extent to which individuals would adopt certain modes of information processing which involve cognitive operations on the semantic content of a connected verbal argument and studying various properties of the temporal course of learning performance for different task-groups so defined.

Naturally, the first problem encountered in this work (and the key problem confronting anyone attempting to study in a direct manner the acquisition of nonverbatim knowledge) was that of obtaining a sufficiently objective and complete specification of the semantic properties of the stimulus passage and obtaining

[1] This research was supported by the Committee on Basic Research in Education, National Academy of Sciences, grant number OEG–0–9–140396–4497(010).

a set of measurements which are sufficient to provide an objective and sufficiently complete description of the properties of the verbal protocols which constitute "learning performance." A starting point for the development of a solution to this problem of formally specifying the semantic properties of a stimulus passage consisting of a connected logical discourse was suggested by Dawes' (1966) experiments on the distortion of meaningful written materials in remembering, and Frase's (1969) demonstrations of the effects of thinking about particular semantic relations present in a text (represented structurally in the form of directed graphs) on recall of elements taken from the text. Dawes developed passages around a number of set relations and attempted to measure *by reference to the set relations specified in the passage* processes of distortion of relationships and selection in memory. Frase's work incorporated the idea that textual materials may be represented in terms of *networks* of set relations symbolized as directed graphs (cf., Harary, Norman, & Cartwright, 1965).

Having decided to try to represent the semantic features of a connected logical discourse as a network of set relations, a set of conventions was developed for the design of a *semantic model* for any connected passage. The model was to be represented diagrammatically and, more rigorously, as digraphs of two sorts: (1) digraphs representing relations among concepts and (2) implication digraphs representing implications among propositions. Incidentally, it was felt that it is not necessary that such a model be unique, only that it be well defined and capable of generating the passage. The problem of scoring semantic or "ideational" features of a subject's written reconstruction of the input could then be treated by reference to the *model* of the input, provided that a satisfactory model is available. At this point another difficulty was encountered. Given a structural model of the input and a subject's written reconstruction of the input (presumably also representable structurally using the same conventions used to develop a structural model of the input), how might the degree of correspondence of these two structures be measured? For example, if a particular relation ARB is present in the input (where R is a directed relation from concept A to concept B) and a relation A'R'B' is present in a subject's written protocol, how might A'R'B' be *identified with* a relation ARB contained in the model of the input, and, given such identification, how might the subject's relation differ from the relation of the model with which it is identified? In the presence of these complexities, it appeared that the development of a solution to the scoring problem just described would require the statement of some sort of outline of a theory of comprehension as well as of memory processes. Since the verbal protocol produced by a subject as a reconstruction of a connected logical argument which he has just read or heard is the result of a sequence of comprehension-memory-reconstruction processes, relations between ARB and A'R'B' ought to be describable in terms of classes of responses resulting from the application of these processes.

This paper will begin by presenting a description of the theoretical model which was formulated (for these very practical purposes) and then proceed to describe our procedures for the measurement of semantic memory and comprehension. Some selected results will be presented concerning effects of task-induced cognitive operations on the content of a connected logical discourse on processes in comprehension and memory which will have been specified in the theoretical model. These cognitive operations define the "arbitrary" and "nonarbitrary" contexts which were the experimental treatments originally proposed. Results will be interpreted in terms of predictions made from the proposed theory.

AN OUTLINE OF A MODEL FOR
COMPREHENSION AND MEMORY PROCESSES

In developing a set of conventions for representing a connected logical discourse in terms of a structural model and in considering the scoring problem just described, it became apparent that a theory of comprehension and memory ought to have certain features. The first such features involve the identification of "units" or *elements* of semantic content which are the object of operations in comprehension and memory. The "smallest" such element arrived at in the development of a semantic model was the *concept* (or class). A concept may be thought of as the intersection of a set of component semantic features and as such there is certainly an issue concerning the size of any particular concept-class for a given discourse. More will be said about this issue in conjunction with the description of our measurement procedures. The approach taken to this problem is a pragmatic one. A second element of content is a relation defined on two or more concepts. Given a specified set of concepts, identification of relations among the concepts is not a difficult matter. Relations may be classified in a number of ways. Among the possibilities are *mode* [e.g., relations assigning properties and thus differentiating concept-classes, relations attributing action, varieties of case relations such as agentive, dative, instrumental, objective, etc. (cf., Fillmore, 1968), order relations of quantity or quality] and *complexity* (e.g., simple relations linking two concept-classes, compound relations linking more than two concepts, and nested relations linking propositions—concepts which are themselves represented as relations). A third element of semantic content is the *implication* defined on two or more propositions. An implication is a transitive relation linking two or more propositions and representing the logical "if . . . then" relation. Further differentiation of implications is possible (and will be presented later). Finally, the most complex class of elements might be referred to as the class of *structures* consisting of systems of relations and/or implications. Subcategories of structures varying in complexity may of course be identified.

Suppose that a text is presented to a subject and that the text is representable in terms of a semantic structure consisting of an organization of structural elements. Suppose also that the subject is asked to write down his reconstruction of the semantic content of the passage—the knowledge which he has acquired and retained in comprehending the passage. Suppose in addition that the passage is sufficiently long that any complete reconstruction of the surface features of the passage is rendered extremely difficult. A protocol which is obtained from a subject is likely to have a number of characteristics. For example, a protocol will generally not correspond in its surface features to the input text; it will contain only some of the semantic elements of the input; these reproduced semantic elements may be linguistically represented in paraphrase; reproduced elements present in the subject's protocol will generally *not* represent a random selection of the input elements; generated semantic elements will be present in subjects' protocols which were never presented explicitly in the input text; many generated elements will represent propositions which may be inferred from those contained in the input text; and many elements will be transformations of, or distortions of, those contained in the text. Any attempt to model cognitive processes in comprehension and semantic memory will have to account for the presence of elements such as these in subjects' recall protocols. A model must also be capable of accounting for effects of conditions "external" to the passage itself such as contextual effects, effects of repeated exposure, and forgetting. Finally, a model must also be generally consistent with the stages of processing that have been found to be involved in human memory in studies of list learning.

In attempting to account for and measure the semantic content of subjects' reconstructions of knowledge acquired from a presented passage, a conception of comprehension and memory processes was developed which is summarized in Figure 1. Stages of processing represented in the process model of Figure 1 are identified and classified in Figure 2. We start with the notion that comprehension involves the construction by the subject of a semantic representation or *semantic model* as an input passage is received. Figure 1 describes processing events that are supposed to occur in temporal sequence as the passage is presented. As the phonetic

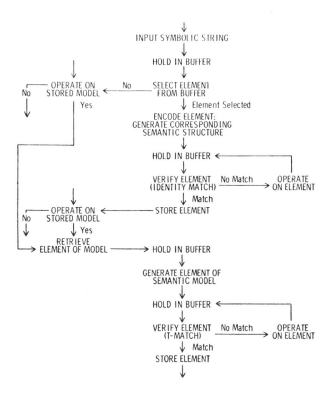

FIG. 1. Processes in comprehension.

STRUCTURAL ELEMENTS OF SEMANTIC MODEL

    Concepts (Classes)
    Relations (Simple, Compound, Nested)
    Implications (Simple, Compound, Nested)
    Structures (Systems of Relations, Implications)

PROCESSES

    Input Linguistic Processes
    Selection:
        Surface Selection
        Inferential Selection
    Production:
        Encoding Processes (Production of Veridical Semantic Elements)
        Generative Reasoning Processes (Production of Inferred Elements)
        Unconstrained Processes (Elaborative Production)
        Null
    Verification:
        Identity Match
        Transformational Match:
            Class Correspondence
            Implication
            Non-Contradiction
        No Verification
    Transformation (Operations on Semantic Model)
    Storage and Retrieval Processes
    Output Expressional Processes

FIG. 2. Classification of possible elements of semantic model
and processes in comprehension, memory, and reconstruction
of connected logical discourse.

string is received, input linguistic processes result in a symbolic string which is held in a memory buffer (working memory). A subset of this symbolic string (e.g., a word, phrase, or sentence) may then be selected for further (semantic) processing. Such *selection processes* may be under the control of surface features of the passage, but cognitive controls of selection (selection strategies) based on semantic features are also possible (Bever, 1970). For example, semantic features might be expected to become increasingly important in influencing the selection of information from the input as the subject proceeds through a long passage and builds his own "semantic model" of the passage. In the present model, a distinction is made between two types of selection processes (see Figure 2). This distinction is based on whether or not selection is the result of evaluative operations on the semantic content of the essay (as, for example when an "idea" is selected because of its relations to other "ideas" in the passage). Selection which is based on such evaluative judgment, and which represents a "decision-to-process" resulting from (possibly complex) cognitive operations on the content of the passage, will be referred to as *inferential selection*; selection which is not based on such inferential evaluation but rather on surface features of the text will be referred to as *surface selection*. Surface selection would result if, for example, a listener selected elements in response to such surface characteristics of a text as inflectional emphasis of a speaker, features of syntax, or sequential or temporal features of the text. In most instances surface and inferential selection processes probably operate in complement to one another. For example, a paragraph structure may influence selection of the topic sentence, while at the same time, inferences based on the content of the paragraph may influence selection of the ideas represented in the topic sentence as central to an understanding of the paragraph.

As the processing sequence proceeds, once an element of the input is selected, then the element is *encoded* through the generation of a semantic element corresponding to the selected element. The phenomenological nature of these generated elements will not be considered here. Such generative operations will be referred to as *production processes*. Since some constraints must govern what is produced, it is supposed next that a generated semantic element must be verified in some way against the selected input element. Processes associated with evaluating the correspondence between a generated element of the semantic model and a selected element of the input string will be called *verification processes*. The simplest sort of verification (which would be expected to occur at the beginning of a passage) is that of an identity match, i.e., verification that the semantic element may be expressed by the corresponding element of the stored surface structure. Following verification (and depending on time constraints), the element of the semantic model may be operated upon and transformed, the result of the transformation verified, *et cetera*. Resulting semantic elements are stored in long term memory.

As this processing sequence recycles with the input of successive elements of the input string, the nature of selection, production, verification, and transformation processes might be expected to change as semantic elements are generated which were not explicitly present in the input text. The stages of such processing involving operations on the semantic content are outlined in the lower half of Figure 1. Thus, in addition to verification based on an identity match, verification processes based on structural features of the stored "semantic model" become theoretically possible as the "model" develops a well formed structure, and thus, operations on the stored semantic model would be expected to occur resulting in the generation of structural elements not present in the input string. The verification of generated structural elements not corresponding to explicitly presented elements must then involve criteria other than that of an identity match. Possibilities include verification of *class correspondence* in which the generated concept includes or is included in the input concept; verification of *implication* in which the generated concept implies or is implied by previously generated semantic structures (or both); and verification of *noncontradiction* in which the generated concept does not contradict previously generated structures.[2] As will be seen later, these categories of verification correspond closely to judgments that must be made in scoring subjects' verbal protocols. An identification of categories of production processes can be made which is based on possible types of verification involving the generated concept. Thus, in addition to *encoding* or *simple production* (production of identities or imperfectly discriminated elements), one can identify *inferential production* (production of inferences or elements which imply and/or are implied by previously generated structures),

---

[2] Verification of class correspondence might be described alternatively in comparison to verification of identity match as a process involving the discrimination of concept classes. Types of verification not involving an identity match might be called weak verification but the general term adopted here is verification of a transformational match since if appropriate operations are applied to generated elements, a match would result.

and *elaborative production* (production of elements which, while they are not inferentially derivable from the previously generated structure, do not contradict that structure). Finally, contradictory elaborative elements may be generated if no verification takes place. Such elements may also be considered to be transformations of inferentially derivable elements and thus their interpretation may be ambiguous. This point will be raised again in describing our scoring procedures.

A great many transformations may be identified. In fact, transformations represent the entire set of possible cognitive operations on any element or elements of semantic content. While categories of transformation will be identified later in terms of the nature of the resulting transformed element, transformations ought better to be defined in terms of particular cognitive operations occurring for a particular task.

Having developed the outlines of a model for processes involved in comprehension and semantic memory, how might processes involved in reconstructing the semantic content of a text, here referred to as *reconstruction processes*, be described in terms of the processes previously identified? In reconstructing a connected verbal argument, a sequence of elements is generated and held in immediate memory. If the task is to reproduce the argument in written or spoken form, the sequence of events is considered to be as follows: first an element is selected from the sequence of elements held in immediate memory; the selected element is possibly transformed; a symbolic string is then generated to represent the selected semantic element and the string is possibly verified; finally, the generated string is output through expressional and motor responses. If the semantic content of the discourse is to be reproduced and then operated upon cognitively (as, for example, if the content or a portion of the semantic content is to be used in solving a problem), the generation of a symbolic string will not necesssrily occur. Recall that the phenomenal nature of a semantic element is not under consideration. Such elements may very well resemble the symbolic products produced overtly in the form of speech or written prose. This model leaves the phenomenal content of "thought" unspecified.

The model which has been presented here is very general. It was developed to formalize the conceptions which we found underlying our thinking in constructing procedures for the measurement of the semantic content of verbal protocols resulting from comprehension, memory, and reconstruction processes, and thus represents a rationale for our procedures. The model raises a host of questions concerning, for example, the nature ("size") of the elements processed and the specific selection, production, verification, and transformation processes which occur in comprehension and memory tasks. Furthermore, it is likely that temporal and individual differences may occur in regard to the answers to these questions. Our immediate purpose in this research is, first, to develop procedures for the measurement of classes of responses implied by this model and, second, to investigate the effects on processes involved in comprehension and memory of certain experimental "contexts" designed to induce particular cognitive operations on the semantic content of a passage. The performance data used to investigate these effects were relative frequencies of occurrences of specific classes of responses implied by the model.

THE MEASUREMENT OF COMPREHENSION
AND MEMORY PROCESSES

The strategy adopted for obtaining measurements of the performance resulting from specific comprehension and memory processes has already been indicated, that is, first, to construct a model of the input passage as a logical network (most rigorously represented in terms of directed graphs representing set relations and transitive implications among propositions), and second, to develop a procedure for scoring an individual subject's verbal protocol (his reconstruction of the passage) against the "template" provided by the constructed model.[3] Presented here will be an abbreviated description of the main features of our scoring procedures in an attempt to convey the "flavor" of our procedures.[4] Needless to say, one encounters many complexities in the development of such a scoring system and detailed rules and "decision algorithms" are necessary to make the more difficult scoring judgments sufficiently objective.

The input essay used in the experimental work reported here was adapted from that of Dawes (1966) and consists mostly of simple declarative sentences. This essay was selected for our initial work because its constructed nature (constructed around certain set relations) and lack of logical or grammatical ambiguity facilitated mapping its structure. A logical analysis of the input essay was made which began with the observation that simple declarative sentences express set relations—that is, they express relations between two denoted sets or concepts. For the purposes of generating a representation of the text in terms of set relations, concept-classes were defined from which the relational structure of the essay could be generated. While it was recognized that many of the defined concepts could be further differentiated (i.e., themselves broken into set relations) and, thus, that the representation is not unique, it was felt that the concepts elected represented reasonably unitary semantic elements and were sufficiently fine to represent essential logical relationships contained in the passage. Surface features of the passage were often used in the definition of concept-classes. For many textual materials, some rather arbitrary decisions of this kind will probably be necessary. However, it was our view that the question of a definition of concept elements does not have a purely *logical* solution since a concept may be regarded as a linguistic and psychological unit of content as well as a logical unit.[5] A diagrammatic model was constructed from these concepts, and certain symbols were utilized to link concept-sets which are represented as phrases in the diagram

---

[3] In work subsequent to that reported in this paper, procedures for representing a text as semantic and logical structures have further developed utilizing principles of semantic analysis similar to those recently discussed by linguists (cf. Fillmore, 1968; Leech, 1970; Simmons, chapter in this volume) and psychologists interested in computer models for semantic processors (cf. Minsky, 1968). The revisions have also been influenced by Crothers' work as represented in this volume. In other respects, subsequent work resembles closely that described in this paper.

[4] A complete scoring manual will be made available through the E.R.I.C. document system of the U.S. Office of Education.

[5] It appears that a considerable amount of arbitrariness can be removed from the procedure of constructing a semantic model of a text when case grammar principles are applied in constructing the model (cf. footnote 2).

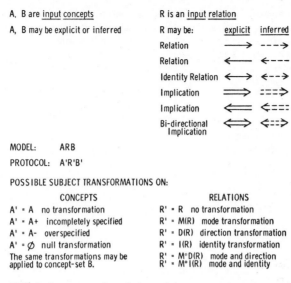

A, B are input concepts

A, B may be explicit or inferred

R is an input relation

R may be:	explicit	inferred
Relation	⟶	---→
Relation	⟵	←---
Identity Relation	⟷	←--→
Implication	⟹	::=→
Implication	⟸	⟸:::
Bi-directional Implication	⟺	⟸::→

MODEL: ARB

PROTOCOL: A'R'B'

POSSIBLE SUBJECT TRANSFORMATIONS ON:

CONCEPTS	RELATIONS
A' = A no transformation	R' = R no transformation
A' = A+ incompletely specified	R' = M(R) mode transformation
A' = A- overspecified	R' = D(R) direction transformation
A' = ∅ null transformation	R' = I(R) identity transformation
The same transformations may be applied to concept-set B.	R' = M°D(R) mode and direction
	R' = M°I(R) mode and identity

FIG. 3. Summary of symbols used in representing connected discourse as directed graphs consisting of networks of set relations, and of possible subject transformations.

(see Figure 3). Represented in the model are concept-sets, in particular, (1) *explicit concepts* (concepts which are explicitly stated in the original passage); (2) certain *inferred concepts* (concepts which, while not stated directly, enter into relationships with explicit concepts which are necessarily true); (3) certain illustrative *elaborative concepts* (concepts which are not stated directly and do not enter into relations with explicit concepts which are necessarily true). Also represented in the model are set relations consisting of *relations* and *implications*, in particular, (4) *explicit relations* (A "has the property" B, where B can be either a property or action); (5) *explicit identities* (bi-directional relations, A "is identical to" B); (6) *explicit implications* (A "implies" B, i.e., "If A, then B", where A and B are propositions consisting of set relations); (7) *explicit bi-directional implications* (A "implies and is implied by" B); (8) *inferred relations and implications* (a relation or implication which, while not stated directly, is necessarily true within the context of the passage); (9) *elaborative relations*; and (10) *elaborative implications*. The decision was made not to represent separately relations involving actions and properties, not to attempt any representation of equivocations (e.g., "might"), and to represent instances of negation in terms of negative concept-sets. From the diagrammatic model, every concept and relation expressed in the original passage may be reconstructed. Each concept and relation in this diagram is identified by a code number which is used in scoring subjects' protocols by reference to the model. The semantic structure graph of two paragraphs of the essay is presented in Figure 4. The corresponding texts of two paragraphs from the Circle Island essay are as follows:

The island is run democratically. All issues are decided by a majority vote of the islanders. The actual governing body is a ten-man Senate, called the Federal Assembly, whose job is to carry out the will of the majority. Since the most desirable trait in a senator is administrative ability, the senate consists of the island's ten best proven administrators—the ten richest men. For years, all senators have been ranchers.

The main opposition to the canal idea came from the ranchers who pointed out that if new farms deprived them of grazing land, they would not be able to export sufficient quantities of beef to match the island's imports. Moreover, this deficit could not be made up by increased farming because farm produce is not in demand in New Hampton or in Beaton's Island which are the countries with which Circle Island can trade. They also pointed out that a large canal would upset the island's ecological balance because it would be a barrier to the several small species which migrate seasonally across the island through its central region. The procanal association calling themselves the "Citizens Development Association" brought the idea of constructing a canal to a vote.

The semantic scoring of subjects' protocols against the constructed model of the input passage involves three steps: verbatim scoring, concept scoring, and relations scoring. Verbatim scoring of a protocol involves reading the protocol and underlining every item of a fourteen-item list of verbatim concepts, each of which occurs in the input passage. Each verbatim concept is scored as either: correct (verbatim criterion), incompletely specified (if a portion of the verbatim concept appears), or absent. Total verbatim elements correct and incomplete are obtained. These totals are the basic verbatim data and are obtained for each subject for each trial. In addition to these scores, the serial position of each verbatim concept in the subject's protocol is recorded.

Concept scoring involves underlining and scoring each of a list of concepts which appear in the original passage and which are numbered and diagrammed in the model. The scoring sheets contain a list of numbered concepts for each section. Each concept is scored as correct, incompletely specified (concept-set not completely delimited, i.e., includes subsets not corresponding to the concept-set of the input), or over-specified (concept-set overly delimited, i.e., represents a subset of the concept-set of the input) (see Figure 3). These scores may be thought of as transformations of the input concept by the subject. In addition to the above scores, the serial position of each concept in the subject's protocol is recorded. Concepts appearing in a subject's protocol are classified as explicit, inferred, or elaborative and are so identified on the scoring sheet. An additional scoring sheet is provided for listing all inferred and elaborative concepts which do not appear on the previous sheets. Each concept which is explicit is scored as correct, incompletely specified, over-specified, or absent; each inferred or elaborative concept is scored as present (meaning subject-produced). Totals for each concept type and scoring category are obtained for each section (the sections correspond to serially located paragraphs in the input passage) and for each trial. This procedure yields a rather large number of scores which represent amount of information, accuracy of information, and transformations on information in the input. Difficult scoring situations sometimes occur involving such aspects as: stating conditions distinguishing situations in which the "over-specified" score category is used versus scoring the concept and the additional words as an additional (subject-produced) inferred or elaborative concept; and stating conditions for the substitutability of identities and the treatment of embedded verbatim concepts (verbatim concepts which are embedded in other concepts).

Section 4

48 GOVERNMENT

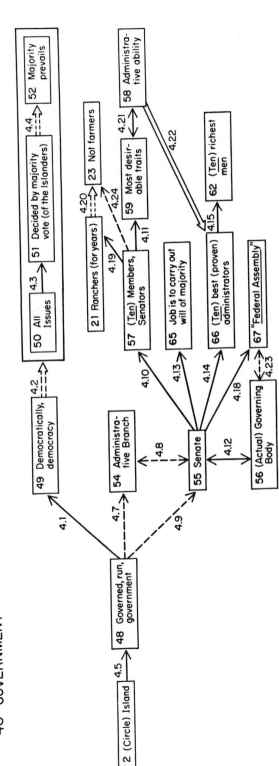

FIG. 4a. Semantic structure graph of first paragraph of the Circle Island essay which was presented to the subjects.

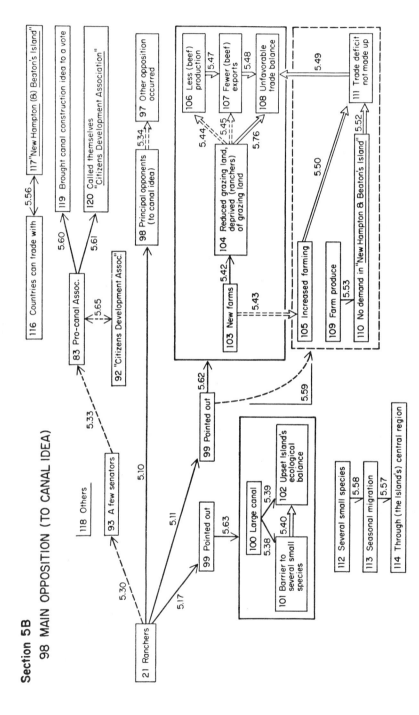

FIG. 4b. Semantic structure graph of second paragraph of the Circle Island essay.

Set relations scoring is considerably more complicated than concept scoring and, like the concept scoring, involves scoring a subject's protocol against the diagrammatic model of the original passage. As in the concept scoring, set relation scoring consists of categorizing a set relation in a subject's protocol in terms of transformations on a set relation in the model with which the set relation in the protocol is identified. A set relation in a subject's protocol is *identifiable with* a stated set relation in the input if the relation appearing in the protocol may be transformed into that in the input passage by one of six possible transformations (see Figure 3) and each concept may be transformed into that in the input passage by one of four transformations. Possible transformations on a relation R are: no transformation; transformation of mode (relation to implication and vice versa); of direction (for unidirectional relations or implications); to or from an "identity" (i.e., a unidirectional relation may become bi-directional, and vice versa); mode and direction; and mode and identity. Four possible transformations on a concept are: no transformations, incomplete specification of the concept-set, over-specification of the concept-set, or deletion. Each triple consisting of two concepts and a connecting set-relation, which appears in a subject's protocol and is identifiable with a set relation in the input passage, then represents one of 96 possible score patterns. In addition, set relations may be explicit, inferred, or elaborative. An elaborative relation is not scored transformationally, but only as to whether or not it contradicts the semantic content of the passage. The scoring sheet for each protocol contains a list of numbered relations and implications (as rows) and three columns headed R', A', and B'. In columns A' and B' the appropriate transformations on A and B (corresponding to the numbered relations in the model) are recorded as previously obtained in the concept scoring. Then a judgment is made as to what transformation has been applied to R and this transformation is recorded. To illustrate some of the complexities which can occur in scoring relations and implications, let us consider two sorts of problems for which detailed scoring rules must be specified. The first involves the scoring of implications involving compound concepts. The scoring procedure involves rules for breaking such relations into parts, or, if this is not allowed under the rules, for scoring the transformation on the compound concept. The second complexity involves the treatment of nested relations. As an example of the kind of scoring rule adopted to handle such complexities, the following statement of the problem and decision procedure is reproduced from the manual.

Nested Relations

Implications often occur in which one of the concepts is itself a set relation. Consider the following two examples taken from *Circle Island*.

Example 1: "Since Circle Island^X has few rivers^Y there is a lack of water^Z."

Generally, we can write this as $[X \longrightarrow Y] \Longrightarrow Z$.   case 1

Example 2: "Since the Island is a democracy,^{Z} all issues^X are decided by a majority vote (of the islanders)^Y."

Generally, we can write this as $Z \Longrightarrow [X \longrightarrow Y]$.   case 2

If a subject's protocol contains a set relation which corresponds to either of these cases or their extensions, the following scoring rules should be followed:

Let A = [X ⟶ Y] and let A' = [X' ⟶ Y']. The implication to be scored is either A'R'Z' or Z'R'A'. *Scoring categories* for scoring A' (which is itself a relation or set of relations) are:

1. Score "1" (*correct*) when, for example, A' = A = XRY, i.e., the set of *relations* and *concepts* which make up A' are all correctly specified by the subject.
2. Score "2" (*incompletely specified*) when, for example, A' = X'RY' and either X' or Y' or both are incompletely specified, i.e., the set of *relations* which make up A' are all correctly specified, but at least one concept is incompletely specified.
3. Score "3" for all other cases, i.e., when any one or more concepts are overspecified. This score is also to be used if any elaborative relations occur involving the set of concepts and relations in A' which are necessarily false within the context the essay.

Note that score category (3) lumps together many possible combinations of subject transformations and elaborations.

4. Score "S" if one (or more) of the concepts or one (or more) of the relations is subject-produced.

Since virtually every concept and set relation produced by a subject in his protocol is scored and recorded, a tremendous variety of classes of responses may be obtained by counting frequencies of occurrences of given response types. Certain classes of response are identifiable as the results of processing operations specified in the model for comprehension-memory-reconstruction processes which was described earlier. A list of response classes obtained from frequency counts of various pooled semantic scores and corresponding to performances resulting from specific comprehension and memory processes is found in Figure 5. These score classes may represent rather direct measurements of the operation of specific processes in comprehension and memory.

EFFECTS OF TASK INDUCED COGNITIVE OPERATIONS ON PROCESSES IN COMPREHENSION AND MEMORY

If comprehension and memory processes are supposed to be in conformity with the model summarized in Figure 1, then the nature and extent of use of specific production, selection, verification, and transformation processes ought to be influenced by task contexts which induce different "superordinate" cognitive operations on the semantic content of a passage. If one could design such contexts and observe their differential effects on the output frequencies of specific classes of response representing performances associated with specific comprehension and

I. DISCRIMINATION

   A. <u>Conceptual</u>   1. veridical (A)
                        2. overgeneralization (A+)
                        3. pseudodiscrimination (A-)

   B. <u>Relational</u>   1. veridical ARB
                        2. overgeneralization   A+RB
                                                    ARB+
                                                        A+RB+
                                                       A-RB+
                                                        A+RB-
                        3. pseudodiscrimination A-RB
                                                        ARB-
                                                        A-RB-

   C. <u>Implicational</u> 1. ARB
                        2. overgeneralization   A+RB
                                                         ARB+
                                                       A+RB+
                                                        A-RB+
                                                       A+RB-
                        3. pseudodiscrimination A-RB
                                                        ARB-
                                                        A-RB-

II. INFERENTIAL PRODUCTION

   A. <u>Conceptual</u>   inferred concepts

   B. <u>Relational</u>   inferred relations among explicit concepts
                        inferred relations among inferred concepts
                        inferred relations including inferred concepts

   C. <u>Implicational</u> inferred implications among explicit propositions
                        inferred implications among inferred propositions
                        inferred implications including inferred propositions

III. ELABORATIVE PRODUCTION

   A. <u>Conceptual</u>   elaborative concepts

   B. <u>Relational</u>   elaborative relations which are not false

   C. <u>Implicational</u> elaborative implications which are not false

IV. TRANSFORMATION

   A. <u>Relational</u>   transformations on R where R is a relation
                        false subject-produced relation

   B. <u>Implicational</u> transformations on R where R is an implication
                        false subject-produced implication

FIG. 5. Classes of responses in reconstructed logical discourse.

memory processes, the results should have considerable importance for demonstrating the nature of comprehension and memory processes. The specification of such task contexts involves selecting a task feature which is likely to affect the probability and extent to which individuals employ certain "superordinate processing" modes involving operations on the semantic content of a connected logical argument (as distinguished from processing modes not involving extensive operations on semantic content). While "parametric" task features such as length of passage, amount of time available for processing, number of concepts, and structural features such as logical structure, features of syntax, redundancy, etc., probably affect mode and extent of superordinate processing, it was decided that a task feature more directly related to the hypothesized processing and thus more likely to produce unambiguously the hypothesized effects on processing modes should be selected. If such contexts indeed produced the hypothesized effects on processing modes, then the effects of "parametric" or structural task features, such as those mentioned, on the nature and extent of use of specific production, selection verification, and transformation processes in   comprehension, memory, and reconstruction could be studied. Indeed, if the model were validated, such investigations could then provide information concerning the locus of effects of structural features in the processing sequence. Of particular interest might be differential studies of social or language group differences in the locus of such effects.

Three "contexts" were finally selected. In every context, subjects were repeatedly presented, by means of a tape recorder, a five hundred word essay entitled *Circle Island*. Three experimental conditions were constructed to define the three contexts. In the first condition (A), subjects were told that the material which they would hear would consist of a passage which describes a socio-political problem on an hypothetical island, involving a canal, a threatened civil war, and the probable collapse of the island's economy, and were instructed only that they were to recount in writing what they had heard. They were also told that they were not expected to reproduce the passage verbatim. In the second condition (B), subjects were told that they were participating in an experiment concerned both with investigating the ability of individuals to remember spoken material and to use this information to solve problems, presented with a problem involving the content of the essay (but giving no additional information), and presented with instructions designed to direct them to think about how to solve the problem while they try to remember information from the essay. The problem involved having the subject generate as many alternate solutions as he could for the island's problems, using the information given in the essay concerning the island's social, economic, and political situation. The problem was designed to cause the subject to operate inferentially on a large number of the logical interrelationships conveyed in the structure of the passage. Since the "level of difficulty" of the passage was about that of a somewhat involved newspaper story, it was felt that if this context produced predictable effects on processes in comprehension and memory, the result would be likely to be generalizable to typical situations involving verbal communication and would certainly generalize to intellectually demanding comprehension tasks.

In the third condition, condition (C), subjects worked only on developing solutions to the problem involving the island. However, after three trials of exposure to the text and work on solutions, on the fourth trial these subjects were asked to recount the essay in writing. Subjects in conditions A and B recounted the story four times, once after each exposure to the text. After the fourth trial, all subjects were presented with the problem solving task. Thus condition A involved "incidental problem solving" and condition C involved "incidental memory." Condition A might be construed as "learning in an arbitrary context." The temporal course of events over the four trials and subsequent problem solving were kept precisely equivalent for the three conditions. In all three conditions, exactly the same prior information about the content of the passage was contained in the instructions.

In addition to the materials just described, a multiple choice test was administered which was a lengthened version of the comprehension test used by Dawes to assess distortions in memory of set relations specified in the passage. Additional items in the test involved implicit set relations directly implied by the passage and elaborative set relations which, while not directly implied by the passage, may be plausibly added to lend coherence to the essay. Finally, all subjects returned one week after the first session to take a battery of ability tests, and were asked at that time (before administration of the tests) to recount in writing their best recollection of the passage. One hundred forty-one subjects were tested, all of whom were undergraduates at California State College at Hayward. Most of the students were enrolled in introductory psychology courses. About fifty were tested in each condition and the sexes were about evenly divided among the treatment conditions. State College students represent a less select population of students than that at Berkeley and thus constitute a more representative sample. The sample size is small for confirmatory analyses on covariance structures (to be described later) but it was felt to be sufficient for an initial exploration of predicted relationships. Subjects were tested in groups varying between ten and fifteen persons in two three-hour sessions held one week apart. Subjects were instructed not to talk about the experiment and were paid for their services. The first session consisted of the learning and problem solving tasks, the test of set relations, and the administration of a strategy assessment questionnaire; the second session consisted of one (unexpected) written recall followed by the administration of a battery of ability tests.

If the contexts just described do successfully induce "superordinate" processing operations on the relational structure of the passage, what effects might the theory lead us to expect these operations to have on specific classes of responses in reconstructed logical discourses (which correspond to specific comprehension and memory processes)? Let us consider the elements and processes of Figure 2 and consider what effects the task-induced cognitive operations might be expected to have on processes identified in Figure 1. To generate hypotheses, it is reasonable to expect that the effect of the contexts will be to order the three experimental groups thus in terms of the extent of task-induced inferential processing of content elements: $A \ll B < C$ (where $\ll$ indicates a "much less than" relation). It is also reasonable to suppose that the separation of these groups on this scale increases with repeated exposures to the text (i.e., increased opportunity to "operate on" the text). Thus the effects to be discussed should increase with repeated exposure to the passage.

The semantic elements which have been identified may be ordered in complexity as: concepts, relations, implications, structures. Here complexity refers to the fact that as one proceeds along this sequence, each successive class of elements contains the previous class as a subelement or special case. If the experimental contexts B and C induce (to different degrees) a subject to operate on structural features of his "semantic model," one expected effect would be to induce the subject to process semantic elements which are more complex than those processed under context A. According to the model of Figure 1, contexts may have effects on the complexity of elements processed for more than one reason. Thus, if a particular context functions in such a way as to induce inferential processing operations on the relational content of an essay, this might affect selection processes (inducing the generation of inferentially produced semantic elements), verification processes (inducing a shift from simple verification to inferential verification or verification of non-contradiction), and/or transformations. An important aspect of any attempt to validate this model will probably involve finding "contexts" which affect these processes individually or differentially.

Since the problem which was used in the present research was designed explicitly to induce the subject to operate inferentially on the content of the essay, it was expected that relative extent of *inferential* and (to a lesser degree) non-contradictory *elaborative production* would increase; the extent of *simple production* was expected to decrease proportionately. With repeated exposures, the relative extent of inferential production should increase at the expense of other forms of production. The import of these predictions should be clear: that the manner in which an individual uses knowledge transmitted in a text will affect the nature of the "semantic model" of the text which he produces, and hence his "comprehension" of the text. In terms of classes of responses obtained from subjects' protocols, the expectation was that inferential production of relations and implications would be greatest under condition C and least under A, and that the trend should be towards increased inferential production over trials; a similar ordering of conditions was expected with respect to elaborative production, with a temporal trend in the reverse direction. To consider the effects of our contexts on simple production (of identities), we expected the effects to be likely to affect *verification processes*: in particular, to induce a shift from simple verification (of identity) to verification of class correspondence, implication, and non-contradiction. Thus the treatment effects expected for inferential production were also expected to occur for frequencies of overgeneralized concepts and relations, and the effects expected for elaborative production were also expected to occur for frequencies of pseudodiscriminated concepts and relations. Parallel temporal effects were also expected to occur.

SOME SELECTED RESULTS

Frequency counts were obtained for each of the categories of responses (listed in Figure 5) from each subject's reconstruction of the logical discourse on each trial for which a protocol was available. Thus, for subjects presented the logical discourse under contexts A or B, protocols were obtained for four trials, and, one week later, for a "reminiscence" trial; for subjects presented the discourse under context C, protocols were obtained only for trial 4 and, one week later, for the reminiscence trial. The predictions just described concern differential effects of the contexts on frequencies of particular classes of responses. No predictions were made concerning the transformations, since it was felt that the frequency of occurrence of transformations would be low, and, second and most important, it was felt that no simple prediction could be made from the model. Thus, while the transformations may be thought of as representing distortions of relations present in the text, this class of distortions is ambiguous with regard to the processes which result in transformations. If one were to make a prediction, it might be expected that greater accuracy would result under contexts B and C (if inferential operations on relational content result in a "semantic model" which is less distorted transformationally), and thus that the contexts would be ordered A $>$ B $>$ C in terms of frequency of transformed relations and implications. It may be that what is needed is a more "functionally-related" classification of transformation types. The classification used in this research was a pragmatic one designed to deal with scoring situations which occurred (albeit infrequently).

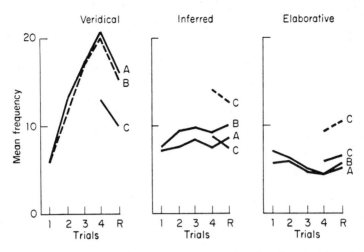

FIG. 6. Plot of mean frequencies of veridical, inferred, and elaborative relations obtained from protocols of subjects under conditions A, B, and C. (R = reminiscence trial, see text.)

Results obtained concerning mean frequencies of various classes of responses in different contexts are presented in Tables 1–3 and Figures 6 and 7. Consider first the predictions concerning the effects of the experimental contexts on relative frequencies of classes of responses resulting from simple, inferential, and elaborative production. Results pertinent to these predictions are found in Figure 6 and Tables 1 and 2. The first graph in Figure 7 is a plot of mean frequencies of *veridical relations* on each trial. There is a general increase in frequency of veridical relations as the learned "semantic structure" is acquired, and a decrease on the reminiscence trial. Frequencies of veridical relations are virtually identical under contexts A and B (even though under context B subjects are working at problem solution) and are considerably lower under context C (the "incidental" memory condition). Mean absolute frequencies of *inferred* and *elaborative relations* are plotted in the other two graphs as solid lines. Since the interest is in inferential and elaborative production *relative to* simple (veridical) production, corrected relative frequencies (relative to absolute frequencies of veridical relations under context A) were computed and are plotted as dotted lines for context C. The obtained results are in every respect as predicted from the model: inferential production increased over trials, while elaborative production decreased; the order of the contexts in terms of relative response class frequencies was in the predicted direction. A summary of the relevant statistical analyses is presented in Tables 1 and 2 for the absolute measures. These analyses indicate: (*1*) that contexts A and B produced significantly different frequencies of inferential production after the first trial, (*2*) that contexts A and B produced significantly different frequencies of elaborative production only on the first trial, (*3*) that context C induced significantly less veridical (simple) production than the other two contexts on trial 4 and in reminiscence, (*4*) that the three contexts differ significantly in absolute inferential production frequencies, and (*5*) that context C induced significantly *more* elaborative production in reminiscence than the other contexts. Sex differences occurred in some instances as

TABLE 1

Mean Absolute Frequencies of Veridical, Inferred, Elaborative, Overgeneralized and Pseudodiscriminated Relations, and Analyses of Variance: Four Trials and Reminiscence Trial, Conditions A and B, Means Pooled Over Sex

| Response Class | Trial | Mean Absolute Frequencies | | Analyses of Variance | | | |
| | | Condition A | Condition B | Conditions | | Sex | |
				F	p	F	p
Veridical Relations	1	5.87	5.92	.024	.877	.104	.7478
	2	13.26	11.92	1.519	.221	.790	.3765
	3	17.32	17.18	.018	.895	3.852	.0528
	4	20.68	20.31	.001	.972	3.736	.0564
	R	16.09	15.59	.058	.810	1.566	.2140
Inferred Relations	1	7.23	7.53	.123	.727	.151	.698
	2	7.64	9.37	5.839	.018	.009	.926
	3	8.38	9.84	5.086	.027	.647	.423
	4	7.64	9.24	5.467	.021	.357	.552
	R	8.62	10.04	3.006	.086	.068	.795
Elaborative Relations	1	5.68	7.08	3.607	.061	1.326	.253
	2	5.89	6.31	.771	.382	.980	.325
	3	4.68	5.04	.303	.583	.478	.491
	4	4.28	4.35	.007	.934	.890	.348
	R	5.34	5.63	.196	.659	.487	.487
Overgeneralized Relations	1	5.00	5.18	0.20	.658	1.04	.311
	2	7.70	8.08	0.80	.373	6.06	.016
	3	7.49	8.18	2.57	.113	8.70	.004
	4	7.91	8.39	0.70	.404	2.49	.118
	R	7.74	8.00	0.41	.523	4.68	.033
Pseudodiscriminated Relations	1	1.79	1.24	4.72	.032	1.07	.305
	2	2.49	1.96	2.40	.125	.15	.697
	3	2.91	2.31	2.48	.119	.06	.812
	4	2.51	2.33	0.30	.583	.02	.886
	R	2.74	2.22	1.14	.288	9.74	.003
		N = 47	N = 49				

main effects but there were no significant interactions of sex with conditions. Particularly striking in these results is the finding that the measure of *absolute* inferential production under context C on trial 4 is higher than that obtained under context A. Also of particular interest is the result that for context C there is a *decrease* in inferential production in reminiscence, while for contexts A and B there is an *increase* in inferential production in reminiscence. This interesting result may indicate that the sort of "distortion" in reminiscence first described by Bartlett (1932), while it occurs in situations in which the subject's "semantic model" is likely to be the result of simple production processes, does not occur in contexts in

TABLE 2

Mean Absolute and Relative Frequencies of Veridical, Inferred Elaborative, Over-generalized, and Pseudodiscriminated Relations and Analyses of Variance for Absolute Measures; Trial 4 and Reminiscence Trial, Conditions A, B, and C, Means Pooled Over Sex

Response Class	Trial	Mean Absolute Frequencies			Mean Relative Frequencies			Analyses of Variance for Absolute Frequencies			
		Condition			Condition			Conditions		Sex	
		A	B	C	A	B	C	F	p	F	p
Veridical Relations	4	20.68	20.31	13.23	20.68	20.68	20.68	14.52	.000	5.88	.017
	R	16.09	15.59	10.17	16.09	16.09	16.09	12.90	.000	2.57	.111
Inferred Relations	4	7.64	9.24	8.93	7.64	9.41	13.96	2.88	.060	.55	.458
	R	8.62	10.04	7.76	8.62	10.36	12.26	4.63	.011	.26	.612
Elaborative Relations	4	4.28	4.35	5.89	4.28	4.43	9.21	3.18	.045	1.74	.189
	R	5.34	5.63	6.53	5.34	5.81	10.33	1.77	.174	.01	.935
Over-generalized Relations	4	7.91	8.39	7.13	7.91	8.54	11.27	1.93	.150	3.03	.084
	R	7.74	8.00	6.72	7.74	8.26	10.63	2.88	.059	8.07	.005
Pseudo-discriminated Relations	4	2.51	2.33	2.17	2.51	2.37	3.39	.59	.558	0.00	.988
	R	2.74	2.22	1.60	2.74	2.29	2.53	5.51	.005	10.56	.002

N = 47   N = 49   N = 47

which the subject's "semantic model" is the result of inferential production processes. Thus, this result may be interpreted as providing additional evidence supporting the notion that the effect of the contexts on processes in comprehension and memory is as predicted from the model.

Now consider the predictions concerning the effects of the contexts on relative frequencies of *overgeneralized* and *pseudodiscriminated relations*. Figure 7 contains graphs of absolute frequencies of veridical, overgeneralized, and pseudodiscriminated relations obtained under each of the three contexts, and graphs of the *relative* frequencies of overgeneralized and pseudodiscriminated relations for context C. The obtained results for frequencies of overgeneralized relations are as predicted by the model; pseudodiscriminated relations appear to have occurred with insufficient frequency to produce the predicted effects (a "bottoming effect"). Analyses of variance of absolute frequencies comparing contexts A and B indicate that the differences between these conditions in absolute frequencies of overgeneralized relations are statistically insignificant; analyses of absolute frequencies of overgeneralized relations for all three conditions indicate that context C is significantly different from contexts A and B, but this difference is reversed in direction when the relative measures are computed. While the absolute level of

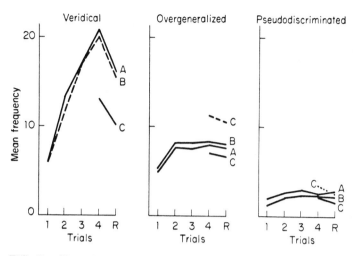

FIG. 7.   Plot of mean frequencies of veridical, overgeneralized, and pseudodiscriminated relations obtained from protocols of subjects under conditions A, B, and C.

production of overgeneralized relations under context C did not surpass that under A (as occurred for absolute frequencies of inferred relations), it is nevertheless striking that the contexts differ as little as they do in absolute frequencies.

Mean absolute and relative frequencies of classes of *concepts* present in subjects' protocols are found in Table 3 together with analyses of variance for the absolute frequencies. Inspection of the absolute frequencies of correct concepts indicates that contexts A and B produced virtually identical performances, while context C resulted in markedly lower absolute frequencies of correct concepts. The frequencies in all three contexts declined in reminiscence. When the absolute frequencies are adjusted to relative frequencies (using frequencies of correct concepts under context A as a reference), the three conditions order themselves as $C > B > A$ in terms of relative frequencies of incomplete (overgeneralized) concepts; in terms of (non-contradictory) elaborative concepts, context C produced greater frequencies than either A or B, A and B being indistinguishable. Overspecified (pseudodiscriminated) concepts occurred with low frequency under all three contexts. Statistically significant differences in absolute frequencies were found for correct concepts, for incomplete concepts, for elaborative concepts, and for overspecified concepts on the reminiscence trial. For the overspecified concepts, the order of the groups in absolute frequencies were different from that obtained from the relative frequencies.

CONCLUDING REMARKS

To conclude this description of our work on effects of task-induced cognitive operations on comprehension and memory processes, two additional empirical approaches to the problem under investigation will be described, both of which have been employed in the present research. The first approach is concerned with extracting structural information relevant to aspects of processes in comprehension and semantic memory from intercorrelations of classes of response measures by fitting certain mathematical models which generate the intercorrelations and which express assumptions about these processes. This approach may be called analysis of covariance structures and has become feasible because of recent developments by Jöreskog (1970a, 1970b, 1970c). The second approach to be described here has been labeled by Cronbach (1969) the "ATI" approach, for "aptitude-treatment interaction," and in the present application involves measuring specific narrowly defined abilities and considering context-induced differences in ability-response class correlations. A rationale for this second approach has been suggested earlier (Frederiksen, 1969). This rationale involves interpreting a high correlation between a specific ability and response class as indicative of the particular process or processes involved in generating responses of that class. Thus, for example, a high estimated correlation of inferential reasoning ability with inferentially produced relations under context C would be expected if context C induced inferential production processes. Let us now briefly consider each of these approaches in more detail.

Evidence has been presented above to indicate that the semantic model which a person develops in comprehending and remembering a text consists of inferred and elaborated semantic structure as well as of veridical elements which were present in the surface structure of the text (in linguistically coded form). Evidence has also been presented to indicate that veridical, inferred, and elaborative structures develop with repeated exposures to a text, that they develop at differential rates,

TABLE 3

Mean Absolute and Relative Frequencies of Classes of Concepts Present in Subjects' Verbal Protocols and Analyses of Variance of Absolute Measures: Three Conditions by Sex, Trial 4 and Reminiscence Trial (R), Means Pooled Over Sex

	Absolute Mean Freq. of Concepts			Relative Mean Freq.			Analyses of Variance for Absolute Frequencies			
	Condition			Condition			Condition		Sex	
Response Class	A	B	C	A	B	C	F	p	F	p
Cor. Con, 4	38.74	38.96	29.71	38.74	38.74	38.74	12.94	.0001	7.90	.0057
Cor. Con, R	33.87	32.82	24.93	33.87	33.87	33.87	12.95	.0001	6.00	.0156
Inc. Con*, 4	9.40	10.71	9.16	9.40	10.66	11.94	2.87	.0604	5.89	.0166
Inc. Con*, R	9.62	10.29	8.27	9.62	10.62	11.23	3.72	.0267	5.03	.0266
Ovrsp. Con**, 4	3.30	3.47	3.31	3.30	3.42	4.32	.23	.7960	1.07	.3033
Ovrsp. Con**, R	4.02	3.59	2.80	4.02	3.71	3.80	3.08	.0491	2.92	.0899
Elab. Con, 4	4.83	4.51	6.07	4.83	4.49	7.92	2.85	.0612	.64	.4240
Elab. Con, R	6.21	5.82	7.27	6.21	6.01	9.88	2.29	.1051	.22	.6421

*Overgeneralized.
**Pseudodiscriminated.
Abbreviations   Cor. Con = Correct Concepts
                Inc. Con = Incomplete Concepts
            Ovrsp. Con = Overspecified Concepts
            Elab. Con = Elaborative Concepts

and that they are differentially affected by contextual conditions. If these statements are accepted, then the following questions may be raised: (*1*) can the production of veridical, inferred, and elaborative structures each be considered to be a growth process (or, alternatively, is the observed growth in inferred and elaborative structure due solely to growth in the veridical structure); and (*2*) are there distinct processes associated with the development of veridical, inferred and elaborative structure and are these processes mutually independent? These questions can all be investigated empirically using available data by expressing the various assumptions indicated above quantitatively as mathematical models which may be fit to the data. The basic data relevant to these questions are the intercorrelations presented in Table 4. Similar questions may be raised concerning processes associated with other response classes. Sample intercorrelations among certain other response class frequencies obtained in our project are reported in Table 5.

The property of a correlation matrix which indicates that a model involving a growth process might generate the data is the *simplex* property—a pattern of correlations in which correlations of adjacent measures are highest with a regular decrease as the measures become more separated in the order. Inspection of Table 4 suggests that the intercorrelations of the veridical relations measured on trials 1 to 4 may represent a simplex; similarly the intercorrelations of the counts of inferred and elaborative relations on trials 1 to 4 may also each have this property. Note that the correlations of veridical relations with inferred relations and the correlations of inferred with elaborative relations appear to vary about zero. The correlations of veridical relations with elaborative relations appear to become negative as the trials progress. The reader is invited to inspect the correlations in Table 5 in the same manner. Empirically, the possibilities raised in the above two questions may be interpreted in terms of the correlations as follows: (*1*) Does the submatrix of intercorrelations of each set of trials within a response class represent a simplex? (*2*) If we allow for the fact that veridical elements contribute to counts of inferred relations, and that both veridical and inferred elements may contribute to counts of elaborative relations, to what extent do the between-response class intercorrelations imply that processes associated with simple, inferential, and elaborative production are independent? Or, put another way, to what extent do they imply that observed growth in counts of inferred or elaborative relations are due to their correlation with (dependence on) production of veridical relations?

A distinction among these possibilities, however, requires more than simple inspection of a matrix of intercorrelations. To illustrate how these questions may be investigated, let us consider a model which was fit to the data of Table 4.

A precise statement of a model which supposes that (*1*) counts of veridical relations reflect a simple production (encoding) process which is a stochastic growth process (more explicitly a nonstationary Markov process with continuous states), (*2*) counts of inferred relations reflect a linear combination of the results of the encoding process and a process of inference which is a stochastic growth process independent of encoding, and (*3*) that counts of elaborative relations reflect a linear combination of the results of encoding, inference, and an elaborative production process which is a stochastic growth process independent of encoding and

TABLE 4

Pooled Within-Group Multi-Occasion Intercorrelations of Response Class Frequencies Based on Veridical, Inferred, and Elaborative Relations

Variate Response Class	Trial	1.	2.	3.	4.	5.	6.	7.	8.	9.	10.	11.	12.	13.	14.
1. Veridical Relations	1	—													
2. Veridical Relations	2	.663	—												
3. Veridical Relations	3	.532	.789	—											
4. Veridical Relations	4	.526	.739	.863	—										
5. Veridical Relations	R	.457	.694	.821	.822	—									
6. Inferred Relations	1	.223	.297	.267	.240	.265	—								
7. Inferred Relations	2	.005	.047	.063	.051	.013	.379	—							
8. Inferred Relations	3	−.029	.119	.083	.101	.076	.338	.524	—						
9. Inferred Relations	4	−.250	−.123	−.181	−.165	−.185	.242	.275	.526	—					
10. Inferred Relations	R	−.064	.039	.041	−.024	.004	.451	.304	.483	.484	—				
11. Elaborative Relations	1	−.140	−.118	−.176	−.149	−.128	.159	.049	.157	.217	.230	—			
12. Elaborative Relations	2	−.388	−.385	−.368	−.352	−.270	−.026	−.126	−.082	.105	.081	.512	—		
13. Elaborative Relations	3	−.192	−.336	−.305	−.263	−.279	−.146	−.175	−.110	.113	−.031	.262	.448	—	
14. Elaborative Relations	4	−.275	−.334	−.288	−.419	−.339	−.059	−.107	−.097	−.063	.035	.253	.390	.458	—
15. Elaborative Relations	R	−.255	−.335	−.314	−.380	−.370	.055	−.072	−.057	.135	.065	.286	.336	.456	.395

$N = 96$

TABLE 5

Pooled Within-Group Multi-Occasion Intercorrelations of Response Class Frequencies Based on Veridical, Overgeneralized, and Pseudodiscriminated Relations

Variate Response Class	Trial	1.	2.	3.	4.	5.	6.	7.	8.	9.	10.	11.	12.	13.	14.	15.
1. Veridical Rel.	1	—														
2. Veridical Rel.	2	.663	—													
3. Veridical Rel.	3	.532	.789	—												
4. Veridical Rel.	4	.526	.739	.863	—											
5. Veridical Rel.	R	.457	.694	.821	.822	—										
6. Overgen. Rel.	1	.394	.430	.368	.382	.233	—									
7. Overgen. Rel.	2	.221	.229	.305	.334	.257	.318	—								
8. Overgen. Rel.	3	.080	.223	.274	.418	.252	.304	.521	—							
9. Overgen. Rel.	4	.006	.060	.219	.162	.124	.250	.217	.401	—						
10. Overgen. Rel.	R	.115	.239	.319	.346	.261	.267	.244	.489	.374	—					
11. Pseudodisc. Rel.	1	.218	.236	.122	-.005	.010	.213	.101	.035	-.012	-.029	—				
12. Pseudodisc. Rel.	2	.147	.067	.169	.150	.153	.113	-.221	.043	.283	.159	.180	—			
13. Pseudodisc. Rel.	3	.119	.130	.060	.104	.096	.236	-.051	.000	.044	.054	.176	.406	—		
14. Pseudodisc. Rel.	4	-.063	.026	.018	-.006	.099	-.083	-.089	-.046	.009	-.009	.063	.157	.220	—	
15. Pseudodisc. Rel.	R	.053	.192	.105	.011	.053	.179	.001	.067	.047	.008	.221	.189	.320	.235	—

TABLE 6

Summary of Model for Veridical, Inferred, and Elaborative Relations:
Hierarchical Additive Encoding, Inference, and Elaborative Production Processes
which are Nonstationary Markov Simplex Growth Processes

Structural Model (a)*

$$X_{tij} = \mu_{ti} + \beta_{ti}^{(G)} G_{tj} + \beta_{ti'}^{(I)} I_{tj} + \beta_{ti''}^{(E)} E_{tj} + \epsilon_{ti'j}$$

$$G_{t+1,j} = \alpha_{t+1}^{(G)} G_{tj} + g_{t+1,j} + \epsilon_{t+1,j}$$

$$I_{t+1,j} = \alpha_{t+1}^{(I)} I_{tj} + i_{t+1,j}$$

$$E_{t+1,j} = \alpha_{t+1}^{(E)} E_{tj} + e_{t+1,j}$$

Assumptions (b)#

1. Scaling Assumptions

$$\sum_j N_j E(G_{tj}) = \sum_j N_j E(I_{tj}) = \sum_j N_j E(E_{tj}) = E(\epsilon_{ti'j}) = E(\epsilon_{tj}) = 0$$

$$\text{var}(g_{tj}) = \text{var}(I_{tj}) = \text{var}(E_{tj}) = 1$$

$$\text{var}(\epsilon_{ti'j}) = \theta_{ti'}^2$$

2. Quasi-Simplex Model: Encoding

$$\text{var}(G_{tj}) = \phi_t = 1 - \psi_t^2 = 1 - \text{var}(\epsilon_{tj})$$

$$\text{var}(g) = \Gamma^{(G)} = D_\xi^{(G)} T \Phi^{(G)*} T' D_\xi^{(G)} + \Psi^2$$

where $\Phi^{(G)} = D_\xi^{(G)} \Phi^{(G)*} D_\xi^{(G)}$

$D_\xi^{(G)}$ is a diagonal matrix containing $\xi_t^{(G)} = \alpha_1^{(G)} \alpha_2^{(G)} \ldots \alpha_t^{(G)}$

T is a lower triangular matrix of one's.

$\Phi^{(G)}$ contains $\phi_t = 1 - \psi_t^2$ (a diagonal matrix)

Ψ^2 is a diagonal matrix containing ψ_t^2

$g' = (G_1, G_2, G_3, G_4)$

3. Simplex Model: Inference

$$\text{var}(i) = \Gamma^{(E)} = D_\xi^{(I)} T\Phi^{(I)*} T'D_\xi^{(I)}$$

where $D_\xi^{(I)}$ is a diagonal matrix containing $\xi_t^{(I)} = \alpha_1^{(I)} \alpha_2^{(I)} \ldots \alpha_t^{(I)}$

* $i = 1, 2, 3$ (response class); $i' = 2, 3, i'' = 3; t = 1, \ldots, 4$(trials); $j = 1, 2$ (group)
# For maximum likelihood estimation, it is assumed in addition that X is distributed multi-normal with mean vector μ_j and covariance matrix Σ. (Note, a lower case letter in italics indicates a column vector while a capital letter in italics represents a matrix).

Table 6 (Cont'd.)

$$i' = (I_1, I_2, I_3, I_4) \text{ and } \Phi^{(I)} = D_\xi^{(I)} \Phi^{(I)*} D_\xi^{(I)}$$

4. Simplex Model: Elaborative Production

$$\text{var } (e) = \Gamma^{(E)} = D_\xi^{(E)} T\Phi^{(E)*} T'D_\xi^{(E)} \qquad \text{as in (3.)}$$

5. Additive Hierarchical Model

$$\sum = \text{var } (X) = B\Gamma B' + \theta^2$$

where

		G_1	G_2	G_3	G_4	I_1	I_2	I_3	I_4	E_1	E_2	E_3	E_4	5	10	15
	1	$\beta_{11}^{(G)}$														
	2		$\beta_{21}^{(G)}$													
	3			$\beta_{31}^{(G)}$												
	4				$\beta_{41}^{(G)}$											
	5													1		
	6	$\beta_{12}^{(G)}$				$\beta_{12}^{(I)}$										
$B=$	7		$\beta_{22}^{(G)}$				$\beta_{22}^{(I)}$									
	8			$\beta_{32}^{(G)}$				$\beta_{32}^{(I)}$								
	9				$\beta_{42}^{(G)}$				$\beta_{42}^{(I)}$							
	10														1	
	11															
	12	$\beta_{13}^{(G)}$				$\beta_{13}^{(I)}$				$\beta_{13}^{(E)}$						
	13		$\beta_{23}^{(G)}$				$\beta_{23}^{(I)}$				$\beta_{23}^{(E)}$					
	14			$\beta_{33}^{(G)}$				$\beta_{33}^{(I)}$				$\beta_{33}^{(E)}$				
	15				$\beta_{43}^{(G)}$				$\beta_{43}^{(I)}$				$\beta_{43}^{(E)}$			1

reminiscence trials

(blanks are zeros)

TABLE 6 (Cont'd.)

6. Assumption of Independent Processes

$$
\Gamma = \left\|
\begin{array}{cccc}
\Gamma^{(G)} & 0 & 0 & \text{cov}\,(G, X_R) \\
& \Gamma^{(I)} & 0 & \text{cov}\,(I, X_R) \\
& & \Gamma^{(E)} & \text{cov}\,(E, X_R) \\
& & & \text{var}\,(X_R)
\end{array}
\right\| \quad \text{(A Symmetric Matrix)}
$$

θ^2 is a diagonal matrix containing θ_{ti}^2

X is a vector of response class frequencies ordered as in Table 4,

$X_R' = (X_5, X_{10}, X_{15})$

---

inference, is summarized in Table 6. The estimated parameter values are presented in Table 7. The first equation in Table 6 states that the frequency of response class i on trial t for context j is equal to the mean for that measure-trial combination (μ_{ti}) plus linear regression on encoding at t trial t for context j (G_{tj}) plus for inferred and elaborative relations) linear regression on inference at trial t for context j (I_{tj}) plus (solely for elaborative relations) linear regression on elaborative production at trial t for context j (E_{tj}). The last term of this equation ($\epsilon_{ti'j}$) represents a measure-specific error component. The next three equations of the structural model represent the growth property defined respectively for encoding, inference, and elaborative production. The remaining equations express assumptions which are necessary to completely specify the model. (It is not necessary to discuss them here; for a detailed discussion of these models see Jöreskog, 1970c).

The fit of this model is quite good (chi-square of 43.68 with 39 degrees of freedom, $p = .279$), indicating that it is reasonable to regard the three processes as independent stochastic processes.[6] In the first three columns of Table 7(a) are estimates of the regression weights for encoding ($\beta_{ti}^{(G)}$), inference ($\beta_{ti}^{(I)}$), and elaborative production ($\beta_{ti}^{(E)}$) for each response class for each trial. Observe that for counts of inferred relations the weights on simple encoding decrease while weights on inference increase with trials. Similarly, for counts of elaborative relations the regression weights on encoding become negative, those on inference decrease with repeated exposure to the text, and weights on elaborative production increase on trial 2 and then decrease on subsequent trials. The numbers in column four reflect the rate of growth of encoding, inference, and elaborative production (small weights represent a low rate of growth). The correlations of Table 7(b) reflect the simplex property for encoding, inference, and elaborative production. Table 7(c) presents the estimated correlations of encoding, inference, and elaborative production with counts of veridical, inferred, and elaborative relations obtained one week

---

[6] Note that a chi-square measure of fit obtained from the likelihood ratio should be small relative to a large number of degrees of freedom and the p value (for rejection of the model) should be large. All three quantities must be considered in evaluating the fit of a model.

TABLE 7

Parameter Estimates for Model for Veridical, Inferred, and Elaborative Relations

Parameter Estimates for Model IV(a)

Trial	Measure	$\beta_{ti}^{(G)}$	$\beta_{ti}^{(I)}$	$\beta_{ti}^{(E)}$	α_t	ψ_t	θ_{ti}
1	Veridical Relations	1.000*			.942	.315	.0*
2	,, ,,	1.000*			.747	.127	.0*
3	,, ,,	1.000*			.816	.162	.0*
4	,, ,,	1.000*			.938	.032	.0*
1	Inferred Relations	.242	.571		1.000*		.795
2	,, ,,	−.009	.714		.896		.700
3	,, ,,	.056	.913		.792		.402
4	,, ,,	−.191	.985		.603		.000
1	Elaborative Relations	−.028	.211	.679	1.000*		.697
2	,, ,,	−.306	−.048	.762	.923		.525
3	,, ,,	−.282	−.113	.677	.586		.665
4	,, ,,	−.383	−.197	.636	.899		.638

*denotes parameter values specified by the model $\chi^2 = 43.6835$, d.f. = 39, p = .279

Intercorrelations of Derived Measures (b)

Simple Production (Encoding) Process

Trial	1	2	3	4
1	1.			
2	.663	1.		
3	.541	.789	1.	
4	.507	.740	.863	1.

Inferential Production Process

Trial	1	2	3	4
1	1.			
2	.896	1.		
3	.709	.792	1.	
4	.427	.477	.603	1.

Elaborative Production Process

Trial	1	2	3	4
1	1.			
2	.923	1.		
3	.540	.586	1.	
4	.486	.527	.899	1.

Intercorrelations of Derived Measures with Measures Obtained One Week Later (tr. 5) (c)

Measure	G_1	G_2	G_3	G_4	I_1	I_2	I_3	I_4	E_1	E_2	E_3	E_4
Veridical Relations	.453	.684	.822	.821	.087	-.052	.004	-.039	-.013	.047	-.037	-.067
Inferred {	.034	.001	.036	-.041	.775	.443	.549	.473	.033	.090	.017	.068
Elaborative { Relations	-.213	-.307	-.318	-.379	.278	-.009	-.016	.006	.243	.206	.525	.347

later. Interestingly, counts of veridical relations correlate highest (.821) with encoding on the last trial, but frequency of inferred relations correlate highest (.775) with inference on the first trial.

The second approach to the study of comprehension and memory processes and the effects of contexts on these processes involves attempting to predict frequencies of each class of response from measurements of abilities and studying the effects of the contexts on these predictive relationships. In the present research, processes in comprehension and memory were classified into input linguistic processes, unconstrained generative processes (associated with elaborative production), generative reasoning processes (associated with inferential production), output expressional processes, storage and retrieval processes, processes associated with buffer storage, and processes associated with the identification and maintenance of semantic elements. Ability measurements related to each of these classes were obtained and used to predict response class frequencies separately for each experimental context.[7]

To illustrate our results, consider the role of reasoning processes in the production of semantic elements. Two tests were selected as measures of reasoning ability: Inference (the test items involve selecting correct conclusions which can be drawn from given statements) and Letter Sets (the task involves finding a rule which related sets of four letters and eliminating a fifth set of letters which does not fit the rule). What the two tests have in common is a requirement that the subject be able to generate and evaluate inferences. The procedure used is to estimate the factor common to the two tests and use this inferential reasoning factor to predict response measures. This factor will be independent of verbal factors since only one of the tests involves verbal content. Thus correlations of response measures with this estimated reasoning factor are not due to common verbal content. Correlations of reasoning ability with frequencies of veridical, inferred, and elaborative relations are found in Table 8. A number of results are apparent: (*1*) frequencies of veridical relations are predictable from reasoning for all contexts; (*2*) with only one exposure to the passage, reasoning correlates highest with veridical relations for condition B, but the correlation for condition A increases with repeated exposures to the text and surpasses that of condition B; (*3*) inferred relations are predictable from reasoning only under condition B; and (*4*) reasoning is negatively correlated with elaborative relations under all conditions. These results would appear to indicate that the generation of relational structures (other than those which are elaborative) in comprehending and remembering a text *necessarily* involves logical operations on the semantic content of the text. Included in the preceding statement are those relations which were explicitly coded in the text. These results also indicate independently of the results on mean frequencies of response classes that the effect of the contexts was in part to induce generative reasoning processes.

One purpose of this paper has been to present a general description of a conception of comprehension and memory processes which developed as this research proceeded and which was found to be necessary for determining measurements of comprehension and semantic memory. A second purpose has been to describe

[7] Tests were selected from the *Kit of Reference Tests for Cognitive Abilities* (French, Ekstrom, & Price, 1963).

TABLE 8

Correlations of Reasoning Ability with Veridical,
Inferred, and Elaborative Relations for each
Condition

Response Class	Trial	Condition		
		A	B	C
Veridical Relations	1	.108	.358	–
Veridical Relations	2	.566	.384	–
Veridical Relations	3	.578	.384	–
Veridical Relations	4	.499	.436	.372
Veridical Relations	R	.453	.345	.313
Inferred Relations	1	.214	.266	–
Inferred Relations	2	.138	.432	–
Inferred Relations	3	.216	.590	–
Inferred Relations	4	.069	.140	.075
Inferred Relations	R	.058	.267	.211
Elaborative Relations	1	−.276	−.103	–
Elaborative Relations	2	−.214	−.479	–
Elaborative Relations	3	−.408	−.128	–
Elaborative Relations	4	−.248	−.276	−.443
Elaborative Relations	R	−.149	−.182	−.302
		N = 47	N = 49	N = 47

methods which have been developed to measure the results of comprehension and memory processes and to present selected results concerning the effects of task-induced cognitive operations on the content of a connected logical argument on classes of responses related to these processes. Any final evaluation of these procedures and results obtained using the procedures will probably have to await future research developments.

CONFERENCE DISCUSSION

Simmons asked for clarification of what Frederiksen meant by inferential production. Frederiksen said it was his belief that more superordinate kinds of processing tend to increase as comprehension of the passage increases. Thus the strategies that may be operating early in the perception of discourse may be different from the ones operating later. This may occur because the semantic resources that are available for strategies to operate on have changed over the course of the discourse. As one gets well into the discourse passage, the frequency with which inferences begin to be made should increase. An additional aspect of inferential production may involve treating the surface structure of discourse in different ways as a function of how far into the text one is—surface structure may become less and less important later in discourse because one should rely more on assessing the significance of content by matching this against one's internalized semantic model of the passage.

Scriven wondered whether Frederiksen equated inferential activities with "pure" comprehension and if so, whether it might not be better to separate them. As an example, suppose one listens to some story. In some sense one comprehends the succession of individual sentences and may be able to give back the story verbatim afterwards. But if one is asked a question about the story, then it may be necessary to carry out an inference. In other words, inferences may not necessarily be occurring while we comprehend the succession of sentences in the story and for that reason we should consider separating memory from inference. Bever disagreed. He thought that the term "comprehension" depends upon an arbitrary decision about what *level* of internal processing one is willing to adopt. For example, one might insist that the presuppositions that go into our use of particular words could, by one point of view, constitute examples of "inferences" whereas another person might reserve the term inference only for higher level (intersentence) processing. By this view, the distinction between pure comprehension and inference is arbitrary. Frederiksen also mentioned in this regard that he was unwilling to separate memory processes from comprehension since this separation too seems to depend upon an arbitrary decision.

Simmons was bothered by a discrepancy between the amount of detail which his own work in computational linguistics required (in moving, say, from surface to deep structure in some of his question-answering programs) and the broad relatively undetailed approach used by others in the conference in characterizing how one matches a subject's recall protocol against the original stimulus passage. Frederiksen agreed that one should be concerned about this relative lack of detail in objectively demonstrating a match or mismatch. Perhaps the only way to accomplish this effectively is to go the computational linguistics route.

In reference to Frederiksen's study which examined the effect of his subjects' searching (versus not searching) for solutions to a social problem that existed in the discourse passage, Rothkopf said he didn't understand why these superordinate tasks (finding solutions to social problems) should increase the inferential processing of the story's information. Frederiksen said that the main assumption was that if a subject was to search for a reasonable solution to the social problem, this should induce him to weigh the discourse information with greater care and more thoroughness (inferential thoroughness) than would be the case if they were asked to simply retell the story in the absence of any other special instructions.

REFERENCES

Bartlett, F. C. *Remembering: A study in experimental and social psychology*. Cambridge: Cambridge University Press, 1932.

Bever, T. G. The cognitive basis for linguistic structures. In J. R. Hayes (Ed.) *Cognition and the development of language*. New York: Wiley, 1970.

Cronbach, L. J., & Snow, R. E. Individual differences in learning ability as a function of instructional variables. (USOE Final Report, Contract No. OEC−4−6−06129−1217) Stanford: Stanford University Press, 1969.

Dawes, R. M. Memory and distortion of meaningful written material. *British Journal of Psychology*, 1966, 57, 77−86.

Fillmore, C. J. The case for case. In E. Bach and R. T. Harms (Eds.), *Universal in linguistic theory*. New York: Holt, Rinehart & Winston, 1968.

Frase, L. T. A structural analysis of the knowledge that results from thinking about text. *Journal of Educational Psychology*, 1969, 60 (6, Pt. 2).

Frederiksen, C. H. Abilities, transfer, and information retrieval in verbal learning. *Multivariate Behavioral Research*, 1969, 69−2.

Frederiksen, C. H. Functional indeterminacy and cognitive processes in learning performance. Paper presented at the meeting of the Western Psychological Association, Los Angeles, April 1970.

French, J. W., Ekstrom, R., & Price, L. *Kit of reference tests for cognitive abilities*. Princeton: Educational Testing Service, 1963.

Harary, F., Norman, R. Z., & Cartwright, D. *Structural models: an introduction to the theory of directed graphs*. New York: Wiley, 1965.

Jöreskog, K. G. A general method for analysis of covariance structures. *Biometrika*, 1970, 57(2), 239−251. (a)

Jöreskog, K. G. ACOVS. A general computer program for analysis of covariance structures. *Educational Testing Service Research Bulletin*, 1970. RB–70–15. (b)

Jöreskog, K. G. Estimation and testing of simplex models. *British Journal of Mathematical and Statistical Psychology*, 1970, **23**, 121–145. (c)

Leech, G. N. *Towards a semantic description of English.* Bloomington, Ind.: Indiana University Press, 1970.

Minsky, M.L. (Ed.) *Semantic information processing.* Cambridge, Mass.: M.I.T. Press, 1968.

10
MEMORY STRUCTURE AND THE RECALL OF DISCOURSE[1]

Edward J. Crothers
University of Colorado

INTRODUCTION

How is human memory organized, and how is this organization used in the learning of new information communicated by linguistic units which are themselves organized? One or another of the "organizations" and "uses" referred to in this question is currently the object of much research in linguistics, psychology, and artificial intelligence. The aim of this paper is to present an interim report of my investigation of the issue. Broader implications as well as the relation to other approaches will be dealt with here only to a limited extent. The reader can consult a previous paper (Crothers, 1970) for a fuller treatment of these matters and also for some technical points assumed in the present paper.

The approach to be discussed is unusual, though not unique (e.g., Frase, 1969; Harris, 1963; Rothkopf, 1969; Sanders, 1969), in that the proper unit of analysis both in memory and in discourse is asserted to be an overall knowledge structure and not a set of independent sentences. On informal grounds this claim is hardly controversial, but for various reasons most linguistic and psychological studies have dwelt on properties of individual sentences. Without denying the contribution of such research, it nonetheless must be maintained that memory and discourse have structures which are no more reducible to independent sentences than a sentence is reducible to individual words. How, then, should one pursue the investigation of the overall structure? Surely this depends on the objective. My aim is to determine the interplay between linguistic structures in prose and structures in memory as

[1] This research was supported by Grant No. OEG8–9–150400–4006(057) from the Committee on Basic Research in Education, National Research Council, and by Grant No. MH–15956 from the National Institute of Mental Health. I wish to acknowledge the assistance of Mr. Charles Jorgensen and Mr. David Huizinga in the running of experimental subjects.

inferred from data gathered in prose recall tasks. It seems that, ultimately, there are four stages to this problem. The first is to formulate a linguistic description of the structure of prose. The second stage is to conduct recall experiments, analyzing both the to-be-read passage and the recalls of it according to the theory developed in the first stage. The third stage involves discovering the empirical relation between structure and recall of it, drawing inferences on the basis of the experimental design. In the final stage, a process model would be postulated to account for the linguistic and, hopefully, also the temporal features of discourse memory.

It is by no means clear how any of these stages can be accomplished because methodological extrapolations from related areas of research must be scrutinized as to their suitability here. Thus progress has been slow. However, a beginning has been made on the first three stages of the problem. As to the discourse structure, a "competence" view is upheld: It seems foolish to seek to write a different theory for each learner when presumably he is unique only in his performance characteristics. The manner of establishing the linguistic analysis has been inductive: It is based on intensive analyses of a few passages with the aim of thereby inferring a general linguistic description. The method seems feasible and intuitively correct for descriptive prose passages of no more than a. few paragraphs though there are basic issues of evaluation and generality which will not be confronted here. The present paper concentrates on the second stage: Experimental procedures and data analyses. A modest quantity of data are presented and analyzed. Some methodological conclusions are reached as to most appropriate experimental designs and data analyses. The further stage of correlating data with structure is currently being explored, but in the absence of any definitive results, it seems premature to attempt a process model.

METHOD

Essentially, the scheme was to present relatively unfamiliar paragraphs to college students who were native speakers of English, and later ask them to recall the passages.

Subjects. Eighteen University of Colorado students served as subjects. Data from four other subjects were discarded because pretesting revealed that they already had some detailed knowledge of the topics. Each subject served in two experimental sessions and was paid $4.00 for his participation.

Design. Four paragraphs were presented in random order. The first was then tested for recall. The second session consisted of testing the four passages for recall with the order of recall randomized over subjects. Two of the passages, one on nebulae and one on oceanography, were basic to the experiment, while the other two were "fillers" included to induce forgetting. Only the nebulae paragraph will be discussed here. Two different textual versions of the same *nebulae* content were given, each to a random half of the subjects. The themes of the filler passages were *steel production* and *the adrenal gland*. Passages were selected to have low preknowledge, minimal overlap with one another, and to be descriptive in their rhetorical mode.

Procedure. Subjects were run individually in a sound-shielded chamber. First, the subject was instructed as to the general purpose of the experiment, and asked to write a brief summary of any preexperimental knowledge he might have about nebulae, oceanography, steel production, or the adrenal gland. Then he was handed an ordered deck of cards, on each of which was a typed sentence of the passage. (The single-sentence card format was used to ensure that the subject attended to every sentence and did not review earlier ones. Also, reading times were roughly measured by the experimenter with a stopwatch, but those data will not be reported.) The subject was instructed to go through the deck "for understanding" just once at his normal speed. Next, the procedure was repeated with each of the other three decks. Finally, he was tested on the first paragraph presented. He was told to write, in his own words, everything he could recall and was allowed unlimited recall time. Seven days later he was scheduled for a second session "similar to the first." Actually, the second session involved only test trials, one per passage.

LINGUISTIC ANALYSIS OF NEBULAE PARAGRAPH

For the corresponding analysis of the oceanography paragraph, see Crothers (1971, pp. 41–44).

Each subject saw either Version A or B quoted below.[2] (Sentence numbers added here to facilitate referral to them.)

Nebulae — Version A.

1. A nebula is any heavenly body which glows and has a relatively fixed location in space and looks fuzzy or nebulous. 2. There are two kinds of nebulae. 3. One kind is the nebulae outside our own galaxy. 4. The ones outside our galaxy are composed of stars. 5. Thus these nebulae are called galaxy nebulae. 6. Galaxy nebulae appear in clusters of from 2 to 30 galaxies. 7. The clusters of galaxy nebulae are spread rather evenly throughout the universe. 8. Galaxy nebulae look fuzzy because the overall nebula is seen, but the nebulae are so remote that their individual stars cannot be distinguished, even with the most powerful telescopes. 9. In fact, only three galaxy nebulae are close enough to be seen at all with the naked eye. 10. The other kind is the nebulae within our galaxy. 11. The ones within our galaxy are clouds of gas or dust. 12. Some of the gas nebulae are evolving to become stars, by expanding and contracting. 13. Gas nebulae glow because the gas itself is luminous, but dust nebulae seem to glow because they are illuminated by nearby stars.

Nebulae — Version B

1. A nebula is any heavenly body which glows and has a relatively fixed location in space and looks fuzzy or nebulous. 2. There are two kinds of nebulae, 3. The ones outside our galaxy and the ones within our galaxy. 4. The nebulae outside our galaxy are composed of stars. 5. Thus these nebulae are called galaxy nebulae. 6. The nebulae within our galaxy are clouds of gas or dust. 7. Galaxy nebulae appear in clusters of from 2 to 30 galaxies. 8. The clusters of galaxy nebulae are spread rather evenly throughout the universe. 9. Some of the gas nebulae are evolving to become stars, by expanding and contracting. 10. Galaxy nebulae look fuzzy because the overall nebulae is seen, but the nebulae are so remote that their individual stars cannot be

---

[2] Several minor syntactic changes were made from the versions quoted in Crothers (1970, pp. 26 and 54) in order to equate Versions A and B on the implicit and explicit frequencies.

distinguished, even with the most powerful telescopes. 11. In fact, only three galaxy nebulae are close enough to be seen at all with the naked eye. 12. Gas nebulae glow because the gas itself is luminous, but dust nebulae seem to glow because they are illuminated by nearby stars.

The linguistic analysis essentially follows that given previously (Crothers, 1970), to which the reader is referred for details. All that will be mentioned here is the general method and some revision in details. The analysis distinguishes an underlying level and a superficial level. The underlying level represents the conceptual structure as a set of semantic hierarchies (also called trees) plus (i) mappings to indicate correspondences between points (called nodes) of different hierarchies and (ii) logical connectives, especially &, OR, ⟹, and the synthetic "connectives," here mainly WHY denoting "because of." This level is depicted as a graph in order to aid in visualizing the structure. For other purposes, it (but not the bare surface structure) could be converted into a linear sequence of quasi-logical predicates or outlines. The plural *outlines* must be emphasized, for the outcome of the analysis differs markedly from a single outline which is conventionally regarded as a description of prose structure. Instead, the outcome is a set of outlines, one for each semantic hierarchy of the graph, along with the mappings between hierarchies. A "semantic hierarchy," as the term is used here, is a hierarchy of propositions such that subordinates logically imply the immediate superordinate, with the important restriction that only those propositions which are explicit or implicit in the text will be included in the hierarchy.

Decisions about the semantic content, such as what the connectives and implicit categories are, rest with the theorist here as in current theories of semantics. Clearly, then, the underlying network of hierarchies is not to be identified with the entire semantic structure of the text: A reader's semantic knowledge will include lexical representations and other information which is neither stated nor implied in the text. For example, the present analysis applied to a passage about the care of cats would represent the fact that they are mammals, but the part of the lexical entry specifying that "cats meow" would be excluded. The rationale for representing only the hierarchic part of a lexical entry is partly objective and partly a matter of expediency. A significant property of prose (at least descriptive prose), is the frequent recurrence of the same semantic concept exemplified by diverse individual members. The element of expediency is that at the present stage of analysis it is not feasible to attempt to analyze each text word into a psychologically acceptable definition, unless the word is in fact defined in the passage being analyzed.

The superficial level characterizes all meaning-preserving operations which have been performed on the underlying level in order to yield the actual text. For the most part, the only syntactic factors treated are those having between-sentence consequences. The aim is to complement, not to duplicate, within-sentence analyses. Thus putative deep structures, even if they exist at all, are not represented in the present analysis. Linguistically speaking, the principal operations are grammatical (e.g., transformations and pro-forms of nouns, phrases, and articles) and semantic (e.g., paraphrases, synonyms, antonyms, and deletion of implied prepositions). However, nonlinguistic textual devices intended to highlight a subtopic (e.g., indentation, underlining, and sentence repetition) should not be overlooked. At present, this analysis of the superficial level has begun to consider only two factors: The sentence order and the explicit vs. implicit forms of reference. Versions A and B of the nebulae passage obviously differ chiefly in their sentence order.

The underlying structure, which is common to both versions, is diagrammed in Figure 1. (Ignore the numbers in the figure for the moment.) The order from left to right in the graph is from subordinate to superordinate. To improve legibility, abbreviations have been employed freely, as noted. Also, each sentence or proposition has been abbreviated by inserting only those words which distinguish it from its immediate superordinate.[3,4] For example, the subgraph

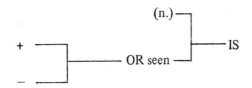

[3] The connective OR as used here denotes a partition of the predicate. Different forms of partitioning are represented by appropriate use of & and OR. For example, S_1 = *The coat was black and gray* and S_2 = *One coat was black and the other was gray* are (i) and (ii) below:

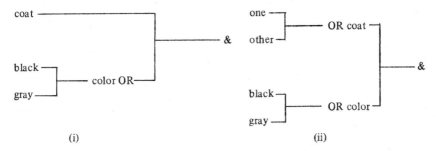

(i)   (ii)

[4] The revisions of the earlier theory (Crothers, 1970, pp. 40–41) are as follows. First, the two revisions tentatively suggested in the latter sections of that report have been adopted here. Second, the subtree headed by *evolve* has been revised as shown, to mark the fact that this verb is here modified by its subordinates *expand*, to *star*, etc. Third, the former graph notation for the case where one tree corresponds to only a subtree of another has proven awkward for expressing a fairly common aspect of recall data, and hence has been replaced. For example, the former notation as in (i) below does not allow a simple way of representing the erroneous response *all nebulae evolve*, whereas

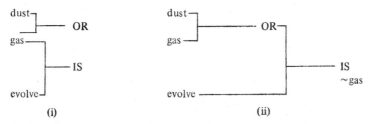

(i)   (ii)

under the revision ii, it simply becomes a special case of a correspondence error. For texts in general, it appears to be somewhat arbitrary as to how far up the main path one should append the restricted subtree.

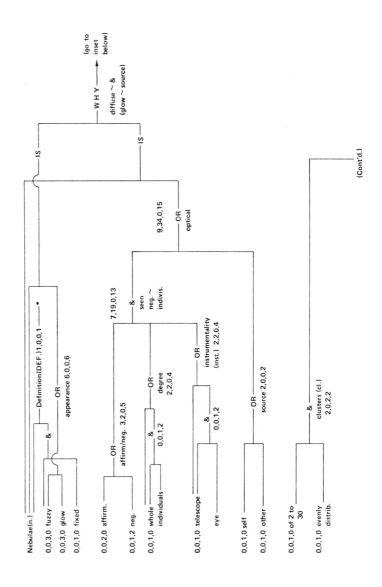

WHY ⟶ (go to inset below)

diffuse ~ &
(glow ~ source)

Nebulae(n.) ══ Definition(DEF.)1,0,0,1 •

IS

0,0,3,0 fuzzy ─┐
0,0,3,0 glow ──┼─ & ── OR
0,0,1,0 fixed ─┘   appearance 6,0,0,6

IS

0,0,2,0 affirm. ─┐
0,0,1,2 neg. ────┴─ OR   7,19,0,13
                  affirm./neg. 3,2,0,5   & ── OR   9,34,0,15
                                              seen   optical
0,0,1,0 whole ──────┐   neg. ~
individuals ────────┴─ &   indivis.
                       0,0,1,2
                       OR
                       degree
                       2,2,0,4

0,0,1,0 telescope ─┐
eye ───────────────┴─ &   OR
                     0,0,1,2   instrumentality
                               (inst.) 2,2,0,4

0,0,1,0 self ──┐
0,0,1,0 other ─┴─ OR
                  source 2,0,0,2

0,0,1,0 of 2 to
30 ──────────────┐
0,0,1,0 evenly ──┴─ &
distrib.   clusters (cl.)
                    2,0,2,2

(Cont'd.)

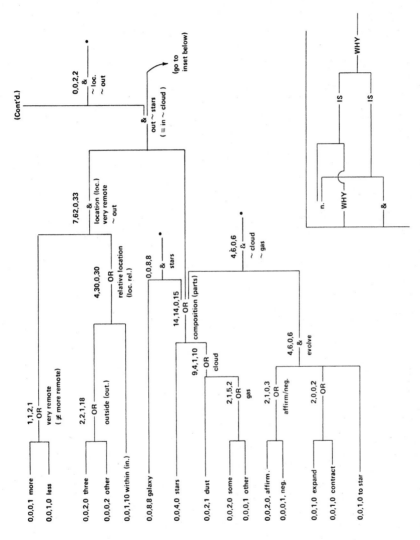

FIG. 1. Nebulae paragraph underlying structure. Abbreviations in parenthesis. Symbol "∉" denotes lines which cross without joining.

is translated *A nebula* (n.) *is (+) or is not (−) seen.* The symbol "~" is used to enumerate mappings between hierarchies and appears at the junction of the hierarchies. For example, consider the & node in the following graph:

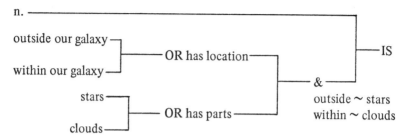

(The node is correctly labelled & rather than OR since a nebula jointly has location and composition.) The expressions *outside ~ stars, inside ~ clouds* specify the mapping between the *location* and *composition* hierarchies. The notation is readily extended to various special cases; in particular, (i) when no mapping is stated or implied within the text or (ii) when one entire tree maps to a subtree of a second tree, leaving nothing to be mapped to the remainder of the second tree.

The figure suggests a simple way of scanning the overall nature of the passage—in other words, of constructing an abstract or summary of the passage. (In fact, it suggests various alternative ways of generating abstracts, but only one will be mentioned here.) By pruning off all but the more superordinate nodes, we are left with:

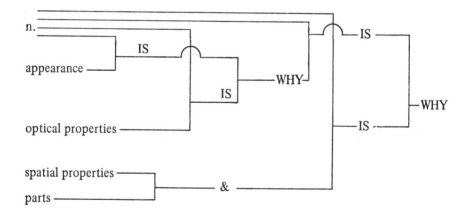

Translating, the embedded (leftmost) WHY attributes the appearance to the optical properties. In turn, the superordinate WHY attributes the optical properties to the conjoined spatial properties and parts. Later we shall discuss the implications of abstracts for theories of memory and linguistic structures. For the present, the one type of abstract is presented merely to help the reader understand the structure of the passage.

In some details, Figure 1 is a revision of the analysis given in the previously cited report (Crothers, 1970, pp. 40–41). (The modifications are discussed in footnote

4). However, for psychological research it is hardly enough to have the underlying structure description given in Figure 1. Superficial structure must be examined also. Among the several such variables there were two—sentence order and frequency of occurrence— which seemed especially worthwhile to examine in view of their established importance in verbal learning. Subsequent analysis may disclose other critical variables, such as the "There are kinds of" sentences to be discussed later. The problem that immediately arises for each structure variable is how to conceptualize it. Any conclusions about how frequency and order affect recall can certainly be expected to depend on how these two factors are defined. Therefore, in the present initial stages of investigation, it seems desirable to propose several indices, at least for the frequency variable, in order to see which one best correlates with data.

Four frequency indices were computed for each node of the graph, and are most easily explained by an example:

$$2, 2, 1, 18 \quad \rule{} \qquad\qquad 4, 30, 0, 30$$
$$\text{relative location}$$
$$\text{out} \qquad\qquad\qquad\qquad (\text{rel. loc.})$$

$$0, 0, 1, 10$$

$$\text{in}$$

The third and four indices count the number of explicit and implicit occurrences, respectively, of the node. Explicit occurrences are determined directly from the text. "Implicit occurrences" appear in the text as pronominalizations, etc., or may even be completely missing from the surface structure. (A grammar is required to mark implicit occurrences, as will be discussed later.) The first and second indices cumulate explicit and implicit occurrences, respectively, of subordinates of the node. For example, the cumulative total for *relative location* above is found thus:

$$2, \quad 2, \quad 1, \quad 18$$
$$0, \quad 0, \quad 1, \quad 10$$
$$\overline{2, \quad 2, \quad 2, \quad 28}$$

explicit   implicit $\quad\quad$ ∴ rel. loc. = (4, 30, ,)

2 + 2 = 4 $\quad$ 2 + 28 = 30

Next, the third index is 0, because *rel. loc.* or synonyms thereof never appear explicitly. According to the grammar being proposed the fourth index—the implicit frequency of *rel. loc.* in this example—is computed as follows. First the *total* occurrences of *rel. loc.*, i.e., the sum of the third and fourth indices, must be at least as great as the sum of all occurrences of immediate subordinates, under the assumption that any occurrence of a subordinate implies the superordinate. Hence the total of the third and fourth indices must equal at least 1 + 18 + 1 + 10 = 30.

But the third index was already found to equal 0, so the fourth index is $\geqq 30 - 0 =$ 30. What remains is to count any excess over the 30. These would be occurrences of the superordinate *rel. loc.* without any subordinate being implied (e.g., if a sentence of the text implied *n. have rel. loc.* with no specification of *out* or *in*). Since this does not occur in the case of *rel loc.*, the total implicit occurrences (fourth index) equals 30 + 0 = 30. Finally, the frequency cumulation has not been extended to the most superordinate nodes because these have minimal semantic content.

Some secondary details of the frequency counting are as follows. First note from Figure 1 that the passage contains five separate trees which can be identified by their dominant node as DEF (*definition*), WHY, & (*clusters*), & (*galaxy*), and & (*evolve*). As discussed in the previous paper, the failure to keep these separate would yield an incorrect description; e.g., neither & (*clusters*) nor & (*galaxy*) is semantically within the scope of WHY. That is, neither is a premise for a conclusion. Tokens of some predicates (e.g., *glow*) appear in more than one tree, raising the question of where their frequencies should be entered. For example:

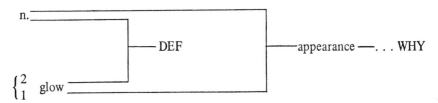

The possible solutions for assigning frequency values of *glow* to DEF and *appearance* are: (i) assign DEF = 2 and *appearance* = 1, to reflect the text predicates; (ii) assign *appearance* = 3 and DEF = 0. (iii) Count *glow* in both trees, so that DEF = 2 and *appearance* = 3. Proposal (i) can be rejected at once since it violates the general principle that all recurrences be counted. Perhaps (ii) could be defended in either of two ways: formally, *appearance* is the node in the main tree of the text; semantically, any lexical representation of glow would specify *appearance*. For the present, proposal (ii) has been adopted, although further examination of texts and of recall data may well suggest that proposal (iii) is preferable. The issue arises only when intersecting trees are involved, since in structures such as

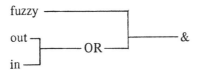

there is clearly no need to separate the *fuzzy* (*out*) frequency from the *fuzzy* (*in*) frequency. The required information is automatically registered in the separate totals for *out* and *in*.

Details of cumulation aside, there are several reasons why even the noncumulative frequency counts suggested here are highly tentative. Perhaps most obvious is the fact that the classification of recurrences into explicit vs. implicit, and especially the counting of implicit frequencies, requires a grammar or at least a parsing algorithm. (The tentative treatment of this question will be discussed below). Less obviously, the frequency counting does not appear to convey enough information about the structure. Unfortunately, attempts to enrich the description tend to render it cumbersome. This remark applies to ideas such as counting pro-forms (pronouns, pro-uses of definite articles, etc.) separately from explicit and implicit recurrences. The present solution was to subsume them under the implicit frequency. Another troublesome aspect of the structure is sentences such as *There are two kinds of nebulae, the ones outside our galaxy and the ones within.* Subjectively, this seems to be establishing *out–in* as a "focus" or "topic" and therefore may well enhance recall (see data analysis on pp. 260 *ff*). Hence such a "disjunction declaration" should evidently be represented somewhere in the description. As argued in my previous paper, the declaration is a superficial property rather than an underlying one because the same semantic content could have been conveyed by a different disjunction declaration of the form *kinds = composed of stars or composed of clouds*, followed by *clouds = loc. (in), stars = loc. (out)*. But where in the superficial description should a declaration be represented? Perhaps this question is resolved in the analysis below of Version A, sentences 3, 5, and 6.

Also, lexical measures familiar from verbal memory studies such as imagery, Thorndike-Lorge count, concreteness, and the like, need to be incorporated in the representation somehow in order to compare memory for different nodes within the paragraph. The present tactic of avoiding the problem by seeking to equate the values across nodes succeeds only in eliminating the most extreme values.

Details Involving Grammar. As mentioned above, a grammar, or at least a rule for determining the explicit and implicit frequencies of each node, is required. The way to approach the question is to formulate a general principle about what constitutes an implicit occurrence. Then if existing grammars satisfy this principle, they can be used to generate "deep" structures which in turn explicate the implicit elements. However, it will be contended that no extant sentence grammar fulfills the appropriate condition, so the operational rule for determining recurrences will be devised on the basis of the underlying structure. Again, the matter is best examined by illustration using excerpts from the passage. Consider this subgraph:

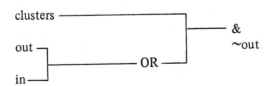

Now suppose that the sentence *The nebulae which are outside our galaxy are spiral-shaped* were to occur. The referent is equivalent to that denoted by *The nebulae which occur in clusters.* But *ipso facto*, the place to represent the equivalence is in the underlying structure, not in the superficial frequency count. Thus *out* but not *clusters* receives a frequency tally (an overt explicit one in this case).

A more problematical situation is as follows. Suppose that sentences 1–5 of Version A have already occurred and the aim is to determine the recurrences implied by sentence 6. (First observe that the mere posing of this question presumes that sentence order affects implicit frequencies; but this point is hardly surprising and simply means that one part of the superficial structure influences another.) Only sentences 3, 5, and 6 are relevant to the issue, and after sentence 5 the structure in question is

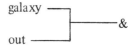

Next occurs sentence 6 = *Galaxy nebulae appear in clusters.* Superficially, this is no different from the preceding example. So apparently *galaxy*, but not *out*, should be assigned an occurrence. Further analysis, however, casts doubt on this interpretation: *out* is syntactically different from the *clusters* in the first example because *out* → *The nebulae outside* + VP in sentences 4 and 5, but *clusters* ↛ *The nebulae in clusters* + VP (where → is an abbreviation for "occurs in the text"). Tentatively, then, the principle might be stated as follows: predicates which undergo transformation into NPs (which in turn need not function as subjects) become thereby included in the deeper structures of other coreferential sentences. If this assumption proves too strong, perhaps one could substitute "disjunction declaration" in place of "transformation into NPs." In any event, the distinction between *galaxy* and *out* is not lost in the frequency tally because explicit and implicit occurrences are recorded separately. Another criterion for assigning implicit frequencies upon encountering a pro-form would be to say that the only antecedent is the most recently stated coreferential node. But the notion of recency seems defensible only as a hypothesis about memory performance, not as a rule of competence.

Another issue in assigning implicit frequencies concerns existential quantifiers. If *some* NP + VP is stated, should the implied *other* NP + neg VP contribute to the tally? Tentatively, it was decided to count this type of implication, on the grounds that a typical reader would draw the intended inference. But such an argument is dubious if the purpose is to derive frequencies that might predict recall data. Merely inserting *some* before each NP can hardly be expected to improve recall of the NP.

Appendix I shows the computation of frequencies for some sentences of the passage. The occurrence frequencies for each node, namely, the third and fourth indices in Figure 1 are then derived as the sums over all sentences in the passage.

Sentence Order. Essentially, the difference between Versions A and B is in the order of occurrence of sentences. Both versions involve identical underlying structures, frequencies of occurrence, and virtually the same syntax. The difference in sentence sequence reflects a different linear organization of the graph. In Version A, the two kinds of nebulae, the ones outside our galaxy and those within, are the foci of organization. That is, first one kind is introduced and then its properties are specified; next, the second kind is treated likewise. Conversely, in Version B one property is first named and then it is elaborated on for each kind of nebulae. Next, another property is treated likewise (of course, not every property is specified for both kinds). This informal characterization can be made into a more precise comparison of the two sequences, as follows. First, a propositional format is more convenient for this purpose than is a graph. A rough translation of the passage into propositions, ignoring some details and adopting abbreviations noted below, is:

DEF. Definition

        Glow
        Appearance: fuzzy
        Location in space: fixed

        Loc. Kinds: Two
           Loc(o) Kind (one):   location (out)
           Loc(i) Kind ((other): location (in)

        Comp. Composition
           Comp(o) Location (out): stars
                          Name: galaxy n.

           Comp(i) Location (in):   clouds
                  Composition: gas or dust
                        Name: gas n. or dust n.

        Dist. Distribution in space
           Dist(o.) Galaxy: in clusters
                     Clusters: from two to thirty
                     Clusters: spread evenly

        Evol. Evolution
           Evol(i) Gas (some):   to stars
                 Gas (some):   by expanding and contracting

        App. Appearance – WHY
           App.(o.) Galaxy: fuzzy
        because   Galaxy: seen, but
                     Galaxy (composition): not seen.
        because   Galaxy: distant.
        And (in fact) Galaxy (three): seen (with naked eye) but
                          galaxy (other): seen (not with naked eye)
        because   galaxy (three):   distant (less)
                     galaxy (other):   distant (more).

         App.(i) Cloud: glow
        because   cloud (gas): glow and
                     cloud (dust): glow
        because   cloud (gas(gas of)): glow   and
                     cloud (dust(dust of)): not glow   but
                     cloud (dust): seem to glow   because
                     cloud (dust): reflect from star which
                                star: glow

TABLE 1

Sequence of Subtopics*

Subtopic	Sentence No.
Version A	
DEF.	1
Loc.(o)	3(&2)
Comp.(o), Dist.(o.), Evol.(o.) = ϕ,	4 & 5, 6 & 7, −,
App. (o).	8 & 9
Loc.(i.).	10(&2)
Comp(i), Dist (i.) = ϕ, Evol.(i).	11, −, 12,
App (i.)	13
Version B	
DEF.	1
Loc.(o), Loc(i)	3(&2)
Comp.(o.), Comp(i.)	4 & 5, 6
Dist(o.), Dist.(i) = ϕ	7 & 8, −
Evol. (o.) = ϕ, Evol. (i)	−, 9
App. (o.), App(i.)	10 & 11, 12.

*Symbol "ϕ" here denotes that the subtopic was not predicated of a particular kind of nebulae.

In terms of this format, the sequences of subtopics in Versions A and B are compared in Table 1. For clarity, only the main headings are listed. This outline is a crude approximation, because it fails to indicate the mappings—the sentence numbers indicate only the new topic introduced.

RESULTS AND DISCUSSION

Mainly, the remarks here center on how a subject's recall protocol is analyzed and on the outcome of the analysis expressed as a total over all experimental subjects. So far, only fragmentary results have been tabulated as to the correlation between structure and recall and between different aspects of recall itself. The effect of the experimental treatments (namely, testing condition and version) will also be mentioned briefly.

Analysis of Recall Protocols. Appendix II gives some sample protocols and their graphic analysis. The data were scored for underlying structure but not superficial structure, since verbatim memory was not of interest.

The first issue is to identify what propositions are assumed to be known at the time of recall although they might not appear (even implicitly) in the data despite instructions to "be explicit." Having read the passage, even the lowest-scoring subjects indicated that nebulae are *in the sky*. Thus, presumably they knew certain other predicates: *glow, + seen, seen-whole, seen-with telescope* OR *telescope & eye, has source of light, has spatial properties,* and *has composition.* For example, a subject would not bother to indicate he knew that nebulae have spatial properties unless he knew some specific such properties (likewise with *source of light,* etc.).

The next problem is how to treat inherent ambiguity in the data. Fortunately, such occurrences were relatively infrequent. (This is probably due to the fact that the stimulus paragraph had been edited to remove both syntactic and semantic ambiguity. A pilot study which used unedited prose revealed a higher incidence of ambiguous data.) The cases that did arise involved ambiguous pronominal reference, elliptic expressions, and uncertainty as to what connective was intended. In scoring the data, the interpretation adopted was the one judged most compatible with the rest of the protocol.

The next question is exactly what to count in scoring the data. The analysis will be clarified with reference to Figure 2 which summarizes some of the main properties of the data. First, the items assumed to be known beforehand (terminals symbolized by "a," others unmarked in the figure) were excluded from the count. Each node's score is a relative frequency, cumulated over all subordinates, plus the node's own contribution, if any, to the total. At any node, the number of observations per subject is found by dividing the denominator by 18. To summarize the outcome of such a calculation, the number of observations per subject is (letting i,j denote nodes and correspondences, respectively.)

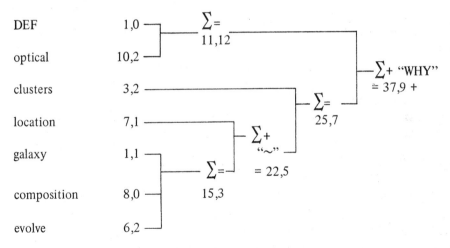

(The "+" in the last term denotes that correspondences at the superordinate WHY have not yet been counted; in this respect the data analysis is incomplete.) Multiplying the 37,9 by N = 18 subjects, there are 666 observations for nodes and 162 for correspondences, or 828 in all.[5] The main rule is that superordinates do not contribute to that count unless either (i) the superordinate is a connective which is not logically obvious from the subordinates, or (ii) the superordinate has its own name. The possible combinations are: (i) present or absent in conjunction with (ii)

[5] The observed frequencies in the format agree with the frequencies per subject. For example, the node total (i.e., excluding correspondences) is 18 (DEF.) + 18 (*galaxy*) + 54 (*clusters*) + 108 (*evolve*) + 468 (WHY) = 666 = 18 x 37.

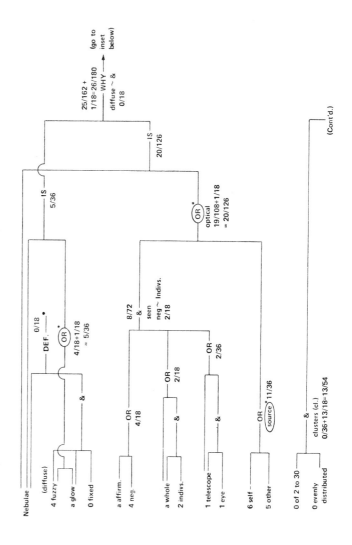

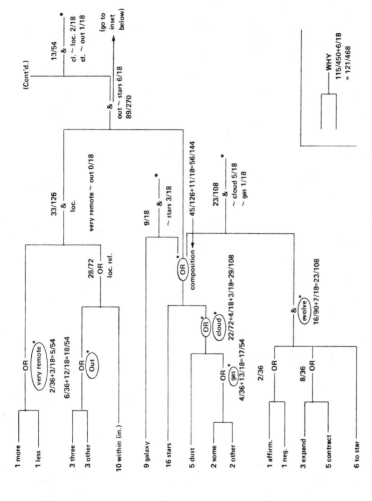

FIG. 2. Nebulae paragraph. Relative frequencies of correct responses. Denominator = 18 unless otherwise indicated. Cumulated over subordinates in the form

a ⌐ c = a + b, d + e
b ⌐

where c = a + b, d = 0 unless superordinate name is starred (*) and e = 0 unless connective is starred.

present or absent, yielding four subtypes illustrated below. For clarity, cases of (i) and (ii) are starred (*).

a affirm.┐
         ├ OR
4/18 neg.┘ 4/18
neither (i) nor (ii)

0/18 2 to 30 ┐
             ├ & (clusters) *
0/18 even────┘ 0/36 + 0 + 13/18 = 13/54
(ii) but not (i)

8/72 & ──────────┐
                 ├ (OR) *
11/36 OR source──┘ 19/108 + 1/18
                 + 0
                 = 20/126
(i) but not (ii)

5/18 dust ┐
          ├ (OR) * (cloud) *
17/54 gas ┘ 22/72 + 4/18 + 3/18
          = 29/108
both (i) and (ii)

Incidentally, it is of interest to note that nearly all of the correspondence errors were reductions of OR to & or else WHY to &, the latter signifying a replacement of causality by correlation.

A couple of other features of the scoring arise from the fact that there were several subtrees. As in the computation of the stimulus frequencies in Figure 1, data from nodes joining two subtrees were cumulated with the main one, i.e., the one dominated by the rightmost WHY. Also, the scoring of correspondence errors had to be examined. Such an error is logically impossible unless the subject stated (or implied) at least two terms of both disjunctions; otherwise the error is regarded as one or more omissions. For example, suppose that the stimulus is as in (i) below.

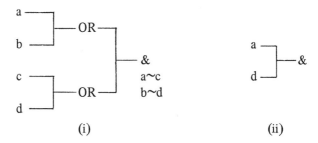

(i)   (ii)

Then if the response replaces "a ~ c, b ~ d" by anything (e.g. a ~ d, b ~ c) but is otherwise correct, a correspondence error is scored. A response of the form (ii) is counted as an omission at b, and likewise at c. Finally, for the sake of consistency, each separate type of correspondence error was tabulated on the basis of N = 18 subjects, even though the N conditional on being correct up to the correspondence would have been much smaller due to omissions and errors on connectives.

An interesting outcome of the present taxonomy of responses was that there remained relatively few errors excluded from the count. That is, what might be called "intrusion errors" whereby a word alien to the passage is substituted in a proposition were quite rare. It might also be noted that "spontaneous comments" which neither contradicted the text nor reproduced it were likewise infrequent. One can sum over entries in Figure 2 so as to obtain, for example, a grand total for

TABLE 2
Sums of Frequencies Cumulated from Figure 2

correspondences 20/162

nodes					nodes	correspondences
nodes		1	{	definition	0/18	--	0/18
definition	0/18			optical	26/180	2/36	28/216
galaxy	9/18		Σ1		26/198	2/36	28/234
clusters	13/54	2	location		33/126	0/18	33/144
evolution	23/108		Σ2		33/126	0/18	33/144
WHY	121/468	3	{	galaxy	9/18	3/18	12/36
Σ	166/666		{	composition	56/144	--	56/144
ΣΣ	186/828			evolve	23/108	6/36	29/144
			Σ3		88/270	9/54	97/324
			Σ2+Σ3		121/396	9/72	130/468
			Σ4 = Σ2+Σ3+Σ2 ~Σ3		121/396	15/90	136/486
			Σ5 = Σ4 + clusters		134/450	18/126	152/576
			Σ6 = Σ5 + Σ1		160/648	20/162	180/810
			Σ7 = Σ6 + superord. WHY		166/666	20/162	186/828

nodes and one for correspondences. Alternatively, the *cluster* data can be added to the *location* data, etc. The outcomes of such computations are summarized in Table 2.

Response Conjunctions and Disjunctions. Other analyses bring out additional properties of the data. One such analysis involves scoring a node as "correct" if at least one node in the subtree dominated by the first node is correct. The correct element in the subtree might or might not be the superordinate itself. Intersecting subtrees are treated as before. Also, a node is scored as "a" if it, or at least one subordinate of it, is regarded as known beforehand. Figure 3 depicts the outcome of this analysis.

As an example of how to read the figure, take this subtree:

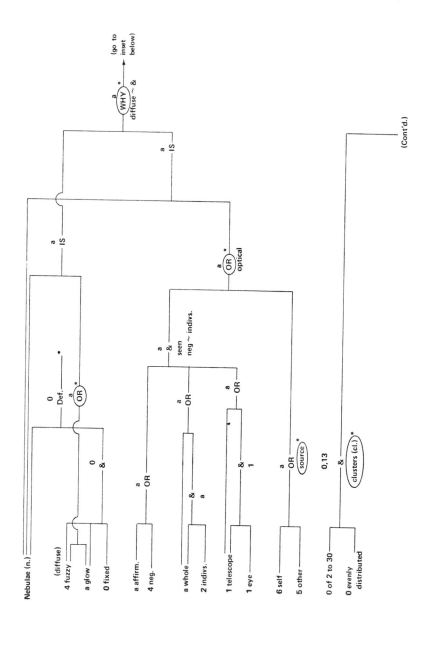

266

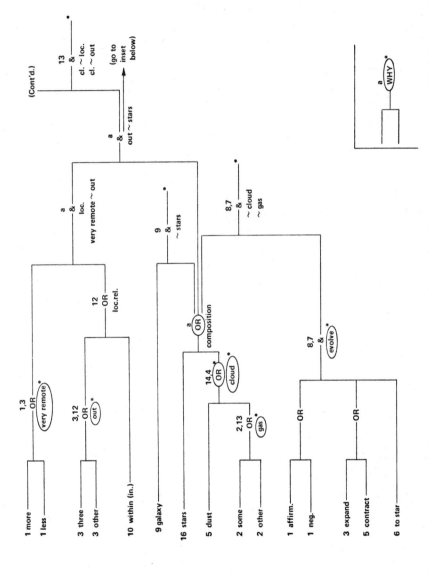

FIG. 3. Nebulae paragraph. Number of subjects, out of 18, who were correct at each node, scoring "correct" if it or at least one subordinate was correct.

Since *composition* is marked "a," all N = 18 subjects are scored as knowing that *nebulae have composition*. Of the 18, there were 16 who gave *composed of stars* and 14 who gave at least one member of the subtree = {*cloud, dust, gas, some gas, other gas*}. In the case of named superordinates, the response frequency of the correct name (e.g., the "3" for *cloud*) is also repeated from Figure 2. Obviously the former frequencies are monotonically decreasing within a path in the direction from superordinate to subordinate.

By contrast with the preceding essentially disjunctive recursion, a conjunctive recursion may be tabulated. The basic idea is simple, although a complication arises in the cases where the superordinate is assigned its own score as a connective or a name. In subtrees lacking this complication, the computation proceeds in the opposite direction to the disjunctive analysis: A superordinate gets a scored "correct" if and only if both subordinates are correct:

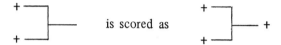

This method seems impractical for the present data simply because when there are so many errors, the analysis degenerates into an "absorbing state" wherein all superordinates above a certain level are marked 0(= omission); e.g.,

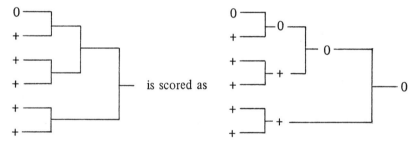

Hence for data containing many errors, a more useful computation involves preserving the conjunction-counting but now proceeding in the reverse direction (top-down). That is, a superordinate is marked "+" if and only if subject has at least one correct response jointly in each path dominated by the node. Thus, instead of the right-hand analysis of the left-hand diagram above, we have all + signs. A more typical example would be:

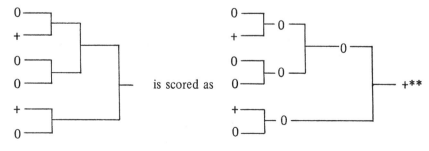

The node marked by the double asterisk (**) is the only superordinate having a +
somewhere in its left branch *and* right branch; thus it is marked "+". What remains
is to include the connective errors and superordinate errors. This will be done by
the following notation; e.g.,

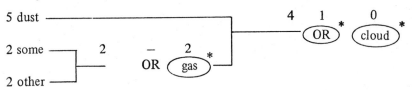

At the rightmost OR node, the frequencies 4,1,0 arise from successively stronger
criteria:

4 = four subjects included *dust* and at least one member of *gas* subtree.
1 = one subject met the above condition and in addition used the correct connective OR at the node.
0 = no subject met the above criteria and in addition gave the superordinate
clouds.
− = assumed known from subordinates (in second position if connective not
circled, third position if superordinate not circled). The converse case, i.e., data
where the superordinate but not subordinates was present, would be scored as
000 (or 0−0), since the superordinate itself is counted at the next higher node in
its path.

For example, the 10 in the 10,9,− entry at *composition* denotes that 10 subjects' protocols included $\{star, X\}$ where $X = \{cloud, dust, gas, some\ gas, other\ gas\}$.
The 9 in this entry denotes that for 9 of these 10 subjects the additional condition
$\{star, X\} \rightarrow \{star\ \mathrm{OR}\ X\}$ was met. The "−" indicates that the superordinate term
composition was not scored. Note that in general the frequencies need not be
monotonic within a path, for example:

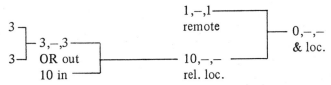

Read σ from left to right in this graph, the numbers of subjects for the left one of
the three indices are (α, β introduced for brevity):

3 = $\{out \cap some\}$ = α 10 = $\{\alpha \cup \beta \cup out\} \cap \{in\}$

3 = $\{out \cap other\}$ = β 1 = $\{remote\}$

3 = $\{2 \cap \beta\}$ 0 = $\{remote\} \cap \{\alpha \psi \beta \cup out \cup in\}$

The outcome of this analysis is shown in Figure 4. Note that if the superordinate
has an "a" somewhere in every one of its paths (excluding the superordinate itself),
it is automatically marked "a" for the first of the three indices.

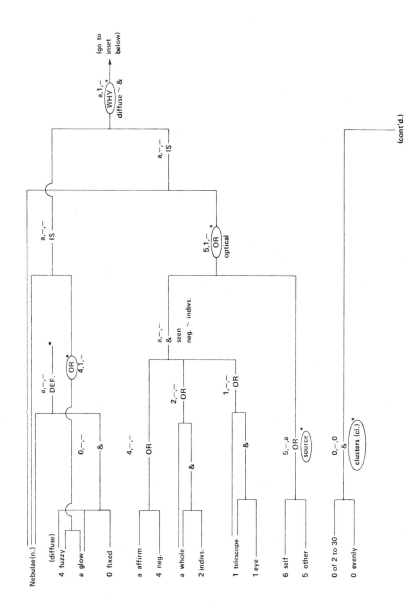

270

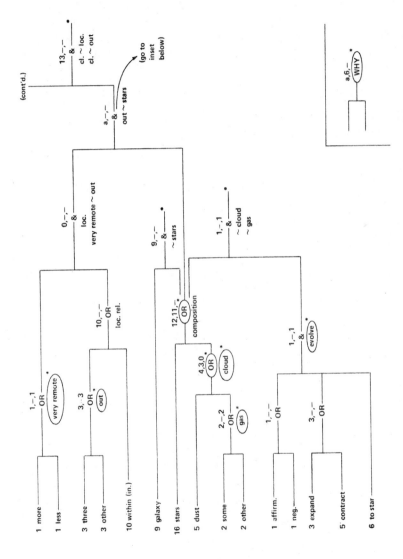

FIG. 4. Nebulae paragraph. Tuples x, y, z, where z = number of subjects jointly correct in at least one node of each path, y = number of these x subjects who also got the connective correct, and z = number of these y subjects who also got the superordinate name correct. Symbol "—" denotes that an error is regarded as impossible.

A limitation of the foregoing analysis is that the order of computing dependencies is given by scanning successive paths of the graph. Many interesting pairs of subtopics fail to be analyzed for dependency by this method; e.g., the various separate trees *DEF*, *galaxy*, *cluster*, etc. Of course, one can compute multiple response correlations among any selected set of subtopics. However, for purposes of model construction independence tests seem more appropriate. Perhaps surprisingly, the conclusion was that the major subtopics are recalled independently of one another. The computation was performed by defining three major subtopics: (i) *definition* (DEF) plus *appearance* plus *optical properties*, (ii) *spatial properties* plus *clusters*, and (iii) *galaxies* plus *composition* plus *evolution*.

In the figures, subtopic (i) consists of the subtrees dominates by the WHY node on the top page of each figure, subtopic (ii) is the subtree dominated by the node *location*, plus *clusters*, and (iii) is everything else in the bottom page of each figure, excluding the two rightmost & nodes joining (ii) and (iii) as well as the dominant WHY node that joins the union of (ii) and (iii) to (i). One reason for performing independence tests on these particular subtopics was that they are the major subtopics in the passage; another reason was that the pooling of all nodes within a subtopic produced sufficient correct responses to allow a meaningful analysis. Each subject's total correct per subtopic was computed, including correspondences which fell within the subtopic (e.g., *evolution* ~ *gas*) but excluding ones which joined subtopics (e.g., *out* ~ *stars*) and excluding the superordinate WHY for the same reason. Then three 2 x 2 tables were constructed, one for each pair of these three subtopics. The tables appear in Table 3. The two rows and columns of each table

TABLE 3

Contingency Tables for Fisher's Tests of Independence among Three Major
Subtopics* (N = 18)

		{location, distribution}	
		< median	≥ median
{DEF,	< median	6	2
optical, appearance}	≥ median	3	7

		{galaxy, composition, evolution}	
{DEF,		< median	≥ median
optical, appearance}	< median	3	5
	≥ median	3	7

		{galaxy, composition, evolution}	
		< median	≥ median
{location, distribution}	< median	4	5
	≥ median	2	7

A subtopic is identified as a set of its constituent subtrees shown in braces.

represent median splits of the 18 subjects. Then Fisher's Exact Test was computed for each table. No table showed a statistically significant departure from independence, although in the top one in Table 3 a shift of 1 in the cell frequencies would have yielded significance at the .05 level. However, the observed independence of subtopics does not necessarily imply that components *within* the same subtopic (e.g., *evolution* and *composition*) are recalled independently. By the nature of the graph, repeated subcategorization inevitably produces progressively more similar subtopics. Thus it might be conjectured that independence would no longer be found at the finer levels of categorization. Unfortunately, here there are inevitably fewer responses per subject. As suggestive but inconclusive evidence, it might be reported that 4 out of 5 subjects who recalled *dust* also recalled *gas*, and every one of the 10 subjects who recalled *nebulae within our galaxy* did recall that there were also *nebulae outside our galaxy*.

STRUCTURE AND RECALL:
EMPIRICAL CORRELATION

Examination of this central issue has barely begun so the conclusions are highly tentative and probably incorrect in many instances. Data from additional passages must be included and subjected to rigorous statistical analysis, especially correlational analysis, before the present suggestions can be evaluated critically. Also, criteria are needed for deciding when to include minor nodes, correspondences, etc., in the analysis, since any decision may well affect the conclusion regarding structural effects. Perhaps the easiest way to undertake a preliminary analysis is to advance hypotheses about the simple effects of single structural variables, with the understanding that such hypotheses are subject to qualification after systematic analyses of interactions have been performed.

Data will be reported here only for the nebulae paragraph. These results were generally corroborated by the data on the oceanography paragraph (Crothers, 1971).

Superficial Structure   This can be disposed of fairly readily, at least for the one variable examined; namely, sentence sequence. It does not appear that sentence order matters—with the important qualification that only the more acceptable orders are being compared. Certainly, a random order would be largely nonsensical. The comparison is between Versions A and B of the passage. The means and N's for the analysis of variance are shown in Table 4. (Recall that the variable of immediate test vs. no immediate test was included orthogonally to the superficial structure variable, creating a 2 x 2 design.)

The difference between means of Versions A and B was not significant ($F(1, 14)$ = 2.4). However, the interaction was significant ($F(1, 14) = 10.2, p < .01$). The explanation of why Version B was better than Version A for subjects also tested on the first day remains uncertain. Statistical tests for possible interactions between the two versions and particular subtopics were not performed because casual inspection of the data indicated that any such effects would be small. Although not of major immediate concern, it might be noted that subjects given the test at the end of the acquisition session were not significantly better on the test after 7 days compared to subjects not given an immediate test ($F(1, 14) = 1.3$), which is a rather

TABLE 4

Frequencies Correct on Test after One Week

		Immediate test		$\bar{X}$	N
		no	yes		
Version	A	$\bar{X} = 8.8$ N = 6	$\bar{X} = 9.0$ N = 3	8.9	9
	B	$\bar{X} = 10.2$ N = 6	$\bar{X} = 15.0$ N = 3	11.8	9
	$\bar{X}$	9.5	12.0		10.3
	N	12	6		18

puzzling result. By the way, from the mean recall of 10.3 out of 46 possible (or 22%) one should not necessarily conclude that acquisition and/or recall of the passage were relatively inefficient. Many of the errors occurred on what could subjectively be judged as secondary information, e.g., quantifiers. Also, the manner of counting denominators in the correspondence data, while it equates the number of observations for all subjects, does inflate the error totals. At any rate, the fact that the data are reported as frequencies rather than proportions in the figures permits various recomputations on any interesting subset of the data.

Psychological Hypotheses about Recall. Two hypotheses about how recall might depend on the underlying semantic structure, as opposed to either the syntax or the idiosyncratic lexical properties of the passage, were proposed earlier (Crothers, 1970). The first says essentially that an overall theme will be recalled better than its details, and the second says that a major theme will be recalled better than a minor theme. Again the graph structure is employed in order to define "theme," "major theme," etc.

Hypothesis 1. Superordinates will be recalled more often than subordinates. This hypothesis originated with the conjecture that people tend to remember only the gist of meaningful material. It is important to realize, however, that a very strong assumption is being made here in order to render the hypothesis testable. This assumption is that the gist is defined graphically as the more superordinate nodes. Surely this assumption need not be correct, ignoring as it does certain customarily important variables, such as frequency of occurrence in the superficial structure. In the nebulae paragraph, the most suitable nodes for testing this hypothesis are ones such that the subordinates are syntactically "independent" of the superordinate (e.g., *dust, cloud* but not *less remote, remote*). In fact, the hypothesis failed to be supported by the data, as a simple comparison of frequencies reveals. In particular, the superordinate *cloud* was given explicitly by only 4 subjects, fewer than the number who gave its subordinates *gas* or *dust* (13 and 5 subjects, respectively).

Hypothesis 2. Secondary subtrees will be recalled less often than the primary subtree. In the graphs, the secondary subtrees are the ones not dominated by the main WHY node. To denote this, they have been depicted as dominated by a node denoted ".". In the data, the secondary subtrees *galaxy* and *distribution* (*clusters*) yielded 9 and 13 correct recalls, respectively, which are at least as great as the corresponding frequencies for the primary subtree. This and similar findings suffice to reject this hypothesis also. Again, a statistical test would be superfluous.

What then might be suggested in lieu of these two disconfirmed hypotheses? At present, we surmise that the fault lies not in the original qualitative notion, but rather in the attendant assumption about how the theme is to be defined in terms of the graph. Apparently additional variables must be included in the definition. Here we shall confine our comments chiefly to one likely candidate, namely, the frequency of occurrence within the paragraph. On this view, one important role of such a superficial variable is to guide comprehension and recall by furnishing what is commonly referred to as "foregrounding" or "emphasis," without otherwise affecting the semantic content.

The analysis is summarized in Table 5. First, a word is needed about how the table was derived. It was tentatively decided to take the total frequency summed over explicit plus implicit occurrences, in order to minimize the effects of any uncertainty as to whether a particular occurrence was explicit or implicit. Also, to highlight the main features of the data, (i) the frequencies were pooled to yield the subtopics given in the table, and (ii) no data on correspondences, connectives, implied quantifiers, or implied negations were included. With the exception of the *optical* subtopic, the rank order of subtopics according to recall frequency agrees well with the ranking on the basis of text frequency. (Perhaps this one discrepancy suggests an error in the semantic analysis.) Altogether, the pattern in Table 5 is rather striking, considering that neither graph structure nor syntax is controlled in the tabulation and, in general, these latter do not always covary with stimulus frequency.

TABLE 5

Frequencies Cumulated by Subtopics*

Subtopic	Data			Paragraph	
	Freq.	Prop.	Rank	Freq.	Rank
DEF., optical, appearance	23/126	.18	6	18	2
distribution (clusters)	13/54	.24	5	4	6
distance (great)	3/18	.17	7	2	7
location (out, in)	22/36	.61	1	30	1
galaxy	9/18	.50	3	16	3
composition (stars, cloud, gas, dust)	38/72	.52	2	15	4
evolution	21/72	.29	4	5	5

*Excludes connectives, correspondence, implied quantifiers and implied negations.

However, it would be premature to conclude on the basis of the fragmentary evidence so far adduced that stimulus frequency is necessarily the dominant determiner of recall. An alternative worth examining is that what becomes foregrounded in the present passage is a *classification* of nebulae; this proposal could be defended by citing the several text statements of the form "There are _____ kinds of _____". On this view, the best remembered predicates will be the ones that are transformed, *in the superficial structure*, into modifiers of nebulae; e.g.,

$$N. \ are \ galaxies \rightarrow galaxy \ .n. \ + \ VP$$

but not *N. appear in clusters → N. which appear in clusters + VP* since the latter NP, though referentially equivalent to the former, never actually appears in the text. The syntactic details of this argument require clarification. It is not claimed that all sentence subjects are well recalled, but only NP or VP constituents which become relative clauses modifying *nebulae*. Finally, the high recall of *out, in* is consistent with this hypothesis (because *The n. outside + VP* appears), though they uniquely allow an alternative explanation to the effect that anything introduced by a "disjunction declaration" (*There are two kinds of n.*) is well remembered. The passage could be modified to test these hypotheses. If a few of the references to *n. out.* or *galaxy n.* were replaced by the semantically equivalent *n. which appear in clusters*, the number of correctly predicated recalls of *clusters* should increase. (The total frequency of *clusters* in the deep structure could be held constant by deleting the *of 2 to 30* and *are evently distributed* constructions.) A more drastic change would be to replace the *kinds = out, in* statement by *kinds = in clusters, not in clusters* in order to decide whether the high frequency or the *kinds* statement is the reason for the high recall of *out, in.*

Also, the data are qualitatively inconsistent with the hypothesis that forgetting is mainly restricted to embedded clauses. For one thing, quantifiers were usually forgotten. More convincing, perhaps, is the low recall for *clusters* (as predicated of *nebulae* themselves) despite its occurrence as a main clause in *The clusters are spread evenly throughout the universe.*

A final phenomenon pervasive in these data was reduction of the semantic (not logical) implication connective WHY, and also the semantic disjunction (e.g., *gas* OR *dust*), to conjunctions. It seems unlikely that this effect is an artifact of the manner of interpreting ambiguous protocols. Whether it is a genuine memory error (perhaps occasioned by forgetting of the very content words that most clearly signal the choice of connective) or instead is a confusion as to the meaning of the connective remains to be determined.

IMPLICATIONS AND CONCLUSIONS

This paper extends the approach, begun in my previous paper, directed toward a formal representation of the structures of memory, prose, and memory for prose as reflected in recall protocols. So far, this work is primarily methodological, with the experiments serving mainly to perfect the methodology. One cannot discover empirical relations between stimuli and responses, much less develop process models, until methods for characterizing stimuli and scoring responses have been established. Moreover, simplicity in the structure is probably an important virtue, for otherwise it would be impossible to go beyond to the empirical and process stages. Conceptually, the present theory is simple despite the aggregation of details. All that is involved are hierarchies and mappings among them. The application to recall rests on the thesis that a protocol reflects a person's competence (not just performance as in language usage), jointly determined by pre-experimental competence and performance within the experiment.

How does this approach differ from others? Artificial intelligence programs contain more comprehensive data bases, but they say little about how a body of new organized information is assimilated and recalled, as a function of the information content itself. Descriptive linguistics and psycholinguistics have gone far toward answering this question, but only in the special case where information is a sequence of independent sentences. To be sure, the insights thus gained about sentence semantics and syntax will be vital to investigations of discourse. But organized discourse is more than a concatenation of sentences. Less obvious, perhaps, it is even more than a concatenation of their deeper structures, however they may be described (in a grammar or else a logical calculus, with or without the "cases" being rediscovered these days). The "even more" is the hierarchic structure. In the present theory, it is a set of trees with mappings between them. Hence the structure resembles an old-fashioned outline, with the notable difference that more than one tree or outline is involved. Thus the present view expressly denies that an outline is a rhetorical relic which is better left to an implicit embedding within some kind of memory network representation. Making the hierarchic structure explicit has several distinct advantages. Most obvious, it represents one's intuitive sense of gist vs. detail, and similarly one's ability to outline a passage more or less in accord with someone else's outline. Likewise, the hierarchic representation is a valuable computational device for analyzing protocols. Responses can be cumulated over any subtree to see how well a particular subtopic is recalled. Moreover, any finding that frequencies of occurrence is a dominant determiner of recall would not destroy the usefulness of the hierarchies, because they are claimed to be the basis for computing the frequencies. As for the details, many problems remain, for example how to treat quantifiers and unmarked verbs, and the role of the specific semantic relations (e.g., a taxonomy tree vs. an instrumentality tree). What has been accomplished to date is an overall framework within which the topic of discourse memory can be investigated with increased precision.

CONFERENCE DISCUSSION

Frederiksen inquired why Crothers maintained that sentence order does not affect meaning. For example if one asserted that "The dog was dead and then the dog barked" this is surely quite different from asserting that "The dog barked and then the dog was dead." The implication of these examples is that order can be of great importance in the analysis of discourse meaning. Coleman cited another example where order can imply causality. "His arm broke and he fell off the horse" versus "He fell off the horse and his arm broke." The first sentence carries with it the implication that he fell off the horse because his arm was broken, whereas the second sentence implies that his arm broke when he fell off the horse. Crothers responded that a semantic implication of order, like any other implied semantic concept, can be represented in the hierarchies regardless of whether or not it is cued by the surface structure ordering.

Scriven suggested that if Crothers was going to place such a load on intuition in arriving at semantic relationships, he should consider moving to a much less formally oriented semantic structure, such as would be found in a simple summary or precis of the discourse passage. A further advantage of this, he suggested, would be an increase in interjudge reliability about what the semantic structure of a passage is. Crothers indicated that while he agreed that this might increase reliability, it would at the same time avoid the difficult issues about what the deep structural relationships are in some passages—hence Crothers felt that the only way to get at these structural relations is to struggle directly with the problem of trying to formalize a system which is adequate to capture these relationships in as explicit a manner as possible.

Bever inquired whether it would be possible to use a more traditional syntactic approach to unraveling the semantic relationships of discourse. This approach would involve rewriting the several sentences of some passage into a single complex sentence; at this point one would draw a tree structure of the syntactic interrelationships of the several clauses and in this manner get at some of the issues that Crothers was concerned with. Crothers said it is well known that current syntactic theory obviously doesn't furnish a ready made semantic theory. To take only one very simple example, syntax fails to mark the fact that the sentences *Baseball + VP* and *Tennis + VP* both refer to sports. Since Crothers indicated that it is precisely such semantic relationships that he is interested in, in untangling discourse relationships, he did not think that current syntactic theory by itself would be of much value to him. Carroll raised a related point: In order to achieve the type of single-sentence interrelationships of what was previously a string of sentences (such as Bever had suggested), it would probably be necessary already to possess a sophisticated semantic theory which would indicate which of several sentences can be placed in subordinate roles.

Simmons questioned Crothers further about whether or not he thought syntactic theory had nothing to offer regarding a semantic analysis. Crothers averred that syntactic and semantic considerations may indeed be interdependent but as a research strategem he thought it justifiable first to examine just how far it is possible to go in accounting for recall data of discourse using only a between-sentence semantic analysis. If this simplification fails, only then would he consider the possibility of introducing additional structural information. Such additional information could include lexical as well as syntactic specifications. At present, the only words actually analyzed within the approach are ones explicitly defined within the passage being analyzed.

REFERENCES

Crothers, E. J. The psycholinguistic structure of knowledge. *In Studies in mathematical learning theory and psycholinguistics.* (Technical report). Boulder: Quantitative Psychology, University of Colorado, 1970. In K. Romney & K. Wexler (Eds.), *Cognitive Organization and psychological processes.* National Academy of Sciences (In press).

Crothers, E. J. Memory structure and the recall of discourse. In *Studies in mathematical learning theory and psycholinguistics.* (Technical report). Boulder: Computer Laboratory for Instruction in Psychological Research, University of Colorado, 1971.

Frase, L. T. Structural analysis of the knowledge that results from thinking about text. *Journal of Educational Psychology Monographs,* 1969, *60*(2), 1–16.

Harris, Z. S. Discourse analysis reprints. Papers on formal linguistics, 1963, *2.*

Rothkopf, E. Z. Concerning parallels between adaptive processes in thinking and self-instruction. In J. F. Voss (Ed.), *Approaches to thought.* Columbus, Ohio: Merrill, 1969.

Sanders, G. On the natural domain of grammar. Paper distributed by Indiana University Linguistics Circle, Bloomington, Indiana, 1969. (Mimeo)

APPENDIX I

Computing Stimulus Node Frequencies

Notation. Sentences are numbered as in Version A. ϕ denotes an implicit occurrence assigned by the analysis, n. = *nebulae*, g = *galaxy*, cl. = *cluster*, and DEF = *definition.*

1. 1 in sky ⌐

    1 glow ── n.   1 + 4 ϕ DEF

    1 fixed

    2 fuzzy ⌐

2.   ⌐ n.   There are two kinds of n.
          ⌐ 1

3. out ──── n.
                                                   The n. outside
    1   1

5. g. ── out ── n.
                                                   Galaxy n.
    1   ϕ 2

6a. =
                                                   galaxy n. appear in clusters.
     cl. ── g. ── out ── n

     1   1 ϕ 1

6b. =   of from 2 to 30 galaxies.

     2 to 30 ── cl. ── g. ── out ── n.

       1   ϕ 1 ϕ ϕ

9a. =   Three galaxy n. are seen
                                                   with the eye.

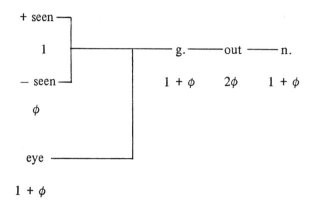

APPENDIX II

Scoring of Protocols

Ambiguity resolution. The most frequent cases are enumerated.

(n. = *nebulae*, cl. = *cluster*)

Response	Interpretation
1. N. are cl.	N. have composition, which is cl. (correspondence error)
2. N. are cl. of stars	(Like #1.)
3. N. are galaxies	N. are composed of stars
4. N. outside our galaxy	⇏ N. outside our galaxy are are galaxies
5. Gases combine	⇏ gases contract, expand
6. some	(*three* scored as correct)
7. groups	(synonym for *cl.*)

Sample protocols.

#2. There are two types of nebulae–galaxy nebulae and gas nebulae. Gas nebulae are luminous and also reflect light from other nebulae.

#8. Nebulae are clusters of stars. They can also be dust particles reflected by light. The Milky Way is a nebula. There are many more nebulae outside our galaxy.

#12. Nebulae are vague heavenly clusters, the elements of which are visible collectively but not separately. Two kinds are visible from earth. The first is composed of large numbers of stars, too far away to be seen individually. The second nebulae are closer, and are composed of dust or gaseous matter. The gaseous nebulae emit their own light, while the dust nebulae reflect light from other sources.

Figure 5 shows the analysis (for compactness, all three subjects' data in same figure). Details of the distinction in Figure 4 between disjunction and name of superordinates are here omitted.

Remarks. For S#2, *glow ∼ source* is not scored as correct because *diffuse* in the *glow* OR *diffuse* disjunction is absent. However, at the inset WHY the *source (other) ∼ closed* is correct because both *other OR self* and *cloud OR star* appear. The further correspondence *other source ∼ dust* cannot be scored because *dust* is absent from the protocol. At the node labelled OR , the OR is scored as correct because the data contain *two types*.

For S#8, *N. are clusters of stars* implies that the correspondence *cl. ∼ loc.* was erroneously rendered *cl. ∼ comp.* Also, *N. is galaxy* is inferred from the last two sentences of the data. And *out ∼ stars* is not scored as correct because no correspondence between *location* and *composition* is implied by the data.

For #12, the *N. are clusters* is treated as in #8. Also, *vague ⟹ diffuse.* The superordinate WHY is scored as correct (see inset) because of the phrase *too far away to be seen individually* in the third sentence. In sentence 4, the clause *The second n. are closer* is not scored. The reason is that, for simplicity, this node was omitted from the graph of the underlying structure. If not omitted, it would have appeared as the doubly starred (**) node below. The *too far away* in the data

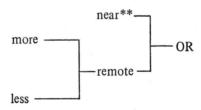

implies that the node *remote* is correct. Also, *other ∼ dust (=self ∼ gas)* is scored as correct because (i) all of the terms *self, other, dust,* and *gas* appear in the data, and (ii) the last sentence in the data states the correspondence correctly. Finally, nothing in the data implies the nodes *outside (within) our galaxy*.

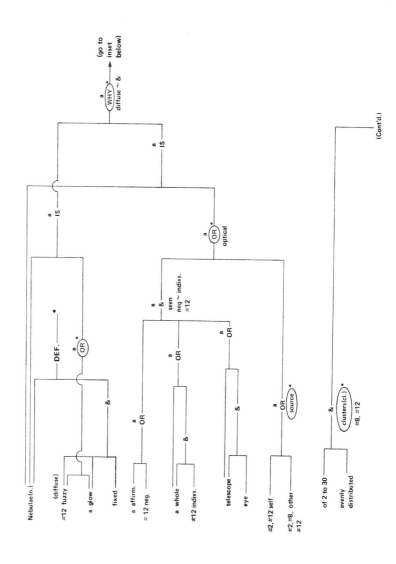

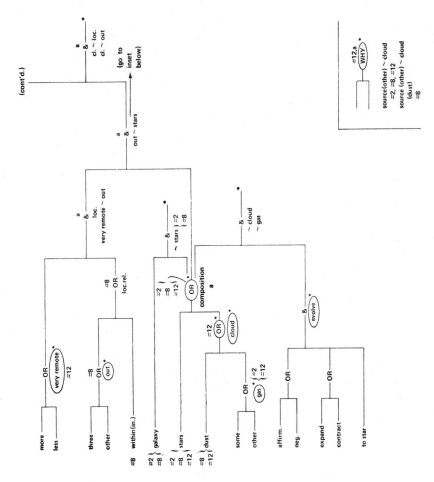

FIG. 5. Nebulae paragraph. Transcription of protocols #2, #8, #12. Only correct responses are shown.

11
LEARNING BY LISTENING[1,2]

Thomas G. Sticht
*Human Resources
Research Organization*

INTRODUCTION

Listening, as the process of comprehending spoken language, is discussed in this paper in relation to a research project concerned with adult literacy. This project, called REALISTIC, had two primary objectives. One objective was to identify functional literacy skill levels for selected Army jobs to which men receiving literacy training within the Army were likely to be assigned. A second objective was to explore methods by which the demands for reading in training schools or on-the-job might be reduced, so as to more effectively train and utilize the less literate personnel.

In attempting to satisfy the first of these objectives, we considered that, although most jobs have certain formally prescribed reading materials, and hence a denotable need for reading skill, many men might learn many job tasks by listening or "show and tell." Hence, whereas reading, as decoding of written symbols into the language sub-system, might be found to be relatively unimportant for learning or performing certain job tasks, it seemed less likely that language per se could be dismissed, and that listening, as the normal mode for accessing spoken messages into the language sub-system, might well be a more generally useful process. For these reasons listening was studied as a subcomponent of literacy.

[1] The research reported in this paper was performed at HumRRO Division No. 3, Monterey, California, under Department of the Army contract with the Human Resources Research Organization; the contents of this paper do not necessarily reflect official opinions or policies of the Department of the Army. Reproduction in whole or in part is permitted for any purpose of the Department of the Army.

[2] Several people were instrumental in accomplishing the research which forms the basis for this paper. I am pleased to acknowledge the contributions of John Caylor, Richard Kern, Lynn Fox, Pat Ford, Don Enderby, and Harry Burckhartt to many and various aspects of the research reported herein. Nina McGiveran has rendered exceptional service in preparing the manuscript.

The study of listening was approached in several different ways. One group of studies, involving questionnaire surveys, personal interviews, and extensive literacy and job proficiency testing, has in common a concern with conceptual and functional relationships of reading to listening and the manner in which reading ability, or lack of it, may influence the use of listening in the acquisition of knowledge. These studies are discussed in the first part of this paper, in relation to a simple model of the development of reading ability. Implications of the model for the measurement of reading and listening abilities are indicated, with emphasis upon certain conceptual issues related to the measurement of outcomes following instruction in learning by listening. A rudimentary model of hierarchical features of spoken messages which may be used by a listener in tracking a message is described and discussed in relation to teaching listening.

A second group of studies on listening was performed in pursuit of the second objective stated above, i.e., the exploration of means for reducing reading demands in training or job situations. One approach to this objective considered the possibility of substituting learning by listening for learning by reading. This led to research and extensive literature review concerning certain message, listener, and situational variables which may affect learning by listening. Aspects of this research are discussed in the second part of this paper.

SOME RELATIONSHIPS OF
READING AND LISTENING

"The child comes to his first reader with his habits of spoken language fairly well formed, and these habits grow more deeply set with every year. His meanings inhere in this spoken language and belong but secondarily to the printed symbols..." (Huey, 1908, p. 123)

Our attention to listening as a component of literacy was based on the common-sense notion, so eloquently expressed above by Huey, that, developmentally, skill in learning by listening precedes and actually forms a basis for the acquisition of skill in learning by reading. A very forceful argument for this point of view is given by Brown (1954).

The consideration of listening as prerequisite to reading led us to conjecture that minimally literate men would: (1) *prefer* to learn prose materials by listening rather than by reading; (2) actually *learn* such materials better with the reading demands removed; and (3) *rely* more on listening than on reading for obtaining job-related information.

Literacy and Preference for Learning by Listening. A survey was conducted to examine relationships of reading ability to preference for learning by listening. In this survey, some 400 men in five classes of three Army training courses were tested for reading ability (Survey Reading Achievement, Junior High Level, California Test Bureau, hereafter referred to as the CTB reading test). The men were also asked the question: "In learning a lesson, would you rather *hear* it from a tape recorder or *read* it from a book." Table 1 presents the results for five reading grade level groupings. Clearly, reduced ability to read led to a greater preference for learning by listening. In fact, for a group of 12 men who read in the 4–5.0 range, 9 (75%) preferred to learn by listening. It is also interesting to note that more than one-half

TABLE 1

Percentage of Men Who Preferred Learning by Listening Over
Reading by Reading Grade Level

Reading Grade Level	N	Prefer to Listen (%)
4 – 6.9	87	45
7 – 8.9	106	25
9 – 10.9	92	23
11 – 12.9	67	12
13 +	49	14

of the men reading below the 7.0 level preferred to learn by reading. This attests to the power of a permanent display of information which can be studied as desired, even if such study is pained!

Reading vs. Listening for Learning. While the foregoing clearly indicates that many of the poorer-reading men *prefer* to learn by listening rather than by reading, the question remains as to whether or not they actually *learn* better by listening rather than by reading. Data bearing on this question were obtained in a study in which the reading and listening test performance of men scoring below the 30th percentile on the Armed Forces Qualifications Test (AFQT)[3] was compared to that of men scoring at the 31st percentile or above on the AFQT (Sticht, 1969). The mean AFQT percentile for the low mental aptitude (LMA) group was 18.3 while that for the average mental aptitude (AMA) group was 63.0. The estimated reading grade level of the LMA group was 7.5; for the AMA group this estimate was 10.0. Estimates were from regression equations for AFQT and reading level on the CTB reading test.

Two tests, A and B, were constructed of brief prose passages of three different Flesch readability levels (Farr, Jenkins, & Paterson, 1951) followed by "fill-in-the-blanks" tests of comprehension. All questions were of a factual nature, requiring memory for details contained in the selection. Both Tests A and B were presented as listening and as reading tests in a counterbalancing design. Listening test questions were read aloud and Ss wrote their answer. Thus, to a degree, writing skill was confounded with listening skill. However, spot checks, wherein Ss were asked for answers, revealed no differences between written and spoken answers. Many similar testing situations led us to believe that the use of a written response did not influence test results. When the tests were given as reading tests, *reading time was limited* to the time required to listen to the test.

Table 2 presents the results of the study. As expected, there were significant differences between AMA and LMA men on both tests, with the AMA scoring higher than the LMA. With regard to the difficulty level of the material, the reading

[3] The AFQT consists of 4 parts of 25 items each: Part 1 is a vocabulary test; Part 2 an arithmetic test using word problems; Part 3 is a tool recognition test; Part 4 is a spatial relations test. Correlation of AFQT and CTB reading test ≈ .65.

TABLE 2

Mean Percent-Correct Scores for Low and Average Mental Aptitude Groups
on the Listening and Reading Subtests

| Aptitude Group | Average grade level of material | | | | | |
| | 6.5 | | 7.5 | | 14.5 | |
	Listen	Read	Listen	Read	Listen	Read
LMA (N=40)						
Mean	52.9	51.7	52.5	43.0	25.5	26.0
SD	20.0	27.4	16.3	19.5	13.4	17.8
AMA (N=56)						
Mean	72.3	72.5	69.5	65.2	44.9	48.7
SD	19.9	21.0	15.9	18.5	19.8	20.6

and listening performance of both groups declined as the difficulty of the material was increased. Thus the readability formula appears to have been appropriate for scaling "listenability" also. There were no differences between reading and listening scores *within* either group. Apparently, men who score low on the AFQT and are of marginal literacy, may learn equally poorly by listening as by reading. This suggests that much of their reading difficulty may result from reduced ability to comprehend language rather than (or perhaps in addition to) lack of ability in decoding written symbols into the language of speech.

Reading and Listening for Job Information. The foregoing studies suggest that preference for learning by one modality or another does not necessarily mean that learning will be best accomplished under the preferred modality (see also James, 1962). It may mean, however, that, when given a choice, men who prefer to listen rather than to read for information might select listening rather than reading sources. Evidence related to this hypothesis was obtained in the course of research to identify job reading tasks (Sticht, Caylor, Kern, & Fox, 1971). Men working as cooks, vehicle repairmen, and supply clerks were interviewed and asked if they could recall a time ". . . in the last month or so" when they were doing some particular job task and had *asked* someone (i.e., listened) for information. They were also asked to provide similar information about times they had used reading materials rather than asking someone. An attempt was made to obtain five examples of the use of listening or reading sources to get job-related information. Men interviewed had been previously tested on the CTB reading test.

For each job, Figure 1 shows relationships of reading ability to the use of listening (closed circles) or reading sources on the job. Listening and reading citations are expressed as a percentage of the maximum number possible if each man had given his full limit of five. Thus the listening citation index of 16 for the cooks reading in the 4–6.9 range means that, on the average, these men reported less than one instance of listening (asking) for job information.

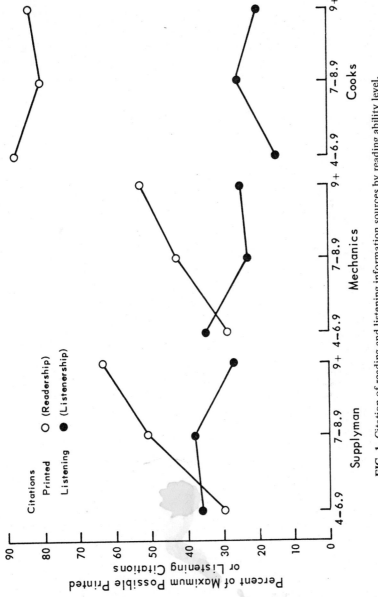

FIG. 1. Citation of reading and listening information sources by reading ability level.

Of particular interest to the present discussion is the fact that, for repairmen and supply clerks, the use of reading materials over listening sources increased with increasing reading ability. Or, stated otherwise, there was a report of proportionally greater use of listening over reading materials for obtaining job information by less apt readers in these jobs. For whatever reasons may be involved, these findings are consistent with the preference study reported above: preference for learning by listening is higher among the poorer readers, and they reported a proportionally greater reliance on listening sources over reading sources in these two jobs.

The data for the cooks differ in showing a high reported use of reading sources by men at all reading levels. It is not certain why this is so, but it is of interest to note that the cooks' reading materials were written at an average readability level of 9.0, while this figure was 14.5 and 16+ for the repairman and supply clerks jobs, respectively. This suggests that the difficulty level of job reading materials may influence the extent to which they are used in preference to asking someone for job information, especially when reading skills are low. In this regard, it is interesting to note that, summing over-all reading levels, the tendency to use listening sources increased from the cook's to the repairman's and then to the supply clerk's job. This parallels the increase in the difficulty levels of the job reading materials.

Another point of interest in Figure 1 is that, within each job, men of all reading levels reported about the same amount of usage of listening sources. Thus, in the repairman's and supply clerk's jobs, the effects of increased reading ability was not so much to suppress the use of listening sources (the slight downward trends for listening citations over reading levels were not significant), as it was to increase the amount of usage of reading materials. Conversely, the poorer readers in these jobs did not compensate for lack of reading input by a proportional increase in their listening input—they simply operated with a total deficit of job information!

Listening, Reading, "Intelligence," and Job Proficiency. If the less literate men seek less job information, as the interview data would suggest, at least for two jobs, do they then *know* less about their jobs and *perform* less well than the more literate men? Summarily, the answer to both of these questions is yes! This was determined by a large-scale study in which literacy and other cognitive test performance was related to paper and pencil job knowledge tests and "hands-on", job sample performance tests, in which cooks cooked, repairmen repaired vehicles, etc. These test data were obtained for some 400 men in each of four Army jobs (Sticht *et al.*, 1971).

Correlations between the literacy and other cognitive tests and the job proficiency measures are given in Table 3. While all correlations are significant, ($p <$ .05), it is apparent that the Maze test[4] is not a useful predictor of job proficiency, whether indexed by job knowledge or by job sample tests. The data also indicate that the two listening tests[4] are slightly less useful than the reading test for predicting job knowledge test performance, although they do as well as the reading test in predicting job sample test performance. In general, then, these data support the

---

[4] The Listening Test involved recall of details from three brief passages presented orally. The Oral Directions Test is the ODT-Form S by the Psychological Corporation, and the Maze Test is a group form of the Porteus Maze Test; see Vineberg, Taylor, and Sticht (1970) for details.

TABLE 3

Correlation Between Predictors and Job Proficiency Measures

Job	Predictor	Job proficiency index	
		Job knowledge	Job performance
Armor Crewman	Reading	.57	.32
	Listening	.53	.29
	ODT[a]	.47	.35
	Maze	.29	.21
Repairman			
	Reading	.47	.26
	Listening	.40	.38
	ODT[a]	.30	.25
	Maze	.13	.10
Supply Clerk			
	Reading	.40	.40
	Listening	.39	.42
	ODT	.29	.34
	Maze	.17	.19
Cook			
	Reading	.56	.34
	Listening	.39	.28
	ODT	.44	.32
	Maze	.20	.21
Average for Four Jobs	Reading	.49	.33
	Listening	.42	.34
	ODT	.38	.32
	Maze	.20	.18

[a]ODT = Oral Directions Test.

statement that less literate men are likely to be less knowledgeable and to perform less well on the job than more literate men (a complete discussion of these data may be found in Sticht et al., 1971).

Evidence for Huey's Developmental Model of Reading

For the purposes of this paper, the data of Table 3 are of special interest because of their relevance to the developmental model of reading acquisition stated by Huey in the quotation above. The model states that reading presupposes and is built upon a foundation of language ability. A simple extension of this model is that language ability presupposes and is built upon a base of preliterate, prelinguistic, perceptual/cognitive, adaptive capabilities collectively referred to herein as "intelligence."

The model thus asserts a hierarchical developmental relationship among intelligence, listening (language), and reading such that language comprehension by reading depends upon and in fact encompasses the prior capability to comprehend language by listening. The latter in turn requires some "core" intellectual capabilities for language to develop. A consequence of this model would seem to be that, with mature readers, i.e., readers at their asymptote, a *measure* of language comprehension *by reading*, must be simultaneously a measure of intelligence, a measure of the ability to comprehend language (usually by listening), *and* a measure of the ability to read for comprehension.

The data of Table 3 present evidence for the foregoing hypothesis. There it is seen that the job knowledge test, requiring reading, language, and intelligence is more highly related to CTB reading test, which has the same three requirements, than to the listening tests, which require both language and intelligence, but not reading, or the maze test, which is our best approximation to a non-reading, non-language measure of "intelligence." This pattern is independently replicated for each of the four jobs.

For the job performance tests, which have few if any specific reading requirements, but do require language and intelligence, the correlations with the reading test, shrink appreciably from those found with job knowledge[5], yet it is seen that both listening and reading variables are about equally associated with job performance. The non-language maze test maintains its low relationships across the knowledge test and the job performance sample test, which would be expected if both tests require "core" intelligence.

Thus, we see from the correlation between reading and job knowledge that a reading measure provides more predictive power when a criterion task which involves reading *and* language *and* intelligence is used, than do language (listening) or intelligence (maze) measures. Furthermore, when the reading measure is used to predict non-reading criterion performance, which nonetheless involves language and intelligence (job sample tests) the correlation shrinks to the size of, but is just as large as, those of the language measures. The suggestion is that in the latter case, the reading component of the reading measure is superfluous to the non-reading criterion, while the language and intelligence components of the reading measure render it equally as useful as the nonreading language (listening) measures, which themselves are measures which include intelligence.

Another way of evidencing that the measurement of comprehension by reading includes the measurement of comprehension by language (by listening in the present case) and the measurement of intelligence is by reference to Table 4. There it is seen that, if job knowledge is predicted by reading test performance (top line), little is gained by adding listening[6] or maze variables. On the other hand, there is a progressive increase in prediction coefficients when variables are added from the bottom of the table as: maze; maze + listening (but note that, in keeping with the model, listening does as well as L + M); and reading + listening + maze. For job

---

[5] The one exception to this pattern is the supply job, a clerical job whose performance tasks make demands on reading.

[6] In this case, only the Three Story Listening Test is included in the analyses. The Oral Directions Test is excluded.

TABLE 4

Multiple Correlations Between Literacy Measures and Job Proficiency Indices

Literacy Variables*	Job knowledge				Job performance			
	Armor	Repairman	Supply	Cooks	Armor	Repairman	Supply	Cooks
R	.57	.47	.40	.56	.32	.26	.40	.34
R+L	.61	.49	.43	.57	.34	.36	.46	.36
R+L+M	.62	.49	.43	.57	.36	.37	.46	.37
(L)	(.53)	(.40)	(.35)	(.39)	(.29)	(.38)	(.42)	(.28)
L+M	.54	.40	.36	.42	.32	.36	.42	.33
M	.29	.13	.17	.20	.21	.10	.19	.21

*R = reading; L = listening; M = maze.

TABLE 5

Predictor Relationships with Education

Predictor	Education			
	Armor	Repairman	Supply	Cook
Reading	.30	.33	.29	.32
ODT	.18	.26	.27	.23
Listening	.19	.15	.16	.14
Maze	−.01	.09	.07	.12

performance, on the other hand, nothing is gained by adding reading to listening + maze, or significantly, vice versa.

One final piece of evidence for the simple developmental model suggested by Huey is given in Table 5. Since reading is generally acquired through formal education, while listening and intelligence are not, the correlations of these latter measures with years of education ought to be smaller than the correlations of reading and years of education, as is the case in Table 5[7].

Implications of Huey's Developmental Model of Reading

One of the implications of Huey's model is that there *do not* exist two kinds of language comprehension, one for reading and one for listening; rather, there is only one, wholistic ability to comprehend by language, and one should be able to comprehend equally well by listening or by reading, *if one has been taught to decode*

---

[7] The years-of-education variable was restricted by a coding system designed for HumRRO Work Unit UTILITY and hence correlations are smaller than might otherwise be expected; but it is the order, not magnitude, of information which is of concern here.

well and other task variables are equalized. There have been at least two studies which claim to have isolated separate listening and reading language comprehension factors (Caffrey, 1953; Spearritt, 1961). However, in neither case were task variables such as examination time (i.e., reading time and listening time) and sequence of presentation (e.g., linear presentation of reading materials without the possibility of forward or backward scanning) equalized. Since these types of task variables are different for the listening and reading situations, they could be expected to produce a constant effect on listening test performance and hence lead to the (erroneous) conclusion that a separate listening comprehension factor exists. In fact, what would exist is what Spearritt claims at one place to have found, a factor he designated as "comprehension of meaningful verbal *passages* presented in *spoken* form" as separate from a factor called "comprehension of meaningful verbal *passages* presented in *printed* form (p. 131). Readers may, however, become confused when, for purposes of convenience, Spearritt talks about "The identification of a separate listening comprehension factor . . ." in his implications section (p. 159). The problem is that, whereas the former factor descriptions stress the *display* (modality) variables, and thus imply *task* differences underlying differential test performance, the latter description implies a special kind of language comprehension which is different when used in conjunction with listening than with reading. We know of no evidence to support this position, and believe that the developmental model suggested by Huey and supported by the data of Tables 3, 4, and 5 argue against this position.

Additional implications from the developmental model include the notion that what can be comprehended by listening sets a limit to what can be comprehended by reading, other task variables being equal; comprehension by listening should exceed comprehension by reading in the pre-school and early school years, and there is evidence that it does [see Brassard (1970) and Duker's (1968) Bibliography, items #1066, 440, 825, 652, 376, 1038, 1316, 1055, 535, 36, 370]; ability to comprehend by listening should be predictive of reading potential, and Brassard's (1970) work suggests it is; and when an *exhaustive* measure of language comprehension by reading is used with people skilled in reading decoding, to predict proficiency on tasks involving or not involving reading, little additional predictive power is to be expected by adding further measures of language comprehension by listening, or measures of non-verbal "intelligence" to the predictive formula.

Implications of the Model for Teaching Learning by Listening

Huey's developmental model brings into focus a distinction that has sometimes been blurred by persons interested in "teaching listening." The distinction is between "teaching listening" and teaching "learning (comprehending) by listening." The distinction is analogous to that between teaching reading and teaching learning (comprehending) by reading. In the former, emphasis is upon the decoding skills involved in reading and the general problems involved in learning the orthography of the written language. In the latter situation, emphasis is upon teaching meanings of words, concepts, reasoning with the information gained by reading, etc.

With regard to listening, teaching speech decoding aspects of listening rarely occurs, because such skills are assumed to be, and generally are, acquired prior to formal schooling (excluding consideration of work with children with speech or dyslexia problems). In most instruction in listening, emphasis is generally given to processing of verbal information presented aurally *for one or another purpose*—such as describing the main idea, describing a sequence of ideas, etc. Since these are exactly the same kinds of things one teaches as "reading to learn," it is not surprising that results of listening and reading tests frequently correlate highly. What is surprising is the number of writers (Russell, in Duker, 1966, p. 191; Spearritt, 1961; Lundsteen, 1969), and designers of tests of learning by listening (Brown, in Duker, 1966, p. 416) who express concern over the fact that such tests appear to be correlated with other measures such as verbal ability and comprehension by reading and hence do not measure some independent "listening ability."

Such concern seems to result from a failure to appreciate that the major task differences between reading (for instance) and listening, i.e., those differences which most sharply focus on the modality being used, are *never* exploited. For instance, if tasks were involved which included listening in the dark versus reading in the dark, or listening in 100 decibel noise versus reading in 100 decibel noise, it is clear that correlations between tasks would be zero (or very low), since one task would be impossible and show no (or only chance) variance.

This not so perspicacious observation also brings to mind the fact that most listening vs. reading vs. verbal comprehension types of comparisons also fail to exploit non-verbal aspects of listening and reading, such as intonation, rhythm, voice quality for listening, and "reading" figures, graphs, and pictures for information. Emphasis is always upon representation of learning by language. If it is learning by language which is of primary concern, and it seems to be, then of course it is possible for such learning to occur through listening, reading, or even touch, feeling, or sign language. In dealing with the deaf and blind, we might, then, speak of "feeling for the main idea," "feeling to note sequence," "feeling for details," etc. These capabilities were in fact obtained by Laura Bridgman and Helen Keller.

It is clear then, that, inasmuch as listening and reading both offer in-roads to comprehension by language, the major factor of concern is comprehension by language as indicated by Carroll (1968). Furthermore, *it is to be desired* and expected that with readers beyond the learning to decode-read stage, learning by listening and learning by reading should be highly correlated, as should these factors with other language (verbal) tests. To the extent that learning by listening or learning by reading are not equal, with subjects skilled in reading decoding, and for similar cognitive tasks, *task* differences (e.g., different vocabulary; difficulty and familiarity of materials, examination time, etc.) should be evaluated to determine just what it is that is resulting in the lack of equivalence.

While there have been many studies which have demonstrated improvement on listening test performance in pre-post-test and experimental versus control group designs (cf. many references in Duker, 1966; Lundsteen, 1969; Devine, 1969; Penfield & Marascuilo, 1970), none have been found in which matched groups were given listening training, and were then compared for performance on the same listening criterion tests, with one group receiving the listening criterion tests presented as reading tests. It would be surprising to find that such training did not transfer to the reading task. In fact, Thorn (1968) presented a close approximation to this design with first graders and reported a transfer of skills gained by listening to reading test performance ($p < .06$). The transfer might have been even greater had the tasks on the reading test more closely resembled those of the listening test, and had the readers been more skillful.

In cases where learning by listening *has* been "shown" to improve, because of admonitions about the importance of listening and paying attention, and instruction in performing various organizational operations (listening for sequence, listening for main idea, judging logical validity, etc.), it seems reasonable to suppose that pupils may have improved simply because schools frequently fail to point out the general usefulness of various organizing schemes, and most instruction in "thinking" is given in conjunction with reading materials. For instance, students are given reading assignments and then are questioned about such assignments; books contain "thought problems" in them; discussion is focused on what was presented in a book; exams ask about information in books, or written lecture notes, etc. "Thinking" in conjunction with written materials is thus likely to be overlearned, while "thinking" about information being presented orally may be underlearned, especially with reticent students in large classrooms. Thus there may be some benefit from explicit practice in "thinking" about material presented orally. If students already know about and use such organizational practices with written materials, there should be little improvement of learning by reading, or performance on written critical thinking tests, etc., following training in doing these things while listening. If this is the case, then it is not surprising that researchers frequently report improved performance on listening tests, without such improvement on reading tests (Devine, 1969). This may merely be a matter of "sensitizing" students to the use of organizational practices in conjunction with listening, which they already use in conjunction with reading.

By these remarks I do not wish to imply that there is no need to teach learning by listening. There are populations who obviously can benefit from and must have such teaching. For example, pre-school children and children in the early grades appear to benefit from training in listening for different purposes (Penfield & Marascuilo, 1970; Thorn, 1968) though many may acquire such competencies "naturally" in the course of their education (Penfield & Marascuilo, 1970). Furthermore, early vocabularies and general language competencies are usually acquired through listening, and we know the negative consequences of restricted experiences in such language development activities (Williams, 1970).

Instruction in thinking and reasoning via listening materials may also be particularly appropriate for persons unskilled in reading. Adults in remedial reading programs might benefit from instruction using listening materials to increase their vocabularies, expand their concepts, and to learn strategies for organizing information received via listening. Such instruction would also be expected to transfer to the reading situation, and to aid in the acquisition of decoding skills. Similarly, the blind constitute another major group for whom training in learning by listening is imperative. Such training would also be expected to facilitate learning from reading braille.

Thus, the main thrust of this discussion is *not* to discourage training in learning by listening within *any* population. On the contrary, the point is that it is neither necessary nor particularly desirable to produce criterion tests for such training that produce test scores which are independent of other (e.g., reading) test results for the same types of cognitive tasks. To justify instruction in learning by listening, it is sufficient that instructional objectives be specified and agreed upon, that a student's ability to accomplish the objective be assessed, and to note whether or not the student can perform the objective. If not, instruction should be provided. The effectiveness of the instructional process can then be evaluated in terms of whether or not the student learns to do what he previously could not. It makes no difference *how* the student acquires the instructional objective, e.g., a person might be taught rules and even improve his learning-by-listening by reading a book; the critical factor is whether or not the instructional objectives can be performed.

A Conceptual Model to Guide Research

The heart of the problem, of course, is to specify the instructional objectives. The scope of the problem is too broad for extended discussion here (cf. Duker, 1966; Devine, 1969; Penfield & Marascuilo, 1970; Lundsteen, 1969). We can, however, discuss the skeletal model which guides our research and instructional program development in teaching learning by listening to language (cf. Neisser, 1967; Norman, 1969; Moray, 1969 for extended discussion of the literature base from which this model is derived).

The problem to which the model is addressed is this: how does a listener continue to fix his attention on a spoken message, and how does he process this incoming aural message in order to subsequently recall all or part of the message? Obviously these are not simple questions. Equally certain is that the answers to these questions are, at best, only fragmented and uncertain. Nonetheless, such answers as have been suggested rest upon an extension body of research and so may direct our activities at the conceptual level, if less so at the procedural level of program design and development.

The model of listening under consideration asserts that a listener can follow along with, or "track" an oral message by attending, as situations demand, to various aspects of the message (Table 6). The paradigm which demonstrates this behavior in its "pure" form involves a listener with different messages in each side of a set of earphones. The listener's task is to attend to only one message. In the model, the attending task is easiest if the acoustic spectrum in the two messages differs, for instance if a female voice is in one ear and a male voice is in the other. In this case, attention can be guided by the spectrum analysis which occurs early in the listening process.

If the signal in each ear is composed of similar acoustic spectrums, then the listener must depend upon a higher order analysis to guide attention—analysis of phonetic constituency and phonemic sequences. An exemplar for this situation is a case in which the same person is speaking the same message in each of the listener's ears, but in one case the speech is in a foreign language. Because the frequency spectrum of the speaker's voice is the same, the higher level of analysis is needed to "track" the target message. Since the phonemic sequences of the foreign language

TABLE 6

A Model of Levels of Analysis of Features a Listener May Use to Track A Spoken
Message and Training Exercises that Might Be Used for Training at Each Level

Level	Examples of exercises
I. Acoustic features	Listening to sounds of various qualities.
Frequency spectrum	Listening to one female (male) voice in a group of
Speech quality	male (female) speakers.
Speech rate	Listening to speech-rate varied recordings.
	Listening to speech with different dialects, accents, etc.
II. Linguistic features	Analysis and synthesis of words using phonetics.
Phonetic constituents	Syllabication of words.
Phonemic sequence	Spelling.
Grammatical structures	Sentence parsing.
III. Semantic features	Vocabulary training.
Meaning of message	Listening to organize information.
	Listening for main ideas.
	Listening for comparative purposes.
	Listening for pros and cons.
	Listening to predict outcomes.
	Listening for affective aspects of message.

would differ from the listener's language, this difference could be used to guide the
listener's attention.

At a third, highest level of analysis, the listener may encounter messages similar
in acoustic and linguistic factors. In this case, the listener may rely upon the
semantic meaning of the message to track the message. Thus, if two messages are
spoken by the same person in the listener's language, the latter must depend upon
the meaning of the message to track it.

The model of the processes used by the listener to track a message thus contains
three levels of analysis: the acoustic, the linguistic, and the semantic. In applying
this model to instruction in learning by listening, we are concerned primarily with
the semantic level of analysis. However, it might be desirable to provide instruction
and practice in attending to "lower level" aspects of the spoken message, such as
training persons to discriminate among speech sounds in male and female voices,
etc., or to provide training in comprehending speech presented at rapid rates. In the
latter two instances, concern would be with acoustic features of the message.

Tracking at the Semantic Level. To attend to listening materials by means of the
semantic level of processing, it is necessary for the listener to understand the
meaning of the message. This means that he must understand the vocabulary com-
prising the message. If a listener is limited in his vocabulary, he will be less successful in tracking at the semantic level. Thus, it is probable that either direct training
in vocabulary or in vocabulary building skills (e.g., inferring meaning from context)
or both may be required in many programs in learning by listening.

A second aspect of the problem of tracking at the semantic level is that of processing the information in some way so as to make it more meaningful and hence more available for later recall. Considerable evidence suggests that listening (as well as reading) materials are remembered best when the listener uses some *organizational procedure* to sort, classify, label, etc., the incoming information. For this reason, training at the semantic tracking level focuses on training for organizing incoming information. Such training should prepare the listener to use different organizing principles when listening to various sorts of materials for a variety of purposes. For instance, the student may be instructed in the "typical" structure of a speech and be given training in listening for different purposes at different places in the lecture or speech. To do this, questions might be strategically placed in the program to attempt to "shape" the occurrence of different organizing practices when listening to speeches, lectures, etc., as discussed in the second part of this paper. Table 6 indicates some of the topics from available programs which may provide training in organizational practices for a variety of purposes. This is not an exhaustive or even extensive list of training topics. The table is meant to suggest possible topics of a listening training course, rather than to enumerate the topics which should be used in any particular program. These can only be determined for particular programs, for particular listeners attempting to accomplish particular learning objectives.

EXPERIMENTAL STUDIES OF LEARNING BY LISTENING TO RATE CONTROLLED RECORDINGS

Research described in the first part of this paper indicated that many men who read poorly preferred to learn by listening rather than by reading. This suggests that the provision of listening materials in addition to reading materials in training programs and in on-the-job training might motivate learning where it otherwise would not even be attempted.

A possible drawback to recorded materials for instructional purposes, however, is that the listener's listening rate is determined by the oral reader's rate of speech. For low aptitude men, the message might be too fast, while for higher aptitude men faster rates of speech might be preferable. Then again, some, perhaps more difficult, listening materials might be best presented at a slow rate of speech and others at a faster rate of speech; or there might be interactions of aptitude, message difficulty, and speech rate.

Information about the effects of such factors, and others, on learning by listening was obtained in experimental studies which had as their general orientation the exploration of the utility of speech-rate controlled recordings in preparing listening materials tailored for different aptitude groups.

In the following pages an experiment will be described which examines interactions of speech rate, level of difficulty of materials, and mental aptitude (AFQT) on learning by listening. Within the context of this experiment, related research by ourselves and others will be discussed to consider certain topics in more analytic detail. Following this, research will be reviewed which concerns methods for preparing listening materials to improve learning.

Effects of Speech Rate, Message Difficulty, and Aptitude on Learning by Listening

As mentioned earlier, our concern with marginally literate, low aptitude men led us to consider the use of rate controlled recordings as instructional materials tailored to individual needs in rate of speech of listening materials. We also considered that the difficulty levels of materials might influence the rate of speech at which the materials could be usefully presented, and, since difficulty is defined by reference to the interaction of materials and users of the materials, it seemed necessary to consider that all three factors (speech rate, difficulty, and aptitude) might combine to influence how well one would learn by listening to recorded messages.

These three factors were included in an experiment (Sticht 1971) using as Ss 204 Army personnel, half of whom were men with AFQT scores at the 30th percentile or below (low mental aptitude, LMA), while the other half were men with AFQT scores at the 80th percentile or above (high mental aptitude, HMA). The Ss in both aptitude categories served in one of six conditions: baseline groups, in which Ss took written, 30 item Cloze tests without listening to the passages; and five experimental groups who listened to the speech materials presented at either 125, 150, 175, 325, or 350 words per minute, and then took the tests. Materials were prepared using the electromechanical method for the time compression or expansion of speech developed by Fairbanks, Guttman, and Miron (1957).

Difficulty of Prose Materials Evaluated by Four Methods. To assess the effects of message difficulty, we used a set of 34 150-word passages which had been scaled for complexity by Miller and Coleman (1967). They had been scaled using a variety of Cloze procedures.

To validate the scaling of the Miller-Coleman passages (MCP) as a scale of difficulty, the present study used direct magnitude estimation and a readability formula by Farr *et al.* (1951). Subsequent to this scaling exercise, work by Aquino (1969) was discovered in which he had validated the MCP as being scaled for difficulty using category scaling techniques. Table 7 compares these four methods

TABLE 7

Correlations Between Measures of Difficulty of Miller–Coleman Passages

	Readability Formula	Judged Difficulty/CS[a]	Judged Difficulty/ME[b]
Bilateral Cloze[c]	−.85	−.93	−.86
Readability formula	−	.84	.82
Judged difficulty/CS		−	.82

[a]CW = Category scale, Aquino (1969); [b]ME = magnitude estimation; [c]In contrast to other measures, Cloze scores are scaled from low (difficult) to high (easy), resulting in minus signs for the correlation.

(Cloze, readability index, magnitude estimation, category scaling) for scaling prose materials. The uniformly high correlations among the scales of difficulty reinforce the use of any one of the procedures for scaling the difficulty of prose materials. Also, they attest to the validity of the MCP as a set of passages scaled for difficulty and hence useful in research requiring materials of defined and differing difficulty levels.

For the present study, six of the MCP passages were grouped into three levels of difficulty, two at each level, selected on the basis of their similarity in Cloze scores, estimated magnitude, and readability. In terms of the latter, the three levels of difficulty were composed of materials of 5th, 8th, and 14th grade difficulty.

Overview of Results. The major results of the study are summarized in Figure 2.

Analyses of variance (excluding baseline groups) confirm the complex interactions of speech rate, message difficulty, and aptitude shown in Figure 2. This complexity is evidence by a significant ($p < .005$) triple interaction of these variables. Interpretation of this three-way interaction is aided by the results of further analyses which indicated that, for HMA Ss, there was no significant difficulty by speech rate interaction, while for the LMA Ss this interaction was significant ($p < .001$). In Figure 2 this difference is evidenced by the observation that the HMA Ss gained about as much when listening to the more difficult materials as when listening to the easier materials, and this was apparently true for each rate of speech. On the other hand, the easier the materials and the slower the rate of speech, the more the LMA Ss appear to have learned.

Examination of Figure 2 also indicates that the HMA Ss may have performed better at 175 words per minute than at 150 or 125 words per minute. In fact, additional analyses confirmed a significant ($p < .05$) quadratic component for the HMA Ss (combining the three levels of message difficulty). This suggests an optimal speech rate for listening for these Ss, and, in comparision with the curves for the LMA Ss in Figure 2, this speech rate may be somewhat faster for the HMA than for the LMA Ss. More will be said about this later on.

With regard to the main effects of speech rate, message difficulty, and aptitude, all three were significant ($p < .005$). From Figure 2 it is seen that the general effect of accelerating speech rate above the "normal" of 175 words per minute was to decrease immediate recall. With respect to aptitude, LMA Ss performed consistently at a lower level than did HMA Ss. Finally, the performance of both aptitude groups improved with reduced difficulty of materials (even on baseline tests). These results are typical of those obtained in other research involving time-compressed speech (cf., Foulke & Sticht, 1969) and, as such, they provide a suitable introduction to a more extended discussion of issues and research related to each factor.

Effects of Speech Rate on Learning By Listening. Studies concerned with speech-rate controlled recordings are interested in discovering the relationship of rate of speech to amount learned by listening. What is this relationship? In their review of the pre-1969 literature, Foulke and Sticht (1969, p. 60) stated: "When these studies are considered collectively, the relationship that emerges is one in which listening comprehension declines at a slow rate as word rate is increased, until a rate of approximately 275 words per minute is reached, and at a faster rate thereafter."

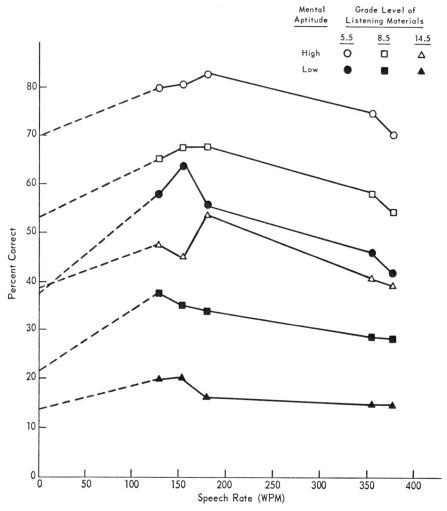

NOTE: The dotted lines mark baseline scores on the ordinate.

FIG. 2. Recall test scores for high and low mental aptitude *S*s for materials of three difficulty levels presented at five rates of speech. The dotted lines connect the data to relevant baseline scores.

The generality of the foregoing conclusion was questioned in a paper by Carver (1970b). The purpose of his paper was to "... present the hypothesis that the amount of information stored from connected discourse is a linearly decreasing function of the average rate at which the information is presented..." Briefly, Carver argued that the slow rate of decrease observed in a number of studies for speech rates from 140 to 280 words per minute resulted from low ceilings on the measurement scales (tests) which do not permit the scale to reflect the increases in information stored at the lower average rates of presentation. This argument obviously fails to account for "ceiling" effects frequently observed with LMA *S*s, (Fairbanks *et al.*, 1957; Sticht, 1971, p. 13; the present study) whose scores level off at speech rates below 250-300 words per minute, but which are not at the same level as those for HMA, and hence certainly not at the test ceiling.

At the present time, there is evidence for both the curvilinear hypothesis of Foulke and Sticht and the linear hypothesis of Carver for describing relationships of speech rate and learning by listening. It seems reasonable to argue that curvilinear results might occur if Ss are habituated to listening comfortably at rates in the range of 125–200 words per minute and simply "try harder" when speech is accelerated up to around 250–300 words per minute. Beyond this range, scores might drop off in a linear manner, in line with Carver's linear hypothesis, because increased effort simply is inadequate to cope with the rapid rate of input. However, changes in listening habits due to extended practice in listening to rapid rates might result in reducing the sharp drop in learning with speech rates above 300 words per minute, as Orr, Friedman, and Williams (1965) have demonstrated (but see Foulke, 1964 for evidence against the trainability of listening to accelerated speech).

As the foregoing suggests, adequate data are not now available to describe empirically *the* relationship between speech rate and learning by listening. The present research even suggests a decrease in learning for HMA with speech rate less than 175 words per minute; see Reid, 1968 for a similar finding for rates less than 275 words per minute. It is reasonable to suppose that the relationship must be an inverted–U when *extremely* fast and extremely slow rates of speech are permitted.

Speech Rate and Pause Time. The work of Goldman-Eisler (1968) has indicated that, in speaking, pauses appear to reflect internal decision making. If this is so, then it seems reasonable that the insertion of pauses into time-compressed materials might improve the comprehensibility of the materials (Carroll, 1967). Such findings were in fact reported by Friedman and Johnson (1969, p. 20) in research in which they inserted pauses of 2 seconds duration into short lexical strings prepared by Miller and Isard (1963) and which were presented at 175, 200, 325, and 450 words per minute. The lexical strings were of three types:

1. Meaningful, grammatical (hereafter designated "grammatical") strings. Example: "Colorless cellophane packages crackle loudly."
2. Meaningless, grammatical (or "anomalous") strings. Example: "Colorless yellow ideas sleep furiously."
3. Meaningless, ungrammatical (designated "ungrammatical") strings. Example: "Sleep roses dangerously young colorless."

Pauses were inserted either at structural junctures (between major immediate constituent boundaries) or at nonstructural loci within each string. Pauses were inserted into ungrammatical strings in such a way as to produce arbitrary segments of approximately equal length.

Their results indicated that spacing at structural boundaries in grammatical strings resulted in the same level of recall for these strings across all four speech rates, whereas recall for nonstructurally spaced and nonspaced grammatical strings declined at the fastest rate, with the latter falling below the former.

This same facilitative effect of spacing was obtained with anomalous and ungrammatical strings, though the effect was not so large. In general, grammatical strings were recalled more easily than anomalous ones, which, in turn, were recalled better than ungrammatical strings, thus replicating previous findings (Miller & Isard, 1963).

These data indicate the importance of pauses in providing time for the decoding of spoken information as well as for the encoding of such messages (Goldman-Eisler, 1968). Friedman and Johnson suggest that the special benefit of spacing between major constituents observed with very rapid speech rates most likely occurs because such pauses aid in the identification of syntactic "units" formed of functionally related words, and such "functional units" are more easily stored than are isolated words, as in the spaced, ungrammatical strings.

In subsequent work, Friedman and Johnson (1969) demonstrated that in listening to compressed speech, the insertion of spaces between major constituents *within* sentences resulted in higher recall test performance than when such spaces were inserted *between* sentences. Also, they showed that spacing between major *phrase* boundaries within sentences produced better recall than spacing between somewhat longer *clause* boundaries. This was true for normal speech rates (175 words per minute) as well as for speech rate accelerated by a factor as high as 2.75. This work confirms the importance of spacing at phrase boundaries (indicated above), and again suggests that such spacing "unitizes" groups of words, rendering them learnable, perhaps, as "chunks" (Miller, 1956). Presumably, since in normal listening phrases must first be identified and then learned, one effect of phrase spacing for rapid listening would be to reduce the time needed for identifying the phrase units. This might also account for the finding by Friedman and Johnson that phrase spacing also improved recall of materials presented at normal speech rates.

Speech Rate and "Chunking". The data of Friedman and Johnson suggest that phrase materials may be learned as units or "chunks." Presumably, such "chunking" could occur whenever pieces of information are grouped together, either by perceptual, linguistic, or associational rules. On the other hand, information which is not conducive to "chunking" may be learned, but only with greater time for organizing the information into some kind of relationship to one's store of knowledge. If a message contains both "chunkable" and "non-chunkable" information, listeners may, at normal rates, learn some of both types of information. With accelerated speech, however, less "non-chunkable" information may be learned for want of adequate processing time.

Data bearing on the foregoing notion was obtained in a study[8] which followed an approach suggested by the work of Rosenberg (1967). His research has indicated that association strength between words affects how well they are learned in a prose selection. Word pairs of high association strength tend to be recalled as pairs, while word pairs of low association strength are learned as separate items. It is as though the high association pairs are learned in "chunks" (Miller 1956) rather than as separate items of information.

For this study, a 350-word listening passage was prepared which contained triplets of nouns embedded within sentences of the connected discourse. Within each triplet of words, there was a stimulus word (S-word) and two response words (R_1

---

[8] Data for this experiment were collected and analyzed by Dr. Douglas Glasnapp while he served as a pre-doctoral intern at HumRRO Division 3 from the George Peabody College for Teachers, 1969–70.

and R_2) which varied according to their interword normative association strengths and proximity to the S-word. R_1 was a high association response (HAR) to the S-word, while R_2 was a low association response (LAR) to the S-word.

The response words were grammatically appropriate in the context of the discourse and each pair was of the same form-class. As an example of the materials, one sentence was: "Inside, the room smelled of *tobacco, smoke,* and *oil.*" In this sentence, *tobacco* is the S-word, *smoke* the HAR, and *oil* the LAR. A total of 18 such word triplets were embedded in sentences throughout the passage. The grade level of difficulty of the passage was 7.0, as determined by the method of Farr *et al.* (1951).

The passage was presented to HMA and LMA men, defined as above, in a baseline condition, in which Ss took a written Cloze test on the passage, and two experimental groups who took the Cloze test after listening to the passage at either 170 or 325 words per minute. In the Cloze test, the response words were deleted from the passage and Ss were instructed to fill in the blanks with the correct words. HARs and LARs were counted as correct if they occurred in *either* of the two response blanks corresponding to the correct S-word.

Figure 3 presents the percent correctly recalled HARs and LARs under baseline and speech rate conditions for both aptitude groups. Of primary interest for the question of the learnability of "chunkable" versus "non-chunkable" information are the differential effects of increasing the speech rate on the learning of HAR and LAR word pairs by the two aptitude groups. Although the HMA group learned more LAR word pairs than the LMA group at the normal speech rate, they learned almost the same number of LAR word pairs at the faster speech rate. Thus, the pressure induced by the acceleration of speech took its greatest toll on the ability of the HMA people to learn the more difficult associations.

This result is consistent with Rosenberg's (1967) suggestion that HAR embedded in prose facilitates storage of information because they are recalled as pairs (chunks), while the LAR word pairs are learned more as individual units. Hence, if the time per unit for learning is reduced, this will have a greater effect upon the learning of LAR than HAR. In the present study, the greater decrease in mean number of LAR word pairs recalled correctly by the HMA subjects under the compressed speech condition indicates that they were not being processed as efficiently as the HAR word pairs[9], i.e., they were "non-chunkable."

The studies of Friedman and Johnson (1969) and the foregoing suggest that the effects of accelerating speech rate are to reduce the time available for perceptual and cognitive processes required for storing sequentially presented information. Such processes apparently include the identification of phrase structures for the economic parsing of sentences into "chunks" rather than strings of words. Other processes which might be brought into play under normal listening conditions when low association or "non-chunkable" information is encountered are imagery or attempts to provide a verbal context for the information. Such activities require time and may be expected to drop out or to be attenuated when the information

---

[9] Unfortunately, since the HAR scores for the LMA Ss returned to baseline at the rapid rate of speech, it is not possible to be certain that they did not lose as many HAR as LAR under this condition.

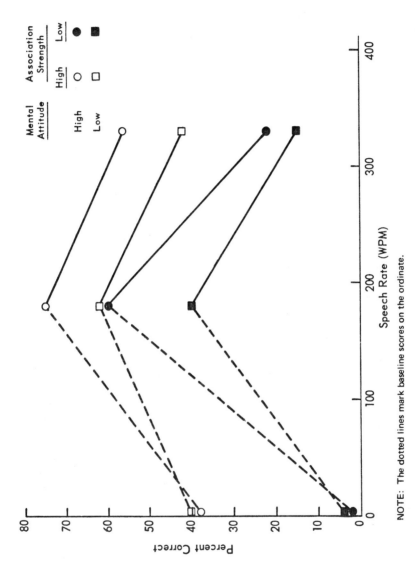

NOTE: The dotted lines mark baseline scores on the ordinate.

FIG. 3. Recall test scores for high and low mental aptitude Ss for a passage containing word pairs of high and low association strength and presented at two rates of speech. The dotted lines connect the data to relevant baseline scores.

rate of presentation is increased. Presumably, the improvement in ability to learn from highly speeded tapes, which may be produced by training (Orr *et al.*, 1965), would result from a change in the manner in which Ss processed the incoming information. Perhaps untrained persons who listen to accelerated speech tend to concentrate on getting information word-for-word, because they feel the pressure of "keeping-up" with the message (in fact, people frequently report that the rapid rate of speech forces them to attend carefully; *cf.* Taylor, 1967). Training might serve to permit Ss to ignore the words and concentrate more on the phrases, thus restoring learning by "chunking," at least to a degree. Additional information related to this idea is discussed below.

Listener Factors in Learning from Rapid Speech. Studies described above indicated that, at various speech rates, HMA persons scored better than LMA persons on the immediate recall test. Thus, verbal ability is realted to the ability to learn at any rate of speech. Are there, however, special abilities related to learning from rapid speech?

This question was asked by Friedman and Johnson (1969) in a study designed to identify some of the correlates of comprehension by listening, at normal and rapid rates, and to identify patterns of change in these correlations with increases in the rate of speech, which might be indicative of some special competence needed to comprehend rapid speech rates.

Using college students, Friedman and Johnson obtained intercorrelations among four criterion variables—listening test performance following passages presented at either 175, 250, 325, or 450 words per minute—and 10 predictor variables—Vocabulary (Nelson Denny Reading Test); Silent Reading Rate (Nelson Denny Reading Test); Space Relations (Differential Aptitude Test, DAT); Sentences (DAT); Clerical Speed and Accuracy (DAT); Verbal (Lorge-Thorndike Intelligence Test); Listening Comprehension (Brown-Carlson); Phonetic Script (Modern Language Aptitude Test, MLAT); Spelling Clues (MLAT); and Best Trend Name Test. The latter requires Ss to infer the semantic relationships among a set of words. For example, the S is given the words "horse-push cart- bicycle- car" and is asked to decide whether the relationship among the four terms is best described as one of "speed," "time," or "size." The correct answer is "time" since the sequence describes an order of historical development; horses were the earliest means of transportation, cars the most recent.

Results of multiple regression analysis identified the Nelson Denny vocabulary measure as the most efficient predictor of learning by listening at all four rates of speech. However, the beta weights for this measure decreased considerably at the fastest rate of speech.

On the other hand, the Best Trend Name Test was of only marginal importance at the normal or near-normal rates of speech, but its correlation and beta weight increased with the fastest rate of speech, thus identifying it as a major source of individual variance in the comprehension of highly accelerated speech.

Factor analysis using the ten tests named above resulted in the identification of three factors which accounted for 70% of the common variance. Of these, one included the Best Trend Name Test, Space Relations, and Clerical Speed and Accuracy, all tests involving the comparison of alternative responses to find one which is most similar to a stimulus.

The Best Trend Name Test, which emerged as an important predictor of learning at rapid rates of speech, calls for the ability to seek out and evaluate the meanings of words so as to match them on the basis of semantic relationships. Efficiency in this ability apparently aids in comprehending rapid rates of speech.

Evidence has also been presented (Carver, Johnson, & Friedman, 1971) to suggest that ability to comprehend rapidly presented speech is related to being field-independent, i.e., having the ability to "keep things apart" in the perceptual field; to be able to disregard superficial aspects of the stimulus field to detect patterning and order; to "see the forest in spite of the trees". Field-dependent people tend to be stimulus-bound, unable to avoid variable aspects of the stimulus field to detect the invariant.

In the work of Carver *et al.*, among other things, correlations were obtained for college students between two paper and pencil measures of field-independence—the Hidden Patterns and Hidden Figures tests—and performance on comprehension tests following each of four speeded listening selections. These correlations for the Hidden Patterns test increased as .22, .48, .64, and .95 for four successive speeded listening tests. For the Hidden Figures test, correlations increased as .04, .24, .46, and .84. Thus, with increasing exposure to rapid speech, the relationship to field-independence increased considerably.

These data are consistent with the above suggestion that untrained persons who listen to compressed speech (like those in the aforementioned study) may attend to the word elements of the message and the rate of speech, while training may result in learning to ignore the rate of speech and individual words and to concentrate more on the concepts being presented. Presumably, field-independent persons who are also skilled in making rapid semantic analyses could comprehend highly speeded speech with little, if any, experience with such speech.

Within the limits of correlational research, the foregoing studies suggest both a special perceptual skill and a special cognitive skill, involving the rapid matching of language elements, in comprehending accelerated speech. For the latter to be effective with respect to a given message, there must be some store of language elements (vocabulary) which match the content of the message. The greater this store, the more likely it will be that any given message can be semantically associated to the stored vocabulary, and hence the greater will be the learning of the message. This emphasizes the role of vocabulary, found by Friedman and Johnson (1969) to be an important factor in learning by listening with normal as well as rapid rates of speech.

Given the importance of the perceptual and cognitive processes identified above for comprehending rapid speech, it follows that structuring of the materials (such as in the spacing studies previously described), to facilitate the perceptual process ("chunking") and to provide time for semantic processing (during the spacing interval), or the provision of high association ("easy" versus "difficult") materials to facilitate semantic matching, should improve the learning of rapidly presented materials. And it does!

Additional research using the speech compression and expansion technique can be expected to further explicate the basic perceptual and cognitive processes involved in learning by listening. Used thus, the focus will be less on the educational utility of rate controlled recordings and more on the usefulness of the technique for studying basic processes involved in listening. However, rate controlled recordings do promise a utilitarian function, and educational technologists are continuing to explore the use of such recordings as instructional media. Explorations of this nature are described next.

Instructional Methods for Improving Learning by Listening (Rapidly or Otherwise)

Interest in improving learning from written materials (cf. Rothkopf, 1970; Frase, 1970; Anderson, 1970; Ausubel & Robinson, 1969) provides some promise for facilitating better learning by listening as well as by reading, because both activities involve learning from meaningful, connected prose. In this section, major concepts advanced to stimulate and guide research on learning from prose by reading are described, and the limited research available on listening to which these concepts can be related is discussed.

Advanced Organizers. A major area of research relevant to the problem of learning from reading or listening materials is that of Ausubel (Ausubel & Robinson, 1969) and his associates. Briefly, Ausubel (1960) assumes "... that cognitive structure is hierarchically organized in terms of highly inclusive concepts under which are subsumed less inclusive subconcepts and informational data." If this is true, so Ausubel reasons, then the learning of new meaningful material ought to be facilitated by insuring that the learner has inclusive concepts which will permit him to subsume the new information under these concepts. To check these hypotheses, Ausubel has had subjects learn reading materials, with and without advance organizers of various kinds which provide the learner with inclusive concepts, and then compared their learning of related materials. A variety of experiments using this general paradigm have been completed (summarized in Ausubel & Robinson, 1969). In general, data supportive of Ausubel's position have been found, but frequently they have been of marginal statistical significance. It is also not certain exactly how an advance organizer is constructed. However, several pertinent findings are: advance organizers are more likely to benefit less verbal subjects; the ability to learn new, but related concepts depends upon the clarity and stability of the previously learned concepts, and general background knowledge can facilitate learning of new material because it acts like an advance organizer.

In the area of rapid listening, Friedman *et al.* (1966, 1967) had Ss read advance organizers in the form of precis of selections to which they would listen. They compared the learning from time-compressed listening selections of groups using or not using the advance organizers. They found no beneficial effects with advance organizers of either a general nature or with those more pointedly directed towards the comprehension test materials. In these studies, however, only college students, more than likely quite high in verbal ability, served as subjects. And, as mentioned, Ausubel's work suggests that advance organizers are likely to be more beneficial for students low in verbal ability.

There have been several studies in which noncompressed recordings were repeated or time-compressed recordings were presented twice in the same amount of time required to present noncompressed materials once, to see if the double presentations would improve test performance (*cf.* Sticht, 1971). In these studies, the first presentation can be viewed as an advance organizer. Results of these studies have generally indicated significant improvement in the comprehension of repeated messages over that obtained with a single presentation of the compressed message, with some facilitating effect of the first listening on the second. However, listening twice to compressed tapes has not improved comprehension over that obtained by listening once to the noncompressed version of the selections. Perhaps careful consideration of Ausubel's theoretical and experimental work on learning from reading materials might facilitate the development of methods for improving listening comprehension of compressed and noncompressed recordings by the use of carefully designed advance organizers.

Mathemagenic and Cybernetic Control

A second area of research which may be fruitfully applied to learning by listening is that involving the studies of "mathemagenic behaviors" as formulated by Rothkopf (1965), and of "cybernetic control" as developed by Smith (Smith & Smith, 1966) and related to mathemagenics by Frase (1968). Rothkopf's term "mathemagenic" is a broadly inclusive term which refers to behaviors that produce learning. The mathemagenic hypothesis is that the acquisition and retention of information from printed material can be related to a variety of ongoing explicit and implicit responses made by the reader. These responses can be brought under the control of test-like events (such as questions) which occur along with the reading materials. Mathemagenic behaviors include a number of postural adjustments of the body and head, eye movements, and various inferred behaviors such as internal speech, echoic responses, the invention of mnemotechnic devices, and others. Rothkopf assumes that functional classes of mathemagenic responses have certain attributes such as topography, rate characteristics, and persistence, and these attributes can be modified or altered by the organization of stimulus events in reading materials. These notions have formed the basis for a number of studies in which stimulus questions are used to elicit various mathemagenic behaviors. Variables explored include the relative value of asking questions before as opposed to after a reading selection, pacing or frequency or questions, etc.

Though no research has been found in which questions have been used to improve learning of time-compressed listening materials, Sanders and Glass (1970) and Sanders (1970) report such research for normal-speed listening materials. Sanders and Glass reported that asking questions of a general type, as contrasted to questions about specific details, *after* a segment of listening materials, produced improved performance on these questions when they were asked later. Such questioning did not facilitate learning of material not directly related to the questions asked. Asking questions *before* listening to a segment produced a somewhat smaller improvement on subsequent testing over the same content.

However, the foregoing effects were *not* replicated in the work of Sanders, who found no differences between questioning before versus questioning afterward in aural presentations. His work did support the finding that questions embedded in the aural presentation focused the learner's attention on question-relevant information. This was indexed by improved performance on these questions when they appeared in the criterion test. One notable aspect of the work by Sanders and Sanders and Glass is the large number of variables which they found could interact to affect student performance, that, as they point out, limits the generalizability of the use of any one of the several variables. Finally, it should be mentioned that in neither of the foregoing studies did questions facilitate performance on criterion test questions which had not been asked during the presentation of the material. Thus, evidence for the inculcation of mathemagenic behavior was not forthcoming. For a more detailed, critical evaluation of the research on mathemagenics, see Carver (1970a).

The cybernetic control model assumes that learning from printed materials involves the ongoing integration of a variety of information processing behaviors. Questions can initiate information processing behaviors which are terminated when the answer is found. If the answer is not found, an implicit error signal response is generated in the reader as negative feedback which controls the reading behaviors until the student answers the question. Questions are best when they increase the probability that the learner will respond discriminately to the printed stimuli. In addition to questions, paragraph headings, typography, and other structural features of the text may aid the reader in integrating his information processing skills.

Research relevant to the cybernetic control model, using time-compressed speech, has been performed by Friedman, Graae, and Orr, (1967). They used the technique of presenting a cueing tone to alert listeners to an important segment of a recorded message. This may be viewed as somewhat analogous to introducing an important concept in printed form by means of an underlined or capitalized key word. Results of criterion tests indicated no facilitative effects due to cueing. Of course, in this study the cueing tone was not coded to signal any particular type of information processing strategy (e.g., listen for main idea, listen for details, form images, make verbal associations, etc.). Thus, listeners would not necessarily know how they were to listen, and hence error signals could not be generated to produce corrective processing. Possibly, a question following the cued passage segment which had to be answered before the student could go on would serve to guide and terminate the processing of the cued information and thereby facilitate learning of the material. As Anderson (1970) has noted, "The trick is to arrange a task that requires full processing from the learner" (p. 364). It is a tough trick to do without mirrors!

CONFERENCE DISCUSSION

To place this discussion in some perspective, the reader is reminded that some papers have a more applied focus. Sticht's paper includes an investigation into pragmatic aspects of language use in conjunction with other on-the-job behaviors which typically involve motor-skills. Thus Sticht's paper is an attempt to study language comprehension in its real-world sense.

Goodman thought that there were at least two aspects to reading in relation to job performance: One involves reading that may be required to learn how to do some job, and another involves reading that may be required in the process of doing some job. For example, one may read about how to become a French chef, and given that one has learned this skill through reading, one may still have to read a recipe in order to make some particular dish. Sticht agreed with this distinction.

Regarding Sticht's comparisons of learning through reading versus learning through listening to tape-recordings of the same material, Bever inquired whether it was legitimate to regard the visual versus aural presentations as comparable. The problem seems to be that in aural presentation, the *pauses* that occur can facilitate (or inhibit) comprehension as a function of where they occur, whereas in written form the reader is always, in a sense, controlling where such pauses occur. Another difference is that some materials are meant to be presented aloud (as in a play); to read them silently makes them seem artificial. Such considerations make it even more difficult to compare learnability of texts presented aurally versus visually. Sticht replied that while one could make a case for Bever's points, the voluminous literature on reading versus listening (see the early portions of Sticht's chapter for the relevant literature review) suggests that the mode of presentation yields no consistent difference in the amount adults learn from prose.

Bever and Sticht agreed that a direct interpretation of the relative frequencies with which different employees make use of available written materials is difficult, but might be attributable to differences in the difficulty level of these materials (for example, in the Army, an auto-mechanics manual usually has a greater difficulty level than a cookbook). Goodman thought that it was not so much the differences in readability indices which accounted for the different frequencies of reading citations across jobs; instead, he emphasized that he thought it was the different purposes for which the several materials were used that probably accounts for the observed differences.

Sticht concluded that his studies of reading and listening comprehension tests indicated that there is but one basic kind of comprehension, not two. Bever didn't agree and thought that there may be many different ways of comprehending. Reading and listening, he thought, probably operate in different ways in terms of the underlying information-processing steps. Sticht replied that it is almost certainly true that the *ways* one arrives at the meaning can be different, but operationally, when one assesses whether the subject can perform correctly using information conveyed by either presentation mode, given adequate reading ability, no difference can be found. It was in this latter sense that he concluded that there was but one kind of comprehension.

REFERENCES

Anderson, R. C. Control of student mediating processes during verbal learning and instruction. *Review of Educational Research*, 1970, **40**, 349–369.

Aquino, M. R. The validity of the Miller–Coleman readability scale. *Reading Research Quarterly*, 1969, 4, 342–357.

Ausubel, D. P. The use of advance organizers in the learning and retention of meaningful verbal material. *Journal of Educational Psychology*, 1960, **51**, 267–272.

Ausubel, D.P., & Robinson, F. G. *School learning: An introduction to educational psychology.* New York: Holt, Rinehart & Winston, 1969.

Brassard, Mary. Direct comparisions between listening and reading as language comprehension abilities in the intermediate grades. Paper presented at the meeting of the American Education Research Association, Minneapolis, March, 1970.

Brown, D. P. Auding as the primary language ability. Doctoral dissertation, Stanford University, 1954.

Caffrey, J. Auding ability as a function of certain psychometric variables. Doctoral dissertation, University of California at Berkeley, 1953.

Carroll, J. B. Learning from verbal discourse in educational media: Some research studies. *Proceedings of Project Aristotle Symposium*, Washington, D.C., December, 1967.

Carroll, J. B. *Development of native language skills beyond the early years.* Research Bulletin RB–68–23), Princeton, N.J.: Educational Testing Service, 1968.

Carver, R. P. A critical review of "mathemagenics" and the effect of questions on the retention of prose materials. Paper presented at the meeting of the American Psychological Association, Miami Beach, September, 1970. (a)

Carver, R. P. The hypothesized linear relationship between the presentation rate of meaningful information and the amount of information communicated. Unpublished manuscript, American Institutes for Research, Silver Spring, Md., 1970. (b)

Carver, R. P., Johnson, R. L., & Friedman, H. L. Factor analysis of the ability to comprehend time-compressed speech. Paper presented at the meeting of the American Educational Research Association, New York, February, 1971.

Devine, T. G. A suggested approach to controlled research in language-thinking relationships. *Journal of Research and Development in Education*, 1969, 3, 82–86.

Duker, S. *Listening: Readings*. New York: Scarecrow Press, 1966.

Duker, S. *Listening bibliography*. Metuchen, N. J.: Scarecrow Press, 1968.

Farr, J. N., Jenkins, J. J., & Paterson, D. G. Simplification of Flesch reading ease formula. *Journal of Applied Psychology*, 1951, 35, 333–337.

Fairbanks, G., Guttman, N., & Miron, M. S. Effects of time-compression upon the comprehension of connected speech. *Journal of Speech and Hearing Disorders*, 1957b, 22, 10–19.

Foulke, E. *The comprehension of rapid speech by the blind: Part II*. (Final Progress Report, September 1961–February 1964). Performance Research Laboratory, Department of Psychology, University of Louisville, Louisville, Ky., 1964.

Foulke, E., & Sticht, T.G. Review of research on the intelligibility and comprehension of accelerated speech. *Psychological Bulletin*, 1969, 72, 50–62.

Frase, L. T. Questions as aids to reading: some research and theory. *American Educational Research Journal*, 1968, 5, 319–332.

Frase, L. T. Boundary conditions for mathemagenic behaviors. *Review of Educational Research*, 1970, 40, 337–347.

Friedman, H. L., Graae, C. N., & Orr, D. B. Further research on speeded speech as an educational medium–effects of listening aids and self-pacing on comprehension and the use of compressed speech for review. (Report No. R67–2), American Institutes for Research, Silver Spring, Md., 1967.

Friedman, H. L., & Johnson, R. L. *Time-compressed speech as an educational medium: studies of stimulus characteristics and individual differences*. (Report No. R69–14), American Institutes for Research, Silver Spring, Md., 1969.

Friedman, H. L., Orr, D. B., Freedle, R. O., & Norris, C. M. *Further research on speeded speech as an educational medium*. (Report No. AIR–E–50–1/166–TR(2)), American Institutes for Research, Silver Spring, Md., 1966.

Friedman, H. L., Orr, D. B., & Norris, C. M. *Further research on speeded speech as an educational medium–the use of listening aids*. (Progress Report No. 3), American Institutes for Research, Silver Spring, Md., 1966.

Goldman–Eisler, F. *Psycholinguistics*. New York: Academic Press, 1968.

Huey, E. B. *The psychology and pedagogy of reading*. New York: Macmillan, 1908. (Republished) Cambridge, Mass.: M.I.T. Press, 1968.

James, N. E. Personal preference for method as a factor in learning. *Journal of Educational Psychology*, 1962, 53, 43–47.

Lundsteen, Sara. Critical listening and thinking: a recommended goal for future research. *Journal of Research and Development in Education*, 1969, 3, 119–133.

Miller, G. A. The magical number seven, plus or minus two: Some limits on our capacity for processing information. *Psychological Review*, 1956, 63, 81–97.

Miller, G. R., & Coleman, E. B. A set of thirty-six passages calibrated for complexity. *Journal of Verbal Learning and Verbal Behavior*, 1967, 6, 851–854.

Miller, G. A., & Isard, S. Some perceptual consequences of linguistic rules. *Journal of Verbal Learning and Verbal Behavior*, 1963, 2, 217–228.

Moray, N. *Attention: Selective processes in vision and hearing*. New York: Academic Press, 1969.

Neisser, V. *Cognitive psychology*. New York: Appleton-Century-Crofts, 1967.

Norman, D. *Memory and attention*. New York: John Wiley & Sons, 1969.

Orr, D. B., Friedman, H. L., & Williams, J. C. Trainability of listening comprehension of speeded discourse. *Journal of Educational Psychology*, 1965, 56, 148–156.

Penfield, D. A., & Marascuilo, L. A. Learning to listen: a broad demonstration study. Paper presented at the meeting of the American Educational Research Association, Minneapolis, March, 1970.

Reid, R. H. Grammatical complexity and comprehension of compressed speech. *Journal of Communication*, 1968, 18, 236–242.

Rosenberg, S. The source of facilitation in the recall of associates embedded in connected discourse. In: H. L. Lane & E. M. Zale (Eds.), *Studies in language and language behavior*. (Progress Report No. IV). Center for Research on Language and Language Behavior, University of Michigan, 1967.

Rothkopf, E. Z. Some theoretical and experimental approaches to problems in written instruction. In: J. D. Krumboltz (Ed.), *Learning and the educational process*. Chicago: Rand-McNally, 1965.

Rothkopf, E. Z. The concept of mathemagenic activities. *Review of Educational Research*, 1970, 40, 325–336.

Sanders, J. R. *Short-term and long-term retention effects of adjunct questions in aural discourse: an extension of research on mathemagenic behavior*. (Report No. 43) Laboratory of Educational of Educational Research, University of Colorado, July, 1970.

Sanders, J. R., & Glass, G. V. Short-term and long-term retention effects of adjunct questions in audio discourse: an extension of research on mathemagenic behavior. Paper presented at the meeting of the American Educational Research Association, Minneapolis, 1970.

Smith, K. U., & Smith, Margaret. *Cybernetic principles of learning and educational design*. New York: Holt, Rinehart, & Winston, 1966.

Spearritt, D. A factorial analysis of listening comprehension. Doctoral dissertation, Harvard University, 1961.

Sticht, T. G. Learning by listening in relation to aptitude, reading, and rate controlled speech. (Technical Report 69–23), Human Resources Research Organization, Alexandria, Va., 1969.

Sticht, T. G. Learning by listening in relation to aptitude, reading, and rate controlled speech: additional studies. (Technical Report 71–5), Human Resources Research Organization, Alexandria, Va., 1971.

Sticht, T. G., Caylor, J. S., Kern, R., & Fox, L. C. *Determination of literacy skill requirements in four military occupational specialties*. (Technical Report 71–23), Human Resources Research Organization, Alexandria, Va., 1971.

Taylor, J. L. Use of compressed speech, tapes and discs and of variable frequency power supply with selected children and adults. In: E. Foulke (Ed.), *Proceedings of the Louisville Conference on Time Compressed Speech*, 1966. Center for Rate Controlled Recordings, University of Louisville, Louisville, Ky., 1967.

Thorn, Elizabeth. The effect of direct instruction in listening on the listening and reading comprehension of first grade children. Paper presented at the meeting of the American Educational Research Association, Chicago, February, 1968.

Vineberg, R., Taylor, Elaine, & Sticht, T. G. *Performance in five Army jobs by men at different aptitude levels: 2. Development and description of instruments*. (Technical Report 70–20). Human Resources Research Organization, Alexandria, Va., 1970.

Williams, F. (Ed.) *Language and poverty*. Chicago: Markham Publishing Co., 1970.

12

STRUCTURAL TEXT FEATURES AND THE CONTROL OF PROCESSES IN LEARNING FROM WRITTEN MATERIALS

Ernst Z. Rothkopf
Bell Telephone Laboratories, Inc.

INTRODUCTION

The path of preference in trying to understand how humans learn from written discourse has been to try to explain phenomena through concepts from simpler learning experiments and psycholinguistic studies. We speak of depth of sentences, of right and left branching structures, and explore the usefulness of elegant, simple models of information processing such as those of Trabasso (see Trabasso, Rollins, & Shaughnessy, 1971) and Clark (1969). The verbal learning laboratory has given us concepts such as organization, familiarity, meaningfulness, and the laws of exercise and effect.

Can these powerful ideas be applied to learning from written text in realistic settings? There are some reasons to wonder about this. Not only is it possible to raise the question whether these concepts can be applied usefully to learning from substantial quantities of written material, but also whether these concepts are relevant to the really big effects in this domain.

Research in psycholinguistic and verbal learning has been dominated by concern with structural variables, i.e., the form of the verbal stimulus and its effect on learning. It is the main thesis of this paper that the most important questions about learning from written discourse need instead to bear on the control of processing activities by S. Emphasis on structural variables is not appropriate for learning from written text because the conditions under which readers attempt to learn from written discourse are usually quite different from the conditions under which verbal learning and comprehension has been investigated in the laboratory. The most salient differences are in the magnitudes of verbal input with which the subject has to deal and in the rate in time in which verbal displays are typically inspected.

Discrepancies of Scale

A single trial in a paired-associate study may involve exposure to a list composed of 6 to 12 pairs of terms. Typically, 1 to 50 trials may take place during an experiment. What are therefore studied in a representative paired-associate learning experiment are the changes in verbal performance that result from experience with anywhere from 12 to 1200 words or similar terms. In a typical psycholinguistic study, the unit for experimentation is usually a sentence, perhaps 4 to 16 words in length. If 20 sentences are involved in such a study, the entire experimental procedure may involve a maximum of about 320 words.

The amount of input investigated in the typical paired-associate or psycholinguistic experiment appears small if compared to the verbal inputs in formal educational settings. A typical school assignment may involve anywhere from 1500 to perhaps 5000 words and it is probably not at all uncommon for scholars to read a 5000-word journal article with considerable care. It is safe to assume that a substantial portion of the literate population has read a passage of 25,000 words (e.g., a short detective novel) within a single, almost continuous, time period.

Very rough calculations suggest that the size of the instructional word swarms through which students travel in order to achieve certain educational ends is formidable. Six million to 12 million words is a reasonable estimate of the word swarm which a college students buys in order to obtain a bachelors degree.[1] These numbers are very large indeed compared to those involved in paired-associate experiments, particularly if one considers that units of conceptual analysis in such experiments are usually the events of a single trial.

Input Rate

The rate of presentation in verbal learning experiments almost never exceeds 60 words per minute. Mature students, on the other hand, inspect text at rates that average between 200 and 300 words per minute. In other words, typical text inspection rates may be 3 to 5 times as large as the fastest rate investigated in the reported verbal learning research.

Perhaps the most important difference between laboratory and the world, however, is that readers normally control their own rate of progress. By contrast, in much of the experimental work on the learning process, exposure of the stimulus is rigorously controlled by the experimenter. This difference in control of exposure may invalidate a number of conclusions about the relative importance of certain learning variables that have been drawn from laboratory studies.

Structure of Stimulus Material and Readability

Syntactic complexity and word characteristics such as familiarity are formal characteristics of verbal stimuli that have been extensively investigated in the laboratory. These two factors are interesting in the analysis of the role of formal structure in text learning because they are related to the widely used readability

[1] The upper limit of this estimate was calculated on the basis of 500 pages of reading per course for 32 courses. Word exposure in lectures was calculated at 3750 words per 50-minute lecture (75 words per minute). Each of 32 courses was estimated at 36 lecture periods.

formulae. Comprehensive and exact characterizations of word factors and syntactic complexity are extremely difficult for substantial prose passages. One approach to the solution of this problem is to obtain a statistical estimate of the formal properties of a passage by counting, or otherwise measuring, features that are correlated with the relevant text characteristics. Readability formulas such as the Flesch reading ease index (Flesch, 1948) contribute one class of statistical approximation of this type. The Flesch readability formula is:

$$\text{Reading Ease (R.E.)} = 207.835 - .946\,wl - 1.015\,sl$$

Where wl is the number of syllables per 100 words, and sl is the average number of words per sentence in a 100-word sample of text. Because of availability of computerized procedures (e.g., Coke & Rothkopf, 1970), reading ease indices can easily be obtained for very substantial passage. More sophisticated statistical estimates of formal text structure than the Flesch Reading Ease Index are undoubtedly not only possible, but desirable. The Flesch formula was chosen for the present discussion because experimental data were readily available.

Schlesinger (1968) has pointed out that readability formulae have lacked theoretical orientation. This is, in part, due to the fact that readability formulae were originally developed for a very specific applied purpose, namely, matching written materials to the educational status of readers. Nevertheless, there are very plausible psychological translations of the main readability factors.

Word length (wl) is related in rather untidy but plausible ways to familiarity and meaningfulness because of Zipf's law (1935). This principle states that word length is negatively related to the frequency of occurrence of that word in the language. Substantial correlations have been found between frequency of use in the language, as determined by the Thorndike-Lorge word count, and meaningfulness in the sense of Noble's (1952) m measure. Similar correlations have been found between word frequency and rated familiarity. Average word length, however, is, not a simple indicator of meaningfulness and familiarity because it is strongly influenced by the number of function words and personal pronouns in the text. In that sense, the work length measure reflects the structure of the sentences used in the text as well as characteristics of the individual words. Average sentence length (sl) is an approximate index of syntactic complexity. Short sentences are rarely complex and long sentences frequently are. The experimental evidence on the effect of word factors and syntactic complexity on performance in simple verbal learning and psycholinguistic experiments will not be reviewed in detail. There is very substantial evidence (see Underwood and Schulz, 1960, for an overview) that word familiarity and word meaningfulness affect both short-term and long-term retention when exposure time is controlled. Research on syntax, on the other hand, has been concentrated on the influence of sentence structure on speed of comprehension (e.g., McMahon, 1963; Gough, 1965) and on short-term retention (e.g., Savin & Perchonock, 1965). Some evidence is available, however, from the work of Coleman (1965) that syntactic factors also play some role in long-term retention. Using controlled exposure intervals that ranged upward to 4 words per second, Coleman found that sentences with an active verb were learned 20–30% more rapidly than sentences containing normalizations of the verb. Active sentences were recalled slightly better than passive sentences, and about 10% more information was recalled about nonembedded than about embedded sentences.

Readability Indices and Prose Learning

Meaningfulness, familiarity, and the complexity of sentences have been shown to be related to learning in a number of laboratory investigations. It therefore seems plausible that the average values of such factors in text or readability indices should predict learning from prose materials. An examination of the experimental literature indicates, however, that evidence for the validity of this extrapolation is weak, particularly for situations in which Ss are allowed to determine their own inspection rate. Clear experimental tests of the hypothesis that learning and reading ease are related are scarce. This is, in part, due to the fact that most work on readability has been concerned with the prediction of comprehension, i.e., performance on open book questions, where memory is not a critical factor.

Another reason why it is difficult to find adequate tests of the relationship between the factors that determine readability and learning ease is that many studies have confounded subject matter difficulty or information content with readability. The experimental control of content in prose is technically difficult and it is hard to find studies in which content is held constant while readability, or the factors that determine it, are varied. One indication of the confounding between content variables and readability is the substantial correlations that have been reported between completion test scores and reading ease.

Completion test scores (sometimes called *Cloze* scores, after Taylor, 1954), i.e., the ability to complete partially mutilated text, have been used to estimate the information content of written material. The ability to fill in a missing word reflects constraints that are due to S's experience with the language and due to his previous experience with the subject matter. Therefore, passages with high completion scores contain relatively little new information. Taylor (1954), Coleman (1971), and others have shown that substantial correlations between completion test scores and readability exist in passages sampled from the population of available written material. The correlation between Cloze score and readability can be interpreted to mean that, in some average sense, highly readable passages tend to be passages about which the student knows a good deal. Control for S's prior knowledge is the key problem in analyzing the available experimental evidence in order to determine whether readability really predicts learnability.

One way to overcome the difficulty posed by the correlation between information content and readability is to analyze samples within a very long passage of relatively homogenous content. This was done in a study by M. E. Smith (1967). Smith analyzed the frame characteristic of a 2200 frame self-instructional program, in order to determine how the frame characteristics predicted learned performance on a criterion test. Two findings from a factor analysis are of relevance. Neither shows a strong relationship between factors that determine readability and learning. A sentence complexity factor (number of modifiers, verbal nouns and adjectives, prepositional phrases, clauses, and number of words per sentence) correlated with r's of .05 and .24, respectively, with learning gains for two sub-samples of the self-instructional program. A word complexity factor (affixed word ratios, number of syllables per word, number of vehicular appearances of key terms) was found to correlate with r's of .08 and .00 with learning gains for the two text samples.

Additional evidence to indicate that the correlations between readability and learning were very modest has been obtained by Smith, Rothkopf, and Koether (1970). They obtained learning data for ten 1500-word passages that had been matched as closely as possible for minimum subject matter content. Learning performance was measured by tests based on carefully specified instructional objectives. The 10 experimental passages were selected from a much larger pool of passages by choosing only those that had at least enough content to satisfy the instructional objectives. This was done by means of an open book procedure in which judges determined whether all the questions of a test based on the instructional objectives could be answered from the experimental passage. The 10 experimental passages had been written by 10 different writers. The passages were therefore equivalent in minimum content but differed in structure and style and thus readability. A group of subjects was exposed to each experimental passage and the achievement of the instructional objectives was then evaluated by both a prompted test procedure (using short answer questions) and a free recall test (essays). Table 1 shows the correlations between certain structural features of the texts and effectiveness. These correlations tend to be small, although average word length correlated $-.50$ with free recall.

It is worthwhile to note here that content features appear somewhat more powerful than the structural features of text as predictors of learning. For example, by use of a fairly reliable scoring procedure, Smith and his co-workers determined the number of items in each experimental passage that were not directly related to the instruction objective. This measure is unrelated to passage length, since length was relatively constant (1500 words) for all passages. Figure 1 shows a plot of performance on a free recall (essay) test as a function of the amount of the irrelevant material in the passage. The calculated rank order correlation between learning and amount of irrelevant material was $-.71$.

Another study in which an attempt was made to control content while varying readability factors was reported by Klare, Shuford, and Nichols (1957). Air Force trainees read two versions of a short passage (about 75 words) on engines that

TABLE 1

Correlations of Text Properties with Measures of Free and Stimulated Recall in Ten 1500-Word Passages Equated for Content (Smith *et al.*, 1970)

Text property	Stimulated recall	Free recall
Reading ease (Flesch)	.28	.30
Average sentence length (words)	−.21	.03
Average word length (syllables per 100 words)	−.24	−.50
Number of technical terms	−.34	−.45
Frequency of technical terms	−.31	−.41
Type/token ratio of technical terms	.06	.08
Number of incidental facts	−.59	−.71

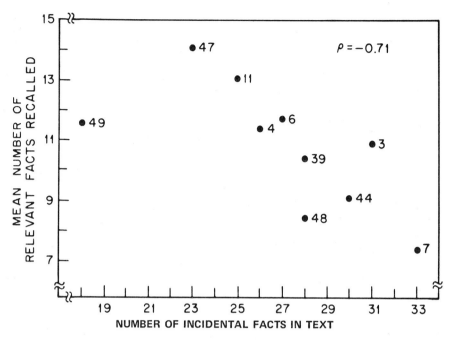

FIG. 1. Correct recall score for ten experimental passages as a function of the amount of material that was not relevant to the instructional objectives in each text.

differed greatly in readability (grades 5–6 vs. 13–15 as calculated from the Flesch formula). The two versions were observed to differ significantly on one retention test (recall) but not on another. Unfortunately, the test averages for the two treatments were not reported.

Klare, in a review of the readability literature, concludes elsewhere (1963, p. 16), "if the reader is not strictly limited in the time he may spend on a piece of writing . . . an increase in readability may not produce a corresponding increase in comprehension."

The number of studies relevant to the effects of readability on learning is too small to allow generalization across the large domain of English texts. But available evidence, bolstered by the absence of strong demonstrations to the contrary, plausibly supports the conclusion that sentence complexity and lexical factors such as frequency of use have *small* effects on what is learned from text by *adults providing that inspection time is not limited.*

Adaption to Text Difficulty

Formal stylistic attributes of text do not appear to affect learning strongly when exposure time is not controlled by the experimenter. One possible explanation for this is that S's process text in a manner that adapts itself to difficult passage constructions. The writer or the experimenter may choose text constructions that have been demonstrated to be difficult in small-scale laboratory experiments using short exposure intervals. But, within some limits, S in self-paced situations, can handle a substantial variety of difficulty levels and reduce them to the same level of internal representation by appropriate processing activities. There is some evidence that inspection is, under some circumstances, adjusted to formal aspects of text.

Klare *et al.* (1957) have reported that when two passages have the same content, the more readable passage resulted in more words per fixation and faster average inspection rate (words/minute) than the less readable text. This finding must be interpreted with some caution, however, because the average number of syllables per word is not the same in the two text versions. The treatments may therefore be equal if inspection rate is calculated in syllables per minute.

The writer (in preparation) has also found relationships between text difficulty and inspection rate. Subjects were allowed to inspect at their own rate a 19-paragraph passage about Thailand. Each paragraph was on a photographic slide and inspection time was automatically recorded for each slide. Two versions of the passage were used, differing in average sentence length and average number of syllables per word. Flesch reading ease as determined by a computer program (see Coke and Rothkopf, 1970) was 51.03 ($\sigma = 10.67$) and 20.14 ($\sigma = 14.38$), respectively. Half of the Ss read the first 10 paragraphs in the normal version, while the remainder read the difficult one. For paragraphs 11−19, half of these groups were switched to the other version so that one quarter of the Ss read, respectively, (a) the difficult version in its entirety, i.e., paragraphs 1−19; (b) the difficult version, paragraphs 1−10 followed by the normal version, paragraphs 11−19; (c) the normal version in its entirety, paragraphs 1−19; (d) the normal version, paragraphs 1−10 followed by the difficult, paragraphs 11−19.

Differences in inspection rate (syllables per minute) due to text difficulty are apparent in the left-hand panels of Figures 2 and 3. The easier version was inspected approximately 50 syllables per minute faster than the difficult form of the text.

A second phenomenon investigated in this experiment was the effect of context on inspection speed. Does the readability of one passage affect the rate at which a subsequent passage is read? The results of the experiment that were relevant to this question are shown in the right-hand panel of Figures 2 and 3. The data in Figure 2 indicate that Ss read paragraphs 11−19, in the "normal" form, more slowly if they read the difficult version of paragraphs 1−10 than if they read paragraphs 1−10 in the "normal" version. A similar, although much smaller context effect, is shown in Figure 3. Paragraphs 11−19, in the more difficult form, were inspected more rapidly by Ss who had the normal version of paragraphs 1−10 than by those who saw paragraphs 1−10 in the difficult form.

The context effects in Figures 2 and 3 were accompanied by small but significant learning effects. On a test covering paragraphs 11−19 that was administered after reading, the groups who read the difficult version of paragraphs 1−10 performed somewhat better than those who read paragraphs 1−10 in the normal form. The learning effect produced by context was more pronounced when the normal version of paragraphs 11−19 was used.

There are two conclusions to be drawn in these studies. First of all, Ss tend to adapt themselves to the difficulty of the materials that they are studying. This tends to neutralize the effect of variables that have been shown to influence learning in experimental situations where exposure time is controlled. Secondly,

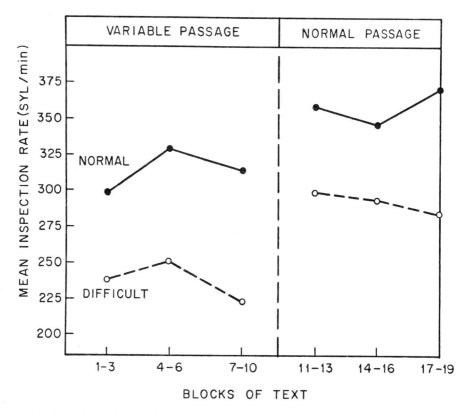

FIG. 2. Mean inspection rate in syllables per minute for successive segments of text. The data in the left-hand panel are for two groups inspecting text of unequal difficulty. In the right-hand panel, both groups are inspecting the same text of average difficulty.

these adaptive processes are not very finely tuned. Inspection rate, and presumably the underlying associated processes, have some persistence. These processes have some determinants other than the nature of the materials that are being inspected at any given time.

These two conclusions imply that laboratory findings relating text characteristics such as sentence structure, word factors, and perhaps the organization of information to learning, may be of lesser importance than usually estimated if realistic study situations prevail and Ss control their own inspection rate. Factors that determine the processing of written discourse may have greater impact on what will be learned from written documents than structural factors.

The Concept of Mathemagenic Activities

The writer (Rothkopf 1963, 1965, 1968, 1970), in theoretical analyses of learning from written discourse, has argued for the critical importance of the distinction between nominal and effective stimuli in this domain. In studying written text, S's activities determine to a very important degree what the effective stimuli will be; i.e., S is the final determinator of the nature of internal representation of the text.   The nature of the internal representation, in turn, determines what is learned. This is almost a truism, and should require little further comment except for the fact that it is so frequently neglected in   psycholinguistic analyses of reaction to   written   discourse.

What is being claimed is that the analysis of the structure of text is not the most important source of prediction about learning. The analysis of the subject's activities while he is exposed to the text is certainly at least as important. The determinants of the subject's processing activities are by no means restricted to text features. Instead, a variety of environmental factors and context effects operate on the subject. This is the central topic for the research that has been carried on during the last few years on so-called mathemagenic activities, i.e., activities that give birth to learning.

Mathemagenic activity is a concept that has proven useful in accounting for various phenomena associated with the subject's control of effective stimulation in written instruction. The concept includes a variety of dispositions that have been studied extensively in the laboratory, such as attention, learning to learn, set, etc.

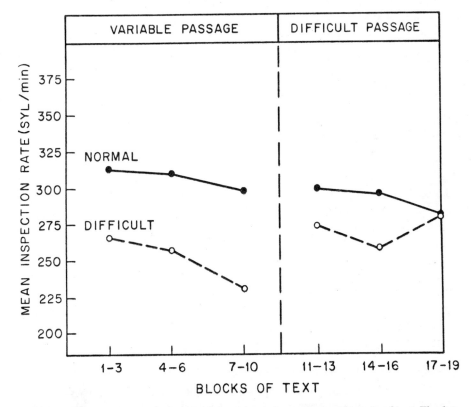

FIG. 3. Mean inspection rate in syllables per minute for successive segments of text. The data in the left-hand panel are for two groups inspecting text of unequal difficulty. In the right-hand panel, both groups are inspecting the same, difficulty text.

and also the ill-defined class of activities that are popularly referred to as reading. Mathemagenic activity is not, strictly speaking, a theoretical construct, but rather a concept that refers to a class of related scientific and practical problems. A working *definition* of mathemagenic activities is that they are those student activities that are relevant to the achievement of specified instructional objectives in specified situations or places (Rothkopf, 1970). No attempt will be made to review here, in depth, the studies concerning mathemagenic activities. In the main, experimental studies have concerned themselves with the control of mathemagenic activities by the use of adjunct questions and direction. The various processing activities that subjects engage in while confronted with text are inferred, in many cases, by indirect methods, mainly by measurement of what learning has taken place. The main tenor of the findings has been that manipulation, such as presenting questions, can produce general learning effects, i.e., that questions affect the acquisition of information other than that narrowly required to answer the adjunct questions. There are some experimental indications that mathemagenic activities are adaptive. Questions and directions are classes of events that exert some environmental pressures on mathemagenic activities.

The shaping through test-like events is thought to work in the following way. Subjects engage in a variety of activities while studying discourse. The consequence of some of these activities is to translate nominal stimuli of the instructional material into effective stimuli. The nature of the effective stimuli determines the substantive learning that results from exposure to the text. Suppose a question is asked of the subject and he is able to answer it adequately. This would be a reinforcing event for the pattern of study activity (mathemagenic activity) that has preceded it and would tend to maintain that pattern of mathemagenic activities during subsequent study. If, on the other hand, the subject fails to answer the question, this would be like an extinction event for all (or some) of the mathemagenic activities that preceded that test failure. This would tend to decrease the likelihood that the same study pattern would be employed in the future and increase the likelihood that other mathemagenic activity patterns would emerge. These, in turn, would be shaped by subsequent test-like events. The hypothesis that mathagenic activities are shaped by questions and other test-like events does not mean that questions are necessarily effective instructional strategies. What it means, instead, is that *S*'s activities tend to adapt themselves to the questions that are asked of him during the course of study. If these questions are representative of the criterion test, then questions are an effective instructional tool. If, on the other hand, questions are *not* representative of the instrument that defines learning, then questions may lead to study activities that have no effect on the desired final performance or that will actually reduce it below the level that could be expected without any questions at all.

Experimental Evidence for the Mathemagenic Concept

The usefulness of the mathemagenic concept has been confirmed by experiments on the use of adjunct questions with written material. The experiments were, in general, conducted as follows. Subjects were asked to read a very long passage (5000—15,000 words) with relatively high factual content. Adjunct questions were inserted in the passage at regular intervals (about every 750 words). The student was directed to answer each question. The correct answer could be supplied to the student immediately following his response, although in some experimental conditions this was not done. The student inspected the text at his own rate. Shortly after inspection of the written passage, the student was given a criterion test in order to find out out how much he had learned.

A technical trick was used to isolate the direct instructive effects of questions from their effect on mathemagenic activities. The questions used on the criterion test were chosen in such a way as to be unrelated to the specific matter from which the adjunct questions that had been used during study were derived. The two sets of questions, the adjunct questions and the questions of the criterion test, were related only in that they were chosen from the same passage and equally from all sections of the passage, and in that they concerned themselves with the same general topic. This was done in the following way. A large pool of questions from all parts of the text was collected. This pool was divided into two subsets, such that there was no transfer of training from the knowledge required for subset A to that required to answer the questions of subset B correctly. This meant that a student who knew enough to answer all subset A questions correctly, would nevertheless perform at chance level on subset B items. This was experimentally verified by having students learn sufficient material to answer all questions in subset A perfectly and then testing to see whether this produced any gain in performance on questions from subset B. Any question in subset B for which even small chance gains were observed was eliminated from use in the experiment. Questions in subset A were then used as adjunct questions. Subset B became the criterion examination.

In this experimental scheme, questions can have two roles. The first is a direct instructive effect. It depends on the information value of questions, and on rehearsal. This aspect of the use of questions depends on the law of exercise. It is measurable by testing subjects on the kinds of materials to which the adjunct questions were directly relevant. The second role of questions is to modify mathemagenic activities. This probably depends on the law of effect although this has by no means been completely proven.

The influence of questions on mathemagenic activities may be measured through test items that are completely unrelated to the material covered by the adjunct questions. Only an existential proof is possible by this method. The measurable effects of changes in mathemagenic behavior depend critically on the relationship between the adjunct questions and the questions on which the criterion test is based. If there is no measurable effect, this does not mean that the adjunct questions do not produce changes in mathemagenic activity, only that suitable conditions for observation of mathemagenic activities have not been arranged. However, if criterion test performance is altered by the use of adjunct questions, this strongly supports the belief that some changes in mathemagenic activities must have taken place.

Several findings from a series of these experiments are of interest. We compared the direct instructive effects and the mathemagenic effects of questions that appeared just before the material to which the questions were relevant to those produced by questions that appeared just after. The experimental facts were clear

Direct instructive effects were produced regardless of the position of the questions, even though it is possible that the direct instructive effect of questions presented just before the material depends on a different mechanism than that of questions asked just after inspection of the relevant material. Effects on mathemagenic activity, on the other hand, were produced only by questions that followed exposure to the relevant material (Rothkopf, 1966; Rothkopf & Bisbicos, 1967; Rothkopf & Bloom, 1970). This suggests that changes in mathemagenic activities are brought about by tests of the knowledge that has been acquired.

These experiments also indicate that informative feedback, that is, "knowledge of results," was important only with respect to the direct instructive effects of questions (Rothkopf, 1966). When knowledge of results was provided after S made his response, performance on the materials to which the question had been relevant was stronger than when no knowledge of results was provided. Knowledge of results, on the other hand, had no effect on changes in mathemagenic activity. This does not mean, however, that outcomes were unimportant with respect to modification of mathemagenic activities. Subjects who cannot answer a question have thereby received information about the adequacy of the knowledge which he has acquired during reading even though explicit feedback has not been provided.

Another finding of these experiments was that the nature of the adjunct questions influences the nature of the knowledge acquired from written discourse (Rothkopf & Bisbicos, 1967). For example, if the adjunct questions contain a large number of items dealing with quantitative terms, recall of quantitative material is enhanced on the criterion test. This suggests that adjunct questions requiring quantitative answers shape the kind of mathemagenic activities that are necessary to recover quantitative information from the written material. We might imagine, for example, that this type of adjunct question makes it less likely that S skips over a sentence that contained numerical terms. There is a strong temptation to think S's intention is somehow related to this phenomenon. It is doubtful that this is really true. There are two reasons for thinking this. First of all, the intention hypothesis says that Ss find out from the adjunct questions what they are supposed to learn. They then govern their study activities accordingly. Yet it was observed that Ss who received their adjunct questions prior to seeing the information to which the questions were relevant did not show any adaptive changes in mathemagenic activities. Certainly, if intention were the critical principle here, this treatment should have resulted in appropriate general performance changes. A second reason for discrediting the intention hypothesis is that there is substantial evidence from the work of Postman and his collaborators (see Postman, 1964) that when adequate arrangements were made to assure that the subject has attended to his environment, learning about the environment took place regardless of intention.

Finally, it has been possible to show by experiment that the persistence of study activities is influenced by the use of adjunct questions (Rothkopf, 1968). The items in the criterion test, administered to the students after reading, were designed so that it was possible to determine from what page in the 36-page text the information necessary to answer each item was drawn. Four items on the criterion test were drawn from each three pages (750 words) of the source text. By looking at performance on items from the various portions of the text, it was possible to map the effectiveness of the mathemagenic activities that prevail throughout the various portions of the text during reading. In this way it was possible to show that when adjunct questions were omitted, mathemagenic activities tend to become less effective, and that the number of adjunct questions asked per text unit probably determines how quickly mathemagenic activity deteriorates after the cessation of questions. This is an important phenomenon which unfortunately is not completely understood. Results from a number of different measures taken on Ss during study, such as inspection time and learning, suggest that when there is little outside support, the effectiveness of mathemagenic activity tends to deteriorate.

Inspection Time and Adjunct Questions

The argument has been made earlier that adjustments in inspection time tend to neutralize the effects of structural characteristics of text on learning. Presumably this is because inspection time is associated with the operation of underlying processes necessary for learning.

Questions constitute one class of environmental pressures that are thought to influence these underlying processes. What are the effects of adjunct questions on inspection time? The relationship between text and environmental variables and inspection time has not been fully explored. Nor has the relationship between inspection time and subsequent learned performance been analyzed to the extent that its potential importance would suggest.

Adjunct questions have been found to have fairly clear-cut short term effects on inspection time. Average inspection time for text segments that just precede an adjunct question tends to be consistently shorter than inspection time for text segments that immediately follow questions. Relevant data of this nature are illustrated in Table 2 which is from a study by Rothkopf and Bloom (1970). The experimental treatment represented in that table have been exposed to one adjunct question after every 6 text slides, or about once every 750 words. The questions were always derived from the set of 6 slides that had just been inspected. Ss in the control condition saw no question whatsoever. It may be noted that for the experimental treatment, average inspection rate in syllables per minute for text slides following questions consistently exceeds inspection rate for text slides that precede questions. For the control treatment, the difference in inspection rate between slides presented in equivalent positions to those compared in the

TABLE 2

Number of Subjects in Each Treatment Whose Average Inspection Rate for Pages Immediately Before Experimental Questions (R_B) was Greater than Average Inspection Rate on Pages Just After the Experimental Questions (R_A)

Item	Oral question	Written question	No question
$R_B > R_A$	18	14	7
$R_B < R_A$	3	7	14
Total	21	21	21

experimental treatments reflects only the acceleration in inspection rate usually observed in the course of prolonged reading.

The situation is somewhat cloudier when the effect of treatment on average inspection time over all pages is considered. There have been no consistent overall treatment effects on inspection time. Treatments involving adjunct questions have tended to produce somewhat longer average inspection times. However, there were a number of notable exceptions within experiments. Nor have the treatments that have produced the best learning results always produced the longest average inspection times. Small positive correlations have been found between average inspection time per treatment and average performance on the criterion test.

It should be pointed out that the inspection time measurement techniques that were used in earlier studies in our laboratory were not very reliable. Subjects simply recorded the time they started and the time that they completed each page in the experimental text. It would seem plausible that this may have accounted for the apparently disorderly data. In more recent studies (e.g., Rothkopf & Bloom, 1970), fully automatic techniques for recording inspection time were used. While Ss were reading a passage approximately 14,000 words in length, inspection time data were measured for 100- to 150-word segments of text. Even with these improved recording techniques, the relationship between treatments that produce average changes in learning performance and average inspection time has been erratic and without apparent pattern.

A recent experiment on the social context in which adjunct questions are used during the studies of written instructive materials (Rothkopf, 1972), has provided further data on the relationships among inspection time, test performance, and adjunct question treatments. This experiment was made possible by the development of better procedures for recording inspection time and by the development of computer techniques for measuring certain text characteristics. Coke and Rothkopf (1970) developed simple computer routines for measuring the number of syllables, words and sentences in passages. This has made it possible to carry out extensive readability analysis for passage segments and has also made it practicable to consider rate of inspection rather than simple inspection time. The following techniques were used to measure S's tendency to change inspection rates during the course of reading.

Subjects read a passage on geology that was approximately 14,000 words in length and that had been photographed on 90 negative slides. The first 24 slides were inspected under the same condition for all Ss. Immediately following slide 30, one group of Ss received adjunct questions at the rate of one question for every six slides. Another treatment group saw no questions. They inspected slides 25–90 under the same conditions as slides 1–24. Inspection time was recorded for each slide. Exactly ten minutes after the inspection of slide 90, learned performance was measured with a 26-item retention test. Subjects under the two treatments were divided into four groups on the basis of changes in inspection rates. (syllables per minute) during inspection of the first 24 text slides. Changes in inspection rate were calculated by subtracting average inspection rate of slides 13–24 from average rate on slides 1–12. In Figure 4, learning gains are plotted for the two treatments as function of change in inspection rate in the first part of the text. Learning gain was

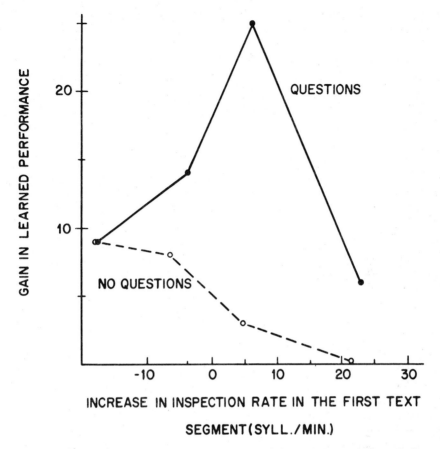

FIG. 4. Gain in learned performance as a function of change in inspection rate during the initial portion of the text. Gain is the difference between average proportion correct response on criterion text items Part I (Slides 1–24) and from Part II (Slides 25–90).

the difference between the proportion of correct responses on criterion test items derived from slides 25–90 and the proportion of correct responses on items from slides 1–24.

The data in Figure 4 indicate that for the *no-question* group learning gains decreased monotonically with initial increases in inspection rate. For the group receiving adjunct questions, on the other hand, the relationship between the initial tendency to change inspection rate and learning gains was considerably more complex. The subjects who slowed down by syllables per minute (or more) during the first 24 slides were hardly aided by questions. This was also true for those who accelerated by more than 20 syllables per minute. Those who slowed down slightly or accelerated by about 5 syllables per minute were substantially aided by adjunct questions.

Figure 5 offers some clues as to how these learning effects came about. It is a plot of changes in inspection rate in the second part of the text (slides 25–90) as a function of changes in inspection rate in the first part (slides 1-24). For the

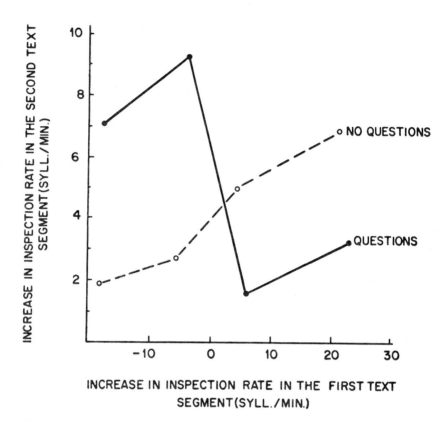

FIG. 5. Change in inspection rate in Part II of the text (Slides 25–90) as a function of inspection rate changes in Part I (Slides 1–24).

no-question treatment, Part II changes are a monotonic, increasing function of changes in Part I. The data for the *question* group indicate that those who slowed down somewhat in Part I show greater acceleration in Part II than those who accelerated in Part I.

The adjunct question apparently had moderated *S*s' initial tendencies to change inspection rate and this proved adaptive to the goals of instruction. The changes in processing activity which this moderation reflects apparently resulted in more effective harvesting of information.

CONCLUSION

This paper explored the thesis that certain formal characteristics of language that have been shown by experiment to affect verbal learning may not be very powerful in determining what is learned from substantial quantities of written discourse. It was proposed that this was true because the experimental procedures that have characteristically been used in fundamental learning research employ experimenter-controlled exposure intervals and very small amount of stimulus material. Realistic reading situations, on the other hand, involve control of inspection rate by S and quantities of written materials that are several orders of magnitudes greater than those typically employed in the laboratory. The subject's control over his own inspection rate allows the operation of processes that tend to neutralize factors that affect difficulty when exposure is controlled by the experimenter.

There are substantial indications that the subject's activities while confronted with written text are crucial determinants of what is learned. The fact that it has been possible to show that environmental manipulations (as contrasted with manipulations of text factors) affect processing activities suggests that these manipulations deserve more careful and energetic experimental attention.

A Creaky Metaphor: The Information Eater

The model of learning and understanding man that has been evolved in the laboratory is that of the information eater. The information eater has a very lively metabolism, perhaps closer to the rapid metabolism of the shrew than that of men or cows. Laboratory experiments in learning have tended to be nutritional studies. The kind of questions that have been asked are, like, "How is daily gain in weight affected by what you place in the feed bin and by how often you do it?". Psycholinguistic studies, on the other hand, particularly those concerned with comprehension, have been asking how digestible certain informational tid-bits were; how long does it take them into nutrients and does this interfere with the digestion of anything else. The question of real gains in weight are often not asked.

The model of the nutritional process based on experiments with daily well-weighted portions does not necessarily shed light on what controls long term weight gains in ad libitum feeding situations. For here, not only food but the innate and/or acquired wisdoms and limitations of the organism about feeding determine what weight is gained and how great the digestive disturbances. Food intakes become interdependent and the limitations and wisdoms of the feeding body serve as an averaging process.

The metaphor creaks a little, but is really quite appropriate for learning from substantial portions of written discourse. The effects of text components become interdependent not only in the sense that there is interference and facilitation among acquired knowledge, but also because inspection of some text segment influences whether and how other text segments are inspected. Furthermore, there are strong averaging effects in inspecting text that tend to change the effects that certain variables have been observed to have in more insulated contexts.

Limitations of Theories

The theoretical analysis of the underlying processes in learning from written discourse is challenging. It is very tempting to trade scientific prudence and modesty for the intellectual titillations of elegant theorizing. Serious theory building is at present limited by the sparse measurement techniques that are available to us.

Anyone who has ever conducted an experiment on learning from written text is struck by the mute and unrevealing posture of the reader. The processes that must be taking place have to be inferred from crude learning measures or from inspection time data in a very indirect manner. The latter are often confounded by a number of extra-experimental factors, such as intelligence. If the content of theories is more elaborate than their observational basis, the theories are unlikely to do more than feed the vanity of their authors.

Much of the tentative character of the arguments proposed in this paper is due to the crude measures of experimental outcomes that are available and due to the difficulty in finding suitable operational definitions for conceptual terms. The latter problem is not the result of difficulty in finding defining operations per se, but rather in phrasing these definitions so that they will have sufficient generality to transcend the confines of a particular experimental situation.

The argument for the limited usefulness of certain laboratory findings for an understanding of the salient phenomena in learning from written text has been illustrated in this paper almost exclusively on the basis of examples involving sentence structure and selected word characteristics. Other factors that have been isolated in the laboratory also probably suffer from the same limitations. Included here should be various organization variables such as sequence of presentations. Frase and Silbiger (1970), for example, have nicely demonstrated that trade-offs are possible between organization factors and environmental controls of study activities. It is not possible, however, to pursue this argument further within the limits of this paper.

The thesis that processing by the subjects compensates for text difficulty in situations where inspection time is not limited raises some questions about the relationship between the concept of *understanding* and learning from written text. Several psycholinguists have treated understanding as a primitive term that requires little further definition. This is a curious metaphysical position since it seems to demand that verbal communications have some *true* content known, perhaps, to some supernatural arbitrator of information exchanges.

The experimental literature, on the other hand, teaches that an instructive communications can have a great many consequences. Many of these can be thought of, in some sense, as being veridical. The full range "true messages" becomes apparent only when the very large domain of possible test questions or situations is fully considered. It seems a more realistic position to assess the effectiveness of a communication in terms of pre-selected, narrowly specified outcomes.

CONFERENCE DISCUSSION

Questions were raised about Rothkopf's study. He showed that if the text to be read consists of a difficult part followed by a moderately difficult part, the reading rate speeds up for the second part, but that if, on the other hand, the first part is very easy and is followed by the moderately difficult part, the reading rate decreases. Rothkopf's conclusion was that the ways we process information are influenced by what has just gone before—or that, to put it another way, we *adapt* to the levels of difficulty of the materials. Carroll inquired whether an alternative explanation might not be that there are confounding effects due to the amount learned across the two halves, such that the reader may have learned less when the hard material came first; when he then turned his attention to the easier second part, his reading rate was retarded because of his incomplete comprehension of the first portion. Rothkopf acknowledged that this might be an alternative explanation. Scriven thought that inspection rate is not a very revealing measure of the degree of comprehension. It is possible, he pointed out, to write down propositions which very few people can understand—even if given an unlimited amount of inspection time. As an example, some people fail to grasp a mathematical proof even when they have all the steps in the derivation explicitly listed and are given an unlimited amount of time to read and reread the proof.

In another group of studies, Rothkopf dealt with the effect that adjunct questions had on what was learned from text. Such adjunct "aids" (questions given prior to exposure to the text) appear to alter the kinds of processing that subjects engage in; thus, they appear to influence what the effective or functional stimulus is upon exposure to the text. Scriven wondered whether these results couldn't be explained by saying that adjunct questions operate as cues telling the subject what is important to remember. [*Editors' note*: Frederiksen's chapter in this volume, though, showed that superordinate processing that occurs when the subject must use the text information to find solutions to a social problem posed prior to reading can be accounted for by examining the particular relationships that this prior question or problem has to the total passage—if the question deals with only a portion and not all of the text, then this *reduces* what is remembered or inferred, but if the question or problem forces the subject to use all or much of the text in searching for a solution, then this *increases* what is remembered and what will be inferred. The reader is also referred to Frase's chapter for a somewhat similar set of results. One might further relate this to the effect that *topic* sentences may have on the degree of processing of text: If a topic sentence is relevant to only a small portion or paragraph of the text, then it might shape a correspondingly small part of what is learned, whereas if the organizing topic sentence helps to state many of the interrelations that will be touched upon in the text, this should correspondingly increase the subject's ability to remember and draw inferences from what he reads.]

Carroll, Scriven, and Crothers thought that Rothkopf may have been overstating his claim that *structural* features of text play almost no role in self-paced instructional settings. As examples, they suggested that sentences that have been thoroughly scrambled, so as to disrupt their structural properties, or in which one has systematically substituted difficult and obscure synonyms for familiar words, will almost certainly be hard or impossible to comprehend, regardless of whether the instructional setting is self-paced or not. Rothkopf suggested that in the extreme cases just mentioned it is probably true that 'structure' can be shown to influence comprehension, but for the kinds of materials he has been dealing with he thought his claim was defensible.

Freedle wondered whether some individuals bring very special previously learned superordinate organizers to bear on materials that they read. For example, if one is given scientific passages to read, it is possible that some subjects will have discovered that temporal and spatial concepts mentioned in the text are virtually always useful as organizing concepts in science. As a consequence, they may pay special attention to assertions in the text which mention particular spatial or temporal aspects of key concepts and may, as well, also use these superordinate concepts of space and time to chunk together in their memory text information that matches these categories. This last effect would be akin to semantic word clustering in memory except that here it involves clustering of propositional content rather than just isolated words. Perhaps repeated training in using such organizing concepts may facilitate comprehension of new scientific materials to which one is exposed. Scriven, however, thought that the discovery of such organizing concepts (if there are such) would not explain the difficulties that his students had in learning to write good précis of complex text. It would appear that his students were failing to find a *match* between the concepts asserted in this complex text and their own current repertoire of concepts. Mere reexposure to the text did not suffice to help them grasp these unfamiliar concepts. However, exposure to good as well as bad examples of précis did apparently aid them in discovering the meaning of these unfamiliar relations, with the consequence that they could then write good précis of the complete text. Crothers, however, partly supported Freedle's comment by mentioning that some of the subjects who responded to his text on nebulae (see this volume) were physics majors. They happened to mention explicitly time and space as superordinate organizers in their recall protocols. This suggests that for materials which assert complex relations that are within the current grasp of students, such organizing principles or strategies may facilitate comprehension and memory when it comes time to recall the passage.

Frederiksen wanted to know how the above results will influence the next steps taken in reading research. Rothkopf replied that he was moving in the direction of searching for better learning measures which are more closely connected to the text content. In this regard he mentioned the following study (Rothkopf & Thurner, 1970): Subjects were exposed to large amounts of physics text and then given a word association test of key terms from this text. A measure of overlap among these key terms was then computed. A somewhat similar overlap measure was defined textually for these key terms by counting the number of co-occurrences of each pair of terms within the same text sentences. A comparison of these two overlap measures suggested that the subjects' word assocations were matching the 'associations' of key terms as they occurred in the physics text; however, additional tests which evaluated the subjects' comprehension of physics theory showed no evidence for learning. Scriven was critical of this and many other studies reported at the conference because he thought they were merely scratching the surface of certain larger issues involved in comprehension: The problems involved in *mastering* a field of study, a theory, or some area of specialization. The problem of understanding what is involved in mastery learning certainly requires more penetrating tools of analysis than that provided, say, by word association studies. Scriven thought that only by redistributing our research emphasis so as to include these larger issues can we hope to increase our scientific understanding of the relationship between knowledge acquisition and language comprehension.

Rothkopf did not deny these limitations; he said Scriven's remarks in part exposed our current inability to satisfactorily isolate *content* variables from other factors that contribute to reading difficulty, such as stylistic clarity or nonclarity of authors. This problem of content difficulty versus, say, stylistic or structural difficulty must still be a relevant consideration even if our attention is directed to such matters as mastery learning.

REFERENCES

Clark, H. H. Linguistic processes in deductive reasoning. *Psychological Review,* 1969,76, 387–404.

Coke, U., & Rothkopf, E. Z. Note on a simple algorithm for a computer-produced reading ease score. *Journal of Applied Psychology,* 1970, 54, 208–210.

Coleman, E. B. Learning of prose written in four grammatical transformations. *Journal of Applied Psychology,* 1965, 49, 332–341.

Coleman, E. B. Developing a technology of written instruction: Some determiners of the complexity of prose. In E. Z. Rothkopf & P. Johnson (Eds.), *Verbal learning research and the technology of written instruction.* New York: Columbia University Teachers College Press, 1971.

Flesch, R. F. A new readability yardstick. *Journal of Applied Psychology,* 1948, 32, 221–233.

Frase, L. T., & Silbiger, F. Some adaptive consequences of searching for information in a text. *American Educational Research Journal.,* 1970, 7, 553–560.

Gough, P. B. Grammatical transformations and speed of understanding. *Journal of Verbal Learning and Verbal Behavior.* 1965, 4, 107–111.

Klare, G R. *The measurement of readability.* Ames, Iowa: Iowa State University Press, 1963.

Klare, G. R., Shuford, E. H., & Nichols, W. H. The relationship of style difficulty, practice, and ability to efficiency of reading and to retention. *Journal of Applied Psychology,* 1957, 41, 222–226.

McMahon, L. E. Grammatical analysis as part of understanding a sentence. Unpublished doctoral dissertation, Harvard University, 1963.

Noble, C. E. An analysis of meaning. *Psychological Review,* 1952, **59**, 421–430.

Postman, L. Short-term memory and incidental learning. In A. W. Melton (Ed.) *Categories of human learning.* New York: Academic Press, 1964.

Rothkopf, E. Z. Some conjectures about inspection behavior in learning from written sentences and the response mode problem in programmed self-instruction. *Journal of Programmed Instruction.,* 1963, **2**, 31–46.

Rothkopf, E. Z. Some theoretical and experimental approaches to problems in written instruction. In J. D. Krumboltz (Ed.), *Learning and the educational process.* Chicago: Rand McNally, 1965.

Rothkopf, E. Z. Learning from written materials: An exploration of the control of inspection behavior by test-like events. *American Educational Research Journal,* 1966, **3**, 241–249.

Rothkopf, E. Z. Two scientific approaches to the management of instruction. In R. M. Gagne & W. J. Gephard (Eds.), *Learning research and school subjects.* Itasca, Ill.: F. E. Peacock, 1968.

Rothkopf, E. Z. The concept of mathemagenic activities. *Review of Educational Research,* 1970, **40**, 325–336.

Rothkopf, E. Z. Variable adjunct question schedules, interpersonal interaction, and incidental learning from written material. *Journal of Educational Psychology,* 1972, **63**, 87–92.

Rothkopf, E. Z., & Bisbicos, E. E. Selective facilitative effects of interspersed questions on learning from written material. *Journal of Educational Psychology,* 1967, **58**, 56–61.

Rothkopf, E. Z., & Bloom, R. D. Effects of interpersonal interaction on the instructional value of adjunct questions in learning from written material *Journal of Educational Psychology,* 1970, **61**, 417–422.

Rothkopf, E. Z., & Thurner, R. D. Effects of written instructional material on the statistical structure of test essays. *Journal of Educational Psychology,* 1970, **61**, 83–89.

Savin, H. G., & Perchonock, E. Grammatical structure and the immediate recall of English sentences. *Journal of Verbal Learning and Verbal Behavior,* 1965, **4**, 348–353.

Schlesinger, I. M. *Sentence structure and the reading process.* The Hague: Mouton, 1968.

Smith, M. E. Prediction of effects with selected characteristics of linear programmed instruction. Unpublished doctoral dissertation, Purdue University, 1967.

Smith, M. E., Rothkopf, E. Z., & Koether, M. The evaluation of instructional text: Relating properties of free recall protocals to text properties. American Educational Research Association Meeting, Washington, D.C., 1970. P. 47. (abstract)

Taylor, W. L. Application of "cloze" and entropy measures to the study of contextual constraint in samples of continuous prose. Unpublished doctoral dissertation, University of Illinois, 1954.

Trabasso, T., Rollins, H., & Shaughnessy, E. Storage and verification stages in processing concepts. *Cognitive Psychology,* 1971, **2**, 239–289.

Underwood, B. J., & Schulz, R. W. *Meaningfulness and verbal learning.* Chicago: Lippincott, 1960.

Zipf, G. K. *The psycho-biology of language.* Boston: Houghton Mifflin, 1935.

13

MAINTENANCE AND CONTROL IN THE ACQUISITION OF KNOWLEDGE FROM WRITTEN MATERIALS

Lawrence T. Frase
Bell Telephone Laboratories

In 1908, Edmund Burke Huey said that " . . . to completely analyze what we do when we read would almost be the acme of a psychologist's achievements, for it would be to describe very many of the most intricate workings of the human mind, as well as to unravel the tangled story of the most remarkable specific performance that civilization has learned in all its history" (Huey, 1908, p. 6). Huey's own experimental work and logical analysis of the reading process clearly reveal that he considered its components characteristic of thinking in general; thus he suggested a broad program of research in an area fraught with pedagogical implications. But at that time scarcely anyone was listening, either in education or in experimental psychology.

After 63 years the situation is beginning to change. The cumulative record of research on prose materials over the past ten years is a positively accelerating function. More important than the number of studies that use the words "prose," "written materials," or "text" in their titles is that the experimental emphasis is shifting toward an analysis of the specifics of the reading process; it no longer seems fruitful to intercorrelate scores from a number of grossly defined variables.

Part of the current trend toward the analysis of process is due to recent changes in what makes for acceptable research. Since Miller, Galanter, and Pribram's book (1960), *Plans and the Structure of Behavior*, and Chomsky's (1957) work on syntactic structure, we have become less uneasy when we talk about complex series of cognitive operations. In many respects educational psychologists can breathe easier. But there is still the demand to make one's research or research ideas somehow relevant to the larger enterprise of instruction. One way to do this is to choose a task with some face validity, like reading, and to focus upon portions of the process that seem especially relevant, bearing in mind that one wants to arrive ultimately at a reasonable conceptualization of a larger process.

In this paper, I would like to describe some studies that originated from a concern with the problem of how test-like events and instructions alter learning outcomes. I suspect that this emphasis on what produces learning, aside from what affects the retrieval of information once it is stored, also mirrors current trends in psychological thinking; see, for instance, Adams and Bray's (1970) suggestion that psychology might now profitably shift its emphasis from memory to acquisition processes. First, I will review some preliminary studies that suggested an experimental model within which to explore selective attention. After these preliminary studies, I will go on to other experiments with adults and children that suggest ways of looking at certain aspects of comprehension.

My general conclusions imply that an adequate conception of the events that produce a particular learning outcome requires that there be some way of analyzing the cognitive operations that a reader performs. Trabasso's recent APA address (1970) and his chapter in this book are examples of the depth of analysis that might be involved. But such an analysis implies that we have some way of characterizing the relationships among internal events (ideas or goals) that alter learning outcomes, the nature of the stimulus materials (their structure and content), and the tests that we use as an index of what is learned. With text materials, this level of analysis is exceedingly complex, but it is a task that must be undertaken if we are to understand how the relationships among the words that represent ideas in a text control and maintain conceptual processing, and consequently how they determine the knowledge that results from reading.

SOME PRELIMINARY STUDIES

Some of the problems that suggested the studies that I will report later were stimulated by research on the learning effects of questions that accompany a text.

Data collected by Rothkopf (1965) implied that under certain conditions adjunct prequestions might exert a selective effect upon learning. In a replication study (Frase, 1968), we found that retention was more restricted to question-relevant text when the question that exerted controls over processing occurred in close contiguity to the related text information. These selective effects were obtained when questions immediately preceded or followed a portion of the text, but the effects were strongest for prequestions.

Patrick (1968), using the same materials as in the previous study (Frase, 1968), theorized that if Ss rehearsed prequestions (making the questions more stable in memory), then the questions would be a salient determinant of processing activities even if the questions were not placed close to the relevant text. He studied the effect of having Ss either write out the adjunct questions, write what they thought were the correct answers, look at the questions a second time, or simply read the text and adjunct questions. A control group studied the text without the adjunct questions.

Figure 1 shows the results of Patrick's (1968) study. It can be seen that incidental learning was depressed mainly for the prequestion groups that had written out the questions or responses. Incidental learning of the postquestion groups was not influenced by these rehearsal activities.

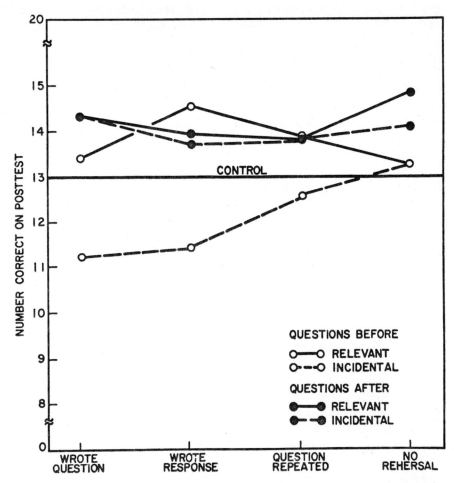

FIG. 1. Retention as a function of retention item, question placement, and rehearsal mode (from Patrick, 1968).

These studies, in the light of the experimental literature on incidental learning (Postman, 1964), suggested that it might be fruitful to explore the effects of asking Ss to perform specific search tasks with text materials. In two studies (Frase, 1969a; Frase & Silbiger, 1970), Ss read a three-page text in order to verify the existence of a conjunctive concept. Several concepts were described in the text, each having similar attributes, but the attribute values differed. The name of each concept and one attribute were given in each sentence of the text, so that Ss would have to combine the information from different sentences. In one organizational scheme, all of the information about a concept was described in one paragraph. We hypothesized that Ss would process the attributes but skip over (scan) the names of the concepts. In another organization, each paragraph described a separate attribute, so that the information about any one concept was scattered throughout the text. Under these conditions, we predicted that Ss would have to process the names in order to gather up the related information. On the basis of this analysis, we could distinguish between three sets of concept names: 1) those that would be scanned, 2) those that would be processed only enough to reject sentences with irrelevant information, and 3) target names which would be stored briefly for searching and which would result in decisions that sentences contained relevant information. Results showed significant differences among the recognition of these names immediately after reading and one month later. Scores were 34% for scanned names, 58% for rejected names, and 69% for target names (Frase & Silbiger, 1970). Analysis of content, without considering the organization of that content and what *S*s were trying to do, would have been insufficient to predict selective processing and consequent retention.

These preliminary studies, which I have not gone into in great detail, were useful in several respects. They suggested, in broad outline, some of the factors that would have to be specified if one were to understand why people learn one thing and not another when they read. Most importantly, in order to describe what effects a question, verbal direction, or explicit statement of learning objectives has upon learning, there must be some way of specifying the content of a text and how that content is related to such verbal directions. For instance, it isn't clear what effects a question will have on learning outcomes unless one can indicate what components of the text are associated with that question and what operations the reader will perform on those text components. Watts and Anderson (1970) have completed a study which indicates that adjunct questions requiring the application of principles to new examples produced higher post-test performance than questions that required identification of names. The latter condition was actually inferior to reading without questions. Rothkopf and Bisbicos (1967) found that adjunct questions produced learning consonant with the category of question, e.g., whether it required a common word or technical term for an answer. Given a technical question, *S*s were likely to learn other technical terms. Both of these studies were predicted on the basis of an analysis of the specific effects of questions in terms of the text content.

Aside from the problem of specifying content, there is also a need to define how that content is presented. The organizational properties of a text can alter the processing demands that it imposes upon the reader (Frase & Silbiger, 1970). Not only organization, but the syntax and semantics of a text are relevant to content representation. Studies of lexical (Perfetti, 1969) and syntactic depth (Yngve, 1960) are relevant here.

Finally, it is necessary to analyze the processing activities that a reader will engage in as a joint consequence of his set to respond and the characteristics of the stimulus materials that he encounters.

These considerations prompted the following series of studies in which some attempt was made to characterize the selective processing effects of inferential search activities, and to gain a clearer view of different levels of learning outcomes.

GOING BEYOND THE INFORMATION IN TEXT

It is clear that different people can learn quite different things when they read a text. At different times, the same reader might learn different things from a particular passage. In the studies that I will cite below, it is also clear that the majority of readers come away from a text with memory mainly for the statements made in that text. But some readers, a very small percentage, take those items of information and combine them in new and useful ways. This kind of intellectual activity is not very well understood, but it must play an important role in thinking in general.

To anyone seriously concerned with this issue, certain problems arise. Chief among them is the problem of content: how are we to conceive of these items of information, these units, that might be combined and recombined to produce statements, the sum of which reflects a reader's knowledge about what he has read? If we succeed in this description, several things become possible. Levels of knowledge might be defined based upon the processes implied by certain combinations. The effect of various alternations of the text upon different levels of knowledge can be studied, as well as the effects of different instructions given to Ss before they read.

One way to do this is to construct passages with known characteristics. Below is an example of such a passage.

> The Fundalas are outcasts from other tribes in Central Ugala. It is the custom in this country to get rid of certain types of people. The outcasts of Central Ugala are all hill people. There are about fifteen different tribes in this area. The hill people of Central Ugala are farmers. The upper highlands provide excellent soil for farming. The farmers of this country are peace loving people, which is reflected in their art work.

Essentially, the passage says that the Fundalas are outcasts. The outcasts are hill people. The hill people are farmers, and the farmers are peaceloving. We might symbolize this structure as $F \longrightarrow O \longrightarrow HP \longrightarrow FA \longrightarrow PL$ or, more simply, in terms of letters of the alphabet: $A \rightarrow B \rightarrow C \rightarrow D \rightarrow E$. The verbal classes thus provide units of analysis from which we can define various levels of assertions that a person might make after he reads the text. For purposes of this analysis we ignore the other information in the text.

The top portion of Figure 2 indicates four levels of assertions that might be produced. Level one includes only text information. For instance, a S might tell us that "A's are B's," or "D's are E's." Level two is composed of assertions that go beyond the information given; they require processing two text sentences, and so on, until, at level four all of the experimental sentences should be processed to produce an assertion of the form "A's are E's." Within this framework, it is thus possible to define different levels of knowledge that are represented by the way in which these verbal classes are combined to produce sentences in free recall. It is also possible to generate all possible pairs of these classes, to put them in sentence form, and to have Ss judge whether or not they follow from the passage they have read.

Given this modest framework, several experimental questions can be explored. For instance, is a reader's ability to put these items together related to the order of the sentences, i.e., does output reflect the order of input in a reasonable way? If so, are higher levels of knowledge affected more by these organizational factors than are lower levels of knowledge?

Another set of problems is concerned with the processing constraints that different instructions impose upon a reader (and hence they relate directly to the earlier studies that I cited). For instance, the level of a question can be defined in terms of the number of items that mediate the answer to that question. The lower

LEVEL OF ASSERTION

ONE	TWO	THREE	FOUR
A → B	A → C	A → D	A → E
B → C	B → D	B → E	
C → D	C → E		
D → E			

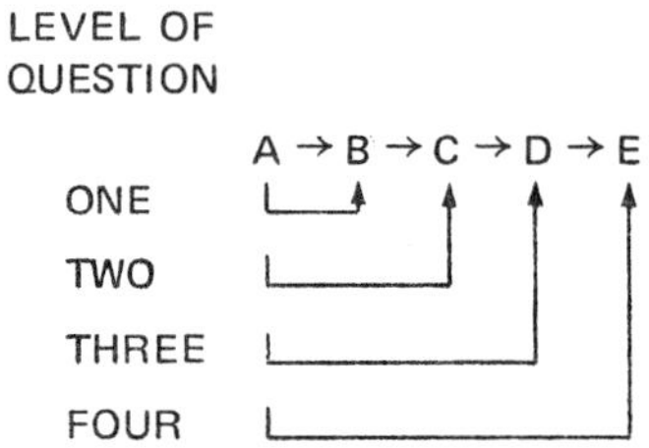

LEVEL OF
QUESTION

A → B → C → D → E
ONE
TWO
THREE
FOUR

FIG. 2. Level of assertion and question in the
simple structure A ——→ B ——→ C ——→ D ——→ E.

portion of Figure 2 indicates these questions. For instance, a level one question of
the form "Are A's B's?" would require processing only one sentence. A level three
question of the form "Are A's D's?" would require processing three sentences.

The answers to several problems can be explored by using questions. For
instance, considering only individual terms, which ones become salient items in
memory as a consequence of evaluating the problem statements? Are items
mentioned in free recall only those contained in the problem, e.g., A and D when S
is asked to determine if A's are D's? Or is S able to tell us about B and C, as well as
A and D, when he answers this higher level question? In short, do items that
mediate the solution to a problem get into memory? One hypothesis is that Ss will
process the text on the basis of these connections among sentences, and that the
most effective stimuli in the text will be those that enter directly into the problem
solving process. Other stimuli (verbal classes) will be processed at a lower level.

Furthermore, we can also answer the question of what effects these different
levels of processing have upon the way Ss combine items to produce assertions at
the time of recall. For instance, given the question "Are A's D's?" will S later
generate "A's are C's" and "B's are D's"? In short, do the inferences that should
mediate the solution of a problem also get into memory?

These are some of the questions that we have tried to answer within this
paradigm. First, I'll report some studies with adults, and then go on to some related
data with children.

STUDIES WITH ADULTS

Level of Assertions Given in Recall. Several studies were run using adult Ss
(Frase, 1969b; Frase, 1970). The experimental text materials consisted of either
three or four passages similar in structure to the example given earlier. Order of
sentence varied across texts. The Ss were told to read the passages and to determine
whether the sentences typed above the passages were valid conclusions.

After completing all passages, the passages were removed and *S*s were given instructions to write down everything that they could remember from the passages, including any inferences that they could generate. The *S*s were instructed not to use pronouns in writing what they remembered, and to use simple active sentences. Recall was elicited in the order in which *S*s had read the passages. In some studies, recognition tests followed the recall tests. The recognition tests included all valid and invalid assertions that could be made by pairing the verbal classes in the texts. For instance, "All A's are B's," "All B's are A's," etc. The *S*s responded "yes" or "no" to indicate whether each sentence could be derived from the passage. Time permitted for reading and testing was subject-paced.

Table 1 shows the number of assertions that *S*s were able to produce in free recall as a function of the number of sentences that would have to be related to each other to produce an assertion between two terms. Several observations can be made concerning Table 1. First, the data are orderly in the sense that an assertion requiring two sentences (e.g., "A's are C's.") was less likely to be mentioned than an assertion requiring only one sentence (e.g., "A's are B's."). In turn, two sentence assertions were more likely than three sentence assertions, and three sentence assertions were more likely than those requiring four sentences. Secondly, this structural dependence was also obtained for invalid assertions of the form, "B's are A's." In general, there was much less tendency for *S*s to produce backward (or invalid) assertions than to produce valid ones, as can be seen in Table 1, but this is partially due to the characteristics of the words used in the texts. Data from additional *S*s were gathered on the pre-experimenal ease of recalling the verbal

TABLE 1

Percentage of Possible Assertions Cited

Structural direction	Number of sentences processed			
	One	Two	Three	Four
Forward (valid)				
Study 1[a]	22.6	4.3	1.1	0
Study 2[a]	23.9	6.8	1.8	1.4
Study 3[b]	16.0	6.5	2.8	1.4
Mean	20.8	5.9	1.9	.9
Backward (invalid)				
Study 1	3.1	1.7	.5	0
Study 2	3.5	3.1	1.5	0
Study 3	6.6	3.7	1.9	0
Mean	4.4	2.8	1.3	0

Note: [a]N = 24; [b]N = 36.

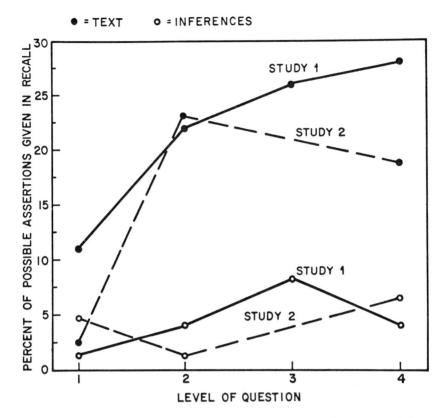

FIG. 3. Production of text and inferential assertions as a function of question level (from Frase, 1969b).

classes and sentences that could be produced from them. These Ss were presented with a recognition test in which they judged the validity of all sentences and potential valid and invalid conclusions from the texts, without their having read the texts. After the recognition test, these Ss were asked to recall all of the sentences they had seen. There were no trends in the data that would suggest differences in recall among the verbal classes, nor among assertions at different levels, but Ss were able to recall more of the valid (forward) assertions, indicating a directional bias. Of course, Ss who had not read the passages scored significantly lower on the recognition test than Ss who had read them.

A third observation concerning Table 1 is that Ss were able to generate sentences that were in the text, but very few higher level assertions. The overall low level of performance shown in Table 1 is due, in part, to the fact that the Ss had read several texts before testing.

Level of Statement Verified. Another question that we explored was the learning effects of having Ss verify statements at different levels of inferential complexity. Figure 3 reports data from two studies and indicates that there was an increase in the amount of text recalled as the level of problem increased. Most of this improvement occurred as a consequence of verifying a statement that required more than one text sentence. There was only a minimal difference when two, three, or four sentences had to be processed to verify a statement.

It is also clear from Figure 3 that higher level problems had little effect upon the inferences that Ss generated from recall. Perhaps recall performance must be relatively high before higher level assertions can be produced. To explore this hypothesis, another experiment was conducted in which Ss verified either two, four, or six assertions with each text (Frase, 1970). Verifying six assertions brought recall scores for text up to 35%, and inferential scores up to 15%. Although text recall was not very high, the slight rise in inferential statements with higher text recall lends some support to the hypothesis that higher level learning outcomes are contingent upon a certain minimal level of text recall. For instance, if Ss recalled two text sentences they might then be expected to produce one inference. In the present study, the six problem statements were related to all possible inferences from the text. Hence, Ss were exposed to as many higher level assertions as they were to text sentences. Bearing this in mind, the number of inferences generated by Ss is not very impressive.[1]

Differences between Recognition and Recall Tests. If Ss experience difficulty in recalling and combining verbal classes from a text, then the mode of testing should influence their performance on higher level learning outcomes. For instance, a recognition test, which explicitly combines all verbal classes from a text, should eliminate problems of recall and/or text segmentation. In two studies (Frase, 1970; Frase, 1971), it was found that there were, in fact, no differences in judging the validity of text assertions and inferential assertions on recognition tests, although the influence of other experimental variables was reflected in those test scores. In the same studies, the usual recall differences between text and inferential statements were observed. Method of testing, then, might obscure important differences in learning outcomes if it eliminates a number of important cognitive operations. In the present studies, it is not clear to what extent the operations are memorial or whether they relate to Ss ability to properly segment elements of a text or to combine them.

Specific Selective Effects of Statements Verified. It is possible to go a step further and to look at the specific effects of the statements that Ss verify. From an analysis of Ss' reasoning activities, predictions can be made about which text items should enter into the solution of a problem and which should not. For instance, in the simple structure A $\rightarrow$ B $\rightarrow$ C $\rightarrow$ D $\rightarrow$ E, confirming that "B's are D's" involves processing B, C, and D, but not A and E. The question is whether the components of the solution to such problems occur more frequently in recall than those which are not part of the solution.

Figure 4 presents relevant data. The arrows in Figure 4 indicate the statement that was verified. Text items that are spanned by the arrows are presumed to be

---

[1] Aristotle was among the first to discuss the dependence of higher level knowledge upon lower levels (see McKeon, 1947, pp. 13–14). The question of how much a text must be overlearned to give rise to stable higher level outcomes is an interesting one. Considering how little people actually remember when they read, it is surprising that any appear at all. Once the text is removed, operations can only be performed on the contents in memory; hence the emphasis in this paper on the processes that occur during reading.

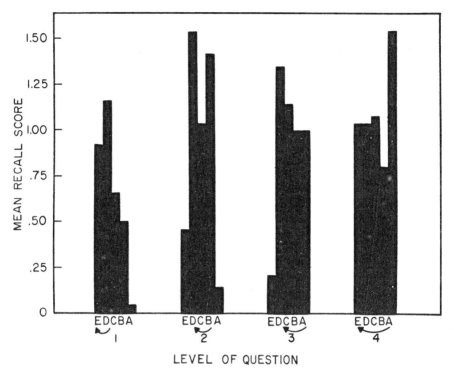

FIG. 4. Specific effects of questions upon recall (from Frase, 1969b).

components of the solution to the problem. It can be seen in Figure 4 that items that were components of the solution to a problem were mentioned most frequently in recall. This was a within-Ss design, hence direct comparisons can be made across levels of problems. Across problems, as well as within a particular level of problem, items that were components of the solution were cited more frequently than those that were not components. There was also a general increase in the number of items that Ss cited in recall as a function of level of problem. Thus, items were selected on the basis of their relationships to the problem sentence and the relationships among the sentences in the text.

Order of Sentences in the Text. Another problem that we wanted to investigate was the effect of the order of sentences upon Ss post-test performance. The aim was to create texts in which the order of sentences corresponded, either more or less well, to the structural "direction" (Harary, Norman, & Cartwright, 1965) which the text represented. The assumption was that the readers would more easily perceive connections between items with an appropriate order because consecutive items in the structure occur close together in the text.

In one experiment (Frase, 1969b) using the texts that I described before, we arranged the sentences so that the terms which mediated connections between items occurred in consecutive critical sentences. There was incidental information interspersed between these critical sentences. The order of the four sentences was, schematically: "D's are E's, C's are D's, B's are C's, and A's are B's." For this text, "D" occurs in the first and second sentences, "C" occurs in the second and third sentences, and "B" occurs in the third and fourth sentences. This was called the *Maximum* order text. For the *Moderate* order text, the second sentence was placed at the end of the passage, violating the rule that mediating links should occur in consecutive sentences. For the *Minimum* order text, two sentences were interchanged.

Thirty-six clerks from the Bell System read several texts, and were tested immediately after they had read the last text. Recognition tests, in which Ss judged the validity of sentences composed of all possible pairs of items, showed that as the order of sentences went from maximum to minimum, there was a decrease in Ss' tendency to accept the sentences as following logically from the texts. With the *Maximum* order, about 47% of the sentences were accepted; with the *Moderate* order, 41%; and with the *Minimum* order, 35%. In other words, the Ss were more likely to feel that verbal items belonged together if the sentences were appropriately ordered. An overall score on these recognition tests indicated that there was no difference between the conditions, because the tests contained an equal number of valid and invalid items. Correct scores on valid items were offset by incorrect scores on the invalid items when the text was well organized. Given a poorly organized text, however, incorrect scores on the valid items were offset by correct scores on invalid items. Changes in the order of sentences, then, affected Ss' bias toward accepting conclusions in general.

In a follow-up study (Frase, 1970), the order of the sentences was improved. Instead of "B's are C's" followed by "A's are B's," the Ss in this follow-up study read, "A's are B's. B's are C's." With this improved order, call it the *Good Order*, "B" not only occurs in two consecutive critical sentences, but it occurs at the end of the first sentence and at the beginning of the second sentence. The purpose of this study was to compare this order with the effects of the reverse order of sentences, which we can refer to as the *Bad Order*. The hypothesis was that the two orders should not create differences in recall of the text sentences, because no matter how one arranges the sentences in the text, the pairs of subject and predicate terms in any particular sentences are not disjoined. But by altering the arrangement of the sentences, one reduces the contiguity between repeated items, and this might affect Ss ability to relate remote items.

Forty-eight college students participated in this study. They each read three texts, after which they were tested. Recognition scores (adjusted for guessing bias) were 33% for the Good Order and 34% for the Bad Order on memory for text sentences. For inferences (which require relating remote items), scores were 41% for the Good Order and 21% for the Bad Order. The Good Order resulted in almost twice as many inferences as the Bad Order. An analysis of free-recall protocols also revealed a significant tendency to reproduce the correct structural sequence in recall with the Good Order, while the Bad Order resulted in generating items randomly from memory. It is possible that the Good Order taught something besides the text information—something about text structure—that could act as a cue for generating appropriate combinations of items.

Conclusions. These initial studies with adult Ss have been useful in several respects. They have provided a scheme for looking at the interaction of several factors that control the effective stimuli in a text. Given a sufficiently rigorous conception of text structure, the set with which a reader approaches his task, and hypotheses about the learning outcomes of his consequent processing activities, it was possible to predict items that would be cited most frequently in recall and how they would be combined to produce and judge assertions. The studies indicate that the breadth of stimuli that are related to goal-oriented processing activities can determine the consequent level of retention, and they place learning behaviors in a context in which they are controlled by the relationships among sentences.

The studies also confirm what is suggested by research on individual sentences: that the production of sentence output is determined by the number of operations that must be performed to produce that output. The present studies are mute as to what portion of this effect is due to acquisition or recall processes.

It was also clear that organizing a text to facilitate linkages among related sentences was likely to influence higher level learning outcomes. In general, readers infrequently produced sentences that went beyond the text, but if the structure was made apparent in some way, then Ss produced as many (or more) higher level assertions as text assertions.

I have referred to these experiments as "initial studies." They are tentative in the sense that no attempt was made to sample from the variety of ways in which sentences in discourse can, in fact, be connected. This is an important point, because relationships among sentences (and ultimately among ideas in a text) are not only signaled by word redundancies, but by the implied semantic subordinates and superordinates of these sentences or ideas. There should be analogues between the factors that we have observed in these studies that I have reported and factors that emerge when the analysis is based upon a broader conception of the semantics of text structure. In this sense, the present analysis is an attempt to oversimplify problems in prose learning so that certain critical issues can be more easily explored and communicated.

But we are still left with the broader problem of how the rational analysis of text structure, in general, might proceed. I believe that Crothers (1970; also chapter 10 of this book) is making important inroads into this area in terms of his analysis of the semantics of ordinary text materials. We can look forward to useful experimental advances in this direction.

STUDIES WITH CHILDREN

Let me turn, now, to some studies with children (Frase & Washington, 1970; Maroon, Washington, & Frase, 1971) that were suggested by the adult studies. Our intention in doing these studies was to determine if primary school children resembled adults in terms of their responses to questions when the text sentences were well or poorly ordered, and the questions required processing one or several sentences.

Because we were working with children, we modified the materials and presentation method. In these studies, the text was available to Ss throughout the experiment, hence relatively long-term recall was not at issue. The Ss were allowed 8 minutes to answer five questions about each of three stories. The following is an example of one of the passages and the questions that Ss tried to answer.

TOMMY'S TREASURE

ONE DAY TOMMY WAS WALKING DOWN THE STREET.
HE LOOKED AT THE GROUND. HE FOUND TWO THINGS.
HE FOUND A BIG THING.
THE BIG THING WAS GREEN.
THE GREEN THING WAS A BOX.
THE BOX WAS EMPTY.
HE FOUND A SMALL THING.
THE SMALL THING WAS RED.
THE RED THING WAS A BAG.
THE BAG WAS FULL OF MONEY.

WHAT DID THE STORY SAY?

CIRCLE THE RIGHT ANSWER LIKE THIS: (YES) OR LIKE THIS (NO)

1. THE SMALL THING WAS RED.   YES   NO

2. THE GREEN THING WAS A BAG.   YES   NO

3. THE SMALL THING WAS A BAG.   YES   NO

4. THE BOX WAS RED.   YES   NO

5. THE SMALL THING WAS FULL OF MONEY.   YES   NO

The relationships involved in these passages were simple equivalencies, for instance, "The red thing was a bag. The bag was full of money." The questions below the passage required processing *one* text sentence, e.g., "The small thing was red."; *two* sentences, "The small thing was a bag."; or *three* sentences, "The small thing was full of money." In addition, there were two false filler items.

Order of Sentences in the Text. The order of sentences was varied. The example passage is organized by concept; the information about the big green empty box is clustered together in the text. An alternate organization grouped the information according to attributes, e.g., "He found a big thing. He found a small thing. The big thing was green. The small thing was red." A passage in which the sentences were scrambled was contrasted with these well-organized passages.

The task was presented as a reading game in class, to second, fourth, fifth, and sixth graders. City and suburban children from the same geographic area were run. After a brief introduction and some practice in answering questions, the Ss read three experimental passages, answering the questions printed below each passage. Each S read a concept, attribute, and scrambled passage.

In two studies (with city and suburban children), errors were greatest when the sentences were scrambled. In addition, there was an interaction between level of question and organization for suburban children, as can be seen in Figure 5. This interaction was not significant for city children. It is possible that this difference is due to the fact that higher level processing of city children was less sensitive to organizational factors.

There was little difference in correct responses between the concept and attribute organizations, a result which is interesting because the information required to answer higher level questions was in separate locations with the attribute organization. It seems that organizational effects were not merely a consequence of placing question-related sentences consecutively in the text.

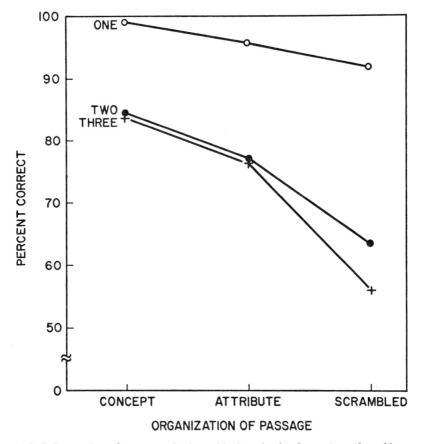

FIG. 5. Interaction of text organization with three levels of questions (from Maroon *et al.*, 1971).

Level of Questions. Table 2 summarizes the data from city and suburban children. They indicate differences between grade level and level of problem. Performance on the questions dropped about 20% when just two sentences had to be processed. There were also large differences between populations of *S*s. At the second grade level, the city children were relatively poor in answering questions that required processing just one text sentence. It is unclear what component of the reading process accounts for this finding. Exploratory data indicated that the vocabulary would not present a problem. By the time the city children were in the fifth grade, however, they were answering the single sentence questions just as well as, or slightly better than, the second grade suburban children, but they were still somewhat below the suburban second graders on the higher level questions. In general, the second graders in the suburbs performed as well as the fifth grade city children.

If the poor performance of city children was not due to vocabulary, then we had to look elsewhere for an explanation of their deficiencies. One hypothesis was that these *S*s did not appropriately segment the text in terms of the equivalencies stated in the text, i.e., intersentence redundancies were not sufficiently salient. In line with this cue salience hypothesis, Washington and Frase (1972) ran another group of 321 fourth grade city children, using the same texts as in the previous studies. He ran two conditions, one of which replicated the instructions of the earlier study. These unprompted Ss scored 86% on questions involving one sentence and 64% on questions involving two text sentences, a result which compares favorably with the data in the earlier study. For the other Ss, he prompted responses to critical text cues by warning the Ss, before reading, to pay special attention to the "small thing, the bag, the red thing," etc. Prompted Ss scored 84% on questions involving one text sentence, but they scored 94% on questions involving two text sentences, which was 30 percentage points higher than the unprompted Ss. Prompting was thus sufficient to wash out the effects of question level, and to put the fourth grade city children above their suburban counterparts in performance on multiple-sentence questions.

The cue salience hypothesis is related to two sets of data that I have reported earlier. First, the effects of prompting bear some resemblance to Patrick's (1968) study in which Ss responded selectively to text information, provided that they had rehearsed a prequestion or practiced the correct response before they read the relevant text material. Secondly, the prompting data with children also relate to differences between performance of adult Ss on recall and recognition tests. On the recognition tests, the differences between level of questions wash out, and this is likely due to the clear segmentation of verbal classes as well as the fact that the entire set of alternatives is presented together to Ss. One is reminded of Cherry's (1953) cocktail party analogy, in which the problem is to select a few relevant messages from among the many that bombard the listener. In reading a text, presumably, the reader must make a prior decision about what is relevant, and he can best do this if some cues are available to tell him about the structural components of the text.

TABLE 2

Percent Correct Solutions to Questions with Text Present

Grade	Area	Number of sentences processed			Mean
		One	Two	Three	
2	City[a]	64.0	45.5	47.0	52.2
2	Sub[b]	90.1	69.0	69.5	76.2
4	City	77.5	54.5	63.6	65.2
4	Sub	97.2	70.8	70.1	79.4
5	City	93.9	59.0	66.6	73.2
6	Sub	99.3	84.7	83.3	89.1
Mean		87.0	63.9	66.7	

Note: [a]N = 22; [b]N = 48.

I would like to present one final set of data, not only because they confirm hypotheses about question level, but because they relate to differences between children from high and low socio-economic (SES) backgrounds; hence they fit in with the other studies on children.

These data were collected by Matz and Rohwer (1971) at Berkeley. Their hypothesis was that, since high-and low-SES children do not differ in their ability to learn noun pairs (Rohwer, 1967), then the poor comprehension of low-SES black students might be a consequence of their not having learned an appropriate conceptual skill. Presumably, this skill involves unitizing chunks of text, e.g., "A's are B's. B's are C's." would become simply ABC. Presenting AB would then elicit the response C. One way of unitizing these items would be to present the information in pictorial form. Matz and Rohwer predicted that pictorial presentation would be especially useful for low-SES black students.

They constructed three passages that had five verbal classes. The sentences asserted relations similar in form to our old friends, "A's are B's. B's are C's. C's are D's. D's are E's." Below is an example of one of their passages.

SOME MONKEYS

ONE TYPE OF MONKEY LIVES IN BANANA TREES. THE BANANAS ARE VERY GOOD TO EAT. ALL THE BANANA TREE MONKEYS ARE KNOWN FOR HAVING CURLY TAILS. THESE MONKEYS WITH CURLY TAILS WANT TO WATCH THEIR CHILDREN. THEY ALWAYS CARRY THEIR CHILDREN ON THEIR NECKS OR KEEP THEM AT THEIR SIDE. THESE WATCHFUL MONKEYS ARE AFRAID OF HUMANS. THEY HIDE WHEN PEOPLE COME NEAR. THESE MONKEYS THAT ARE AFRAID ARE VERY BUSY ALL DAY LONG. THEY LIKE TO GATHER SMALL STICKS AND MAKE DESIGNS WITH THEM ON THE GROUND.

A DIFFERENT TYPE OF MONKEY LIVES IN COCONUT TREES. THESE MONKEYS BREAK OPEN THE COCONUTS BY DROPPING THEM ON THE GROUND FROM HIGH IN THE TREES. THESE COCONUT TREE MONKEYS HAVE LONG STRAIGHT TAILS. THESE MONKEYS WITH STRAIGHT TAILS LIKE THEIR CHILDREN TO TAKE CARE OF THEMSELVES. THEY LIKE THEM TO WANDER OFF ALONE AND BE FREE. THESE MONKEYS WITH CHILDREN WHO WANDER OFF ALONE ARE VERY FEARLESS WITH HUMANS. THEY COME RIGHT NEXT TO PEOPLE AND ASK FOR FOOD.

There were two methods of presentation—text and pictorial. In each mode the passages were read to Ss via tape. The presentation was cumulative; in the text condition, each successive sentence was added to the ones preceding. In the pictorial condition, successive parts of a picture, corresponding to sentences in the text, were added onto each other.

There were also two testing conditions, either with the final stimulus materials present or with them absent. Each S answered eight yes-no questions for each passage.

The Ss were 64 low-SES black fourth graders and 64 high-SES white fourth graders.

The results indicated that the availability of the stimulus materials at the time of testing did not affect performance. Population, presentation mode, and level of question were significant. As predicted, population interacted with presentation mode. These data are shown in Figure 6. The figure shows that there was an

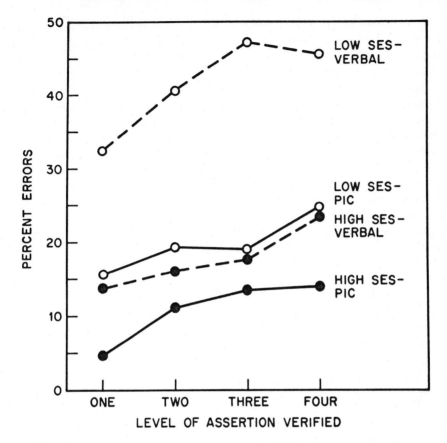

FIG. 6. Effect of structure, presentation mode, and SES upon performance
(from Matz & Rohwer, 1971).

increase in errors as more information had to be processed to answer a question. A
chance score would be 50%.

Figure 6 also shows the influence of pictorial presentation on the performance
of low-SES black students. With information in this form, they did about as well as
high-SES white children who had read the text material.

Conclusions. Let me summarize briefly these studies with children. First, they
confirm the adult data, showing that errors increase as more sentences must be
taken into account. In these studies, however, relatively long-term memory was not
an issue because the text was available to *S*s when they answered questions. But
these acquisition effects were also reflected in memory when testing occurred with
the stimulus materials absent in the Matz and Rohwer study (1971).

The data also confirm that young children, in the second grade, are sensitive to
the organizational properties of text. Higher level processes (relating several sentences in a text) seem to be most affected by organizational factors. This was true
for adults as well as children.

There were also substantial differences between *S*s from different populations in
terms of their ability to answer simple and complex questions. There was a slight

tendency for city or low-SES children to be especially poor on the questions that required relating several sentences. Some of the data indicate that cue salience might be important, implicating factors of selective attention. But if decisions must be made about relevant and irrelevant components of a text, they must arise as a consequence of analyzing the structural characteristics of a text. Hence, the reader is faced with the same problem as the experimenter, i.e., coming to grips with the analysis of content.

The studies also suggest that it is possible to gather useful comprehension data from children in a group setting. The effects of several variables were reflected in test scores. Although the form of the texts and questions that I have described are extremely simple, it should be possible to introduce other variations, such as semantic and syntactic transformations, and to explore the specific effects of various processing constraints upon memory and comprehension tasks. Bormuth's (1970) recent book on the theory of writing achievement test items and his research with others (Bormuth, Manning, Carr, & Pearson, 1970) help to usher in a long awaited age of analysis of these problems. Although such analyses have existed in the experimental literature, these intellectual tools have only recently begun to be seriously applied to instructionally relevant tasks, such as reading. Incidentally, the Bormuth *et al* (1970) data also indicate that questions that involve processing more than one sentence present special difficulties for the reader.

SUMMARY

The studies that I have reviewed reflect, in broad outline, critical problems in the study of learning from written materials. These problem areas concern, (1) the analysis of content, (2) textual representation of that content, (3) consequent processing activities, and (4) the measurement of learning outcomes. Each of these factors is intertwined with the others, and without a precise analysis of their relationships we cannot hope to make much progress in understanding how people learn from written materials.

Several factors in the learning situation exert controls over the acquisition of knowledge. The organization of information is one of these factors, and some of the studies that I have reviewed suggest that organization may be especially relevant for higher level outcomes. But these learning outcomes can vary with the form of testing, e.g., recall or recognition.

Presumably, the process of reading is controlled and maintained by critical text cues, which are more or less critical, depending upon the reader's set. Connections among sentences can be obscured or facilitated depending upon the organization of a text. The salience of certain cues might also be manipulated by verbal prompting (which may take the form of exhortations, problems, or objectives) that results in selective processing activities. The learning outcomes of these verbal directions were seen to be a consequence of processing sentences according to their interconnections, with the consequent rejection of information that was not a component of those interconnections. The level of learning outcome, in general, reflected the amount of information that had to be processed to produce that particular item of knowledge.

All of these factors taken together support the importance of the analysis of structure and processing activities in relation to instructional materials.

This analysis has been based upon the assumption that comprehension, in the ordinary sense of "grasping together," is an important intellectual achievement and that it is worthwhile to explore it in a simple form in the reading process. Just how simple this form should be is a complex question. At present, we might descend to the level of individual words or letters. In the future, we may be able to soar to the experimental heights of complex paragraphs, chapters, or books. But until then, the possibility for connections between just a few sentences provides a useful challenge.

CONFERENCE DISCUSSION

Olson wondered how Frase explained the fact that even when questions were asked *after* subjects had already finished reading some material, they would still exert some slight selective effects on memory. Frase suggested that this could happen if the subjects selectively rehearsed just the parts pertinent to the questions. He cited some related studies by Ed Patrick (1968) at the University of Massachusetts where one group of subjects rehearsed test questions prior to exposure to the material by writing out the questions; another group wrote out what they thought the correct responses would be; another group simply repeated the questions without writing them out; and a control group was not exposed to the questions. The incidental material which was unrelated to the rehearsed questions was best retained by the control group, whereas incidental learning for the three experimental groups was much lower. This suggested that the experimental subjects were selectively attending only to the parts of the text which matched the content of the test questions, and thus did more poorly on their retention of the incidental material.

Rothkopf mentioned the additional result that in some of his own work the type of question asked will make a difference in the degree to which one can manipulate selective attentional processes. For example, one group of questions emphasized numerical kinds of content. If the text contained only a *few* such numerically-oriented sentences, a strong selective attentional effect was obtained. But if one used questions containing frequently used types of content and the text also contained many such sentences dealing with this content, then the degree to which one obtained a selective effect was much reduced.

Freedle inquired whether one could not use the shaping effects induced by questions to get subjects to selectively pay 'attention' to the main ideas in a text. Rothkopf thought that might be possible but that the types of specific-content questions which he and Frase have studied thus far do not permit a definite answer on that. Sticht thought that some programs dealing with self-improvement study or speed-reading may have already tried out such special shaping instructions, such as reading for the main idea, etc. Goodman suggested that a way to get young subjects to read for the main idea is to ask them to search for a good title while they read; here finding a good title would probably necessitate finding the key ideas in the passage. Rothkopf recalled an early study by Postman and Senders (1946) which contrasted instructions to either read for the main idea or read for the details; the results were somewhat counterintuitive inasmuch as those subjects instructed to read for the main ideas did more poorly at recall than those asked to read for details. Carroll also recalled a study by King and Russell (1966) which gave essentially the same result. Olson suggested that perhaps the reasons subjects who were asked to read for the main idea did more poorly than subjects reading for details is that instructions to read for the 'gist' are not clear-cut enough; they don't provide a clear enough *plan* to guide the person with an explicit decision strategy as he reads the material. Regarding Olson's comment, Trabasso said that there is probably no mechanical procedure for discovering the main idea—the main idea may very well depend upon who is reading the material and what *he* thinks the most relevant, salient topic is. Scriven reminded the discussants that the main idea need not always be a simple concept; sometimes, it may be a complicated cluster of concepts such as the exposition of some theory. This observation raises the problem that what can function as the main idea may very well depend upon the type of discourse that one is dealing with. If the discourse is expository (as in stating a theory) there may be no simple way to state the main idea; whereas if the discourse is a narrative type then the main idea *may* be easy to state. Trabasso interjected that Scriven's method of guiding comprehension by giving examples of the kind of understanding that is sought from students (and by giving additional examples of the kind of understanding that is *not* sought) would seem to qualify as another way to shape people's selective processes in defining what their goal should be in reading some particular text. Scriven agreed.

Crothers suggested that one reason why some people have trouble finding the main idea in a text (granted that there is one) is that they may be distracted by particular words in the text which have very high imagery value; these words compete for the reader's attention, thereby interfering with their ability to discover the 'gist' of a passage.

Several people thought that Frase's stimulus sentences concerning the fictional Hill People (and especially the sentences used to convey information about fictional planets) were somewhat artificial and perhaps confusing to subjects. There were numerous suggestions that one way to make at least the Hill People passage read more naturally would be to pronominalize across successive sentences. What they meant can be conveyed by the following: Instead of asserting "John found a ball. The *ball* was green," it is more natural to say "John found a ball. It was green." Frase agreed that this would be an interesting variation to study. Incidentally, Frase cited some additional studies wherein children were given the following types of sentences: "John found a ball. The ball was green. The green thing was big." The children had to answer whether or not the *ball* was big. They couldn't do it. However, if one instructed the children before presenting the task to "Pay attention to the *ball*" then they found it very easy to answer the question. This suggests that, in certain simple experimental settings, it may be possible to get the subject to focus upon the main idea (here a simple concept, ball) with the consequence that one facilitates his ability to carry out a simple inference.

REFERENCES

Adams, J. A., & Bray, N. W. A closed-loop theory of paired-associate verbal learning. *Psychological Review*, 1970, 77, 385–405.

Bormuth, J.R., *On the theory of achievement test items.*. Chicago: University of Chicago Press, 1970.

Bormuth, J. R., Manning, J., Carr, J., & Pearson, D. Children's comprehension of between- and within-sentence syntactic structures. *Journal of Educational Psychology*, 1970, **61**, 349–357.

Cherry, E. C. Some experiments on the recognition of speech, with one and with two ears. *Journal of the Acoustical Society of America*, 1953, 25, 975–979.

Chomsky, N. *Syntactic structures.* The Hague: Mouton, 1957.

Crothers, E. J. The psycholinguistic structure of knowledge. In *Studies in mathematical learning theory and psycholinguistics.* (Technical Report) Boulder: University of Colorado, 1970.

Frase, L. T. Effect of question location, pacing, and mode upon retention of prose materials, *Journal of Educational Psychology*, 1968, 59, 244–249.

Frase, L. T. Cybernetic control of memory while reading connected discourse. *Journal of Educational Psychology*, 1969, 60, 49–55. (a)

Frase, L. T. Structural analysis of the knowledge that results from thinking about text. *Journal of Educational Psychology*, 1969, **60** (Monograph Supp. 6). (b)

Frase, L. T. Influence of sentence order and amount of higher level text processing upon reproductive and productive memory. *American Educational Research Journal*, 1970, **7**, 307–319.

Frase, L. T. Effect of incentive variables and type of adjunct question upon text learning. *Journal of Educational Psychology*, 1971, **62**, 371–375.

Frase, L. T., & Silbiger, F. Some adaptive consequences of searching for information in a text. *American Educational Research Journal*, 1970, 7, 553–560.

Frase, L. T., & Washington, E. D. Children's ability to comprehend text. *Proceedings of the 78th Convention of the American Psychological Association*, Miami, 1970.

Harary, F., Norman, R. Z., & Cartwright, D. *Structural models: An introduction to the theory of directed graphs*. New York: Wiley, 1965.

Huey, E. B. *The psychology and pedagogy of reading*. New York: Macmillan, 1908. (Republished) Cambridge, Mass.: M.I.T. Press, 1968.

King, D. J., & Russell, G. W. A comparison of rote and meaningful learning of connected meaningful material. *Journal of Verbal Learning and Verbal Behavior*, 1966, **5**, 478–483.

Maroon, S. J., Washington, E. D., & Frase, L. T. Text organization and its relationship to childrens' comprehension. Paper presented at the Annual Meeting of the American Educational Research Association, New York, 1971.

Matz, R. D., & Rohwer, W. D., Jr. Visual elaboration and comprehension of text. Paper presented at Annual Meeting of the American Educational Research Association, New York, 1971.

McKeon, R. *Introduction to Aristotle*. New York: Random House, 1947.

Miller, G. A., Galanter, E., & Pribram, K. H. *Plans and the structure of behavior*. New York: Holt, Rinehart & Winston, 1960.

Patrick, E. M. Prose learning: Induced question and response rehearsal, and question repetition. Unpublished manuscript, University of Massachusetts, 1968.

Perfetti, C. A. Lexical density and phrase structure depth as variables in sentence retention. *Journal of Verbal Learning and Verbal Behavior*, 1969, 8, 719–724.

Postman, L. Short-term memory and incidental learning. In A. W. Melton (Ed.), *Categories of human learning*. New York: Academic Press, 1964.

Postman, L., & Senders, V. L. Incidental learning and generality of set. *Journal of Experimental Psychology*, 1946, **36**, 153–165.

Rohwer, W. D., Jr. *Social class differences in the role of linguistic structures in paired-associate learning: elaboration and learning proficiency*. Final report, U.S.O.E. Basic Research Project # 5–0605, Contract OE6–10–273. November, 1967.

Rothkopf, E. Z. Some theoretical and experimental approaches to problems in written instruction. In J. Krumboltz (Ed.), *Learning and the educational process*. Chicago: Rand McNally, 1965.

Rothkopf, E. Z., & Bisbicos, E. E. Selective facilitative effects of interspersed questions on learning from written materials. *Journal of Educational Psychology*, 1967, 58, 56–61.

Trabasso, T. Reasoning and the process of negative information. Paper presented at the 78th Annual Convention of the American Psychological Association, Miami, 1970.

Washington, E. D., & Frase, L. T. Effects of prompting and relevant reading upon childrens' comprehension and recall of logical content. Paper presented at Annual Meeting of American Educational Research Association, Chicago, 1972.

Watts, G. H., & Anderson, R. C. Effects of three types of inserted questions on learning from prose. Unpublished manuscript, University of Illinois, 1970.

Yngve, V. A model and an hypothesis for language structure. *Proceedings of the American Philosophical Society*, 1960, **104**, 444–466.

14

LANGUAGE COMPREHENSION AND THE ACQUISITION OF KNOWLEDGE: REFLECTIONS

Roy O. Freedle
and
John B. Carroll
Educational Testing Service

It could hardly be expected that a volume such as this could fashion an entirely new and precise theory of language comprehension. Nor could it promise novel insights into how knowledge is acquired and retained. Nevertheless, certain aspects of these problems have been highlighted, progress in research endeavors has been noted, and suggestions have been made towards ways of extending our knowledge of processes in language understanding. In this overview of the volume we would like to draw attention to certain major themes and problems. We shall not attempt to comment on or allude to every chapter in this book. Rather, we take our cues from the dominant issues that emerged from a consideration of all the papers. The views expressed here are our own and are not necessarily those of the other contributors.

We find it necessary, pondering the broader context of language as a communicative medium, to treat problems of language *production* alongside problems of language *reception*, even though the processes involved may be in many respects quite distinct. Many of the difficulties in language understanding stem from difficulties introduced at the point of producing a verbal message, not only in the actual form and organization of the message, but also in the failure of the message producer to relate his message adequately to the total communication context.

LANGUAGE COMPETENCE AND LANGUAGE UNDERSTANDING

Little has been said in these papers regarding the role of language competence in language understanding. Most of the contributors have taken for granted that the hearer or reader is, in fact, a mature speaker and reader of the language, and thus is endowed with the basic knowledge of the language, which enables him to understand anything said or written in it. Such an assumption is obviously faulty, for many reasons. The individual's knowledge of the lexicon, grammar, and semantics of a language develops only gradually, even though some sort of "basic" competence is normally achieved at a fairly early age. Therefore, a child's comprehension of a verbal message is inevitably constrained, to a large extent, by his level of competence with respect to the vocabulary and syntax of the message. In typical tests of reading or listening comprehension, the examiners present passages that are graded in difficulty with respect to vocabulary and syntax, and in this way attempt to determine at what level the examinee begins to meet serious difficulties stemming from inadequate language competence. At the same time, there is evidence that language competence develops only as the individual is exposed, over long periods of time, to increasingly difficult materials; somehow the individual is able to use this material as a basis for increasing not only his general knowledge and understanding, but also his basic linguistic competence. To a degree, the material itself can teach him new lexical items, new meanings, and new and complex syntactical constructions. But he can also be helped by instruction in understanding, by use of the dictionary, and by discussion of the content. In stating these generalities, however, we realize that actually we do not know enough about how the individual's linguistic competence is developed and how it can be fostered. The fact that little has been said here about the development of language competence and its role in language understanding should not be taken as denying that these matters are of great importance, either in teaching or in research.

SOME COVERT SEMANTIC ASSUMPTIONS AND PRESUPPOSITIONS IN LANGUAGE DISCOURSE

In retrospect, the chief concern of many of the papers presented here seems to have been with the often unrecognized role of the "presuppositions" built into language discourse. Understanding language nearly always involves not only comprehending the words and grammatical structures of a message as linguistic symbols, but also taking account of those knowledges, facts, or ideas that underlie the message but are not explicitly built into it. Throughout the volume contributors repeatedly emphasized that much of the semantic content of discourse is not to be found in the spoken or printed words themselves, but in the prior knowledge that the producer of a message assumes the hearer or reader to have.[1] Sometimes, but not always, the producer of a discourse attempts to supply at least some of the knowledge he wants the receiver to have, so that the receiver fully understands the message. This may be done by developing a context for the message, by organizing its ideas in a particular way, or by supplying definitions and referents for the terms of the discourse. But for several reasons it is impossible, or at least impractical, for the speaker or writer to supply *all* the necessary context required for understanding a message; he must assume that the hearer or reader already possesses an appreciation of a large part of the required context.

This is so because it would be well-nigh impossible, in any case, for the message producer to make explicit *all* the assumptions and presuppositions underlying his discourse. He elaborates his statements only to the level of detail required by the

[1] There is considerable disagreement among philosophers and linguists as to how to define the term "presupposition" (see Fillmore & Langendoen, 1971).

overall purpose of the discourse, by the situation in which the discourse occurs, and by his estimate of the message-receiver's appreciation of the assumptions underlying the message. If the listener is very young he may go into greater detail than if the listener is an older person. If the listener is perceived to be relatively unfamiliar with the subject-matter (regardless of age), the speaker may supply more background knowledge than if the listener is perceived as his equal in general familiarity with the topic.

There are two very common assumptions underlying verbal messages, usually shared by both speaker and listener. One is that the message as a whole is to "make sense" and exhibit a certain consistency, even if on later examination this is found not to be the case. Thus, it will frequently happen that the speaker can omit certain details, on the expectation that the listener can fill the gap and resolve any apparent inconsistencies. The other common assumption is that whatever is asserted is assumed to be "true," in some sense. If the discourse relates to some actual state of affairs, the speaker assumes that the listener can recognize this fact and utilize his knowledge of that state of affairs to interpret his utterances. Even if the discourse has to do with some fictional state of affairs, that state of affairs will bear sufficient resemblances to actual reality to enable the speaker to utilize those resemblances as presuppositions of his message.

Some simple examples may make these points clear. Suppose Frank and Joe are walking down the street and are about to pass a hamburger stand. Frank says, "Would you like to eat here?" Such a question contains assumptions of at least time and place: The time is not "right now" but "pretty soon, after we get served," and the place is not "right here on the street" but "at the counter of the hamburger stand." Yet if Frank and Joe are walking in the park and carrying a picnic basket, the question "Would you like to eat here?" would assume that the time is "right now, as soon as we can unload the basket" and the place could be "right here." In either case, the total situation supplies the context which evokes the semantic assumptions that are most consistent with the utterance.

Similarly, if we read in a novel the statement, "The villagers were hard-working people," the presupposition is that the statement refers only to those villagers of an age who were expected to be capable of working—it surely does not refer to infants, children, and the aged and infirm who could not be expected to work. It cannot even be taken to imply that *all* those capable of working were indeed hard-working; normally, it would be interpreted as a generalization implying only that the people in some particular village tended to work harder, on the average, than, say, people in some other villages that might have been mentioned. In fact, if we try to be too literal, as by saying, "*Some* of the villagers were hard-working," we might convey the false impression that there were some real slackers in the village. This example illustrates the fact that in normal discourse the reader or hearer is expected to adjust the range of reference of a statement to whatever makes "cultural sense" in the light of his normal expectations, or perhaps in terms of the "naive psychology" (Heider, 1958) which sums up the layman's belief system concerning human behavior in Western culture.

Another type of semantic assumption is illustrated by the surface ordering of statements about events, as in the sentence "He fell off the horse and broke his leg." The culture teaches us to make inferences about whether something has caused something else to happen. In the sentence just cited, it teaches us to conclude that the man broke his leg because he fell off the horse, even though this cause-effect relation is not explicitly stated in the sentence.

Or suppose someone tells us that his dentist has had to give him a shot of penicillin because he had had rheumatic fever. If the person is complaining about the bad experiences he has had at the dentist's, we might interpret this statement as merely a reference to the painful experience of the penicillin injection. But a deeper processing of the sentence would be possible only if we happen to know that persons who have had rheumatic fever are likely to have a quantity of the rheumatic fever bacillus in the mouth, and that dental work for such persons is likely to bring on a serious reinfection unless an appropriate antibiotic (such as penicillin) is used.

Presuppositions and/or covert semantic assumptions invade the structure and semantic import of discourse at every conceivable level, from lexical items to larger units such as sentences and paragraphs. Some types of presuppositions and assumptions may be considered as having the status of formalized aspects of the language structure, such as those discussed by Fillmore (1968) and Chafe (this volume). Other presuppositions and assumptions may or may not be considered to have a formal status in the language: There is a grey area where one might claim that a presupposition is merely an arbitrary choice, inadequately signaled by the words themselves, of the interpretation of a "figure of speech" in either a literal sense or in a sense that is consonant with the prior context. Possibly these less formally determined presuppositions should be regarded as constituting a separate category—let us call them *semantic biases*—so that they are not confused with those which appear to have a more formalized status in the language system. As such they may represent perceptual strategies at the molar levels of discourse comprehension in somewhat the same way that perceptual strategies exist at the more "molecular" single-sentence level, as Bever's (1970) survey of psycholinguistic theory would seem to illustrate. Both Bever's perceptual strategies and the "semantic biases" suggested here can be argued to represent the merging of prior knowledge about the world with one's language competence, to result in the deep comprehension of discourse. Thus all presuppositions, semantic biases, and language perception strategies probably fall under the very general rubric of language and thought. Yet it would be satisfying to be able to break down and classify these presuppositions further, thereby giving structure to the several operations of mind which have produced these structures in the first place. Their very profusion and the apparent ease with which we operate with them make it all the more difficult to discover their existence. We believe that more work on this problem is of the utmost importance for furthering the development of discourse comprehension theory.

INFORMATION-PROCESSING
APPROACHES TO DISCOURSE

Several of the chapters in this volume draw heavily upon what may be called an information-processing approach, whereby the language user is viewed as an organism that accepts and processes input stimuli through various stages or subprocesses; at each stage or subprocess, decision mechanisms are postulated that act to interpret one or more aspects of the linguistic signal. Most of the models used have been highly particularized and focused at the level of specific experimental outcomes, for example, the individual's evaluation of the truth of simple sentences vis-a-vis simple perceptual displays. (See Trabasso, this volume). We believe these approaches deserve further study and application.

Naively, one might suppose that all the semantic information that a reader (or listener) extracts from a discourse passage is contained in the strings of words on the page (or the spoken string of words). An information-processing approach might be a relatively simple one if this were the case. But we have argued above that in most discourse-understanding situations the perceiver must contribute his background knowledge and his presuppositions to the understanding of the message. What is explicitly given in discourse represents only cues to underlying semantic structure. If this is so, the study of the manner in which "information" is processed must take into account not only the surface structure of discourse, but also what the language perceiver must contribute to its understanding. Nevertheless, there is a sense in which our study of this process must attend primarily to the stimulus input, i.e., the discourse itself, since this is most readily controlled and observed, and the information-processing organism must operate at least *initially* upon that input.

Miller, Galanter, and Pribram (1960) define an Image as follows: "The Image is all the accumulated, organized knowledge that the organism has about itself and its world" (p. 17). They define a Plan as "...*any hierarchical process in the organism that can control the order in which a sequence of operations is to be performed*" (p. 16, italics in the original). In addition, they refer to strategies or heuristics which guide the organization of the molar aspects of Plans (while tactics help guide the more molecular aspects of Plans). They also point out that Plans and Images are not mutually exclusive concepts, since Plans can be learned and so can be considered to be part of the knowledge (Image) system; also, knowledge becomes incorporated into decisions about which Plans to execute and hence aspects of the Image can be considered as part of Plans. Perhaps these ideas of Miller *et al.* can help us untangle some of the complexities of discourse structure and discourse comprehension.

Specifically, what we would like to suggest is that the structure of a discourse can be regarded as a ready-made Plan to help the reader understand it, be persuaded by it, or be inspired by it. This is particularly true if the discourse is structured with unusual intelligence or artfulness. To illustrate, suppose that a particular paragraph in discourse begins with a topic sentence that informs the reader of the main premise of the paragraph. This information can serve as a cue as to how the passage will be structured; that is, it provides a tentative Plan for the language user to test out the information that follows the topic sentence in order to assess whether the assertion in the topic sentence is valid or not. The topic sentence itself can be considered as a statement of what the total "problem" is, while the remaining sentences in the paragraph can be considered as substeps in the process of "proving" or demonstrating that the topic sentence assertion is correct. (Of course, closer analysis may disclose that the "proof" is fallacious or otherwise unsatisfactory.) This is analogous to a heuristic called "means-ends analysis" that has been of much use in computer studies of artificial intelligence (see Miller *et al.*, 1960, p. 189). A means-ends heuristic seeks to solve a general problem by analyzing it into a sequence of subproblems; if the gap between the stated problem and the desired solution seems too great, an attempt is made to break the large problem into smaller ones. Finding the solutions to the smaller ones, and putting the results together, leads to a solution of the large problem.

Structuring written discourse into paragraphs, and paragraphs into sentences, may represent a way of formally incorporating this heuristic into language structure—it becomes, as we have said, a Plan for the flow of information. This also suggests that if some assertion is immediately or easily apprehended by the reader, the paragraph will be short—it may consist of just a single sentence, if the topic sentence is so clear that it needs no further demonstration. But assertions that are judged (by the author) to be not readily believed may be expanded into a long string of sentences which seek to convince the reader of the correctness of the original assertion. Of course, the amount of justification is likely to be influenced by the author's intended audience and their judged degree of knowledge or expertise in the subject-matter.

As we read, then, our knowledge structure (Image) is advanced by the organization of the discourse into paragraphs, topic sentences, and explanatory sentences. It has in fact been demonstrated that readers can rather consistently segment an unparagraphed discourse into paragraphs, and recognize topic sentences among the scrambled sentences of a paragraph (Pfafflin, 1967; Koen, Becker, & Young, 1969); thus paragraphs, topic sentences, and explanatory sentences appear to have recognizable characteristics. First we grasp, and presumably entertain a belief of, the essential point that is asserted by the topic sentence. Then we go on to examine the sequence of explanatory sentences that may prove to us why the assertion is correct. At a more general level we may also have learned the principle behind applying the heuristic itself—that is, that an effective way to present and prove a difficult proposition is to break it down into a series of easier propositions.

To illustrate, consider the following paragraph:

"General Knucklehead might have won the battle at Smithtown if he had had a better blacksmith. For want of a good blacksmith a horse lost its shoe. For want of a shoe, the horse was lost. For want of the horse, the rider was lost. For want of the rider, a crucial message was not delivered. For want of the message, the general failed to move his troops to the proper positions. For want of proper troop emplacements, the battle was lost."

From a strictly logical viewpoint, the above string of sentences is not a proof of anything in particular; however, it is not atypical of the kinds of loosely structured arguments that one finds in texts that seek to justify general assertions. It exemplifies an appeal to a means-ends heuristic whereby each sentence supplies a link in a presumptive causal analysis. Whether any paragraph selected at random would also fit this pattern even approximately is doubtful, but this illustration does, at least, convey the type of paragraph analysis that might be adaptable to an information-processing analysis of discourse. It may be suggested that the study of comprehension processes might be advanced by devising means to index the reader's state of knowledge as he progressively reads the successive sentences of such paragraphs.

The means-end heuristic is not the only type of heuristic that may be built into a paragraph. Consider the following account of a television commercial, cited by Tversky (1971, pp. 60–61):

"[The announcer starts] 'There are more than two dozen companies in the San Francisco area which offer training in computer programming.' The announcer puts some two dozen eggs and one walnut on the table to represent the alternatives, and continues: 'Let us examine the facts. How many of these schools have on-line computer facilities for training?' The announcer removes several eggs. 'How many of these schools have placement services that would help find you a job?' The announcer removes some more eggs. 'How many of these schools are approved for veterans' benefits?' This continues until the walnut alone remains. The announcer cracks the nutshell, which reveals the name of the company and concludes: 'This is all you need to know in a nutshell.' " This commercial pitch reveals quite clearly the workings of another heuristic, one that we may call the elimination-of-aspects. Actually, the topic sentence in the commercial does not *explicitly* state the problem, but certainly it is implied in the context: Which school is the best one? The elimination-of-aspects heuristic is a central concept in Tversky's general theory of choice, which is concerned with the problem of trying to choose the best of a set of available alternatives. At each (covert or overt) substage of the process, an aspect is selected with the consequence that all the alternatives that do not include that aspect are eliminated from further consideration. Finally one alternative remains, and that is the chosen one. Again, we have not been able to assess the extent to which this heuristic is employed in paragraph organization, but we expect that its use may be widespread.

The types of paragraphs studied by Crothers, Frederiksen, and Frase, all discussed in this volume, seem to represent still other heuristic procedures for understanding discourse. For example, Crothers' paragraphs about nebulae and Frederiksen's paragraph about Circle Island prompt a classification heuristic on the part of the reader, while Frase's paragraphs about types of monkeys prompt the reader to extend the list of attributes that are asserted to be characteristic of particular types of monkeys. From an information-processing point of view, we are suggesting that the particular types of heuristics inherent in the structure of a discourse may have an important influence on the manner in which the information in paragraphs are processed. Implicit in this suggestion is the notion that discourse comprehension cannot be studied adequately when only one type of heuristic is contained in the materials; rather, different discourse structures must be presented and their effects compared.

This line of thought may also have important applications in the analysis of how speakers or writers plan and develop their discourses. Speakers and writers can have a wide variety of purposes—to describe an experience, to persuade the audience of the validity of a certain proposition, to explicate cause-effect relations, and so forth. Frequently these purposes are mixed; for example, the writer may allege certain cause-effect relationships in order to support the validity of a certain proposition, as in: "You should vote for candidate X because he will do so-and-so, and these actions on his part will bring about such-and-such events that will have such-and-such desirable consequences." At any stage of developing a discourse, a good speaker or writer has to judge what type of heuristic will best advance the hearer or reader towards the goal of understanding, conviction, feeling, or whatever, that he has in mind. Despite centuries of writing and speculation in classical rhetoric, we feel that no adequate analysis of discourse development and understanding has been offered, and we suggest that psycholinguists turn their attention to this endeavor, utilizing as far as possible the insights that contemporary linguistic and psychological analysis can offer.

THE MAINTENANCE OF
COMPREHENSION BEHAVIOR

One more predominant theme of the volume, especially in some of the later papers, is that of how attentive listening or reading can be secured. Comprehension as such was not the issue here, for it was taken for granted that the listener or reader could comprehend if the stimulus was adequate and if he could maintain a proper set to observe the verbal stimulus with attentiveness. Rather, the question was, how could the language perceiver be motivated to attend to the message or to its salient features?

Stimulus adequacy was touched upon in Sticht's paper, where it was implied that there might be a point, in increasing the rate at which a message is presented, at which the rate of presentation might be too fast to permit adequate processing of the verbal information, whether because of difficulties in perceiving and segmenting the message itself or because of difficulties in processing and interrelating the perceived information. We are left with the impression that the study of the perception of rate-controlled speech is far from complete, because there are still questions as to how best to compress speech. Granting that a near-optimum method of compression has been achieved, there is inadequate information as to how different language materials can be processed by the human mind at this rate. In spite of this, it would seem that rate-controlled speech offers an excellent vehicle for studying all sorts of interesting questions concerning language comprehension, because it allows the experimenter to force processing times down to threshold values.

The roles of attention and of motivation, as inferred intervening variables, in causing the listener or reader to observe and retain particular aspects of text information were dominant issues in the papers of Sticht, Rothkopf, and Frase. At least, this would be our rendering, into terms of a more cognitive type of psychology, of the concepts of "mathemagenic activities," and "maintenance and control," as used by these writers. From an operational point of view, the actual manipulations of variables—such as the positioning of adjunct questions in text materials—provide concrete bases for the effects that are observed. Nevertheless, from the standpoint of attempting to construct a general model to account for these effects, it seems necessary to postulate intervening variables. What, for example, is the real effect of adjunct questions on the learner's strategy in reading a passage? The evidence, such as it is, suggests that it is a heightening, expansion, or focusing of the observational powers of the reader, in the sense that he pays attention to more aspects of the text—both those that may be immediately critical in the light of the questions themselves *and* those that the reader may *expect* to become critical upon being tested. Thus the effects of these manipulations may be taken to be means of controlling the reader's expectancies concerning what may be critical in the text, and thus of his attention to particular classes of details. All of this is predicated upon the assumption that the reader in an experimental situation can be induced, some, to care about how he performs. This caring constitutes the motivational component.

We may suggest also that the work in memory for prose passages should include attention to the reinforcing effects of comprehension itself and of the student's discovery that he *can* answer questions successfully. When prose comprehension and memory for prose are viewed and treated as purely passive processes there is difficulty in tying performances to what is known concerning more active, reinforced memory processes.

CONCLUSION

We have emphasized three themes—linguistic presuppositions and semantic assumptions; information-processing; and attentional processes—that we personally found were given impetus in the papers and discussions in the volume. Possibly there were important themes that we have neglected or overlooked; perhaps we should have highlighted the considerable attention to semantic analysis of a purely linguistic character that was discussed, or perhaps we should have attempted to develop Scriven's (this volume) idea for a more general behavioral analysis of understanding than that afforded by a language-dominated analysis of the comprehension process. Be that as it may, we believe that the three themes we have tried to expand on are among the more promising entry points for further research on the process of language comprehension.

REFERENCES

Bever, T. G. The cognitive basis for linguistic structures. In J. R. Hayes (Ed.), *Cognition and the development of language*. New York: Wiley, 1970.

Fillmore, C. J. The case for case. In E. Bach and R. T. Harms (Eds.), *Universals in linguistic theory*. New York: Holt, Rinehart, & Winston, 1968.

Fillmore, C. J., & Langendoen, D. T. (Eds.), *Studies in linguistic semantics*. New York: Holt, Rinehart, & Winston, 1971.

Heider, F. *The psychology of interpersonal relations*. New York: Wiley, 1958.

Koen, F., Becker, A., & Young, R. The psychological reality of the paragraph. *Journal of Verbal Learning and Verbal Behavior*, 1969, 8, 49–53.

Miller, G. A., Galanter, E., & Pribram, K. H. *Plans and the structure of behavior*. New York: Henry Holt, 1960.

Pfafflin, Sheila M. Some psychological studies of sentence interconnections in written English prose. *Psychonomic Bulletin*, 1967, 1(2), 17.

Tversky, A. Elimination by aspects: A probabalistic theory of choice. *Research Bulletin of Michigan Mathematical Psychology Program* (MMPP70–12), 1971.

AUTHOR INDEX

Numbers in italics refer to the pages on which the complete references are listed.

A

Aborn, M., 19, 23, *28*
Abrams, K., 105, *111*
Adams, J. A., 338, *356*
Anderson, H. E., Jr., 2, *27*
Anderson, R. C., 309, 311, *312,* 340, *357*
Aquino, M. R., 300, *312*
Arnheim, R., 161, 163, *165*
Ausubel, D. P., 309, *312*

B

Bach, E., 73, *96*
Bartlett, F. C., 7, 23, *26, 96,* 230, *244*
Bateman, D., 2, 20, *26*
Becker, A., 364, *367*
Begun, J. S., 135, *136*
Beilin, H., 158, *165*
Bem, S. L., 160, *165*
Bever, T. G., 105, 106, 107, *111, 112,* 114,
   115, 117, 135, *136,* 155, *165,* 166, 215,
   244, 362, *367*
Bisbicos, E. E., 326, *335,* 340, *357*
Blake, R. R., 127, *136*
Blommers, P. J., 3, *26*
Bloom, R. D., 326, 327, 328, *335*
Bormuth, J. R., 3, 4, 18, 20, 24, *26,* 163,
   165, 354, *356*
Braine, M. D. S., 159, *166*

Brassard, M., 294, *312*
Bray, N. W., 338, *356*
Brown, D. P., 286, *312*
Brown, J. I., 2, *26*
Brown, R., 99, *111,* 143, *166*
Bruner, J. S., 141, 144, *166*
Burger, J. F. 73, 89, 92, *96*

C

Caffrey, J., 294, *312*
Cairns, H. S., 105, *112*
Caplan, D., 106, *111*
Carbonell, J. R., 73, *96*
Carlsen, G. R., 2, *26*
Carnap, R., 71, *96*
Carr, J., 4, 24, *26,* 354, *356*
Carroll, J. B., 8, 11, 23, *26,* 99, *111,* 295,
   303, *312*
Cartwright, D., 212, *244,* 346, *357*
Carver, R. P., 21, *26, 27,* 302, 308, 312, *313*
Casagrande, J. B., 99, *111*
Caylor, J. S., 288, 290, 291, *314*
Celce, M., 77, *96*
Chafe, W. L., 42, *69*
Chapin, P., 70, *96*
Chase, W. G., 113, 114, 116, 117, 118, 120,
   128, 130, *136*
Cherry, E. C., 351, *356*
Chomsky, C., 18, *26*

Chomsky, N., 71, *96, 136,* 156, 159, *166,* 337, *356*
Christophersen, P., 56, *69*
Clark, H. H., 8, *26,* 113, 114, 115, 116, 117, 118, 120, 121, 128, 130, 131, 135, *136,* 149, 161, 162, 164, *166,* 315, *334*
Clark, K. B., 22, *26*
Clifton, C., Jr., 20, *27*
Coke, U., 317, 321, 328, *334*
Coleman, E. B., 18, 19, *27,* 300, *313,* 317, 318, *334*
Collins, A. M., 114, *137, 166*
Collinson, W. E., 82, *96*
Cronbach, L. J., 233, *244*
Crothers, E. J., 247, 249, 250, 251, 254, 273, 274, *278,* 348, *356*

D

Danks, J. H., 5, 13, 16, *27*
Darby, C. A., Jr., 21, *27*
Davis, F. B., 2, 8, 9, 20, *27*
Dawes, R. M., 170, 191, 194, *209,* 212, 218, *244*
Dedmon, D., 2, 20, *26*
de Laguna, G. A., 144, 148, *167*
Devine, T. G., 295, 296, 297, *313*
Donaldson, M., 161, *166*
Downey, R. G., 23, *27*
Duker, S., 294, 295, 297, *313*

E

Edfeldt, A. W., 5, *27*
Egeth, H. E., 131, *137*
Eisenberg, K., 160, 161, *166*
Ekstrom, R., 242, *244*
Epstein, W., 6, 23, *27*
Ertel, S., 107, *112*
Estes, W. K., 179, *209*

F

Fairbanks, G., 300, 302, *313*
Farr, J. N., 287, 300, 305, *313*
Feldman, C. F., 26, *27*
Filby, N., 142, 145, 153, *167*
Fillenbaum, S., 6, 7, 20, *27,* 123, *137,* 155, *166*
Fillmore, C. J., 43, *69,* 73, 75, 89, 94, *96,* 148, *166,* 213, 218, *244,* 360, 362, *367*
Fishman, J. A., 108, *112*
Flesch, R. F., 317, *334*
Fodor, J. A., 11, *27,* 105, *112,* 115, *137,* 155, 156, 166, *167*
Follettie, J. F., 23, *27*

Ford, W., 144, 145, *166*
Forster, K. I., 105, *112*
Foulke, E., 301, 303, *313*
Fox, L. C., 288, 290, 291, *314*
Fox, R., 127, *136*
Frandsen, K., 2, 20, *26*
Frase, L. T., 191, 209, 212, *244, 247, 278,* 309, 310, *313,* 332, *334,* 338, 339, 340, 342, 344, 345, 346, 347, 348, 350, *356,* 357
Frederiksen, C. H., 211, 233, *244*
Freedle, R. O., 170, 185, *209, 313*
Frege, G., 140, *166*
French, J. W., 242, *244*
Freshley, D. L., 2, *27*
Friedman, H. L., 303, 304, 305, 307, 308, 309, *313, 314*

G

Galanter, E., 337, *357,* 363, 364, *367*
Garner, W. R., 201, *209*
Garrett, M., 105, 106, *111, 112,* 115, *137,* 155, *166*
Gelman, R., 141, *166*
Gibbons, G., 72, *97*
Gibson, J. J., 142, 163, *166*
Glaserfeld, E. Von, 88, *96*
Glass, G. V., 310, *314*
Gleitman, L. R., 18, *29*
Glucksberg, S., 147, *166*
Goldman-Eisler, F., 303, 304, *313*
Gombrich, E., 163, *166*
Gomulicki, B. R., 7, 22, *27*
Goodman, N., 163, *166*
Gough, P. B., 17, *27,* 116, 118, 119, 132, *137,* 149, 158, *166,* 317, *334*
Graae, C. N., 309, 311, *313*
Greene, F. P., 18, *27*
Greene, J. M., 120, 121, *137*
Grieve, R., 120, *137*
Guilford, J. P., *27*
Guttman, N., 300, 302, *313*

H

Hakes, D. T., 23, *27,* 105, *112*
Halford, G. S., 141, *166*
Harary, F., 212, *244,* 346, *357*
Harris, Z. S., 247, *278*
Heider, F., 361, *367*
Henderson, E. M., 22, *27*
Herman, E., 106, *112*
Herriot, P., 154, *166*
Hildyard, A., *167*
Holmes, V. M., 105, *112*

Huey, E. B., 286, *313*, 337, *357*
Hunt, E., 130, *137*
Hurtig, R., 106, *111*
Huttenlocher, J., 160, 161, *166*

I

Isard, S., 303, 304, *313*
Ivins, W. M., 143, *166*

J

Jack, O., 6, 22, *28*
Jackendoff, R., 108, *112*
James, N. E., 288, *313*
Jarvella, R. J., 106, *112*, 155, *166*
Jenkins, J. J., 20, *27*, 287, 300, 305, *313*
Jöreskog, K. G., 233, 239, *244*, *245*
Johnson, R. L., 303, 304, 305, 307, 308, *313*
Johnson-Laird, P. N., 135, *137*, 164, *166*, *167*
Jones, R. L., 23, *28*
Jones, S., 18, *27*, 113, 121, 122, 127, *137*, 161, *167*

K

Kahneman, D., 110, *112*
Kaplan, E., 24, *28*
Karttunen, L., 56, 60, *69*
Katz, J. J., 11, *27*, 72, 79, 86, *96*, 101, *112*, 156, *167*
Kay, M., 73, 85, *96*
Keller, B., 5, *28*
Kelly, C. M., 2, *27*
Kern, R., 288, 290, 291, *314*
Kershner, A. M., 17, *28*
King, D. J., 7, 22, 23, *28*, 355, *357*
Kingsley, P., 170, *209*
Kingston, A. J., 18, *29*
Kirk, R., 105, *111*
Klare, G. R., 319, 320, 321, *334*
Koen, F., 364, *367*
Koether, M., 319, *335*
Krauss, R., 111, *112*, 147, *166*
Kruskal, J. B., 187, *209*
Kurcz, I., 20, *27*

L

Lackner, J. R., 105, *111*
Lakoff, G., 71, 73, *96*
Langendoen, D. T., 106, *111*, 360, *367*
Lappin, J. R., 127, *136*
Lee, W., 20, *28*

Leech, G. N., 94, *96*, 218, *245*
Lenneberg, E. H., 99, *111*
Levin, H., 24, *28*
Levitt, E. E., 22, *28*
Lindquist, E. F. 3, *26*
Longacre, R. E., 191, *209*
Luce, R. D., 187, *209*
Lundsteen, S., 295, 297, *313*
Luria, A. R., 159, *167*
Lyon, D. O., 22, *28*
Lyons, J., 9, *28*, 89, *96*

M

McCawley, J. D., 73, *96*
McGuigan, F. J., 5, *28*
MacKay, D. G., 19, *28*
McKeon, R., 345, *357*
Maclay, H., 207, *209*
McLuhan, M., 143, 163, *167*
McMahon, L. E., 118, 119, 120, 127, 136, *137*, 317, *335*
McNeill, D., 115, 137, 159, *167*
Madill, J., 23, *28*
Manning, J., 4, 24, *26*, 354, *356*
Marasuilo, L. A., 295, 296, 297, *314*
Marin, J., 130, *137*
Marks, E., 20, 25, *28*
Marks, M. R., 6, 22, *28*
Maroon, S. J., 348, 350, *357*
Martin, J. E., 107, *112*, 147, *167*
Martin, J. G., 23, *28*
Martins, G. R., 73, 85, *96*
Matz, R. D., 352, 353, *357*
Myer, D. E., *167*
Miller, G. A., 10, 22, 23, *28*, 115, 124, *137*, 140, 156, 163, *167*, 300, 303, 304, *313*, 337, *357*, 363, 364, *367*
Miller, G. R., 18, 19, *27*
Minsky, M. L., 38, *39*, 218, *245*
Miron, M. S., 300, 302, *313*
Moore, T., 105, *112*
Moray, N., 297, *313*
Morris, C. W., 94, *96*
Mundy-Castle, A. C., 144, *167*

N

Neisser, V., 297, *314*
Newman, S. E., 20, 207, *209*
Nichols, W. H., 319, 321, *334*
Noble, C. E., 317, *335*
Noll, G. A., 20, 25, *28*
Norman, D., 297, *314*
Norman, R. Z., 212, *244*, 346, *357*
Norris, C. M., 309, *313*

Norton, L. M., 70, *96*

O

Odom, P., 20, *27*
Oléron, G., 19, *28*
Olson, D. R., .77, *96,* 139, 142, 145, 148, 153, 162, *167,* 169, 170, 171, *209*
Orr, D. B., 303, 307, 309, 311, *313, 314*

P

Paivio, A., 115, *137*
Papert, S., 38, *39*
Paterson, D. G., 287, 300, 305, *313*
Patkau, J. F., 23, *29*
Patrick, E. M., 338, 339, 351, 355, *357*
Paul, I. H., 7, 23, *28*
Pearson, D., 4, 24, *26,* 354, *356*
Peisach, E. C., 18, *28*
Penfield, D. A., 295, 296, 297, *314*
Perchonock, E., 6, 23, *29,* 317, *335*
Perfetti, C. A., 340, *357*
Pfafflin, S. M., 364, *368*
Piaget, J., 162, *167*
Postman, L., 326, *335,* 339, 355, *357*
Pribram, K. H., 337, *357,* 363, 364, *367*
Price, L., 242, *244*

Q

Quillian, M. R., 73, 87, *96*
Quillian, M. R., *96,* 114, *137, 166*

R

Randhawa, B. S., 147, *167*
Rankin, E. F., Jr., 18, *28*
Raphael, B., 75, *96*
Reichenbach, H., 139, *167*
Reid, R. H., 303, *314*
Richards, I. A., 140, 141, 143, *167*
Robinson, F. G., 309, *312*
Rohwer, W. D., Jr., 352, 353, *357*
Rollins, H., 113, 114, 118, 120, 124, 125, 126, *137,* 315, *335*
Rommetveit, R., 155, *167*
Rosenberg, S., 23, *28,* 304, 305, *314*
Ross, J. R., 55, *69*
Rothkopf, E. Z., 247, *278,* 309, 310, *314,* 317, 319, 321, 322, 324, 326, 327, 328, *334, 335,* 338, 340, *357*
Rubenstein, H., 19, 23, *28*
Russell, B., 124, *137*
Russell, G. W., 7, 22, 23, *28,* 355, *357*

S

Sachs, J. S., 7, 20, *29,* 105, *112,* 155, *167*
Saltz, E., 20, *28*
Sanders, G., 247, *278*
Sanders, J. R., 310, *314*
Savin, H. B., 6, 23, *29,* 317, *335*
Schlesinger, I. M., 24, *29,* 317, *335*
Schulz, R. W., 317, *335*
Schwarcz, R. M., 73, 89, 92, *96*
Scriven, M., 31, *39*
Selfridge, J. A., 23, *28*
Senders, V. L., 355, *357*
Shaughnessy, E., 113, 114, 118, 120, 124, 125, 126, *137,* 315, *335*
Shepard, R. N., 20, *29*
Shipley, E. F., 18, *29*
Shuford, E. H., 319, 321, *334*
Silbiger, F., 332, *334,* 339, 340, *357*
Simmons, R. F., 73, 80, 81, 89, 92, *96, 97*
Slamecka, N. J., 23, *29*
Slobin, D. I., 17, 22, 23, *29,* 116, 127, 128, 129, *137,* 149, 154, 155, 157, 158, *167*
Slocum, J., 73, 80, 81, *97*
Smith, C. S., 18, *29*
Smith, K. U., 310, *314*
Smith, M. E., 310, *314,* 318, 319, *335*
Snow, R. E., 233, *244*
Sparck-Jones, K., 87, *97*
Spearritt, D., 3, *29,* 294, 295, *314*
Spontak, G., 158, *165*
Stanton, E., 5, *28*
Stein, G., 99, *112*
Sternberg, S., 114, 126, *137*
Sticht, T. G., 301, *313*
Sticht, T. G., 287, 288, 290, *291,* 300, 302, 310, *314*
Stoltz, W., 105, *111*
Stone, P., 130, *137*
Strauss, S., 160, 161, *166*

T

Tarski, A., 71, *97,* 139, 163, *167*
Taylor, J. L., 307, *314*
Taylor, W. L., 18, *29,* 318, *335*
Terman, L. M., 22, *29*
Thompson, F. B., 72, *97*
Thorn, E., 296, *314*
Thurstone, L. L., 2, *29*
Trabasso, T., 113, 114, 116, 118, 120, 124, 125, 126, *137,* 149, 157, 161, 167, 315, *335,* 338, *357*
Tulving, E., 23, *29*
Turner, E. A., 155, *167*

Tversky, A., 365, *368*
Tversky, B., *137*

U

Underwood, B. J., 21, *29,* 317, *335*

V

Valian, G., 105, *112*
Vendler, Z., 56, *69,* 107, *112*
Vineberg, R., 290, *314*

W

Wales, R. J., 9, *28,* 120, *137,* 161, *166*
Washington, E. D., 348, 350, *357*
Wason, P. C., 17, *29,* 113, 115, 121, 122, 123, 127, 136, *137,* 164, *167*
Watts, G. H., 340, *357*
Weaver, W. W., 18, *29*
Weinreich, U., 144, *167*

Welsh, C. A., 22, 23, *29*
Werner, O., 203, *209*
Wesemann, A. F., 23, *27*
White, J. H., 87, 88, *97*
Whorf, B. L., 99, 100, *112*
Williams, F., 296, *314*
Williams, J. C., 303, 307, *314*
Wittgenstein, L., 140, *167*
Woods, W. A., 72, 75, 89, 94, *97*
Wright, P., 119, 135, *137,* 153, *167*

Y

Yngve, V., 340, *357*
Young, R., 364, *367*
Yu, K. C., 22, *28*

Z

Ziff, P., 14, *29*
Zipf, G. K., 317, *335*

SUBJECT INDEX

A

Adaptability
  cognitive, 34
  to text difficulty, 320-322
Adjectival modification, 77-78
Adjectives
  use by children in experiments, 144-147
  prenominal ordering, 107
Adjunct questions
  and attention, 366
  as strategies, 367
  and learning from texts, 327-330
  effect on recall, 326
  and affect on amount learned, 333
Adverbs, 80
Ambiguity
  in recall protocols, resolution of, 280-283
  sentence, 12
Analogical patterning, 36
Analysis by synthesis, 104
Analytic truth, 69
Aptitude treatment interaction and comprehension, 233
Artificial intelligence, 277
Articles and definiteness, 56-58

Assertion, 116
Attention
  and listening, 296, 366
  and reading, 366

B

Base grammar, and propositional thinking, 139
Bilingualism, 100

C

Case grammar, 75
Case relation, 75
Chunked comprehension test, 21
Chunking, 304
Classification learning and sentences, 134
Clause
  as primary perceptual unit, 104
  embedded, 81-82
  relative, 65-67
  segmentation, 105
Cloze procedure, 18, 318
Codability
  and thought, 110-111
  and message content, 172

Cognitive adaptation, 34
Cognitive theory of semantics, 169
Communication Tasks, 139-165
Comparing operations, 113
Competence, 359
Complex learning, 211
Comprehension
    ability, 3
    and general behavior approach, 367
    and stage theory, 363
    and task-induced operations, 224-228
    and templates, 37
    complete comprehension, 39
    definition, 5
    effects of pause time on, 303
    model for, 213-217
    of stories, 191-201
    studies with children, 348-354
    subjective judgements, 58
    testing of, 14-24
Comprehension strategies, 362
Comprehension theorem, 31, 38
Compressed speech, 304
Computational linguistics, 95
Concepts, 35
    and different languages, 101
    word-sense meaning, 74
Concreteness measures, 257
Conjunctions, 79, 265-273
Connectives, sentential, 75
Conservation task, 141-142
Constancies, 35
Context effects on inspection speed, 321
Contextual features, 43
Contextual rule, 42
Contradiction, 101
Control processes in learning from prose,
    315-334
Conversion model, 121
Creativity and innovation, 36
Cultural ideas, 101
Cultural knowledge and comprehension,
    170
Cybernetic control, 310

D

Decision rule, 130
Deductive thinking, 162
Deep structure
    and semantic networks, 95
    of paragraphs, 277
    relations, 105
Definiteness, 56-69
determiner and number, 82
Developmental aspects of language use,
    139-164

Digraphs
    and relations among concepts, 212
    implicational, and relations among
        propositions, 212
Dimensions
    and message construction, 171
    salient, 173
Direct object, 95
Discourse, 41-68, 71
    structure, 211-244, 247-283
Discrimination processes
    conceptual, 225
    implicational, 225
    relational, 225
Disjunction, 265, 273

E

Efficiency and an information-acquisition-
    storage-retrieval system, 31
Elaborative production, 225
Embedded clauses, 81-82
Encoding
    active versus passive voice, 133
    and classification, 131
    and processing, 131-132
    classification learning, 132
    model of, 114
    pictures, 132
    stages in, 115-116
    subject versus object, 133
Entailment, 101
Environment, informational, 35
Epistemology, 31
Error correction, 169
Error detection, 37, 169
Ethnoscience and comprehension, 170,
    203-205
Exhaustive search of memory, 131
Existential quantifiers, 258
Explanation theory, 31
Extrapolation, 32, 36
Eye-voice span, 24

F

Factor analysis, 2, 25
Features
    contextual, 43
    inherent, 43
Feature-usage and messages, 171,
    178-179
Foregrounding, 50-55, 68
    and pronominalization, 51
Frequency counts, 257

G

Generalizations, 35
Generic noun, 59-60
Gist, reading for, 355
Graph theory and discourse structure, 212

H

Heuristics
    and paragraph organization, 363
    classification, 365
    elimination of aspects, 365
    means-ends analysis, 364
Hierarchical additive encoding model, 237
Hierarchical structure of discourse, 247-283

I

Imagery, 257
Images, 363
    and knowledge, 364
Implication transformation, 90
Implicational structure, 162
Incidental learning, 355
Inconsistency, 34
Individual differences and learning from
    rapid speech, 307
Inference, 8-9, 38
    and logical quantifiers, 361
    cause-effect, 362
    converse relation, 89
Inferential complexity, level of, 344-345
Inferential production, 225
Information
    expressive, 100
    in text, going beyond the, 340-342
    logical, 100
    new, 51
    processing, 363
    processing, treatment of errors in,
        169-209
    processing models, 113-136
Informationally rich environment, 35
Inferent features, 43
Insight, 37
Inspection time and learning from texts,
    327-330
Instruction and language, 139-165
Instrumentalism, 36
Internal representations, 113-114, 117,
    131
    and concept learning, 131
Interpolation, 32, 36
Intrusion errors in recall of paragraphs,
    264
Invariants, 35

K

Knowledge, 41-68
    formalization of, 67
    of results and adjunct questions, 326
    retention of, 359
    of grammar, 360
    of lexicon, 360
    of semantics, 360

L

Language
    and effects of context, 139-165
    and semantic structure, 72
    and syntactic structure, 72
    and thought, 362
    concept structure of, 74
    implicational structure of, 89-94
    implicit structure of, 72
    influence of, on perception and
        thought, 99-112
    lexical structure and, 83-93
    logical structure, 77
    pragmatics, 94
    production, 359
    reception, 359
    tree structure, 76
Latency and processing models, 149-156
Laws, 35
Learning
    by listening, 285-312
    complex information, a model for,
        204-205
    mastery aspects of, 334
Level of assertion, 350-354
    and recall, 342-344
Lexical structures, 83-93
Lexical nodes for words and word senses, 84
Lexicon and propositional thinking, 139
Linguistic idea, 101
Linguistics
    computational, 95
    descriptive, 277
Listening
    and comprehension factors, 294
    and expansion of speech
        by temporal means, 300
    and intelligence, 290
    and job information, 288
    and job proficiency, 290
    and task variables, 294
    and time compression, 300
    comprehension, 2, 3
    measures of, 295

Listening *(Cont'd.)*
  training, 295, 297-299
Literacy, 285-312
Logical contradiction, 37
Logical converses, 89
Logical structure of language, 77
Logical quantifiers, 82
  and story comprehension, 192-201

M

Markov processes for encoding
  and inference, 237
Mathemagenic activities, 322-327
Mathemagenic control, 310
Meaning, 10
  acquisition of, 102
  and idiosyncratic experience, 102
  and reference, the problem of, 165
Means-Ends analysis, 364
Measures of listening ability, 295
Memory, 3, 6-8
  and recall of discourse, 247-283
  processes, 211-244
  processes, a model for, 213-217
  search, exhaustive, 131
  structure, 247-283
Mental operations and language, 113-136
Message
  construction, experiments on, 174-182
  context and comprehension, 360
  detail and age of recipient, 361
  detail and topic familiarity, 361
Mind and language, 99
Minimum feature hypothesis for messages, 171
Mnemonic, 36
Modeling, 32, 36
Morphemes and problem of language
  and thought, 99
Multidimensional analysis of topic-confusion
  matrix, 187-189

N

Negation, 114
Negative sentences and implicit negatives,
  162
New information, 51
Nominal stimuli of text transformed into
  effective ones, 324
Noun
  generic, 59-60
  proper noun, 57
Novelty, 33

O

Object, direct, 95
Organization, 33
Organizers for learning by listening, 309

P

Paired associate learning, 316
Paradigmatic, 102
Paragraph structure
  and plans, 363
  linguistic analysis of, 249-260
Parallel processing, 131
Paraphrase, 23
Parts of objects, 61-64
  and analytic truth, 69
  and synthetic truth, 69
Pattern construction, 35
Pattern recognition, 35
Perception, influence of,
  on thought and language, 99-112
Perceptual chunking, 304
Perceptual strategies, 362
Perceptrons, 38
Personal ideas, 101
Philosophy of science, 37
Plans
  and cultural knowledge, 203-205
  and prose recall, 355
  and the structure of paragraphs, 363
Polar opposition and the lexicon, 163
Pragmatics, 94
Prenominal adjectives, ordering of, 107
Prepositions, 87-89
Presuppositions, 116, 360
Process model, 136
  encoding and comparing model, 114
  for active and passive sentences,
    149-156
  response change model, 114
  optional recoding model, 114
Production processes, 216
Pronominal usage hypothesis, 171
  and message construction, 179-182
Pronominalization, 51, 356
  and foregrounding, 51
  as implicit semantic repetition, 255
Proper noun, 57
Propositional thinking, 139

Q

Quantifiers, logical, 82
Quantitative models of comprehension, impli-
  cation of, 201-202
Questions, 19, 24-25

R

Rapid speech perception and individual
    differences, 307
Rate of input and verbal learning, 316
Reaction time to auditory clicks
    and sentence processing, 105
Readability, 18
    and prose learning, 318-320
    and stimulus material structure, 316-318
    formula, 288, 300
Reading
    and eye-voice span, 24
    and intelligence, 290
    and job proficiency, 290
    and listening, relationships of, 286-294
    correlations with education, 293
    developmental model of, 291
    remedial reading, 296
Recall
    for superordinates versus subordinates,
        274
    of secondary subtrees versus primary
        subtree, 275-276
    versus recognition tests, 345
Recall protocols, scoring of, 260-273
Recoding
    of clause, 104
    of context and sentence, 148
    optional model, 121-131
Recognition
    message recognition, 20
    versus recall tests, 345
Reconstruction processes, 217
Redundancy, 13, 34, 39
    filter, 37
    hypothesis for messages, 171
Reference, 100
    and meaning, the problem of, 165
    quantitative model for, 181
    theory of, 139-165
    word-sense and token, 76
Relations
    complex, 92-94
    elaborative, 229-232, 237
    implication, 213
    inferred, 229-232, 237
    nested, 223-224
    overgeneralized, 230-232
    pseudodiscriminated, 230-232
    types of, mode, 213
    veridical, 229-232, 237
Relative clause, 65-67
Representation conventions, 73
Response change model, 116-121
Rhetoric, 366
Rules, 35

S

Salient dimensions, 173
Scoring of discourse recall protocols,
    260-273
Search model and self-terminating search,
    131
Selective attentional effect, 355
Selection processes, 215
Selection restrictions, 87
Self-instructional program, 318
Semantic
    bias, 361
    consistency, 361
    constraints, 44-48
    definition, 102
    error detection, 169, 190-191
    error correction, 169, 190-191
    implication and hierarchies, 278
    implication and sentence order, 277
    marker, 86
    model and digraphs, 212
    networks, 73
    networks and deep structure, 95
    presuppositions, 360
    programming, 32
    relations between phrases, 104
    resources, 42-48
    selection restrictions, 87
    structure, 42-45, 71
    variability, 46-48
Sensory processing load, 105
Sentence
    comprehension and effects of context, 148
    complexity
        and adjectives, 318
        and clauses, 318
        and learning, 318
        and modifiers, 318
        and number of words, 318
        and prepositional phrases, 318
        mapped onto other sentences,
            156-164
        mapping onto perception, 139-156
        order effects, 258-260, 346-349
        recoding and development, 162
        sequences as superficial structure,
            273-274
Sentences
    and classification learning, 134
    as descriptions, 139-156
    as propositions, 156-164
    equivalence among, 163
    verification of, 114-115
Sentential connectives, 75
Set relations and story comprehension,
    191-201

Sets of alternatives, effects on language behavior, 169-209
Simplex matrix and language comprehension data, 234
Speaker, role of, 53-55
Speech decoding, 295
Speech perception, 100, 104
and rate-controlled tasks, 299
Standardized tests, 103
Statement verification, selective effects of, 345-346
Strategies at paragraph and sentence levels, 362
Story comprehension, 191-201
and network of relations, 170
model for explicit information, 198-201
model for inferred information, 201
Structural description, 11
Structural features of text and self-paced instruction, 333
Subject-matter identification as topic identification, 182-189
Subjective judgments, 16
Subordinate clause, 106
Superordinate organizers in learning from text, 333
Superordination, 163
Supposition, semantic, 131
Surface order, influence on concepts, 108
Surface selection, 215
Synonymy, 101
Syntactic order, 100
Syntactic versus semantic approaches to discourse, 278
Syntax as representation convention, 73
Synthetic truth, 69

T

Target items and message content, 172
Tasks, theory of, 38
Templates and comprehension, 37
Tense, 48-50
Tests, 2
of job knowledge & performance, 290
Text features and learning from prose, 315-334
Text length and recall, 319
Thought
and language, 99-112, 139-165, 362
and perception, 99-112
and reasoning, instruction in, 296
Theory, limitations of, 331-332
Theory of tasks, 38
Token and word-sense reference, 76

Topic identification, 169-191
factors affecting, 182-189
Topic sentences
and paragraphs, 363
as organizers, 333
Transformation processes, 225
Transformational grammar, 3-4, 119
Transformations and process models, 114
Translation, 23, 100
Tree structure, 76

U

Uncertainty
and ease of comprehension, 15, 148
and message content, 172
Understanding, 37
and general behavior approach, 367
Universals of language, 106

V

Venn diagram and discourse structure, 193
Verb
and tense, 48-50
Be and essive relations, 78-89
case grammar, 75
case relation, 75
Have, 79
optional arguments for, 86
required arguments for, 86
Verbal memory measures, 257
Verbalization, 4
Verbatim reproduction, 22
Verification
and class-inclusion decisions, 136
of class correspondence, 216
of implication, 216
of noncontradiction, 216
processes, 216
time for negative and passive sentences, 157
time for adults versus children, 157

W

Whorfian hypothesis, 99-112
Word
familiarity and retention, 317
meaningfulness and memory, 317
referent, 139-156
referent relations, 170-171
Words and problem of language and thought, 99